"Silence" in Translation

1 Corinthians 14:34–35 in Myanmar and the Development of a Critical Contextual Hermeneutic

Anna Sui Hluan

© 2022 Anna Sui Hluan

Published 2022 by Langham Academic (Previously Langham Monographs)
An imprint of Langham Publishing
www.langhampublishing.org

Langham Publishing and its imprints are a ministry of Langham Partnership

Langham Partnership
PO Box 296, Carlisle, Cumbria CA3 9WZ, UK
www.langham.org

ISBNs:
978-1-83973-216-4 Print
978-1-83973-807-4 ePub
978-1-83973-809-8 PDF

Anna Sui Hluan has asserted her right under the Copyright, Designs and Patents Act, 1988 to be identified as the Author of this work.

All rights reserved. No part of this publication may be reproduced, stored in a retrieval system or transmitted, in any form or by any means, electronic, mechanical, photocopying, recording or otherwise, without the prior written permission of the publisher or the Copyright Licensing Agency.

British Library Cataloguing-in-Publication Data
A catalogue record for this book is available from the British Library

ISBN: 978-1-83973-216-4

Cover & Book Design: projectluz.com

Langham Partnership actively supports theological dialogue and an author's right to publish but does not necessarily endorse the views and opinions set forth here or in works referenced within this publication, nor can we guarantee technical and grammatical correctness. Langham Partnership does not accept any responsibility or liability to persons or property as a consequence of the reading, use or interpretation of its published content.

Contents

Preface xi

Acknowledgments xiii

Abbreviations xv

Chapter 1 1
  Introduction
    1.1 Statement of the Problem 2
    1.2 Research Methodology 4
    1.3 Limitations of the Study 7
    1.4 Significance of the Study... 7
    1.5 Literature Review.. 8
        1.5.1 Literature on Interpretation in Myanmar 9
        1.5.2 Literature on Contextual Theology in Myanmar ...10
        1.5.3 Three Western Hermeneutical Approaches 12
        1.5.4 Literature on Contextual Hermeneutics................ 14

Part One: The Myanmar Context

Chapter 2 21
  Silence in Myanmar
    2.1 The Historical Background of Silence in Myanmar....... 22
        2.1.1 The Precolonial Period.. 23
        2.1.2 The Colonial Period 29
        2.1.3 The Postcolonial Period 34
    2.2 The Impact of Missionaries on Myanmar Interpreters and
        Their Understanding of Silence 43
        2.2.1 Overview of Christian Missionaries in Myanmar... 44
        2.2.2 The Influence of Adoniram Judson 45
        2.2.3 The Influence of Women Missionaries on the Role
            of Women 50
        2.2.4 Myanmar Women's Reflections on the Role of
            Women Missionaries... 56
        2.2.5 The Impact of Missionaries and Culture on Biblical
            Interpretation in Myanmar 59
    2.3 Conclusion 63

Chapter 3 65
   A Textual Analysis of 1 Corinthians 14:34–35 in Myanmar Bibles
      3.1 The Judson Burmese Bible and the Myanmar Common
          Language Bible 67
         3.1.1 The Judson Burmese Bible 67
         3.1.2 The Myanmar Common Language Bible 71
      3.2 Textual Analysis of 1 Corinthians 14:34–35 73
         3.2.1 Variances in the Judson Burmese Bible (JB) 73
         3.2.2 Analysis of 1 Corinthians 14:34–35 in the Judson
            Burmese Bible 77
         3.2.3 The Translation of Silence in the Judson Burmese
            Bible and the Myanmar Common Language Bible 97
      3.3 Historical Influences Affecting Judson's Translation 112
      3.4 Conclusion 120

Part Two: Hermeneutics and Context

Chapter 4 125
   Silence in Contemporary Scholarship
      4.1 The Hermeneutics of Contemporary Scholarship 126
      4.2 Points of Comparison 129
         4.2.1 Pauline Authorship 129
         4.2.2 The Corinthian Context 132
         4.2.3 Silence: Women and the Church 138
         4.2.4 Speaking 143
         4.2.5 Silence and Submission 148
         4.2.6 Silence and the Law 152
         4.2.7 Paul's Expectations 155
      4.3 Hermeneutical Keys of Contemporary Interpreters 161
         4.3.1 Hermeneutical Methodology 161
         4.3.2 Hermeneutical Presuppositions 169
         4.3.3 Hermeneutical Processes Relating to
            1 Corinthians 14:34–35 187
      4.4 Conclusion 202

Chapter 5 205
   A Critical Contextual Hermeneutic for Myanmar
      5.1 Hermeneutical Schools 206
         5.1.1 Evaluation of Three Hermeneutical Schools 206
         5.1.2 Evaluation of Contextual Theology 213

5.2 Toward a Satisfactory Contextual Hermeneutic 222
    5.2.1 The "Critical Contextualization" of Paul Hiebert..............222
    5.2.2 The Components of a Critical Contextual Hermeneutic 225
    5.2.3 The Presuppositions of a Critical Contextual
    Hermeneutic 226
    5.2.4 Criteria for a Satisfactory Hermeneutic for Myanmar 227
5.3 Conclusion 242

Part Three: Revisiting the Context and the Text

Chapter 6 245
Revisiting the Context
    6.1 An Interplay of Contexts 245
    6.2 Cultural Obstacles to Developing a Myanmar Contextual
    Hermeneutic 247
        6.2.1 Problems with the Culture of Obedience 247
        6.2.2 Problems with the Virtue of Submission.........................250
        6.2.3 Problems with the Passive Acceptance of Biblical Texts ..251
    6.3 Rethinking Our Approaches to Interpretation.............................252
        6.3.1 Rethinking the Culture of Respect in Interpretation........254
        6.3.2 Rethinking Language Study 259
        6.3.3 Rethinking Comparative Studies 261
        6.3.4 Rethinking Hermeneutical Methods 262
        6.3.5 Rethinking Leadership...264
    6.4 Obstacles to a Critical Contextual Myanmar Hermeneutic 265
        6.4.1 Need for Increased Exposure to the World......................266
        6.4.2 Rethinking Judson's Translation 269
        6.4.3 Rereading the Text in Light of the Historical Context 274
        6.4.4 The Need to Embrace Servant Leadership 276
    6.5 Conclusion 278

Chapter 7 279
Revisiting the Text through Critical Contextual Hermeneutics
    7.1 Interpretive Keys in Revisiting the Text 279
        7.1.1 Women in Corinth...281
        7.1.2 Paul's Attitude on Women in the Church.......................288
    7.2 Revisiting 1 Corinthians 14:34–35.......................................291
        7.2.1 Pauline Authorship 291
        7.2.2 Silence: The Context..293
        7.2.3 Silence: The Women..296
        7.2.4 Silence: The Speaking...299

   7.2.5 Silence: Submission 304
   7.2.6 Silence: The Law 307
  7.3 Contextual Application of the Text 313
  7.4 Conclusion 318

Chapter 8 321
 Summary and Conclusion
  8.1 Culture and Hermeneutics 321
  8.2 Hermeneutics and Translation 323
  8.3 Schools of Interpretation 325
  8.4 Critical Tools for a Contextual Hermeneutic 327
  8.5 The Example of Katharine Bushnell 328

Bibliography 333

List of Tables

Table 1. Variances of the Text of 1 Corinthians 14:34–35 in Judson's Burmese Bible 74

Table 2. Changes in the Judson Burmese Translation of 1 Corinthians 14:34–35 76

Table 3. Texts of 1 Corinthians 14:33 78

Table 4. The Greek, English, and JB Texts of 1 Corinthians 14:34a 79

Table 5. Women and Silence in 1 Corinthians 14:34a 82

Table 6. Speaking in 1 Corinthians 14:34b 84

Table 7. The Greek, English, and JB Texts of 1 Corinthians 14:34c 87

Table 8. The Greek, English, and JB Texts of 1 Corinthians 14:35a 93

Table 9. The Greek, English, and JB Texts of 1 Corinthians 14:35b 95

Table 10. The Greek, English, JB, and MCL Texts of 1 Corinthians 14:33–34a 100

Table 11. The Greek, English, JB, and MCL Texts of 1 Corinthians 14:34a 102

Table 12. The Greek, English, JB, and MCL Texts of 1 Corinthians 14:34b 104

Table 13. The Greek, English, JB, and MCL Texts of 1 Corinthians 14:34c 106

Table 14. The Greek, English, JB, and MCL Texts of 1 Corinthians 14:35a 107

Table 15. The Greek, English, JB, and MCL Texts of 1 Corinthians 14:35b 109

Table 16. A Comparison of the JB, KJV, and NIV Translations of 1 Corinthians 14:34a 262

List of Charts

Chart 1. Robert Schreiter's Map of Constructing a Local Theology 235
Chart 2. Flow Chart of a Critical Contextual Hermeneutics..........................236

Preface

The social significance of silence used as a sign of submission to the powerful, or to anyone in a position of authority, gained importance in Myanmar over a prolonged history of imperial, colonial, and postcolonial authoritarian rule. The culture of silence in the face of power reinforced the position of the powerful in their control of the people and impacted not only the political sphere between the rulers and the ruled, but also relationships between men and women, parents and children, and religious leaders and followers. For Christians, silence as a sign of women's submission to authority gained importance through the teachings of nineteenth-century missionaries, of whom Adoniram Judson was the most important, particularly through the terms used in his translation of the Burmese Bible. Myanmar Christians read its references to silence and the role of women through the lens of their own experience of the cultural and social significance of silence and submission and tended to uncritically accept the expectation of silence for women in the church as well as in society.

Taking interpretations of the text of 1 Corinthians 14:34–35 and adjacent verses as an example of the hermeneutical issues raised by the interaction between translation and social context and the issue of silence, the first question this work seeks to address is, "What is the impact of these verses on Myanmar Christians' views of the role of women in the church?" It examines how this text and its statements about women and silence have been translated, particularly in Judson's Burmese Bible, and also in Greek versions and other translations into English and Burmese. The uncritical acceptance of Judson's translation illustrates how the common hermeneutical approach in Myanmar of interpreting the text literally reinforces cultural assumptions and fails to account for the contexts of the text itself, the translator, and the readers of the translation. There is a lack of awareness of issues of hermeneutics, including how translated texts, even scholarly ones which pay careful attention to what an author was trying to say, embody a translator's interpretive viewpoint, and may contribute to a misunderstanding of the intended scope and meaning of the text.

The need for a critical analysis of hermeneutics leads to a second major question, "What would a satisfactory contextual hermeneutic in Myanmar today look like in order to interpret passages that concern women today?"

In order to answer these questions, this work looks at how these verses have been interpreted by three representative contemporary schools of interpretation: literal traditional, feminist, and egalitarian, and points out the importance of the starting point for determining the meaning of the text.

These three schools of interpretation represent views about the role of women in the church current in Myanmar. They are analyzed in order to develop hermeneutical principles which are more appropriate for Myanmar today – a critical contextual feminist hermeneutical methodology for Myanmar which takes the Bible seriously as the rule of faith and life. This includes exegesis of the text and the evaluation of three contexts: Myanmar culture, the Scriptures, and Judson's Burmese Bible translation.

The intention is to promote an informed response that makes it possible for Myanmar Christians to evaluate and implement appropriate contextualized practices. Critical keys for evaluation in analyzing the text include Jesus's example of servant leadership and Paul's general acceptance of women's involvement in the church. This challenges traditional readings of the concept of silence and raises questions of relevancy in the contemporary context of Myanmar.

Acknowledgments

First, I would like to give thanks to my Lord and my God for enabling me to write the thesis which is now being published as a book.

I want to thank my supervisors Dr. Paul Trebilco, Dr. John Roxborogh, and Dr. Lynne Baab. You have been my source of encouragement throughout this PhD process. Thank you for all that you have done for me.

The final writing was enhanced by the detailed reading and corrections by Lydia Johnson, who read and corrected all my manuscripts with much care. Thank you so much.

Furthermore, thanks to LeaDev-Langham of New Zealand for choosing me as your first Langham Scholar. Thank you for trusting and investing in my study. Special thanks to Tony Plews, former executive director of LeaDev-Langham of New Zealand, for all that you have done for me.

Also, I would like to thank all my friends, both in Dunedin and abroad, whose prayers and encouragement helped me to keep moving forward during many difficult times. I especially want to mention my heartfelt gratitude to Rev. Richard Dawson and all friends from the Leith Valley Presbyterian Church, my prayer partners Peter and Jessica Crothall, my friends from the Theology and Religion department at the University of Otago, and also to Myanmar Christian communities throughout New Zealand. Your friendship made this journey bearable.

Last, words cannot adequately express my gratitude to my family for their support especially during these PhD years. To my father Rev. Dr. Ral Buai and my mother Mary Sung Kui, who died one month after I started my writing. Thank you for always believing in me. My heartfelt thanks to my husband Henry Van Thio, who resigned from his job so that I could pursue this further study. Without your support through encouragement and love, I truly could not have done this. Also, I am so thankful to my children, Jesse, Jennifer, and Joseph for their love, understanding, and patience during the course of writing the thesis. I am so blessed!

Abbreviations

BDAG	Bauer, *A Greek-English Lexicon of the New Testament and Other Early Christian Literature*
ESV	English Standard Version, 2001
GNB	Good News Bible/Today's English Version
JB	Judson Burmese Bible, 2007
KJV	King James Version
LXX	Septuagint
MCL	Myanmar Common Language Translation, 2005
MT	Masoretic Text
NA[27]	Aland and Nestle, *Greek-English New Testament*
NA[28]	Nestle and Nestle, *Novum Testamentum Graece*
NASB	New American Standard Bible, 1995
NET	New English Translation
NIV	New International Version, 1984
NKJV	New King James Version, 1982
NLT	New Living Translation
NRSV	New Revised Standard Version, 1989
REB	Revised English Bible
TR	Textus Receptus
UBS[4]	*The UBS 4 Greek New Testament*, 2007
UBS[5]	German Bible Society, *The Greek New Testament*

CHAPTER 1

Introduction

My interest in the interpretive issues surrounding 1 Corinthians 14:34–35 and adjacent verses, along with other scriptural texts bearing on the role of women in the church, began when I decided to pursue my theological education. The two schools where I studied in the United States both held a traditionalist or fundamentalist view on the role of women in the church, and as a woman, this led me to question my place in the church and wonder if I would ever be able to use my theological education after graduation. Nevertheless, despite many challenges, upon my return to Myanmar, I became a pastor, an academic dean of a Bible college, and a Greek language teacher at two seminaries. My fourteen years of experience in these fields, especially teaching the New Testament in Bible colleges in Myanmar, deepened my interest in the hermeneutical issues surrounding biblical passages concerning women.

In my initial inquiry into the hermeneutical issues facing interpreters, one text in particular, 1 Corinthians 14:34–35, became the focus of my attention. I had decided to undertake research for a Doctor of Ministry degree among sixty women alumnae of six evangelical theological seminaries in Myanmar.[1] The main purpose was to determine the percentage of women alumnae who went into church-based ministry and the challenges they faced. During this research, 1 Corinthians 14:34–35 was often included among the reasons given why women were not allowed to preach in churches and it was mentioned more than 1 Timothy 2:12–15, whose interpretation raises similar issues.

---

1. Hluan, "Analysis on the Leadership Challenges Facing the Women Alumnae among the Evangelical Seminaries of Yangon" (DMin Thesis, Asia Graduate School of Theology-Philippines, 2007).

When I got the opportunity to do further study at the University of Otago, New Zealand, I decided to examine 1 Corinthians 14:34–35 more closely, looking particularly at the critical hermeneutical issues affecting the ways that different churches and scholars were interpreting this text.

Although hermeneutics is generally referred to as a "science of interpretation," it is not a straightforward process. It involves bridging the gap between the world of the biblical text and the world of the interpreter, and differences arise when interpreters living in different cultures and periods of history experience the gap between their world and the world of the Bible in different ways. Many also bring to the task a personal search for meaning, in which their own needs and questions are important elements in what they understand the Bible to be saying. Even when one seeks to be primarily concerned with the intentions of the original authors, editors, and translators, assumptions and questions arising from one's own culture, context, and experience lead to the same text having different meanings. It is possible for the best of interpreters to misunderstand the message of a particular text and for deeply felt conflicts to develop around different understandings.

The reference in 1 Corinthians 14:34–35 to women and silence is a significant instance of such a "conflict of interpretation."[2] Although many scholars, including conservative scholars, do not see this text as prohibiting women from exercising Christian leadership and ministry, a significant number do. The issues are compounded when both conservative and less conservative readings are reinforced by cultural attitudes and deep-seated beliefs about the role of women in society. Even scholars attempting to interpret this text simply with the aim of identifying its original intention draw different conclusions. This situation underlines the difficulties that interpreters in Myanmar face with the meaning of 1 Corinthians 14:34–35 and other New Testament texts in their own context.

1.1 Statement of the Problem

A key issue in interpreting 1 Corinthians 14:34–35 concerns the translation by Adoniram Judson, where he translated λαλέω as "preaching" instead of what I will argue is the better translation, "speaking." From his choice of

---

2. Ricoeur, *Conflict of Interpretations*, xv.

λαλέω as referring to "preaching," especially in the context of σιγάω, "silence," Myanmar interpreters generally take this text as prohibiting women from authoritative forms of speech, specifically "preaching." This has significantly influenced perceptions of the role of women in the Myanmar churches due to the respect people have for Judson and his translation of the Bible. I am not aware of anyone in Myanmar raising linguistic issues surrounding the 1 Corinthians 14:34–35 text, although the translation of Judson is still used widely in the church.

The linguistic issues relating to Judson's translation highlight two areas of concern for hermeneutical practices in Myanmar. The first is the influence of the Burmese Bible translation in forming theological meanings. It is only recently that biblical scholars in Myanmar such as La Seng Dingrin, John De Jong, and Naw Eh Thar Gay have begun to dialogue critically with the Judson translation.

The fact that only a few scholars have interacted with the Judson Bible translation highlights the need for critical dialogue in Myanmar between biblical studies and contextual realities. It is necessary to engage not only with the Judson Burmese Bible translation itself, but also with its historical and contextual background and its reception by Myanmar Christians. The attitudes of reverence that people have toward this translation, along with their embrace of a literal interpretational method, have contributed to its uncritical acceptance. Biblical interpreters have hardly questioned Judson's translation, yet without seriously engaging with this translation from within the context of Myanmar, the effectiveness of Christian communication of the gospel is questionable.

The next area of concern is the role of an interpreter's presuppositions shaped by their context including their religious, sociopolitical, and cultural background. The concept of silence, for example, is deeply rooted in the cultural background of Myanmar and reinforces understandings and practices in the present time. This historical-cultural background plays a significant role in the way 1 Corinthians 14:34–35 has been interpreted.

The interpreter's presuppositions influence their understanding of the translated texts, and their translations made in the light of those cultural assumptions are likely, in turn, to reinforce the commonly accepted applications of the texts. In the past, the role of the interpreter's presuppositions has not been acknowledged. Myanmar interpreters relied on the imported approaches of Western biblical interpreters, often reinforced by missionaries whose inherited denominational teachings are still promulgated by many interpreters in Myanmar today. There has been a failure to realize that these missionary interpreters were themselves products of their own cultural worldviews, which were different from the Myanmar worldview and experience, but in some respects, as in relation to the role of women in society, had parallels which made their assumptions difficult to challenge. It is therefore necessary to seek to identify these key presuppositions and influences, both Western and local, which have shaped present-day Myanmar Christians' approach to biblical texts such as 1 Corinthians 14:34–35.

This situation contributes to the complexities that interpreters in Myanmar face in interpreting 1 Corinthians 14:34–35, and further underlines the importance of biblical hermeneutics in present-day Myanmar. Without a critical dialogue with the Myanmar context and the issues interpreters bring to biblical texts from their own contexts, biblical hermeneutics in Myanmar will continue to be dependent on the interpretations of outsiders. In this light, this work seeks to develop a contextually relevant hermeneutic for Myanmar.

1.2 Research Methodology

The challenges that interpreters in Myanmar face in interpreting 1 Corinthians 14:34–35 are analyzed through a context-critical hermeneutic informed by a combination of feminist interpretations and principles gleaned from contextual theology. The Myanmar historical and cultural context is surveyed to identify deeply rooted assumptions about the role of women and the significance of silence. Christian traditions of interpretation that have influenced and shaped the role of women in the Myanmar church are evaluated. This approach has affinities with broader approaches to contextual theology which examine every context carefully through the lens of social analysis and makes use of key texts in contextual theology and contextual biblical studies.

These challenges and the proposed solution are addressed in eight chapters, comprising an introductory chapter and seven chapters grouped in three parts.

This introductory chapter sets out to present why the issue of silence and the interpretation of 1 Corinthians 14:34–35 is an important problem and discusses the focus and scope of the study and the significance of approaching the issue through the process of developing a critical contextual hermeneutic for Myanmar. The issues are highlighted by the influence of traditional interpretations in the history and culture of Myanmar itself and the questions which continue to be asked about the place of women in church leadership. Issues include the significance of the cultural context of Myanmar and the influence of historic Bible translations. This is viewed from a perspective that acknowledges the cultural context (or the "cognitive environment") of the interpreter is the contextual lens through which interpretations are made which shapes the "hermeneutical assumptions" of the interpreter.

Part One (chapters 2 and 3) highlights the need for such a hermeneutic in Myanmar. It discusses the cultural worldview and ideological orientations of Myanmar that lie behind interpreters' understandings of the word "silence" and the impact of Bible translation on Myanmar Christians' views of the role of women in the church.

Chapter 2 addresses the cultural and historical background of the concept of "silence" in Myanmar and the impact of Bible translation on the role of women in the Myanmar church. It outlines the historical background of Adoniram Judson and the theological and cultural factors that influenced his hermeneutical decisions.

Chapter 3 looks at the influence of the Burmese Bible translation in forming theological meanings and details differences between Judson's translation of 1 Corinthians 14:34–35 and those of other Burmese translators, paying attention to the Greek text available to Judson, as well as currently available Greek texts and their variant readings. The underlying perspective is one that views the Myanmar interpreter's understanding of words as functioning together with Bible translations in forming the theological meanings and social implications of the text.

In Part Two (chapters 4 and 5), the interplay between the understanding of what silence means and who it applies to is explored by examining the issues of interpretational conflict exposed by a comparative study of three schools of biblical interpretation represented by Wayne Grudem, Elisabeth Schüssler Fiorenza, and Ben Witherington III.

Chapter 4 looks at the reasons for considering the three scholars and the influences behind each of these in order to understand the presuppositions underlying each school of thought. This notes their divergent starting points in approaching biblical texts and their usage of other Scripture passages to interpret the 1 Corinthians 14:34–35 text. This chapter then provides detailed interpretations of 1 Corinthians 14:34–35 from each of the three schools. This lays the foundation for the question of what a satisfactory context-sensitive hermeneutic in Myanmar might look like.

Chapter 5 addresses the question, "What are appropriate hermeneutical principles for Myanmar when interpreting passages that concern women in the church?" in order to identify key components for constructing a satisfactory contextual hermeneutic for Myanmar in interpreting passages like 1 Corinthians 14:34–35.

Part Three (chapters 6, 7, and 8) introduces a context-sensitive hermeneutic and then seeks to demonstrate how this methodology can be applied in the context of Myanmar today. It revisits the contexts of Myanmar and of the 1 Corinthians 14:34–35 text, by considering the particular challenges of the Myanmar situation and key elements in the interpretation of 1 Corinthians 14:34–35.

Chapter 6 looks at the problematic nature of hermeneutics in Myanmar which are important for understanding the obstacles that interpreters encounter, and how these hinder analyzing the Bible translation of Adoniram Judson. It highlights the principles of contextual hermeneutics based on analysis relating to three contexts: those of the Myanmar interpreter, the Bible translator, and the context of the Bible in its historical setting.

Chapter 7 revisits the 1 Corinthians 14:34–35 text through principles learned from the proposed context-sensitive hermeneutic mentioned in chapter 5 and explores what an interpretation that follows a context-sensitive hermeneutic might look like. It seeks to answer the question, "What are the practical means of approach to 1 Corinthians 14:34–35 using the principles of a contextual hermeneutics for Myanmar?"

Chapter 8 provides a summary of a proposed contextual hermeneutic for Myanmar and demonstrates how this methodology can be applied, the contributions it offers, and the challenges it faces. It notes the encouragement provided by the example of Katharine Bushnell as a nineteenth-century Christian woman ahead of her time who took a particular interest in the way in which the Bible was being interpreted and its impact on women.

1.3 Limitations of the Study

The scope of this study is limited by its focus on the Myanmar context, particularly Protestant churches and institutions using the Bible translation of Adoniram Judson. It is also limited by the documents which were available at the time the research was undertaken, and the current state of the history of the translation of the Bible at an exegetical level. I was not able to locate material on the training in biblical interpretation Judson may have received at Brown University or elsewhere. Further work on placing Judson within the history of interpretation, following William Smalley,[3] would be an interesting avenue for further study.

There are almost no written documents representing the views of Myanmar interpreters on 1 Corinthians 14:34–35, although they are voiced through preaching and teaching in the church. To my knowledge, it is only recently that a very few Myanmar theologians have raised issues regarding Judson's translation. In 2015, I searched the two largest libraries in Yangon but could locate only a few sources, mostly written by Western historians. I was not able to locate any studies in Myanmar that parallel the concerns of this thesis, and in particular I was not able to locate any written materials about Judson's interpretation of 1 Corinthians 14:34–35 and its importance for the role of women in the Myanmar church, nor any which addressed interpretation issues in the New Testament texts of Judson's Burmese translation.

The literature in Myanmar on contextual hermeneutics has been limited, and there are only a few books on contextual theology. As a result, hermeneutical principles have been explored through a comparison of traditional, feminist, and evangelical feminist/egalitarian hermeneutical schools of thought. Due to limits of space, the views of those who have advocated for the total silence of women in church have not been included.

1.4 Significance of the Study

To my knowledge, this is the first written hermeneutical study of 1 Corinthians 14:34–35 carried out from the context of Myanmar. My hope is that it will encourage others in the study of how key passages of Scripture have been translated and understood and help interpreters in Myanmar, whether male or

---

3. Smalley, "Translation as Mission."

female, understand more fully the issues surrounding such texts. It is also my hope that this work will contribute to supporting the work of women pastors in Myanmar, the focus of my earlier DMin research, and all those who are asking sincere questions about the place of women in Christian leadership.

The need for dialogical conversation between interpreters and sacred texts is crucial and timely because Myanmar is in a new phase of its history as a country. Recent political and economic changes mean that the role of women in society is undergoing changes. More than ever before in the history of Christianity in Myanmar, women are now being trained in theological institutions. Yet, although theological institutions have accepted these women, church traditions still make leadership in ministry difficult, if not impossible. This study is an invitation to biblical interpreters in Myanmar to reflect together on these issues as a community of believers.

Moreover, this study can offer to hermeneutics a new approach to understanding the Bible in the context of Myanmar. It is my hope that this study will challenge interpreters to seriously consider a fresh approach to biblical interpretation that is relevant for Myanmar. It is important to raise awareness of the role of the interpreter's presuppositions in biblical interpretation, including the relevance of cultural understandings, social location, and theological traditions as important factors that influence the decisions of the interpreter. I hope that by applying the questions raised here, we will discover new insights from the Bible that we have missed because we have followed traditional ways of reading texts. It is my belief that, through this new way of reading the Bible, we will discover new ways of doing contextual theology in the context of Myanmar.

Consideration of these issues has practical value in contributing to the work of the churches in Myanmar and their theological institutions, including their theologizing, hermeneutics, mission, translation, social analysis, assessment of the role of women in church and society, and New Testament studies.

1.5 Literature Review

Material on Myanmar was located in the libraries of the Myanmar Evangelical Graduate School of Theology (MEGST) and the Myanmar Institute of Theology (MIT). Resources on biblical hermeneutics and contextual theology came mainly from the University of Otago library. John England's *Asian Christian Theologies: A Research Guide to Authors, Movements, Sources* was particularly helpful in identifying relevant authors.

The books and articles consulted can be divided into four categories:

(1) material on Myanmar which deals with interpreting the Bible in general or interpretation done by Myanmar authors;

(2) material relating to contextual theology in Myanmar and the formulation of a contextually engaged hermeneutic;

(3) material on the three representative hermeneutical schools of thought, and in relation to the history and culture of first-century Corinth; and

(4) material on similar contextual studies in other contexts.

1.5.1 Literature on Interpretation in Myanmar

It is only recently that scholars in Myanmar have begun to dialogue critically with Judson's translation and there are only a few articles which deal with aspects of his translation work rather than exegetical analysis of the translation itself.

La Seng Dingrin has raised questions[4] from the perspectives of mission and linguistics, highlighting the terminology borrowed by Judson from Burmese Buddhism which includes terminology for God and ways of making references to God. He attributes Judson's failure to reach many Burmese, to his negative attitude toward Buddhism despite his willingness to use Buddhist terms. Although La Seng Dingrin's focus is different from the one I have taken, it is helpful for identifying some of the influences behind Judson's translation choices.

Other issues related to Judson's linguistic usage are highlighted by Khoi Lam Thang[5] and Eh Tar Gay.[6]

From the perspective of translation, Khoi Lam Thang, general secretary of the Bible Society of Myanmar, examined Isaiah 40:31, where Judson translated the term for eagle as *shwe lin ta* ("golden vulture") instead of *lin yung* ("eagle"). He defended Judson's choice while acknowledging its problematic aspects.

---

4. Dingrin, "Adoniram Judson's Tracts." See also his "Conflicting Legacy of Adoniram Judson."
5. Thang, "Eagle in the Myanmar Bible."
6. Gay, "Authority and Submission."

From the perspective of postcolonial hermeneutics, Eh Tar Gay's PhD thesis raises the issue of missionary influence on the role of women in the church of Myanmar. She examines several New Testament texts dealing with authority, power, and submission in people's social, political, and religious life and discusses how these have been exegeted by mainstream scholars, missionaries, Asian liberation theologians and feminists, and by Myanmar Christians.

Gay's work is particularly helpful in understanding the role of Judson's translation in shaping Myanmar churches' views on the status of women in the church. It is also helpful in informing our understanding of how words such as authority, power, and submission gained importance in the Myanmar church based on the broader political situation, social and cultural traditions, and religious teachings. She notes the influence of Judson's translation of 1 Corinthians 14:34–35,[7] but does not investigate the linguistic differences between Judson's translation and the Greek text, which is the primary interest of this study.

John De Jong raises linguistic questions about Judson's translation from the perspective of Old Testament studies.[8] He notes that in Genesis 4:7, Judson translates the Hebrew word *hattat* as "sin offering" rather than "sin." He sees Judson's translation as similar to that of Matthew Henry (1662–1714) and Adam Clarke (1762–1832), whose rendering of Genesis 4:7 was widely held during his lifetime. However, as De Jong notes, this is no longer considered an accurate rendering, even if it is the one that most Myanmar Christians know. In the light of this, De Jong asks Myanmar interpreters to accept the reality that "Judson was affected by the understanding of the time."[9] My work shares some similarities with De Jong's in terms of linguistic analysis, but it differs with respect to other aspects of his methodology.

1.5.2 Literature on Contextual Theology in Myanmar

Literature[10] on contextual theology in Myanmar generally focuses on communication from the perspective of mission, rather than on contextual

---

7. Gay, 284.
8. De Jong, "'Sin Offering'?"
9. De Jong, 91.
10. For example, Lwin, "Contextualization of the Gospel." See also Khawsiama, *Towards a Ludu Theology*.

hermeneutics. It nevertheless contributes to an understanding of the role of context in shaping the Myanmar worldview and way of life. Theologians such as Tha Din (1963), Pau Khan En (1995), Peter Thein Nyunt (2010), and Samuel Ngun Ling (2014) address Christian communication approaches, missionary strategies, and issues relating to indigenous Christians, especially in relation to Bamar Buddhists. Two of these authors were former Bamar Buddhist monks, while the others are from a Christian background.

Tha Din trained in the scholarship of Buddhist monks before his conversion. His book *Comparative Study of Buddhist and Christian Scriptures* raises awareness of the role of Buddhism in the Myanmar worldview and daily life. From this, he developed a comparative approach between the teachings of the Bible and the teachings of Buddhism, but highlighting the similarities between the two religions rather than their differences. Din's work is a serious treatment of the teaching of Buddhism in conversation with Christianity, however, it does not include exegetical analysis of the sacred texts of either religion.

Pau Khan En's thesis, "*Nat* Worship: A Paradigm for Doing Contextual Theology for Myanmar," sees *nat* (spirit) worship highlighting the need for Myanmar Christians to think seriously about contextual theology. He argues that since an aspect of *nat* worship is widely practiced among Buddhists in their daily life, it should be considered theologically by Myanmar Christians in order to address issues relating to spirituality and worship. This is helpful in raising awareness of a contextual influence on the Myanmar worldview, though it does not provide principles and methods for contextual hermeneutics, which is our primary interest.

In his book, *Mission amidst Pagodas*, Peter Thein Nyunt examines past and current Protestant approaches to Burmese Buddhists. He agrees with Tha Din and Pau Khan En about the influence of Buddhism in forming a Myanmar worldview based on religious values, which directly influences how the Bamar people make daily life decisions, including decisions about changing their faith. He notes how Protestant missionary endeavors to communicate with Burmese Buddhists failed to enter into the worldview of the people, and regards approaches to communication which continue to imitate Western churches as inadequate and contextually irrelevant. He proposes a missiological strategy based on principles of contextual communication. Although his work differs from my concern for contextual hermeneutics, he clarifies the role of the interpreter's worldview in the hermeneutical process.

The work of Samuel Ngun Ling, who is president of the Myanmar Institute of Theology and a Baptist, is very relevant since he is also searching for a critical form of analysis that takes the context of Myanmar seriously. In *Christianity through Our Neighbors' Eyes*,[11] Ling analyzes the way theology and mission are understood and practiced by Baptist churches in Myanmar, though his work is relevant for church life in Myanmar generally. He sees conventional approaches to theology and mission as still dependent on missionary teaching and imported theologies from the West, and argues that they are no longer relevant to Myanmar's religious, cultural, and sociopolitical contexts.[12]

Ling calls for the deconstruction of Western traditions and practices in the church, and the reconstructing of these in a "Burmese way and thought forms with the use of Burmese religious cultural resources."[13] In order to do this he proposes a cross-textual hermeneutic[14] that interprets Christian and Buddhist texts dialogically, as a part of an interreligious dialogue.[15] This is helpful as another way of doing contextual study, though it is not concerned with developing a critical contextual hermeneutical method.

1.5.3 Three Western Hermeneutical Approaches

The hermeneutical approaches of three Western biblical interpreters are examined to discover principles for the articulation of a contextual Myanmar hermeneutic since there is almost no literature that explores the interpretation issues surrounding 1 Corinthians 14:34–35 written by interpreters in Myanmar. I was able to locate only one exegetical paper relating to women's silence in the church, written by Eh Tar Gay, on 1 Timothy 2.[16]

The three schools of thought were selected because of their influence on contemporary views in Myanmar. They were also selected for their

---

11. Ling, *Christianity through Our Neighbors' Eyes*.
12. Ling, 177.
13. Ling, 129.
14. Lee, "Cross-Textual Hermeneutics."
15. Ling, *Christianity through Our Neighbors' Eyes*, 295.
16. Gay, "Exegesis on 1 Timothy 2:11–15."

similarities in understanding the historical context of 1 Corinthians 14:34–35 in relation to prophecy.

Wayne Grudem[17] is a complementarian[18] and is taken as representative of the literal-traditional school. He sees male headship as "biblical manhood"[19] and argues that Paul was seeking to preserve male leadership as the norm in the church. He provides insights into the theological reasoning used by those whose views about women's roles relative to men[20] are similar to those which have been normative in the Myanmar church. His book, *The Gift of Prophecy in 1 Corinthians*, is explored, including his examination of 1 Corinthians 14:33–35.[21]

As a representative of feminist hermeneutics, the work of Elisabeth Schüssler Fiorenza is also explored. Her book, *In Memory of Her: A Feminist Theological Reconstruction of Christian Origins*,[22] is examined along with other writings which address interpretive issues in 1 Corinthians 14:34–35.[23] *In Memory of Her* introduces her "hermeneutics of suspicion" and draws attention to the patriarchal context of biblical texts and their androcentric presuppositions. She traces how the role of women has been impacted by the patriarchal presuppositions which lie behind some New Testament texts, as well as the patriarchal influences that resulted in a forgetting of women's history in the church. She calls for a historical recovery of the place of women in the New Testament and argues from the perspective that Paul was not himself a hierarchialist.

For an egalitarian or evangelical feminist hermeneutical point of view, the work of Ben Witherington is examined.[24] His book, *Conflict and Community*

---

17. http://www.waynegrudem.com. He was involved in the translation of the ESV and was the general editor of the ESV study Bible.

18. Complementarians consider the roles of women and men to be complementary and that their functions in leadership and ministry are different, with headship reserved for men. Piper and Grudem, *Biblical Manhood and Womanhood*.

19. A term often used by Grudem. See Grudem, *Biblical Foundations*, and Piper and Grudem, *Biblical Manhood and Womanhood*.

20. Grudem, *Evangelical Feminism*. See also his *Gift of Prophecy*.

21. Grudem, *Gift of Prophecy*, 239–255.

22. Schüssler Fiorenza, *In Memory of Her*.

23. Schüssler Fiorenza, "Rhetorical Situation."

24. http://www.benwitherington.com/. The suffix III after his name is often but not always used.

in Corinth: A Socio-Rhetorical Commentary on 1 and 2 Corinthians,[25] is examined along with his other writings[26] which analyze 1 Corinthians 14:34–35. Witherington pays attention to historical critical analysis and places the cultural and social context of 1 Corinthians 14:34–35 in historical perspective alongside a literary reading of the passage. He argues that Paul was neither hierarchical nor feminist and views the issues highlighted in 1 Corinthians as more cultural and rhetorical than theological.

Other commentaries that I consulted include those by Anthony Thiselton,[27] Roy Ciampa and Brian Rosner,[28] David Garland,[29] Gordon Fee,[30] Phillip Payne,[31] Craig Keener,[32] Jerome Murphy-O'Connor,[33] as well as the Asian scholar, Edgar Ebojo.[34] Female scholars include Antoinette Wire,[35] Cornelia Crocker,[36] and Lucy Peppiatt.[37] Bruce Winter[38] has also been useful for his perspectives on the sociohistorical context of Corinth.

1.5.4 Literature on Contextual Hermeneutics

Contextual theologians who have been helpful include the Roman Catholic scholars, Stephen Bevans and Robert Schreiter, and the evangelical scholars, Paul Hiebert and Dean Fleming. Each of them highlights the contextual character of all theology, but they are also concerned about theological integrity. Their concern for evaluation as well as contextually sensitive interpretation and application are important foundations for constructing a critical contextual hermeneutic for Myanmar.

---

25. Witherington, *Conflict and Community*.
26. Witherington, *Women in the Earliest Churches*, also his *Women and the Genesis*.
27. Thiselton, *First Epistle to the Corinthians*.
28. Ciampa and Rosner, *First Letter to the Corinthians*.
29. Garland, *1 Corinthians*.
30. Fee, *First Epistle to the Corinthians*.
31. Payne, *Man and Woman*.
32. Keener, *Paul, Women and Wives*.
33. Murphy-O'Connor, *Keys to First Corinthians*.
34. Ebojo, "Should Women Be Silent?"
35. Wire, *Corinthian Women Prophets*.
36. Crocker, *Reading First Corinthians*.
37. Peppiatt, *Women and Worship*.
38. Winter, *Roman Wives, Roman Widows*.

Stephen Bevans in his *Models of Contextual Theology* clarifies a core concern of this book – namely, the role of context in hermeneutics generally. Drawing on his experience as a missionary in the Philippines and his work as professor of historical and doctrinal studies at the Catholic Theological Union in Chicago, Bevans provides a helpful explanation of the differences between the perspectives, assumptions, and methods of Western theologians compared with Majority World theologians. He points out that theology in the Majority World has traditionally been dictated by Western perspectives and has thus failed to address contextual issues and concerns. He invites readers to enter into a creative dialogue by examining five models of contextual theology: "translation," "synthetic," "praxis," "transcendental," and "anthropological." He takes seriously the role of contemporary experiences and questions in all theological conversations. His work aids in analyzing the influences of Western biblical and theological perspectives in Myanmar, though he does not directly approach the hermeneutical issues surrounding the interpretation of biblical texts in Myanmar.

Robert Schreiter's *Constructing Local Theologies*[39] is helpful for articulating principles of contextual hermeneutics. Like Bevans, he is a former missionary and also a professor of theology at the Catholic Theological Union in Chicago.[40] Schreiter affirms how cultural context functions as a source of the questions that interpreters bring to their theological conversations. He has observed how, in many Majority World contexts, these questions often emerge out of experiences of colonialism and dissatisfaction with colonial interpretations. He sees these questions as valid starting points for theological conversations and proposes a theological method which takes such local questions seriously. He calls for a theology that seeks to answer questions which people "on the ground" grapple with, rather than the institutional agendas of the church. His method of "dialogical analysis" between the contemporary context and the Bible is particularly helpful.

From the perspective of evangelical scholarship, Paul Hiebert and Dean Flemming raise similar issues. Paul Hiebert was professor of mission and anthropology at Trinity Evangelical Divinity School and a former missionary

---

39. Schreiter, *Constructing Local Theologies*.
40. https://ctu.edu/faculty/robert-schreiter/.

in India. His 1987 article "Critical Contextualization"[41] advocated a contextualization which took the Bible seriously in responding to questions about traditional beliefs and practices and the assessment of how some may be judged appropriate and others not. He highlighted the importance of analysis of culture alongside exegesis so that it is possible to respond critically when applying biblical texts in different cultural contexts. Critical contextualization makes it possible to discuss what practices are relevant for a given context, as well as checking them against the risks of inappropriate syncretism, or confusion of religious loyalties. Although he is primarily concerned with contextual theology, his work is helpful for understanding the need to include a critical form of analysis in any contextual hermeneutic.

Like the other three contextual theologians, in his *Contextualization in the New Testament: Patterns for Theology and Mission*, Dean Flemming[42] believes that the contemporary questions which interpreters bring to the biblical text are an important beginning step of the interpretive process. The next step is discovering the meaning of the text in its original setting, in ways which allow the text to confront the presuppositions and assumptions that interpreters bring to the text. He addresses patterns of contextualization found within the New Testament itself and calls for a critical as well as a transformational study of the Bible. He sees Paul engaged in a dynamic interplay between "Israel's Scriptures, the gospel as an interpretive matrix, and the life situation of the mission churches."[43]

Lastly, the literature I consulted includes sources written by Western scholars on the translation of the Bible. Given the questions which arise from the linguistic usage of the Judson Burmese Bible, the work of William Smalley has been particularly helpful, especially his *Translation as Mission: Bible Translation in the Modern Missionary Movement* which outlines the historical development of Bible translations and discusses translation issues such as the theology and principles of translation, including dynamic equivalence.

This is helpful also in understanding how translations are related to a range of hermeneutical issues.[44] Smalley highlights the issue of an interpreter's

---

41. Hiebert, "Critical Contextualization." See also in his *Anthropological Reflections, Transforming Worldviews*, and *Gospel in Human Contexts*.

42. http://www.mnu.edu/faculty/profile/dean-flemming.html.

43. Flemming, *Contextualization*, 167, 172.

44. Smalley, *Translation as Mission*, 177.

personal experiences and preferences in interpreting theological meanings within a text and traces the source of many interpretive problems to the interpreter and the presuppositions brought to their examination of biblical texts, including in the context of Myanmar.

Part One

The Myanmar Context

CHAPTER 2

Silence in Myanmar

The Historical and Cultural Context

The contextual setting of Myanmar is complex. According to the 2014 census,[1] Myanmar, formerly known as Burma,[2] is a homeland for over 51 million people. There are eight major ethnic groups – Kachin, Kayah, Kayin, Chin, Mon, Bamar, Rakkhine, and Shan and some 135 spoken languages. The Bamar form the majority group at 68 percent of the population, with the Shan at 9 percent , Kayin 7 percent, Rakhine 4 percent, Mon 2 percent, Kachin 1.5 percent, Chin 1 percent, Kayah 0.75 percent, and the remainder Chinese and Indians.[3]

Myanmar is also marked by its religious diversity. The 2014 *Census Report* states that Buddhists constitute 87.9 per cent of the total population, Christians 6.2 per cent, Muslims 4.3 per cent, Animists 0.8 per cent, and Hindus 0.5 per cent. Other religions are 0.2 per cent, and 0.1 per cent of the population does not follow any religion.[4]

This diversity of ethnicities and religions has made the country culturally rich, but at the same time it has created ethnic, religious, and political

---

1. The Republic of the Union of Myanmar, *2014 Myanmar Population and Housing Census*, 1. See also Spoorenberg, "Myanmar's First Census."
2. Steinberg, *Burma the State of Myanmar*, xi.
3. Guo, ed., *Understanding Burma (Myanmar)*, 24.
4. The Republic of the Union of Myanmar, *2014 Myanmar Population and Housing Census. The Union Report: Religion, Census Report Volume 2-C.*, 4.

complexities and conflicts. This reality provides the conceptual framework or lens through which the Myanmar interpreter approaches biblical texts. It is the backdrop to the assumptions they bring to any interpretation of 1 Corinthians 14:34–35.

In this light, this chapter introduces the contextual background of Myanmar in terms of three major historical periods, and notes how the worldview revealed in this cultural and political history has predisposed the people of Myanmar, including Christian biblical interpreters, to understand the concept of silence.

2.1 The Historical Background of Silence in Myanmar

In Myanmar, as in other contexts, the prior understanding of biblical interpreters of the concept of silence cannot help but influence their interpretation of silence in 1 Corinthians 14:34–35. Burmese people generally understand the concept of silence as a sign of submission, as well as a sign of respect for the powerful, meaning anyone in a position of authority. This concept has been socially constructed within the historical realities and cultural worldview of Myanmar. It has gained significance in Myanmar due to its prolonged history of imperial, colonial, and postcolonial authoritarian rule. It is also rooted in and reinforced by the religious teachings of the major religion (Buddhism) and the cultural values that are intertwined with these religious teachings.

This chapter thus traces the development of the concept of silence in Myanmar from a historical and political perspective, including the background of relevant religious teachings, and how this has influenced the status of women in present-day Myanmar. The focus is on the silence that is imposed by the powerful upon those who are less powerful through factors such as the use of power, particularly how respect is enforced by the powerful over the powerless, and through actions that create fear in people, thereby preventing them from voicing their concerns. These factors are cross-examined with particular reference to the status of women in key historical periods.

2.1.1 The Precolonial Period

The earliest known settlements in Myanmar were Mon and Pyu.[5] The Mon people settled in the Irrawaddy Delta and Tennesarim coastal areas around 2500 – 1500 BC,[6] and the Pyu (present-day Yunnan)[7] set up the first known city-states in the central part of Myanmar around the second century BC.[8] It was only in the ninth century AD that the Burmans/Bamar people founded a small settlement at Pagan (Bagan), and they later overwhelmed the Pyu.[9] Pagan gradually grew in power, and this led to the beginning of the first Bamar empire. The precolonial period from around the second century AD to 1824 when Myanmar came under British rule[10] was a period of kings and kingdoms, where kings generally practiced an absolute form of authoritarian rule.

The Pagan empire, from AD 1050 to AD 1287, was founded by King Anawrahta, who introduced Theravada Buddhism into the kingdom in AD 1050.[11] The Mongols defeated this empire in AD 1287, and this led to a series of smaller kingdoms such as the Shan, the Mon in the Hanthawaddy kingdom, and the Bamars in the Ava kingdom.[12] The Taungoo empire was founded in 1522 by the third king of the Taungoo dynasty, who was known as Bayinnaung.[13] He conquered a wide swath of mainland Southeast Asia.[14] However, the empire unraveled soon after his death in 1581 and fell into the hands of the Mon in 1752.[15]

---

5. Guo, *Understanding Burma (Myanmar)*, 4.

6. Guo, 4.

7. Moore, *Early Landscapes of Myanmar*, 236. The cities were Thayetitaya, Bekthano, and Prome.

8. Guo, *Understanding Burma (Myanmar)*, 4.

9. Seekins, *Historical Dictionary of Burma*, 13; Guo, 4.

10. Guo, *Understanding Burma (Myanmar)*, 10.

11. Guo, 6, notes that the rulers from this period of the Pagan Empire were exceptionally powerful and wealthy and built over 10,000 Buddhist temples in the Pagan capital zone alone. Many are still standing. During this reign, the Burmese language and culture gradually became dominant in the upper Irrawaddy. See also Topich and Leitich, *History of Myanmar*, 156.

12. Seekins, *Historical Dictionary of Burma*, 13.

13. Guo, *Understanding Burma (Myanmar)*, 7; Topich and Leitich, *History of Myanmar*, 30.

14. He conquered the Shan states, Lan Na, Manipur, the Chinese Shan states, Siam, Lan Xang, and southern Arakan; Guo, 7.

15. Seekins, *Historical Dictionary of Burma*, 13.

The Konbaung empire, from AD 1752 to AD 1824,[16] was the last kingdom of Myanmar. The Konbaung king, Mindon, was a proponent of formal education, and modernized the kingdom. However, during his son Thibaw's reign, three wars were fought with the British, the first in 1824.[17] After the third war, the country became part of British India in 1885.[18]

The social structure of these precolonial period societies was strongly hierarchical, placing the king at the center of power and the village unit at the bottom. The kings, as well as the chiefs or headmen of the villages, were known for their authoritarian use of force which paralyzed and terrorized the lives of ordinary people. In these three periods, while there were a few benign kings, most were known for their cruelty and their demands for respect that forced people into submission. They "could remove or even execute their officials at any time, for the slightest offence."[19] The legends of the thirty-seven talented individuals[20] killed by kings due to jealousy and suspicion are testimonies to the unbridled power and authority of the kings. Legends describe these kings as turning into powerful spirits, called *nats*. These were believed to have influence over human affairs, and many in Myanmar still worship them today.

Seekins describes this precolonial period as a time of "absolute monarchy."[21] Kings were believed to have obtained their positions due to their birth and meritorious deeds in past lives,[22] following the religious concept of *kutho*, or *karma*,[23] which teaches the importance of doing good deeds in order to achieve a better life through reincarnation. This not only legitimized the king's power and authority, it also legitimized the suffering of the people, which was assumed to be the result of their lack of meritorious deeds in past lives.

Kings were further thought to have entitlement to *hpoun* (charismatic glory or innate power), since *hpoun* was endowed only to men, who possess

---

16. Seekins, 13; Guo, *Understanding Burma (Myanmar)*, 8.
17. Seekins, 12–14. The first Anglo-Burmese War was from 1824 to 1826, the second from 1852 to 1853, and the third in 1885.
18. Guo, *Understanding Burma (Myanmar)*, 8.
19. Fink, *Living Silence*, 15.
20. Fink, 16.
21. Seekins, *Historical Dictionary of Burma*, 50.
22. Fink, *Living Silence*, 16. Also Harriden, *Authority of Influence*, 61.
23. The doctrine of *karma* asserts that the present life of a person is the result of merit accumulated in previous incarnations.

let-yon (military force) and *a-na* (authority).[24] The downfall of a king was viewed as the result of weakness in his *karma* and *hpoun*. After a victory in battle, cruelty toward the defeated was considered a sign of the king's *hpoun*.[25] These concepts were introduced concurrent with the installation of Buddhism in the kingdoms and became strongly integrated into the belief system of the people. They continue to exert a powerful influence on the worldview of people, and especially on the daily lives of women in Myanmar.

Despite the absolute power of kings, there is also the suggestion that, relative to other societies at the time, women enjoyed some degree of freedom in their social roles during the precolonial period. According to Jessica Harriden, the social roles and status of women during the Pagan period were determined by class as much as by gender.[26] She notes that class distinctions were less rigid than in other Asian societies, and were based on "differences of birth, wealth and profession."[27] Women who were born into the ruling class, which included the royal family and high-ranking officials, had power and status over commoners derived from their family lineage. Although the highest offices in the court were reserved for men, during this period educated women, especially those of higher status, served as lower level officials, royal secretaries, and clerks in the court.[28]

Among commoners, the wives and daughters of rich traders had rights to inheritance and property, and were able to work in any profession, albeit with much lower wages than men. However, a woman's status was typically linked to her relationship to a powerful man. A prime example of this is the only woman monarch, Queen Shinsawbu (AD 1453–1472), from the Hanthawaddy kingdom, a major Burmese state.[29] Her rule was made possible

---

24. Lieberman, *Burmese Administrative Cycles*.
25. Seekins, *Historical Dictionary of Burma*, 208.
26. Harriden, *Authority of Influence*, 55.
27. Harriden, 55, notes four categories of commoners: *Asan* ("unbounded people who earned their livelihood through private business"); *Kwyan-to* ("people in the royal service"); *kwyan* ("people bonded to private individuals") and; *pura kwyan* ("those dedicated to Buddhist establishments"). *Kywan* was not precisely equivalent to slavery, as some people became *kywan* out of obligation and a relationship formed between "a client and his or her patron."
28. Harriden, 55.
29. Seekins, *Historical Dictionary of Burma*, 405.

only when there were no male relatives of the king left to rule, and she was the wife of the late king.[30]

The role and status of women in the precolonial period can thus be described as both somewhat liberated as well as limited. This can be seen in marriage during this period, where the standard for husbands was different from that of wives. Although a man could have many wives, a woman could not have more than one husband. This polygamy "created unequal power between men and women"[31] and was related to the concept of *hpoun* which assumed that only men could possess inborn glory and *karma*. Men are viewed as being of a higher spiritual order and thus superior in status to women. This concept continues to influence the worldview of both men and women to this day.

Built on this concept, the husband is referred to as *ain-oo-nat*, meaning "spirit head of the house," while the wife is referred to as *ain-shin-ma*, meaning "lady, house owner."[32] The customary law of *Dhammathat* even allows a husband to chastise his wife by beating her with a stick.[33] Although motherhood is highly esteemed,[34] mothers are expected to view their "son as lord and husband as god."[35]

According to the Burmese Buddhist female writer Mi Mi Khaing, the concept of *hpoun* still influences the lives of women today.[36] It can be seen in the daily lives of all women, especially wives who are expected to respect the glory of men and to protect this glory by not standing or sitting on a higher level than a man, not thrusting their feet in his direction, and not sleeping on his left side because his *hpoun* resides on his right side. A woman is even expected to treat a man's clothes with the same respect as the man himself. A woman's clothes must also not be placed over anything connected with a

---

30. Harriden, *Authority of Influence*, 71.
31. Harriden, 58.
32. Khaing, *World of Burmese Women*, 194.
33. Gay, "Authority and Submission," 44.
34. Children are taught that the care given by parents is beyond repayment. It is often said that even though Buddha showed his mother "the way to nirvana, he did not manage to repay more than a minute portion of what he owed her." Kyi, *Freedom from Fear*, 75.
35. Khaing, *World of Burmese Women*, 16.
36. Khaing, 16.

man, including his clothes.[37] Ma Sein Sein, a prominent Burmese Buddhist, summarizes in the following way:

> It has always been believed that men have a kind of in-born power of glory called *phon* [*hpoun*], regarded as a distinctive feature of men, and which keeps them on a different plane from that of women. The women have not this *phon*. This *phon* [*hpoun*], according to the belief, must in no way be harmed or weakened. A woman's skirt is supposed to be a dangerous article. As such, no man will touch the skirt of a woman, unless it is his mother's or grandmother's, once it has been worn. He will never bathe in water from the same jar or tub which the female members or the household used for themselves.[38]

Since the concept of *hpoun* entrenches the glory and holiness of males, it also affects the religious lives of Burmese women, reinforcing the religious hierarchical structure that restricts women from religious spheres.[39] Since the thirteenth century, the *sangha*,[40] which is the highest spiritual authority in Theravada Buddhist societies, has excluded religious women (nuns) from being fully ordained *bhikkhuni*, meaning "female Buddhist monastics," instead designating them as *thilashin*, or "owners of virtue."[41] Male monks are referred to as *pongyi*, meaning "great glory."[42] This distinction means that only boys can go through the ceremony of *shinpyu*, which is initiation into the *sangha*.[43] Girls merely go through an ear-piercing ceremony during the time of the

---

37. Khaing, 16.
38. Sein, "Position of Women," 76.
39. Khaing, *World of Burmese Women*, 71.
40. The *sangha* is the community of monks who are voluntary members of monasteries. They have the responsibility of conserving and teaching *dhamma*, the teachings of Buddha. They follow a strict monastic rule, including the study of religious texts, the *Tipitaka*, and practicing meditation in order to prepare for entry into *nirvana* (*neikban* in Burmese), which is liberation from *samara*, the cycle of rebirth, and suffering. Seekins, *Historical Dictionary of Burma*, 334.
41. Ikeya, "'Traditional' High Status of Women."
42. Seekins, *Historical Dictionary of Burma*, 389.
43. *Shinbyu* is a "ceremony marking adolescence for boys, when they spend a short time as novices in a monastery." This is done with great celebration, usually by the parents or sponsors, in order to gain *kutho* (merit). Boys who go through the ceremony also gain *hpon*. Khaing, *World of Burmese Women*, 197.

shinpyu ceremony, a ritual that is considered only social, without the spiritual significance of *shinpyu*.[44]

This hierarchy of value has created perceptions of the family and the communal and social order that have sanctioned a view of women as inferior to men. This was used by men as the "ground of social, political and religious hierarchy to legitimize women's oppression and subordination."[45] Although women were allowed to participate in gaining merit (*kutho*)[46] by practicing generosity (*dana*),[47] including building monasteries and temples as well as making small donations, only men were able to attain "enlightenment."[48] In other words, a man is considered to be spiritually higher than a woman.[49] Womanhood is seen as a stage of low *karma* due to misdeeds or lack of *kutho* (merit) in the past. For a woman to attain such enlightenment, she must be reincarnated as a man first to attain the state of *nirvana* or *nibban*.[50] Women are also seen as hindrances for men in achieving the state of *nirvana*.[51] For these reasons, many women during the precolonial era expressed their desire to be reborn as a man or a *nat* (spirit).[52]

---

44. Khaing, 197. The first pair of earrings is given to a girl to symbolize "her entry into a woman's world and ending her days of careless play in the company of boys."

45. Aye Nwe, "Gender Hierarchy in Myanmar," 131.

46. Seekins, *Historical Dictionary of Burma*, 389. Buddhism teaches that everyone must work out their own liberation through observation of precepts, and performing good deeds of merit, and meditation. The monks are not responsible for laypeople's liberation.

47. *Dana* is an act of offering to the monks by donating daily food (*soon*) to the monks when they go out daily with bowls. When a monk refuses to receive the "daily food offering," it is a form of religious protest and it affects laypeople negatively, as they then lose their opportunities to gain merit.

48. Harriden, *Authority of Influence*, 57; Tin, "Women in the Inscriptions of Pagan."

49. Khaing, *World of Burmese Women*, 16. "For us it is no less than a glorious truth to recall that the greatest concentration, clean thought, and enlightenment was attained by the Buddha as a man, who had discarded his family ties ruthlessly. So, there is no doubt in our minds that, spiritually, a man is higher than a woman."

50. Khaing, 16. This is a state where there is no more *Samsara*, the cycle of birth and rebirth.

51. "Monks, I see no single form so enticing, so desirable, so intoxicating, so binding, so distracting, such a hindrance to winning unsurpassed peace from effort – this is to say monks, as a woman's form. Monks, whatever clings to women's form – infatuated, greedy, fettered, enslaved – for many a long day shall be . . . snared by the charms of a woman." Nikaya, *Book of the Gradual Sayings*, vol. 3, 93.

52. Tin, *Women in the Inscriptions of Pagan*, 412, notes that the female donor of a pagoda in Pagan had it inscribed that: "I wish to be freed from this state of a woman and when in future existence I pass through the abodes of men and of spirits I wish to be born a man endowed with virtue, understanding, truth and faith."

The absolute authority of rulers over the lives of their subjects created an atmosphere of fear. The people accepted the rule of the kings, as well as their own servitude, as the result of the meritorious deeds of the kings in their past lives, and they obeyed kings without question. Although the social status of women was in certain cases somewhat on a par with men, their religious role and social position relegated them to an inferior status. Their silence sealed this status.

2.1.2 The Colonial Period

The status of women in Myanmar during the colonial era has affinities with racial and gendered patterns in other colonized countries where the organization of society was based on colonial constructs of power and control.[53] The colonial period in Myanmar started with the first Anglo-Burmese war with the British in 1824.[54] There was a second war in 1852. After the third war and the fall of Mandalay, Myanmar came under British rule in 1885,[55] and was regarded as part of British India until 1937.[56] Due to growing anti-British sentiment and nationalism,[57] the Burma Independence Army fought against the British with the help of the Japanese, and the colonial era ended in 1942.[58] The Japanese occupied Myanmar from 1942 until 1945, when the

---

53. Harriden, *Authority of Influence*, 110.
54. Seekins, *Historical Dictionary of Burma*, 14.
55. Seekins, 14.
56. Seekins, 14. In 1937, Ba Maw became the first prime minister and premier of Burma. The British moved the capital to Yangon, which was called Rangoon at that time.
57. Seekins, 301. The wars led to anti-British feeling, but British attitudes (for example, refusing to remove their shoes in Buddhist temples) also fueled this sentiment. British policy was to have two separate kinds of government in the one country. They administered "Ministerial Burma" where the Burmese dominated, and the "Frontier Areas" controlled by traditional chiefs, as separate territories. Ethnic battalions were used to crush uprisings which created further tensions between the ethnic groups and Burmese Buddhists. This "divide and rule" policy exacerbated relationship problems between the ethnic groups the British favored, and Burmese Buddhists, and thus reinforced a growing religious polarization. Buddhist-centered nationalism was a response to the spread of Christianity among the other ethnic groups and the favoritism displayed by the British. The arrival of Indians who took over businesses from the Burmese also increased tension.
58. Seekins, 22, notes that this was led by student leaders such as Aung Sang, who organized student groups and called for independence. In 1940, before Japan formally entered the Second World War, Aung San formed the Burma Independence Army in Japan. In 1942, the Japanese formed the Burmese Executive Administration headed by Ba Maw.

unified Burma National Army,[59] allied with the British army, defeated the Japanese.[60] Myanmar became an independent country on 4 January 1948.[61]

The effects of the colonial era on women's roles and status were both positive and negative effects: socially, economically, and politically. A positive effect was the opening of doors to formal education for girls,[62] which in the precolonial period had only been available through monastery education to mostly male and elite children. The first school for girls was established by Christian missionaries in 1827, and the British authorities introduced coeducational schools in Lower Burma in 1868.[63] This provided new economic and social opportunities whereby women were able to become involved in journalism, law, nursing, and teaching, and some later became influential figures in the nationalist movement against colonial rule.[64]

However, although education enabled Burmese women to make "great advances," some Burmese women writers have accused the colonial educational system of instilling "conceptions of femininity and domesticity in Burmese girls" and training them primarily to be good wives and mothers.[65] A popular perception of parents was that the education of their daughters would increase their value in the "marriage market."[66] Therefore, female education during the colonial era must also be evaluated as limited to, in general, equipping women mainly with domestic skills and British colonial morals rather than scholarly or open-ended skills.[67] It also became a movement away from the traditional economic role that Burmese women enjoyed in the precolonial period. Before colonization, many women were economically independent, being involved in agriculture, trading, weaving, and textile

---

59. Seekins, 22–25. This agreement was officiated by General Aung San with ethnic leaders, as a commitment to live together in a new country side by side. The treaty was signed in Panlong, a town in what is now Shan state, at their second conference, and is known as the Panlong agreement. The decisions were embodied in the Constitution of 1947, which combined the features of a federal and a unitary state.

60. Seekins, 22.

61. Seekins, xxvi. General Aung San did not live to see the independence of Burma. Political rivals assassinated him and eight other cabinet members on 19 July 1947.

62. Harriden, *Authority of Influence*, 118.

63. Harriden, 118.

64. Harriden, 142.

65. Harriden, 119. See also Delap, "Uneven Orientalisms," 406.

66. Khaing, *World of Burmese Women*, 93.

67. Delap, "Uneven Orientalisms," 403.

manufacturing.⁶⁸ Due to rapid commercial expansion during the colonial era, many women lost their traditional businesses to Indians, who were brought from India by the British as soldiers, civil servants, construction workers, and traders, and who also became moneylenders.⁶⁹ The dominance of Indians in business further fueled resentment toward colonial rule. Many women who lost their land and businesses later joined the nationalist movement against British colonial rule. This loss of women's economic power "reinforced gender differences."⁷⁰

The impact of colonialism on the role and status of women cannot be separated from the Buddhist-led nationalism which developed as a response to the religious favoritism displayed by the British toward ethnic minorities.⁷¹ When Christianity became prominent among the ethnic minorities, it appeared to the Buddhist majority as a foreign religion and a threat to national identity. A popular catchphrase was "to be Burmese/Burman is to be Buddhist."⁷²

When educated Burmese Buddhist men formed the Young Men's Buddhist Association in 1906,⁷³ many women participated in their nationalist activities, especially village women who had lost their businesses under colonial rule.⁷⁴ However, given "the religious divide between monks and women and the cultural emphasis on male political authority,"⁷⁵ women's involvement was restricted to supporting male leaders of nationalist groups. In 1920, female students also joined the first students' strike,⁷⁶ which protested against the educational system teaching more about the kings and queens of Britain than their own history.⁷⁷ This was seen as fostering dependence on and submission

---

68. Harriden, *Authority of Influence*, 19.

69. Harriden, 117.

70. Harriden, 117.

71. During the Third Anglo-Burmese War, some missionaries encouraged Karen to cooperate with the British in suppressing Burmese rebels.

72. Seekins, *Historical Dictionary of Burma*, 11.

73. Harriden, *Authority of Influence*, 123. The name was modelled on the Young Men's Christian Association. It began in response to concern about Christian missionary movements among the ethnic minorities.

74. Harriden, *Authority of Influence*, 123.

75. Harriden, 125.

76. Seekins, *Historical Dictionary of Burma*, 425; Harriden, 132.

77. Many mission schools maintained their Westernized curriculum, together with Christian religious education, as instruments for evangelizing Buddhists. Even though

to British authority.[78] Women also played an important role in the 1930 strike,[79] both as journalists and publishers as well as in supportive roles such as cooking and cleaning.[80]

Although women actively participated in these protests, the growing involvement of the movement in militant nationalist activities "reinforced the view that they [women] needed men's protection and guidance."[81] Once again, the role of women was restricted to supporting the male leaders, since militant activities were considered as masculine. This view of women was further reinforced during and after World War II by the British as well as the Japanese. Although a women's army unit, consisting of one hundred female soldiers, was formed to join the anti-Japanese resistance in 1945, only seven women were chosen to serve in minimal duties, such as cooking and providing moral support for the male soldiers. This regiment only lasted three months. Harriden notes how it provoked "no significant shift in men's perception of women's (limited) capabilities."[82]

In evaluating the role and status of Burmese women throughout the colonial period, it was not only Burmese men who relegated women to a submissive and subordinate role derived from patriarchal cultural and religious beliefs. British colonial attitudes also reinforced the ideology of women as inferior to men. Even though some colonial writers portrayed Burmese women as possessing more freedom, independence, and equality with men than in the neighboring countries and the West,[83] they also pointed out that

---

missionaries themselves were not from Britain, the work of the missions was seen as a colonial invention. Christianity is still perceived as a Western religion.

78. Kyi, *Freedom from Fear*, 54. In 1920, the male student leaders started *Dobama Asiayone* (meaning "We Burmese Association") and were known as *thakhins* ("masters"). The women who joined the movement were known as *thakhimas* (mistresses). During the colonial era, the term *thakhin* was used to address British people. By appropriating this term in the *Dobama Asiayone,* they are asserting that "the Burmese rather than the British were the true masters of the country." Seekins, *Historical Dictionary of Burma*, 445.

79. The anti-British spirit was sparked by dissatisfaction toward the rule of British Commissioners and officials as well as Indian junior staff. This led to several uprisings. The colonial authorities ruthlessly crushed the revolt led by Saya San with unarmed peasants in 1930–1932.

80. Harriden, *Authority of Influence*, 131.

81. Harriden, 133, notes that "in both the 1936 and 1938 strikes, male nationalist and student leaders emphasized the need to protect the female participants."

82. Harriden, 139.

83. Fielding-Hall, *Soul of a People*, 215; Hall, *History of South-East Asia*, 3.

women's independence and influence was seen as not "feminine,"[84] as a mark of "uncivilized and backward society,"[85] and as undermining their husbands' "authority" and "power."[86] Given this view of Burmese women, colonial officers were warned not to take Burmese wives or mistresses, and intermarriage between the British and the Burmese was significantly lower than in other colonial societies in Southeast Asia.[87]

The colonial authorities also at times depicted Burmese women as possessing a traditionally "high status"[88] compared with other colonial countries, especially India. Pointing out this relatively higher status of Burmese women was one way in which the colonials could indoctrinate Burmese women into believing that they enjoyed a privileged position, in comparison to the more "backward" Indian women.[89] Colonial writers often pointed out that Burmese women did not have to practice "*sati* and *purdah*"[90] like women in India, that they had the right to receive an inheritance, and the right to receive property in a divorce settlement.[91] On the other hand, colonial writers also highlighted the low literacy rate of Burmese women and the high infant mortality rate as evidence of their failures in education.[92] Missionaries such as Ann Judson also claimed that Burmese women had a high status, but concluded that they still lacked education since these women allowed men to oppress them.[93] The

---

84. Harriden, *Authority of Influence*, 108. An example is Supayalat, the last queen of Burma. Most historians portray her negatively as being domineering over her husband, King Thibaw. Her use of power and influence was described as like that of men and not feminine, but she was also accused of using her sexuality to dominate her husband. Many colonial writers saw the fall of the Kongbaung dynasty as the result of her interference in political and military matters which were reserved for men.

85. Harriden, 111.

86. Harriden, 112.

87. Harriden, 113–114.

88. Ikeya, "'Traditional' High Status of Women," 51.

89. Ikeya, 76.

90. *Sati* is the practice of widow-burning and *purdah* is the wearing of a veil. Ikeya, 60.

91. Ikeya, 58.

92. Ikeya, "Gender, History and Modernity," 18.

93. Delap, "Uneven Orientalisms," 389, notes that in 1823, Ann Judson described Burmans as "a lively people, oppressed by 'despotic rulers,' whose way of life was in sharp contrast to their 'Hindoo' neighbours." "They have none of the habitual indolence of the natives of Hindostan, nor are they addicted to that gloomy jealousy which prompts so many eastern nations to immure their females in the solitude of a harem. The sexes have equally free intercourse as in Europe." Ann Judson wrote to her American supporters that Burmese women "are on an equality with ourselves. Wives are allowed the privilege of eating with their husbands."

influence of the missionaries on the role of women in Myanmar will be discussed in greater detail in the next chapter, which addresses the history of interpretation in Myanmar.

In assessing the impact of the colonial period, one could conclude that colonial attitudes toward Burmese women were conflicting and led to mixed results.[94] On the one hand, women's greater access to education and the colonial narrative about their having a "high status" contributed to their participation in nationalist movements to contest colonial rule in Burma. Women advocated for independence, yet they were not given important roles in the nationalist movements.[95] The nationalists also condemned the intermarriage of Burmese women and Indians as unpatriotic and an abandonment of their "high status."[96]

In short, the presumed "high status" of Burmese women was used as a political tool by both colonial men and Burmese men. A positive view of women's involvement in economic life and education existed side by side with negative ideologies that restricted women to a limited and subservient role in society. Ikeya notes that "the very attribute that gave women their autonomy and power subordinated them to men religiously, politically, ritualistically, and ceremonially."[97] Despite some gains in terms of greater access to education, women were once again restricted to obeying and submitting to authority, as in the precolonial period.

2.1.3 The Postcolonial Period

The status of women in Myanmar during the postcolonial period was determined by gender-appropriate ideals, membership in the elite class, and ethnic identity as seen in similar societies with military dictatorships, where the structure of society is "hierarchical,"[98] "authoritarian," and androcentric.[99]

Nonetheless, she stressed the need for strenuous action on their behalf: "Show us the situation of our tawny sisters on the other side of the world, and though the disgusting picture breaks our hearts, it will . . . excite us to stronger exertion on their behalf." She considered that Burmese women lacked education and "were tyrannized by their male kin."

94. Harriden, *Authority of Influence*, 111.
95. Ikeya, "'Traditional' High Status of Women," 64.
96. Ikeya, 74.
97. Ikeya, 55. See also Ikeya, "Gender, History and Modernity," 9.
98. Harriden, *Authority of Influence*, 180.
99. Harriden, 180.

The period in Myanmar has been described as one of a drastic "decline in women's status"[100] – politically, economically, and socially.

After gaining independence from the British in 1948, Myanmar enjoyed a brief period of parliamentary government until 1958.[101] However, serious problems began with a rebellion by some ethnic minority troops,[102] which led to the "Burmanization"[103] of the military. Various ethnic groups considered this to be a violation of the Panlong agreement[104] and it led to many other insurgencies. Tension increased with an attempt by the government to promote Buddhism as the state religion,[105] resulting in a military coup on 2 March 1962.[106] The military then ruled the country under a one-party socialist system until 1988.[107]

Failure to provide adequate education and economic opportunities led to further poverty, and students led massive protests against military rule, beginning in August 1988.[108] In response, the military formed the State Law and Order Restoration Council and seized power in September 1988.[109] In the face of continuing political unrest, free elections were held for the first

---

100. Harriden, 174.

101. Seekins, *Historical Dictionary of Burma*, 29, 78.

102. In 1949, the Karen, with the help of other ethnic troops, started an uprising, but the majority of officers who were Burmans, and some ethnic troops, remained loyal to the government. This ended the mixed multiethnic army that the British established in 1945. Seekins, 29.

103. The Burmanization of the army was instigated by General Ne Win to include only the Burman ethnic group in the military, especially at the command level. Harriden, *Authority of Influence*, 308.

104. This was signed on 12 February 1947 at Panlong in Shan State by General Aung Sang with ethnic leaders of the Kachin, Chin, and Shan. They agreed to incorporate Burma Proper and the Frontier Areas into one independent Burma. They also agreed to ensure "fair and equal treatment of the Frontier Area peoples through representation in the highest levels of government and economic development." Seekins, *Historical Dictionary of Burma*, 352.

105. Seekins, 29. U Nu, the first prime minister of the country, was in office during this time.

106. Seekins, 30.

107. This government was called "the Socialist Republic of the Union of Burma." During its rule, ethnic minorities lost the special status guaranteed in the Constitution of 1947 and after implementation of the Constitution of 1974. Seekins, 419.

108. This demonstration was known as the "Four Eights Movement," named after a general strike that began on 8 August 1988. It was organized by student activists joined by thousands of citizens and led to a violent crackdown by the military. Seekins, 192.

109. Known in abbreviated form as SLORC. Later, they changed their name to SPDC, the State Peace and Development Council. Seekins, 419.

time in May 1990.[110] Yet, despite the fact that the National League for Democracy achieved a landslide win, the military continued to rule the nation.[111] After the so-called "Saffron revolution" led by Buddhist monks in 2007,[112] a process of political change was again initiated and a new constitution was published in 2008.[113] Military rule was dissolved in 2011[114] and a parliamentary democratic system of government was reinstated.[115]

The role and status of women in postcolonial Myanmar is tied to the entire experience of repressive, authoritarian military rule described above. During both the socialist phase and the State Peace and Development Council period, military leaders controlled the whole country and silenced opponents by imposing severe restrictions on the media, closing independent newspapers or nationalizing them, prohibiting criticism of the government, and imprisoning and torturing anyone who spoke out in any way.[116] Any opposition was illegal in this period. During the socialist period, the party leadership did not tolerate "public dissent or criticism from party members, let alone from anyone outside the party."[117] Government workers and civil servants were ordered not to engage in politics, and people were, in general, too afraid to participate in any case. It became even harder for ordinary women in Myanmar to express any political views.

Conditions during the latter period of military rule were described in October 1996 by Judge Rajsoomer Lallah, the United Nations Special Rapporteur of the Commission on Human Rights, in stark terms: "There is essentially no freedom of thought, opinion, expression or association in

---

110. Seekins, 323.

111. General Saw Maung led the State Law and Order Restoration Council from 1988 to 1992. See Skidmore and Wilson, *Dictatorship, Disorder and Decline*, 30; Rogers, *Than Shwe*.

112. Rogers, *Than Shwe*.

113. *Constitution of the Republic of the Union of Myanmar (2008)*.

114. Skidmore and Wilson, *Dictatorship, Disorder and Decline in Myanmar*, 13. General elections under the new constitution were held on 7 November 2010. The name was changed to the Republic of the Union of Myanmar and Thein Sein became the first president on 30 March 2011.

115. The parliament consists of two legislatures, the *Pyidaungsu Hluttaw* (House of Representatives, 440 seats) and the *Amyotha Hluttaw* (House of Nationalities, 224 seats). Twenty-five percent of seats are allocated to military personnel. Aung San Suu Kyi and forty-two other National League for Democracy members who won in the April 2012 by-elections later joined the parliament.

116. Harriden, *Authority of Influence*, 181.

117. Harriden, 179.

Myanmar. The absolute power of SLORC is exercised to silence opposition and penalize those holding dissenting views or beliefs."[118]

Under this government, the economic status of women declined as the whole country suffered through mismanagement of the economy and corruption. Ordinary wives struggled alongside their husbands to provide for their families, although the wives of the top military leaders, and those who were close to the elite, prospered.

During this period, the use of force by the army to force people into submission was the normal way of life. Several major violent crackdowns occurred: on unarmed university students in 1962, on thousands of protestors in 1988, during peaceful demonstrations by monks in 2007, in wars against ethnic groups, the imprisonment of anyone who attempted to express dissent, in displaced villages, forced labor, and the forbidding of freedom of speech and expression. These were routine occurrences during this period.

As in Myanmar's historical past, the role and status of women depended on their having connections to powerful men. This was the case for both the wives of senior military officers who were given significant roles in politics during military rule, and for Aung Sang Suu Kyi, who was asked by the opposition groups to be their leader due to her connection as the daughter of the national hero of Myanmar.[119] However, although Aung Sang Suu Kyi and the wives of the military elite had connections to powerful men, their experiences differed because of their positions relative to authority and power. The women who were closely related to the military elite enjoyed social, economic, and political opportunities that other women did not have. Through their connection to military leaders, these wives and other women in the elite circles experienced great advances in their economic wealth and influence in society.

In an attempt to curb international criticism of discrimination against women, top military leaders gave leadership opportunities to their wives. In 1998, they formed the Myanmar National Working Committee for Women's Affairs (MNWCWA),[120] albeit with males in the top leadership positions. After the United Nations Convention on the Elimination of All Forms of

---

118. Houtman, *Mental Culture*, 213.
119. Harriden, *Authority of Influence*, 308.
120. Houtman, *Mental Culture*, 139, 244.

Discrimination Against Women (CEDAW) committee session in 2000 pointed out the failure of the military government to address women's rights, and reports from ethnic women's groups[121] which accused the military of rape and violence against women in ethnic regions, the military formed the Myanmar Women's Affairs Federation (MWAF) with wives of generals in leadership roles.[122] All wives of military personnel and government officials, and all female government employees were expected to join,[123] but the leadership positions were restricted to the wives of the ruling elite.

This organization supported and defended the military regime's policies and actions and promoted "social welfare and traditional culture"[124] in ways that reinforced the already existing stereotypes of women's role in society with programs that focused on women's nurturing role, vocational training in skills such as sewing and weaving, and promoting the concept of feminine culture through beauty pageants.[125] Women's empowerment was encouraged only to the extent of mobilizing women to defend the military. Members were warned not to get involved in politics, and women in opposition politics were condemned,[126] especially Aung San Suu Kyi,[127] who was the most prominent voice of resistance during this time and who was placed under house arrest for extended periods of time.[128] After the 1988 demonstrations, there were more female political prisoners than ever before.[129]

The military encouraged women to only pursue professions considered appropriate for females. Ordinary women were involved in agriculture,

---

121. Harriden, *Authority of Influence*, 256. The report was assembled by the Shan Human Rights Association (SHRF) and the Shan Women's Action Network (SWAN) and entitled *License to Rape: The Burmese Military Regime's Use of Sexual Violence in the Ongoing War in Shan State*. The military denied the charges and asked women in the MNCWA and women's NGOs to work harder to defend the government.

122. Daw Kyaing (wife of Military Council Chairman Than Shwe), Daw Mya San (wife of Vice-Chairman Maung Aye), and Dr. Daw Khin Win Shwe (wife of Prime Minister Khin Nyunt) held administrative positions.

123. Harriden, *Authority of Influence*, 261.

124. Harriden, 263.

125. Harriden, 253.

126. Harriden, 258.

127. Seekins, *Historical Dictionary of Burma*, 98.

128. She was under house arrest from 1989 to1995, 2000 to 2002, and 2003 to 2010. In 1991, she was awarded the Nobel Peace Prize for her nonviolent struggle for democracy. She was released on 13 November 2010.

129. Fink, *Living Silence*, 167.

industry, service sectors, and professions such as nursing and teaching. In line with their nationalist ideology, the military appropriated the nationalist discourse of the colonial era and condemned Burmese women who married foreigners.[130] Although the government did not officially make Buddhism the state religion, they vigorously promoted it. As with the nationalist rhetoric from the colonial period, the Buddhist religion was used to control people through the promotion of devotion to senior monks and the allocation of huge resources for pagoda projects, which led to public support for the religious majority.[131] And as in precolonial times, the religious concepts of *hpoun* (glory of authority), maintaining *hpoun* by merit, and making *kutho* in order to gain good *karma* in the next life were manipulated to legitimize the authority of those in power. The military made people believe that military rule was part of their *karma*.[132] Aung Sang Suu Kyi pointed out that there is another aspect of *karma* that promotes creating one's own *karma*.[133]

In addition to appealing to *karma* and *hpoun*, the military also used the cultural concept of respect for authority to enforce obedience. From childhood, children in Myanmar are taught to submit to the "five reverent ones"[134] – Buddha, *dhamma* (the teachings of Buddha), *sangha* (the community of monks), parents, and teachers. Teachers and parents are to be regarded with "awe, love and respect."[135] Paying regular homage to them[136] and obeying their

---

130. The military used Aung Sang Suu Kyi's marriage to Michael Aris against her in their nationalist discourse.

131. Seekins, *Historical Dictionary of Burma*, 378.

132. A person's *kan*, which is the Burmese version of *karma*, is one of the key concepts that lies behind the understanding of authority in Myanmar. Although *kan* is generally understood as "luck" in English, it is more about a person's destiny or fate. This is determined by an individual's merit (*kutho*) or demerit (*akutho*). There is a common saying, "a person's good or ill fortune is the 'fruit' of good or bad *karma* from a previous life." As a result, a person would generally accept the control of authoritarian figures over them without question. Seekins, 239, 389.

133. Kyi, *Voice of Hope*, 168 and 186. "I remind the people that karma is actually doing. It's not just sitting back." "You create your own karma. And in a sense, I believe in destiny, it's something that I create for myself."

134. Kyi, *Freedom from Fear*, 66.

135. Kyi, 67. Burmese children are taught from an early age that the care given by their parents is beyond repayment.

136. The culture of showing gratitude and reverence to parents, teachers, and monks is manifested collectively as well as individually. During *Thadingyut*, the festival of light that marks the end of the Buddhist Lent around mid-October, and on the Burmese New Year's Day called *Thingyan* in the middle of April, the proper way of showing respect is called *gadaw* –

instructions without question are marks of proper respect. The military rulers used this to enforce silent submission and obedience.[137]

This leads to the question whether women in the ethnic groups understand submission and silence in the same way as Burmese women. In both the cultures of the ethnic minorities and the Burmese, the ideology of patriarchy is accepted. In Chin society, women traditionally enjoyed even fewer social opportunities than Burmese women, because the cultural mores of the Chin do not accord women inheritance rights. Men can divorce their wives at any time, for any reason. The father has the sole right to retain custody of the children in the event of divorce. Caring for children and domestic duties are considered women's duties alone.[138] Like the veneration of men in the concept of *hpoun*, women's role in Kachin society is considered to be one of lowly drudgery. As they are considered impure or unclean, women are not allowed to participate in religious ceremonies, and are "prohibited to climb trees lest the fruit fall before it is ripe, or to enter a newly built house because they might defile it." The traditions and cultural practices among the ethnic groups support a hierarchical worldview in which men are at the top and women at the bottom.

Proverbs and popular sayings among the ethnic groups also portray negative attitudes toward women. Chin sayings include the following: "Wives and gongs: the more you beat, the better the sound"; "the voice of women is worthless and meaningless"; "a woman's word cannot reach up to the gate"; and "the price of a woman is equal to a smoking pipe." Similar attitudes are found in Burmese proverbs. Some examples include: "The sun rises when roosters crow, but never with the clucking of hens"; "the voice of women never reaches beyond the gate"; "as the bun (hairstyle) follows the head, the

---

bowing down deeply before parents, teachers, or monks to receive their forgiveness and blessings. A person of lower social standing always pays respect to a person of higher standing by kneeling and paying obeisance with joined hands and bowing. Fruits, tinned foods, candles, and other articles are placed in decorated baskets before the teachers, parents, and monks as a token of respect.

137. Steinberg, *Burma the State of Myanmar*, 53, says the "government . . . is the parents; the people are the children who must obey the parents and must be punished when they do not do so. If recalcitrant children (e.g. the insurgents) repent, then as wayward sons and daughters they would be welcomed back into the fold."

138. Pa, "Asian Feminist Theology," 21.

wife must follow her husband"; and "buffalo and woman, the more you beat them the better they work."[139]

All of these patriarchal cultural values were reinforced by the military government which used them to ensure women's silent obedience. In this milieu, women in the ethnic groups understood submission and silence in the same way as the Burmese women, for they share a culture that silenced people from speaking out against anyone in authority.

During this period, the decline in women's access to economic and political power was endemic for minority groups in Myanmar, whether ethnic or religious. Due to the increase and severity of the wars with ethnic groups, not only did women's access to economic participation decline sharply in those regions, but as in all wars they also suffered mentally and emotionally. A study among these women revealed decades of conflict and experiences of torture, shootings, interrogations, and forced labor which resulted in their deeply ingrained sense of fear.[140] Creating and sustaining such fear was a strategy that was used by the military to impose silence and submission and reinforce the social hierarchies.

The experiences of ethnic women in the war regions was intertwined with religious minority experiences, since most of these women are Christians. As in the colonial period, Christianity was considered an alien Western influence. In 1962, foreign missionaries were banned from living in the country.[141] Christians were still portrayed as having supported British colonial rule, and Christians found it difficult to rise to high-ranking positions in the army or the civil service.[142]

The role and status of Christian women during this period is linked to the experiences of other Christians across Myanmar. Fink observes that "although Christians in the cities and towns in central Burma have not faced physical persecution, they have been harassed in various ways."[143] Some of the very difficult problems that Christians encountered during the military period included being denied building permits for churches, new churches being

---

139. Pa, "Boundary Crossers and Risk Takers," 83.
140. Ma and Kusakabe, "Gender Analysis of Fear and Mobility," 253.
141. Seekins, *Historical Dictionary of Burma*, 302.
142. Fink, *Living Silence*, 167.
143. Fink, 167.

pulled down even after proper permits were obtained, difficulty in getting passports for church leaders, crosses being taken down and churches replaced with Buddhist temples, forced conversions to Buddhism among ethnic children in Buddhist monastery schools, forced labor on Sundays, physical abuse of Christian clergy, prohibiting the import or publishing of religious materials, and many other similar difficulties.[144] Among the Christian ethnic minorities, persecution relating to religion has been more dominant than other ethnic-related issues, and Christians view their struggle as necessary "not only to protect their ethnic rights but also their religion."[145] As a minority population, Christians have found it very difficult to have any public voice.

Christians have also struggled theologically in this period over whether they should accept unjust rule as "God's will." An example of this occurred during the 2007 demonstrations when the most prominent churches in Myanmar remained silent. One author attributed the churches' silence to their interpretation of Romans 13:1–7 as equating silence in the face of an unjust government with following God's will.[146] Many Christians, pastors as well as church members, accepted suffering as God's will and took a passive role. Christian women's acquiescence in this silence echoed their silent submission to their husbands, fathers, and other men in authority over them.

We may conclude that while the role of women in the colonial era was a mixture of positive and negative experiences, in the postcolonial period the role of women was more negative than positive. Christian women's role and status during this period was centered on their gender, ethnic identity, and religious identity. Although Christian women shared the struggles of women in general, their ethnic and religious backgrounds added an additional layer of suffering. As the system of government turned more repressive, the nationalist religious-based (Buddhist) traditional values it embraced further diminished the status of women. The domestic and submissive roles of women were strengthened, and women's empowerment and independence diminished. The result of oppression on the mentality of women was silent obedience to authority.

---

144. Chin Human Rights Organizations, *Threats to Our Existence*, 18. Also in Partners Relief and Development, *Crimes in Northern Burma*.

145. Fink, *Living Silence*, 224.

146. Nan, "Submission to the Government," 7.

We can conclude that throughout the history of Myanmar, there have been aspects of liberation as well as of repression. The political history of Myanmar highlights a "culture of power"[147] which is deeply rooted in the religious teachings of Buddhism. This concept of power was reinforced by authoritarian rulers who forced submission on the people and used fear to silence them and legitimize their rule. This concept of silence greatly influenced the underlying ideology and identity of the people. The effects of this concept were manifested in the political sphere in the relationship between the rulers and the ruled, in the social sphere in relationships between men and women and parents and children, and in the religious sphere in relationships between the leaders and followers of different religions.

All these contributed to the ideological framework within which Myanmar biblical interpreters have understood the concept of *silence*. This cultural and historical understanding of the concept, grounded in submission to authority, was reinforced by the early missionaries. Hence, it is important to examine the role of missionaries in buttressing the culture of silence for women in the church.

2.2 The Impact of Missionaries on Myanmar Interpreters and Their Understanding of Silence

As the previous section made clear, silence as a sign of submission to anyone in a position of authority derives from a collective history and worldview steeped in a religious orientation. This integral role of religion and culture shapes the thinking of both men and women in Myanmar regarding authority and the status of women. This has strengthened the control of every perceived authority over people in all areas of life, including the political, societal, and religious spheres. Much of Myanmar women's self-image and social image derives from "religious values," and the dominant Buddhist religious worldview has had a profound effect on women, whether one views this as one of "oppression or liberation."[148]

Christianity in Myanmar has also been significantly shaped by the cultures and worldview of Western missionaries. The historical backgrounds of

---

147. Steinberg, *Burma: The State of Myanmar*, 50.
148. Mananzan, "Woman and Christianity."

Adoniram Judson and the women missionaries of his period had a huge impact, including on the role of women in the church. Even after missionaries left Myanmar, Christians continued to follow their teaching and example. To the present day, churches still depend on "imported theologies inherited from the past centuries and eras without critical appraisal of their relevancy and empowering vitality."[149] Nearly two centuries after the first missionaries arrived, their ideological presuppositions have continued to influence the church in terms of its "God-talk (theology)," "form of worship," "structure of church organization," and "strategy of mission outreach."[150] For this reason, studying the history and legacy of the missionary era is important in order to help understand the current worldview and attitudes of the Myanmar church.

2.2.1 Overview of Christian Missionaries in Myanmar

Christian missions in Myanmar began in 1554 with the arrival of Father Pierre Bonfer, a French Franciscan who left in 1557.[151] He was followed in 1600 by Jesuit fathers who arrived with the Portuguese adventurer, Philippe de Brito, when he established a colony at Syriam (Thanlyin).[152] Their most famous convert was the Taungoo king, Natshinnaung, a renowned poet, who was killed in 1613.[153] Catholic presence further developed following the arrival of Italian Barnabites in 1721 who began work on translation and printing.[154] Father Vincentius Sangermano was one of the most notable of these priests.

The first Protestant mission to Burma was in 1807, initiated by Rev. Chater and Felix Carey, son of William Carey.[155] However, Protestant missions only began to flourish following the arrival of Adoniram and Ann Judson in 1813. After little success among the Buddhist Burmese, following the First Anglo-Burmese War the Judsons moved to Moulmein in British-occupied territory. Large numbers of Karen were converted.[156] Later, other Baptist missionaries,

---

149. En, *Called to Be a Community*, 15.
150. Ling, "Encounter of Missionary Christianity."
151. Chain, "Wives, Warriors and Leaders."
152. Seekins, *Historical Dictionary of Burma*, xxiv.
153. Seekins, 300.
154. Chain, "Wives, Warriors and Leaders," 1.
155. Sunquist, *Dictionary of Asian Christianity*, 59–61; Clement, *Adoniram Judson*, 39.
156. Seekins, *Historical Dictionary of Burma*, 300.

Karen and foreign, evangelized other ethnic groups such as the Kachin[157] and Chin.[158]

Anglican mission work in Myanmar is often dated from the establishment of the Diocese of Yangon in 1877, although British Anglican chaplains were present from 1852.[159] Anglicans started mission schools in the lower and middle part of Myanmar. Methodists arrived in 1879.[160]

The church in Myanmar grew in numbers despite many hardships and challenges, especially during World War II, but after 1962, when General Ne Win established the Revolutionary Council, all missionaries were ordered to leave the country. The last missionaries left in 1966,[161] and their schools were nationalized. The government regarded missionaries as "accomplices of British colonial oppression and agents of cultural imperialism, robbing indigenous people of their authentic beliefs and ways of life."[162] However, others have highlighted their positive contribution in promoting "health, education and literacy, and a new national identity for ethnic minority peoples, especially among the Karen, Kachin and Chin."[163]

2.2.2 The Influence of Adoniram Judson

Of all the missionaries who came to Myanmar, Adoniram Judson[164] was the most influential in the history of the church, and he continues to be highly

---

157. S'Peh, a Karen, and Josiah Cushing, an American, were the first missionaries to the Kachins in 1878. Moffett, *History of Christianity in Asia*, 577.

158. The American Baptist, Carson, and his wife, accompanied by the Karen evangelist Saw Win, started work among the Chin in 1899. Sunquist, *Dictionary of Asian Christianity*, 61.

159. Sunquist, 27.

160. Sunquist, 542.

161. Sunquist, 577.

162. Seekins, *Historical Dictionary of Burma*, 300.

163. "Missionary activity among non-Burman indigenous populations was one of the most important factors in the development of ethnic nationalist movements during the colonial period. Under missionary and British guidance, Christian ethnic minorities could advance – educationally, socially and politically – to gain far greater influence than that warranted by their numbers." Harriden, *Authority of Influence*, 123.

164. Secondary sources for research on Judson include biographies by his contemporaries such as: Knowles, *Life of Mrs. Ann H. Judson*, 1830, and *Memoir of Ann H. Judson*, 1844; Clement, *Adoniram Judson*, 1852. Wayland, *Memoir of the Life*, 1853; Middleditch, *Records of the Life, Character, and Achievements*, 1854; Judson, *Life of Adoniram Judson*, 1883. Twentieth century biographies include: Warburton, *Eastward!*, 1937; Brumberg, *Mission for Life*, 1980; Anderson, *To the Golden Shore*, 1987. More recent biographies, based on original research, include: Hunt, *Bless God and Take Courage*, 2005; Hulse, *Adoniram Judson*, 2007; Duesing,

regarded. His influence extends to the theology and practices of the church and its mission, and, significantly for our interests, on the language and terminologies still used in the church today.

Samuel Ngun Ling has said that Judson "dominated whatever theological thinking there was among the ethnic Christians and early Burman converts of the nineteenth century."[165] His contributions include translating the Bible into Burmese as well as a Burmese-English dictionary,[166] a Pali dictionary,[167] and several tracts[168] on basic Christian beliefs. These sources are important for understanding the influence of his translation of 1 Corinthians 14:34–35.

2.2.2.1 Historical Background

Judson arrived in Yangon (Rangoon at that time) on 13 July 1813,[169] with his wife, Ann Hasseltine.[170] They devoted three years to the study of spoken Burmese language and to Pali, the sacred religious language of Theravada Buddhism.[171] In 1816, Judson began to translate the Gospel of Matthew from Greek into Burmese, a task he completed in 1817.[172] A Burmese governor was surprised to find that it was the work of a foreigner, who had only learned and used the language for four years.[173] Judson also published several tracts

---

Adoniram Judson, 2012; Christie, *Adoniram Judson*, 2013, and; Burns, "*Supreme Desire to Please Him*," 2015.

    165. Ling, "Encounter of Missionary Christianity."

    166. Judson, *Dictionary of the Burman Language*, 1823, and Judson, *Dictionary, English and Burmese*, ed. Edward Abiel Stevens, 1852, published after the death of Judson.

    167. Seekins, *Historical Dictionary of Burma*, 351. Pali is the sacred language of Theravada Buddhism, in which the Tipitika is written.

    168. His tracts include: *Threefold Cord* and *Septenary, or Seven Manuals*. See Judson, *Life of Adoniram Judson*, 563–64; Burns, "Spirituality of Adoniram Judson," 76. Judson wrote two works on doctrine: *Burman Liturgy* and *Digest of Scripture*; Wayland, *Memoir of the Life*, vol. 2, 467–475; Judson, *Digest of Scripture*.

    169. Wayland, *Memoir of the Life*, vol. 1, 125; Clement, *Adoniram Judson*, 33.

    170. Knowles, *Life of Mrs Ann H. Judson*; Wyeth, *Ann H. Judson*; Robert, "Judson, Ann"; James, *My Heart in His Hands* and "Life and Significance of Ann Hasseltine."

    171. Knowles, *Life of Mrs. Ann H. Judson*, 83. Ann noted that after two years, "Mr. Judson has obtained a tolerable knowledge of the construction of the language, and only needs time and practice to make it perfectly familiar. I can read and write, but am far behind Mr. Judson in this part, though in conversation I am his equal."

    172. Clement, *Adoniram Judson*, 58; Duesing, *Adoniram Judson*.

    173. Walsh, "Adoniram Judson," in *Modern Heroes of the Mission Field*, 74; Pleasants, "Beyond Translation."

in Burmese, translated the Epistle to the Ephesians, and preached in *zayats* despite the unfriendly attitude of the Burmese monarch during this period.[174]

The first convert, Maung Naw, was baptized in 1819[175] and the translation of the New Testament was completed in 1823.[176] That year, Judson was awarded a Doctor of Divinity degree by Brown University but he was troubled by the status and in 1828 renounced the title in order "to rid himself of his perceived self-love."[177] In 1824 the Judsons moved to Ava, where he preached until war broke out between the English and the Burmese. Suspicions that all foreigners were spies for the British meant that in June he was imprisoned for two years in conditions of extreme cruelty.[178] After he was released,[179] the Judsons moved to Amherst, a new British settlement. For a time, he returned to Ava as an interpreter for the British to help negotiate a treaty between the English and the Burmese.[180] However, this contributed to a nationalist view of him as pro-British and of missionaries as representatives of colonialism rather than purely religious teachers.[181] While he was in Ava, Ann died in Amherst in October 1826,[182] and their daughter died soon after in 1827.[183]

Realizing the need to distance the message of the gospel from associations with the British colonial rulers, Judson ceased his affiliation with the British in 1828.[184] In 1829, he moved to Moulmein to work with George and Sarah Boardman, and several converts were added to the church.[185] On 31 January 1834, twenty-one years after arriving in Burma, he finished his translation

---

174. A *zayat* is a resting place for travelers often found in Burmese villages. Clement, *Adoniram Judson*, 71.

175. Clement, 75; Duesing, *Adoniram Judson*, 143.

176. Clement, 95; Duesing, 85.

177. Burns, "Spirituality of Adoniram Judson," 170; Clement, 192.

178. Clement, 184–185; Duesing, *Adoniram Judson*, 90.

179. Clement, 172; Duesing, 90.

180. Trager, *Burma Through Alien Eyes*, 27.

181. Nyunt, "Toward a Paradigm," 141; Trager, xi.

182. Clement, *Adoniram Judson*, 182; Duesing, *Adoniram Judson*, 85.

183. Clement, 186–188; Duesing, 115. After Ann's death, Judson became depressed and gave his property to the American Baptist Mission Board. Wayland, *Memoir of the Life*, vol. 2; Duesing, 79–81.

184. Clement, 186–188.

185. Judson went on evangelistic tours to Rangoon, Prome, and among the Karen in jungle areas during 1830 and 1831. Duesing, *Adoniram Judson*, 81.

of the entire Bible into Burmese.[186] That year he married Sarah, by then the widow of George Boardman. He spent seven more years revising his translation and on 24 October 1840, it was ready for the press. In 1842, he began to prepare his English to Burmese and Burmese to English dictionary for publication, but Sarah's illness interrupted the work. While returning to America in 1845, Sarah died and was buried on St. Helena Island in the South Atlantic.[187] Judson remarried in 1846 and returned to Moulmein with his new wife, Emily Chubbuck.[188] The dictionary was still unfinished when he died on 12 April 1850, on a ship three days out from Moulmein. He was buried at sea.[189]

The American Baptist work that Judson had started continued to grow. By 1854, there were 63 missionaries (including their wives), 154 Burmese preachers and assistants, and 8,836 members.[190] The Burmese and English dictionary was completed by Edward Abiel Stevens and published in January 1852.[191] Together with his Pali dictionary, Burmese grammar, and his Burmese Bible, these are Judson's great contributions to the church in Myanmar. Although there are at least five other translations or revisions[192] and translations in eighteen ethnic minority languages, Judson's translation remains the most popular.[193]

2.2.2.2 The Influence of Judson's Bible

Judson's Burmese Bible translation is still "the most widely read version in the Myanmar language"[194] and remains highly regarded as "classic literature."[195] It is often referred to as "the authorized Bible in Myanmar."[196] "Like the KJV

---

186. Clement, *Adoniram Judson*, 221; Duesing, 85.
187. Clement, 188, 242; Duesing, 95; Wah, "Outstanding Baptist Women Leaders," 7.
188. Clement, 288; Duesing, 97.
189. Clement, 237; Duesing, 149.
190. Wa, Sowards, and Sowards, *Burma Baptist Chronicle*, 135.
191. Clement, 320, *Adoniram Judson*; Duesing, *Adoniram Judson*, 85; Judson, *Dictionary, English and Burmese*.
192. Thang, "Eagle in the Myanmar Bible," 195. The other translations or editions discussed by Thang are: (1) U Tun Nyein's translation of 1906, (2) the British and Foreign Bible Society version in 1928, also known as the Anglican Version, (3) the McQuire version in 1933, (4) the Myanmar Common Language version in 2005, and (5) the Eagle edition in 2006.
193. Chain, "Wives, Warriors and Leaders," 1; Thang, 195.
194. De Jong, "'Sin Offering'?" 91.
195. Thang, "Eagle in the Myanmar Bible," 195.
196. Gay, "Authority and Submission," 21.

in English, whether or not people understand all its linguistic usages today, many feel that its language is sacred, and should not be changed."[197] Judson's success is seen as "rare in the history of Bible translation."[198]

However, at the same time, there are some problems, including those arising from his decisions to use Pali vocabularies and honorific language which not everyone understands. Pali is considered a "dead" language. It is derived from Sanskrit and is only used by Buddhist monks. Judson learned Pali and used it in his translation after noting that Pali terms were commonly used in Burmese books at the time.[199] He also used honorifics which were used in reference to royal persons and members of the Buddhist *sangha*.

Judson's scholarship was indisputable and his decisions were aimed at maximizing the expansion of Christianity. He intentionally incorporated Buddhist terms from culture and religion into his theological language, but his hope of attracting educated Buddhists by incorporating their sacred language left a "conflicting legacy,"[200] especially when Christianity flourished among ethnic minorities rather than among Buddhist Burmese.

2.2.2.3 Judson's Influence Relating to Gender

Another problematic aspect of Judson's legacy concerns the role of women in the church, where inclusion as well as restriction of women in ministry occurred. Although Judson allowed women missionaries, including his wives, to be actively involved in church work, his translation of passages like 1 Corinthians 14:34–35, where he translated λαλέω as "preaching" in the context of women's silence, precluded women from preaching in most instances. This translation no doubt influenced the missionary women of his era, including his wives, who were actively involved in evangelism and teaching in the church but who, for the most part, refrained from preaching.

His hierarchical and patriarchal notion of authority has also been influential. This is seen in his translations of the word "κεφαλή" in Ephesians. Instead of translating "κεφαλή" as simply "*oo khaung*," meaning "head," relating to the headship of Christ over the church in Ephesians 1:22, he chose to

---

197. Smalley, *Translation as Mission*, 50.
198. Smalley, "Language and Culture," 61.
199. Pleasants, "Beyond Translation," 2.
200. Dingrin, "Conflicting Legacy of Adoniram Judson."

translate it as "*a choke a char oo Khaung*,"²⁰¹ meaning "absolute head."²⁰² Since the word "absolute" is attached referentially to the head, it influences how contemporary interpreters in Myanmar understand power.

Judson implies that the meaning of this passage is that "Christ has absolute power over man as man has over woman." Later, in Ephesians 5:23, Judson translated the same word, "κεφαλή," as "*oo khaung*," meaning "head" only where the relationship of Christ, man, and woman are mentioned. Elsewhere, in 1 Corinthians 11:3–10, when speaking of head coverings, and in Colossians 1:18–19, speaking of Christ as the head of the church, Judson refers to "κεφαλή" as "head" only.

Although Judson translated some words into stronger terms than we find in most English translations, in other passages he used words that are weaker than in the English translations. For example, about the relationships of husbands and wives found in all his translations of the Epistles, he translated the term "ὑποτάσσω," as "*won khan*," meaning "to consent, agree to, or comply with,"²⁰³ which is milder in meaning than the English translation of "be subject" or "submission."

In general, however, his linguistic choices reflect the patriarchal view of authority and submission embraced by the missionaries, mission boards, and sending churches at that time. These understandings are the background to Judson's translation of 1 Corinthians 14:34–36, discussed in chapter 3. The following section explains how they influenced women missionaries and how these women in turn influenced the formation of the Myanmar contextual understanding of the role of women in the church.

2.2.3 The Influence of Women Missionaries on the Role of Women

In the nineteenth century, despite the cultural challenges and limitations imposed upon them, many women in the United States and Great Britain

---

201. The Anglican Version translates "head" as "*a tut a tate*" meaning "the ultimate," thus authorizing a male's authority as ultimate. Gay, "Authority and Submission," 120.

202. The usage in the Judson Bible 1834 version is the same as in the version printed in 1840.

203. Judson, *Dictionary of the Burman Language*, 348. The Anglican Version is milder than Judson's as it translates the term as "*a non a tar*," meaning "tolerance" or "forbearance." Gay, "Authority and Submission," 120.

became involved in "evangelistic, missionary, benevolence, and reform societies founded and led by women."[204] The legacy of women missionaries is paradoxical. Their influence had empowering as well as limiting effects on the role of women in the church. These women missionaries influenced the role of women in the church through their teaching as well as their actions, which reflected the beliefs and teachings of the male missionaries as well as the sending mission agencies.

Among the missionary women who came to Myanmar, those most often mentioned are Ann Hasseltine and Sarah Boardman, the first two wives of Adoniram Judson. They were involved alongside Judson in teaching, preaching, and, to some extent, translation. Their involvement in the work of mission not only set examples for women in Myanmar, but it also inspired many women from their home country to make a commitment to mission work.

After Ann Hasseltine Judson arrived in Myanmar with Adoniram in 1813, they learned Burmese together and her language skill was said to exceed his.[205] With the help of Ma Min Lay,[206] the first Burmese Christian woman convert, she founded in 1821 the first Christian school where both boys and girls in the villages could be taught to read and write. Education at that time was only available to boys and a few females from the higher classes of society.[207] Although she started the school mostly for girls because no attention was given to female education, it soon became co-educational. Through this school many students were converted to Christianity.[208]

Due to ill health, Ann returned to America in June 1823 and helped to publish the first book about the work in Burma, *An Account of the American Baptist Mission to the Burma Empire*.[209] She assisted Adoniram with translating several tracts into Burmese as well as the books of Daniel and Jonah.[210] She also translated the first New Testament in Thai.[211] Ann returned to Burma in December 1823 only to discover that Adoniram was in prison. When she

---

204. Groothuis, *Good News for Women*, 49.
205. Clement, *Adoniram Judson*, 58.
206. Wah, "Outstanding Baptist Women Leaders," 10.
207. Judson, *Account of the American Baptist Mission*, 4.
208. Khai, *Cross amidst Pagodas*, 40.
209. Judson, *Account of the American Baptist Mission*.
210. Robert, *American Women in Mission*, 45.
211. Wah, "Outstanding Baptist Women Leaders," 5.

found out that government officials were to confiscate their house, she put the drafts of the New Testament translation in a pillow and gave it to him in prison with the result that they survived.²¹² She endured many hardships with Judson, including the death of their children, and suffering serious illnesses, but she committed her life faithfully to mission work. She died on 24 October 1826 and was buried in Amherst (*Kyait-kha-mi*).²¹³

Sarah Hall Boardman, who married Adoniram Judson in 1834, was another outstanding woman missionary.²¹⁴ She had come to Burma with her husband Rev. George Boardman in 1827 and they started mission work among the Karen people around Tavoy.²¹⁵ She continued this after her husband's death in 1831 and started a school in 1833.²¹⁶ She completed a translation of the New Testament into the Mon language and also translated Bunyan's *Pilgrim's Progress* into Burmese.²¹⁷

Through the stories of these pioneer women missionaries, not only Myanmar women, but also many Western women, were encouraged to become involved in mission work. Ruth Tucker notes that from 1861 onwards, "women's missionary boards sent out a host of unmarried female missionaries; in less than fifty years there were two women for every man on the mission field." She adds that "the women's missionary movement was unique in that for the first time in history women could take up leadership positions in evangelistic outreach on a large scale" – and they did so with the support of millions of people from their home churches.²¹⁸

However, while these women missionaries had a positive influence on women regarding teaching and education, they also reinforced a traditional understanding of a limited role for women in the church, based on their own understanding of authority and submission,. The following shows the traditional expectations they reinforced and affirmed through their teaching and activities.

---

212. Wah, 4.
213. Clement, *Adoniram Judson*, 188.
214. Wayland, *Memoir of the Life*, vol. 2, 82.
215. Wayland, vol. 1, 423. Ko Tha Byu, the first Karen pastor, was the first fruit of their mission.
216. Wayland, 427, 524.
217. Stuart, *Lives of the Three Mrs. Judsons*, 312.
218. Tucker, *Women in the Maze*, 180.

2.2.3.1 *Women as Supporters and Homemakers*

First, the women missionaries helped reinforce the role of women as supporters of husbands and homemakers. Pierce Beaver notes that the American Mission Board of that time made decisions about missionary marriages and encouraged males to have wives while working on the mission field. They saw the main duty of women as "being a helpmeet and companion" to men and a "mother of children," and that the only suitable jobs outside of the home were teaching their children and other women.[219]

A general rule among American mission boards during this period was to allow only married couples as missionaries, which prevented the appointment of single women. Although this policy changed, and Adoniram Judson lived to welcome Sarah Cummings, the first single woman as a missionary to Burma,[220] these attitudes and policies in turn influenced the general understanding of women's role in the church in Myanmar.

Rosalie Hall Hunt rightly argues that Judson's wives contributed greatly to his work and that his accomplishments were not his alone. Ann Judson "translated tracts and kept Adoniram alive while he was in prison." Sarah "proved a remarkably adept linguist and evangelist." Emily was a "talented writer and expositor of her husband's career."[221] Nevertheless, they appear to have been more admired for their supportive role in relation to their husband's work than for their individual contributions.

2.2.3.2 *Women's Ministry as an Exception*

Judson thought that restricting single women from missionary service was "probably a good" rule, but when Sarah Cummings was appointed, he said that "our minds should not be closed" to making exceptions.[222] Mission boards had begun to consider the employment of single women as an "exception," to be permitted when male missionaries were unavailable, but for some time, translation, literary work, and itinerant evangelism were still seen as "the

---

219. Beaver, *All Loves Excelling*, 52–53.

220. Vuta, "Brief History of The Planting and Growth," 73. Sarah Cummings arrived in 1832 and started work in Chumerah, about sixty miles above Moulmein on the Salween (Thanlwin) river. She died of jungle fever at Moulmein in 1834.

221. Hunt, *Bless God and Take Courage*, 337.

222. Moffett, *History of Christianity in Asia*, 328.

responsibility of missionary men."²²³ Mission board policy, for example, "precluded women from working in Bible translation."²²⁴

The work of Ann Judson as an evangelist and translator alongside her husband was seen as an exception due to the lack of male missionaries. Although Ann was instrumental in opening the door to theological education and ministry for Myanmar women when she introduced co-educational schools, in other respects, she reinforced the traditional roles of women as homemakers through the domesticating curriculum for girls in those schools. She was also involved in teaching in women's groups, meeting regularly with groups of women who were interested in learning about the new religion and teaching them to read the Bible for themselves instead of having it read to them. Although she emphasized the importance of educational opportunities being available to girls not just boys, she also promoted the ideology and theology of the headship of men over women.²²⁵ She avoided preaching to men until her husband's captivity, but during that period, her preaching to gender-mixed congregations was acceptable since she was without a male protector.²²⁶

This was also the case with Adoniram Judson's second wife, Sarah Boardman. Although Sarah assumed the work of her late husband, George Boardman, by preaching to Karen men and women on several occasions, when she was remarried to Judson, she again took on the role of homemaker and gave up her role as evangelist and preacher. Her translation of Bunyan's *Pilgrim's Progress* was praised by Judson as "one of the best pieces of composition we have published,"²²⁷ and although she began the Mon (Pequan) Bible translation and finished the New Testament, she gave up this translation work to a male missionary as soon as one became available.²²⁸ However, she still taught Bible classes and led prayer meetings for women, directed the co-educational school, and instructed native women in "maternal and social

---

223. Robert, *American Women in Mission*, 51.

224. Robert, 51. The Amercian Board of Commissioners for Foreign Missions (ABCFM) was founded in 1810 to support Presbyterian and Congregationalist missionaries. Judson was originally sent out by the ABCFM before he became a Baptist.

225. Robert, 56.

226. Gay, "Authority and Submission," 53.

227. Stuart, *Lives of the Three Mrs. Judsons*, 312.

228. Stuart, 308. James Haswell carried on her work and the translation was published in 1847.

studies."[229] Like her predecessor, Sarah Boardman contributed to the development of women while at the same time affirming the societal expectation of women as homemakers.

2.2.3.3 Obedience to the Authority of Men

Almost all the women missionaries, whether married or unmarried, through their teachings and their personal example, emphasized the importance of obedience to the ultimate authority of men.[230] Nevertheless, there were some Baptist missionary wives like Deborah Wade and Calista Vinton who were noted for their outstanding evangelistic preaching. Deborah Wade was a contemporary of Ann and worked among the Karen people with her husband and when her husband left to preach in remote areas, she preached and taught both men and women.[231]

In 1834, Calista Vinton[232] also came with her husband to work among the Karen, along with the Wades. Given the need, the Vintons began traveling to separate locations, taking assistants and going from village to village. Both Calista Vinton and Deborah Wade preached and taught in mixed congregations. While Deborah Wade refused to call what she did "preaching," Calista Vinton accepted that preaching was her calling.[233] This was accepted by the Vinton's home church in America because it was done in modesty and so was not seen to contradict their understanding that women were not to "usurp authority over the man."[234] Again, this was connected to the idea of making an exception and maintaining the principle that women were only allowed to participate in ministry on the condition that they remained obedient to the authority of men.

Ellen Mason's[235] legacy was different. Her teaching aroused controversy and she was expelled from the mission charged with not following the instruction of the proper authority on the issue of "indigenous leadership and

---

229. Stuart, 305.
230. Gay, "Authority and Submission," 52.
231. Wyeth, *Wades: Jonathan Wade, Deborah B. L. Wade*, 111–122.
232. Robert, *American Women in Mission*, 54; Calista V. Luther, *Vintons and the Karens*.
233. Robert, 55.
234. Luther, *Vintons and the Karens*, 25.
235. Womack, "Contesting Indigenous and Female Authority."

the role of women."²³⁶ She was the third wife of the American Baptist missionary, Francis Mason, who had a successful ministry among the Karen. She had spent her first year in an area supervised by the first single woman missionary, Sarah Cummings, who was a teacher and evangelist and assumed similar roles for herself when she moved to Toungoo with her husband in 1847.

Ellen Mason was accused of doctrinal errors and of causing division²³⁷ and her husband was accused of "sustaining" her "in the exercise of an authority in the church with which, according to the teaching of the Apostle, no woman ought to be entrusted." He was also blamed for not controlling her with marital authority to curb her overzealous leadership.²³⁸ Their support was withdrawn until her husband renounced her errors. Although some of what she taught was indeed controversial, Womack points out that the main reason for her dismissal was her strong "interest in politics and the politics of gender."²³⁹

When examining the work of these missionary women, we see that the attitudes and policies of the sending mission agencies were deeply connected to the perception that the role of women was as supporters of husbands and homemakers, that their forays into the sphere of male missionary work was an exception, and that obedience to the authority of male leadership was unquestioned. Although most of the missionary women complied with the rules, a few resisted. The compliant attitudes and activities of these women further legitimized the authority of men in the church. We can conclude that these missionary women had a profound influence on the role of Myanmar women in the church, both positively and negatively.

2.2.4 Myanmar Women's Reflections on the Role of Women Missionaries

Regarding the positive influence of missionary wives on Myanmar Christian women, Eh Eh Wah argues that missionary wives encouraged Burmese women to be actively involved in mission work. She notes the influence Ma Min

---

236. Womack, 543, 554.
237. Womack, 554.
238. Toungoo Baptist Mission, "Minutes of a Council Held at Toungoo 8 October 1863."
239. Womack, "Contesting Indigenous and Female Authority," 543–559.

Lay, who in 1820 became the first female Burmese Christian and the tenth Burmese convert, as an impressive example of indigenous female involvement in mission work.[240] Ma Min Lay helped Ann Judson found a co-educational school which opened on 20 January 1821.[241] After Ann Judson died, and until she herself died in 1827, Ma Min Lay carried out the work of the mission based in Amherst and extending to the eastern part of Tennesarim. After Ma Min Lay's death, another Burmese woman, Hpwa Tee,[242] took her place in teaching and carried out her duties alongside other missionaries.[243] Since 1983, a "Ma Min Lay Day" has been observed annually in the second week of September in U Naw's Memorial Baptist Church, by the Burmese Women Missionary Society.[244]

However, although these women envisioned new possibilities for women through Christian teaching and education, and the women missionaries were seen as personal examples to follow, a major emphasis was on the traditional roles of women and being subordinate to men. Despite these patriarchal restrictions, "many of the (women) graduates became teachers, bible women and pastor's wives,"[245] but in Myanmar today, the normative view of churches continues to be that the role of women in church is as wives, homemakers, and supporters of male leadership.

Aye Nwe is one who traces this tradition in the Baptist church to the "patriarchal tradition" of the missionaries. She notes that the church is still following this tradition by restricting "women's ordination, leadership, [and] priesthood ministry," and only allowing women to aspire to the highest role as "assistants of male pastors."[246] Khin Thida Nyunt also explicitly traces this traditional view of the role of women as wives and homemakers to the wives of the nineteenth century women missionaries and argues that this legacy is one of the reasons women tend to assume a quiet role in the church and not

---

240. Wah, "Outstanding Baptist Women Leaders," 10.

241. Judson, *Account of the American Baptist Mission*, 256.

242. Wah, "Outstanding Baptist Women Leaders," 13. Hpwa Tee and her husband Nai Mehm Boke were the second converts among the Mon people. She was baptized in December 1828.

243. Wah, 13.

244. Wah, 11.

245. Beaver, *All Loves Excelling*, 121.

246. Nwe, "Women's Roles, Rights," 30.

a leadership role.[247] Thus, most of the women in Myanmar churches serve in the church as Sunday school teachers, secretaries, women's group leaders or youth leaders, rather than pastors, even though they may be educated at the same level as or higher than male pastors.

When a few women do end up in leadership positions, it is still considered an exception, just as women missionaries in responsible leadership roles were considered exceptions in the nineteenth century. Most churches allow women to teach other women, but not mixed congregations or male audiences.

Anna May Chain sees the strategy of women teaching other women as a direct legacy from these missionary wives. It was the reason that the Myanmar church started training schools for "Bible women,"[248] who would teach the Bible to women and children only. Eh Tar Gay notes that this was also the reason for turning these training schools into Women's Bible colleges, even if they are now becoming co-educational.[249] Although the numbers of women students are increasing in most theological institutions in Myanmar, the "women graduate(s) still have to struggle to find places as pastors, theological educators, and executives in associations, conventions, and synods."[250]

In sum, although educated Myanmar women can see new possibilities for themselves in the light of Christian teaching, they still find that their ministry opportunities are limited. They remain under the authority of men in the home and in the church, and silent submission to authority continues to be legitimized not only by Burmese culture, rooted in its patriarchal history and Buddhist religious teachings, but also by the examples of their "new liberators, the missionaries,"[251] who used the Bible as their authority so that silence as a sign of submission found legitimacy in the teaching and examples of missionaries.

---

247. Nyunt, "Myanmar Women in Church and Society," 19.
248. Chain, "Wives, Warriors and Leaders," 1.
249. Gay, "Authority and Submission," 53.
250. Gay, 53.
251. Gay, 53.

2.2.5 The Impact of Missionaries and Culture on Biblical Interpretation in Myanmar

The influence of missionaries, combined with hierarchical and patriarchal cultural perceptions about the role of women, has had an extended effect on present-day biblical interpreters. Their interpretational tradition has supported the hierarchical and patriarchal culture in the church as well as an uncritical understanding of the issues involved in the translation of the Bible. In particular, Judson's translation is regarded as a literal translation from the original languages, and there is little awareness of how all translation involves issues of interpretation.

With few exceptions, the interpretational tradition of the Myanmar church has prescribed the place for women as in the home and the role of women as subordinate to men. This continues to make it difficult for women to speak for themselves or to critique others, especially men, and encourages them to remain silent in the face of abusive situations.

The following writings by Myanmar interpreters are examples of views that a woman's place is in the home, the encouragement of silence even in cases of domestic violence, and beliefs that women's role in the church should be limited. As noted in chapter 1, literature is limited. What is cited here was found in the MIT[252] and MEGST libraries[253] only, but it is reasonable to suggest that it represents prevailing attitudes in the church.

An example of the belief that a woman's place is in the home can be seen in a series of articles published in *Myanmataman*, a Christian monthly magazine published by the Myanmar Baptist Convention. In a 2016 article entitled "Wanted: Christian Daughter-in-Law,"[254] Aung Din describes an ideal wife as someone who lives a virtuous life, who takes good care of her husband and children, and who fulfills all the household responsibilities. A wife should be a supporter of her husband, a protector of his honor, and a follower of his leadership.[255] Earlier, in 2000, Din, writing on preparation for marriage, stated

---

252. The Myanmar Institute of Theology (MIT) in Yangon belongs to the Myanmar Baptist Convention. It was founded in 1927 and is the largest seminary in Myanmar.

253. The Myanmar Evangelical Graduate School of Theology (MEGST) in Yangon was founded in 1995. It is an interdenominational school of the Myanmar Evangelical Christian Alliance (previously known as the Myanmar Evangelical Christian Fellowship).

254. Translation from the Burmese title.

255. Aung Din, "Wanted, Christian Daughter-in-Law," 1–15.

that young men should prepare to be able to lead and feed their households, and that young women ought to prepare to take care of their children and the household.²⁵⁶ In 2004, he wrote that a wife should do the domestic work in the home, save the money that is earned by her husband, and teach children to live a good moral life.²⁵⁷

In these articles, Din maintains that the place for women is in the home, that work for women is domestic work, and that women must be submissive and obedient to their husbands' leadership. As I wrote in the conclusion of my DMin dissertation,²⁵⁸ such teachings influence women to remain silently in the background and to stay away from vocational ministry.²⁵⁹

Another writer, Samo Thoung, also emphasizes the leadership role of the husband. He argues that since men are created in the image of God (Gen 1:26), men alone have the Spirit of God (Gen 2:7). Since Adam was the first receiver of God's commandment (Gen 2:16), therefore husbands should be the leaders of the family. Using these passages to prove men's place of leadership, he concludes that all men should be providers and protectors of their children, wives, and the church.²⁶⁰

Some writers such as Khin Maung Myint even encourage women's silence in cases of domestic violence. In an article in *Myanmataman*, Myint argues that the basis for women to submit to the ruling of their husbands, even in the case of domestic violence, is based on 1 Peter 3:1–5. While acknowledging that this passage was referring to the married women of unbelievers, he insists that the passage instructs all wives "to love, revere, respect, obey and submit to the ruling of the husband. Even if the husband is not religious and a cruel man, the wife is to submit to his ruling."²⁶¹

According to Myint, the prime example of such obedience is Christ's obedience until death. He therefore admonishes wives that, even if their husbands are violently abusive to them, they should "remember that God alone is the

---

256. Din, 7–9.
257. Din, 11–12.
258. Hluan, "Analysis on the Leadership Challenges," 186.
259. This was the main reason given in my research among women alumnae of evangelical seminaries. The question focused on why women seminary graduates did not go into ministry and 40% said that marrying someone who thinks a woman's place in the home was the main reason.
260. Thoung, "Being a Man," 11–12.
261. Myint, *How to Choose Your Mate*, 82.

judge and ask God for strength to be able to endure it."[262] Myint advises wives to be a helper to their husbands in everything, based on Ephesians 5:22, and never to disobey their husbands,[263] warning that wives should "not be like Jezebel, who was a bad woman that died with violent death."[264] He equates wives' disobedience of their husbands to "rebellion against God," since he sees this act as rejecting the authority whom God has appointed to rule.[265]

Finally, a disapproving view of women's participation in the church is also found in other writings from Myanmar. A well-known Christian writer, Thanlwin Pe Thwin, who was a member of the Translation Supervising Committee for the Myanmar Common Language Bible, sees women's leadership in the church as negative. Although he gives no specific scriptural text, his article suggests passages like 1 Corinthians 14:34 and 1 Timothy 2:12. He sees women as drawn to gossip and creating arguments in the church. He describes women's preaching and praying as long and boring. He believes women are more easily attracted to worldly things than men and thus more easily tempted than men. He concludes that women tend to have more difficulty concentrating on spiritual things and are thus not suitable for leadership roles.[266]

These sentiments are shared by an anonymous writer in the journal *Golden Balance* who believes that leadership in the church is reserved only for men and characterized women who aspire to be in leadership roles in the church as being too bold, like Eve, reaching out for something that is not for them. He describes men who allow their wives to lead as acting cowardly, like Adam.[267]

In the many churches in Myanmar that share these views, women's participation is limited, even if in certain situations women can contribute in some ways to some ministries. Although the restrictions vary from denomination to denomination, Baptist, Anglican, Catholic, and Evangelical-Pentecostal women in Myanmar have all stated that the very idea of women's

---

262. Myint, 82.
263. Myint, 82.
264. Myint, 82.
265. Myint, 82.
266. Thwin, *Myanmataman*, 1–15.
267. Anonymous, *Golden Balance 21*, 2.

leadership is a continual challenge in today's churches.[268] Men find it difficult to see women as "co-equal, much less to submit to women in higher authority."[269] For this reason, there are few women in pastoral roles in Myanmar churches today and these women face tremendous challenges, beginning with the right to ordination. Even though women work hard for many years to achieve their theological education, ordination is not permitted for women in some churches, and others require more years of probational ministry than is required for men.

In the churches, Anna May Say Pa highlights some of the problems these teachings create for achieving ordination for women. She describes how because of "strong ideas of [the] pollution of menstruation, elderly women have a greater chance of ordination than younger women. Some men will not take communion served by a woman because of this factor. Whereas a man, just a few years out of seminary, will easily get ordination."[270]

The realities described above indicate the general view of men toward women's roles in the church in Myanmar, but the view that sees women as inferior to men influences the attitudes of women as well. Even in the cases when women in the church are given some opportunities, they find it difficult to take up leadership roles because they lack confidence. Say Pa links this lack of confidence to the teaching of women's subordination and submission.[271] She points out that taking a leading role for a Myanmar woman is "to go against upbringing and training,"[272] because throughout her life she has been taught to think of herself as not as valuable as a son, acculturated from girlhood to be submissive and passive, and told repeatedly that a good girl is never assertive in any sector of society.[273]

Further, Say Pa notes that the silence passages of Paul in 1 Corinthians 14:34–35 and 1 Timothy 2:11–15 are used as "proof texts for limiting women's ministry in the church and restricting women's pastoral leadership role in

---

268. Cing, "Engagement, Women Roles,," 21–38.

269. Cing, 38.

270. Pa, "Asian Feminist Theology," 25.

271. Anna May Say Pa was principal of the Myanmar Institute of Theology from 1998 to 2005 and a pioneer of feminist theology in Myanmar.

272. Pa, "Place at the Round Table," 18.

273. Pa, 18.

the church."[274] Thus, a Christian feminist writer like Aye Nwe raises the need for "reading the Bible critically and reinterpretation for women's emancipation"[275] to challenge the perceptions of both men and women in the church. There are also serious implications in society to be addressed. Nang Thuzar Mon links the kind of teaching from Genesis that men are masters of women because the first woman was created out of the rib of a man, to the problem of sex trafficking of Myanmar girls into Thailand. She sees these teachings as contributing to women's feelings of being undervalued, further influencing a woman to believe that "she cannot raise her voice against violence (since) she has been taught not to."[276]

2.3 Conclusion

Our examination of the contextual setting of Myanmar provides a framework for understanding how biblical interpreters in Myanmar have understood silence in 1 Corinthians 14:34–35. The contextual background of silence in Myanmar is inextricably linked to its hierarchical and patriarchal culture and the symbols that embody that cultural worldview. This worldview forces people into submission, and it is rooted and has been reinforced throughout Myanmar's history by authoritarian political rulers and religious teachings. In the church, this cultural worldview that legitimizes women's silence was reinforced and strengthened by Adoniram Judson and the women missionaries of his era, who affirmed the prevalent cultural concept of the domestic and subservient role of women. This background helps explain the assumptions that Myanmar interpreters bring to their interpretation of women's silence in the most popular Bible in Myanmar, the Judson Burmese Bible translation.

Just as the interpreter's understanding of words in biblical texts is contextually conditioned, the same dynamic occurs in the translator's choice of words. In the Judson Burmese Bible translation, the passage on women's silence in 1 Corinthians 14:34–35 is a great example of such conditioning. Judson's understanding of the role of women contributed to his choice of words in his translation. The following chapter will therefore analyze the

---

274. Pa, 18.
275. Nwe, "Women's Roles, Rights," 33.
276. Mon, "Victimization of Women," 43.

Judson Burmese Bible translation of 1 Corinthians 14:34–35 to show how his choice of words continues to have an impact on Myanmar Christians' views of the role of women in the church.

CHAPTER 3

A Textual Analysis of 1 Corinthians 14:34–35 in Myanmar Bibles

Among Protestant churches in Myanmar, there are six different Burmese Bible translations in general use. Khoi Lam Thang[1] notes five others in addition to the Judson Burmese Bible (JB)[2]: (1) the U Tun Nyein version[3] based on the English Revised Version of 1881 to 1895 and published in 1906[4]; (2) the British and Foreign Bible Society version of 1928,[5] also known as the Anglican Version or the Garrard Bible[6]; (3) the McQuire version of 1933 which was a revision of Judson's Bible by a committee of the Baptist

---

1. Thang, "Eagle in the Myanmar Bible," 195.

2. The Myanmar Catholic Bible version is not included in this list, but see Fr. John Aye Kyaw, *New Testament, Psalms and Proverbs*, and Gunanto, "Biblical Apostolate in Southeast Asia." Prior to the publication of a Catholic New Testament in 2005, the Catholics were using Judson's translation. Other Burmese translations include the "Easy-to-Read" New Testament produced by Bible League International in 2006, and the Myanmar Standard Bible published online by The Global Bible Initiative.

3. U Tun Nyein was a government translator and member of the Plymouth Brethren. He based his translation on the ERV – a revision of the KJV completed between 1881 and 1894.

4. Warburton, *Eastward!*, 155; McLeish, *Christian Progress in Burma*, 98.

5. Pwint, "Ceremony Celebrates Revised Bible Translation," *Myanmar Times*, 3 December 2012.

6. Charles Edward Garrad, William Sherratt, and George Kya Bin made use of U Tun Nyein's version as well as their own translations. This project started in 1911 and was completed in 1928.

mission[7]; (4) the Common Language version of 2005 (MCL); and (5) the Eagle edition of 2006.[8]

Judson's Bible remains the most popular translation. When asked about other translations relying on Judson's translation, Khoi Lam Thang responded that Judson's translation was "undoubtedly consulted or even used as a basis for other Bible translations done in Myanmar even though none of them mentioned it in their translations."[9] He also noted, in his article "'Baptism' in Myanmar Bible," that even after almost two centuries Judson's Bible is still "the only popular Bible in Myanmar" and that "in spite of criticisms and revisions, no other version can supersede it."[10] These statements underline that Judson's translation is likely to have been used, consciously or unconsciously, as a source of proof texts, including for limiting women's ministry and women's pastoral leadership in Myanmar churches.

In this chapter, the Myanmar Common Language translation (MCL) is compared with the JB to highlight Judson's linguistic choices. The MCL translation project of the New Testament began in 1966 and was published in 2005. It emerged out of dissatisfaction with some of the terms used in the JB and a desire to use contemporary language. At the dedication service of the MCL on 12 January 2006, it was noted that the meaning of some words used in the JB were "no longer the same today," or had "became archaic," and that "a lot of phrasal expressions are hard to understand for modern Myanmar speakers." The MCL is used fairly widely, though it has still not displaced the popularity of the JB.

The first part of this chapter examines the historical backgrounds of the JB and the MCL. The second part analyzes the linguistic choices of the JB in 1 Corinthians 14:34–35. It will show that Judson normally follows the Textus Receptus (TR), like many translators in the nineteenth century,[11] although with some revision using Johann Jacob Griesbach,[12] the first scholar to present

---

7. Warburton, *Eastward!*, 155. The main contributors were John McGuire, W. F. Thomas, U Tha Din, and U Lu Din.

8. Thang, "Eagle in the Myanmar Bible," 195.

9. Thang, personal conversation, 8 April 2020.

10. Thang, "'Baptism' in Myanmar Bible," 5.

11. Stringer, "Word of God for All Nations."

12. McKim, "Griesbach, Johann Jakob," in *Historical Handbook*, 319–324; Metzger, *Text of the New Testament*, 165.

a revision of the TR, the Elzevir edition,[13] and also Georg Christian Knapp.[14] Hence, the JB is also compared with the TR and Knapp. The chapter then also analyzes the text of NA[28], which is the most recent contemporary critical Greek text, to further highlight differences and similarities with the linguistic choices of Judson.

The third part of the chapter compares the linguistic usages of the JB with the MCL. The differences and similarities illustrate the linguistic choices in Burmese language usages of 1 Corinthians 14:34–35. The chapter ends with a summary of the prevailing view of women in Judson's American church context that would have influenced his own view.

3.1 The Judson Burmese Bible and the Myanmar Common Language Bible

3.1.1 The Judson Burmese Bible

Judson completed his translation of the New Testament in 1823,[15] ten years after his arrival in Burma. The entire Bible was printed in 1840[16] and after his death, a second edition was printed in 1883 which was a reprint of the first edition with the addition of Edward Abiel Stevens' references. Many still agree with the assessment that this was Judson's "greatest literary achievement."[17] His other literary works, such as dictionaries,[18] derived from his work for his Bible translation.

Despite a number of more recent translations among the Protestant churches of Myanmar, Judson's Bible is still the most popular.[19] For many, it

---

13. Baird, *History of New Testament Research*, 142. In his *Novum Testamentum Graece*, Griesbach questions the reliability of the old TR. Aland and Aland, *Der Text Des Neuen Testaments*, 9.

14. Clement, *Adoniram Judson*, 237. Knapp's publications include: *Novum Testamentum Graece*, 1797; *Hē Kainē Diathēkē*, 1813, and *Lectures on Christian Theology*, 1831. See also https://www.catalogus-professorum-halensis.de/knapp-georg-christian.html.

15. Clement, *Adoniram Judson*, 95.

16. Clement, 237.

17. Warburton, *Eastward!*, 156.

18. Judson, *Dictionary of the Burman Language*, 1823; Judson, *Dictionary, Burmese and English*, ed. Edward Abiel Stevens, 1852.

19. Chain, "Wives, Warriors and Leaders"; Thang, "Eagle in the Myanmar Bible," 195.

is considered to be better than the versions which attempted "to revise or replace it."[20] A recent biographer of Judson, Rosalie Hall Hunt, records that when some Burmese biblical scholars met to develop a new edition of the Bible, they unanimously decided not to pursue the project since Judson's translation was remarkably beautiful and they "could not improve upon its accuracy and purity,"[21] and gave up the effort to revise his translation before they had even started. Smalley describes this as a "King James Version effect" as many felt that his linguistic usages should not be changed even if they are no longer easily understood by everyone in the present day.[22]

However, as noted previously there are some significant problems, including Judson's use of honorific language and Pali vocabulary. In the nineteenth century, the honorific form of language was used for the royal family and Buddhist teachers. It indicates the rank of the speaker and the person addressed by the choice of personal pronouns as well as nouns. Examples of Judson's use of honorific language include his saying that Jesus's tears "fall royally" in John 11:35, and that Jesus is "sleeping royally" in Mark 4:38.[23] Since the end of the Burmese kingdom, this form of language has only been used by Buddhist teachers, but in 1853, Judson's use of honorific language was not seen as problematic by Wayland, for example, who saw Judson's translation as "free from obscurity to the Burmese mind. It is read and understood perfectly," and he considered that the style and language choices of Judson were "elegant."[24]

Although Pali was already considered a dead language in Judson's day, Pali terms were used widely among Buddhists more so than today, especially among Buddhist teachers, "similar to the way Latin continues to occupy a key place in Roman Catholic theology and liturgy."[25] Judson felt it was an absolute necessity to learn the Pali language, and he used Pali words in his

---

20. Smalley, *Translation as Mission*, 50.

21. Hunt, *Bless God and Take Courage*, 254–255. Hunt does not indicate the year or location of this meeting, but it could be the Translators' Conference held in Yangon in 1953. Eugene Nida attended that conference where the possibility of revising the Judson Burmese Bible was discussed but abandoned. Willans, "Translators' Conference in Burma."

22. Smalley, *Translation as Mission*, 50.

23. Vincent, "Use of Honorifics in Burmese," 196–197.

24. Wayland, *Memoir of the Life*, vol. 2, 168.

25. Duesing, *Adoniram Judson*, 86.

translation to draw the attention of the educated and Buddhist teachers.[26] Although Judson's intention was to facilitate the expansion of Christianity, it is ironic that Christianity flourished only among the ethnic minorities, not the Bamar, which created difficulties and prompted questions for some seeking to understand his linguistic choices.

As a result of developments since the nineteenth century in biblical scholarship, textual criticism, and interpretation, some have also claimed that there are "mistakes in Judson's translation."[27] Others have argued that he allowed himself "to be turned aside from the accurate translation of a word or a passage by his presupposition as to the meaning."[28] However, accusing him of committing "mistakes" and not being "accurate" can create a misleading impression about the quality of his scholarship in the light of the resources available to him at the time, and his hopes for the future of the church in the country. In a letter he sent to the printers, Judson noted:

> I have bestowed more time and labor on the revision than on the first translation of the work. . . . Long and toilsome research among the biblical critics and commentators, especially the German, was frequently requisite to satisfy my mind that my first position was the right one.[29]

In this light, the question of the differences in Judson's translation compared with how particular words and phrases might be translated today, needs to be considered with similar care.

There are two major reasons for such variances. First, although the TR was very much the standard in his day, Judson used other Greek texts as well, not just the TR. This was apparent in a study done on Bible translations following the TR when the researchers quickly discovered that there were variances between the TR and Judson's Bible.[30] At first it was assumed that these must have come from others, but as they are present in the first editions as well as later printings (1823, 1907, 1926, 1933), this was ruled out "since

---

26. Pleasants, "Beyond Translation," 2.
27. Warburton, *Eastward!*, 155.
28. Warburton, 155.
29. Judson, *Life of Adoniram Judson*, 406.
30. Stringer, "Word of God," 28.

Judson was very much alive when the New Testament was [first] printed."[31] His use of a range of critical Greek texts was also explained by Judson himself.

> In the first edition of the Old Testament, I paid too much regard to the critical emendations of Lowth,[32] Horsley,[33] and others.[34] In the present edition, I have adhered more strictly to the Hebrew text. In my first attempts at translating portions of the New Testament, above 20 years ago, I followed Griesbach, as all the world then did; and though, from year to year I have found reason to distrust his authority, still, not wishing to be ever-changing, I deviated but little from his text, in subsequent editions, until the last; in preparing that which I have followed the text of Knapp (though not implicitly), as upon the whole the safest and best extant; in consequence of which the present Burmese version of the New Testament accords more nearly with the received English.[35]

This clarifies how Judson's Burmese Bible was based on both the TR and on other critical Greek texts available at the time. For the New Testament, the fact that Judson first consulted Griesbach[36] indicates that Judson's base text for the TR was the Elzevir edition, not the older Stepanus edition.[37] The critical works of Griesbach were based on the Elzevir edition[38] and Knapp's text was also based on Griesbach's work. He was known for correcting the punctuation of Griesbach's text.[39] It is likely that Judson's comment about consulting German scholars refers to them. Later in our analysis, the Elzevir

---

31. Stringer, 28.

32. William Lowth (1660–1732), in Wilson, *History of Merchant-Taylors School*, 885.

33. Samuel Horsley (1773–1806), in Lee, ed., *Dictionary of National Biography*, 383–385.

34. "Stuart, Robinson, Stowe, Ripley, Bush, Noyes and such like, with some of the best German works." Judson, *Life of Adoniram Judson*, 406.

35. Clement, *Adoniram Judson*, 237.

36. McKim, "Griesbach, Johann Jakob," in *Historical Handbook*, 319–324; Metzger, *Text of the New Testament*, 165.

37. Robinson, *Stephen's 1550 Textus Receptus*.

38. Robinson, *Elzevir Textus Receptus (1624)*. The Stephanus and Elzevir editions of the TR are explained in Aland and Aland, *Der Text Des Neuen Testaments*, 3–10.

39. Schaff, *A Religious Encyclopaedia*, 275, mentions that Knapp leaned toward the TR. See also Planck, *Introduction to Sacred Philology*, 262.

edition of the TR is presented alongside Knapp's texts to highlight the differences.

Variances found in Judson's translation are also linked to the role of the translator's interpretation in translation. De Jong sees these as indicating how "Judson was affected by the understanding of the time," and describes Judson's translation of Genesis 4:7, for example, as an "exegetical fossil."[40]

Smalley's exposition of translation theory stresses the importance of the translator's "culture, attitudes, education, and experience," and argues that a translator's "theological assumptions" are "foundational" in translation.[41] This dynamic can be seen in the way in which Judson's contextual and theological assumptions influence his translation. This contributes to our understanding of the role of the translator's background in shaping theological assumptions that influence the translation of biblical passages, such as those concerning women's silence in the churches.

3.1.2 The Myanmar Common Language Bible

The Myanmar Common Language Bible project was started in 1966 to provide a translation that contemporary people would be able to better understand and in particular to reconsider terminology in the JB many considered to be archaic. The chief translator, U Sein Pe,[42] was a headmaster of mission schools, a well-known teacher and a state education officer. Through his competency in Burmese and English, and with the expertise of Harold Moulton[43] and Norman Mundhenk[44] in Greek and Hebrew, the translation was finished in 1981. The *New Testament with Psalms and Proverbs in Myanmar Common Language* was published in 1984. A second corrected edition was published in 2001. The whole Bible was completed in 2005.[45]

---

40. De Jong, "'Sin Offering'?" 3.
41. Smalley, "Language and Culture," 61.
42. Thang, "Eagle in the Myanmar Bible," 196.
43. Moulton was a member of the *Good News Bible* translation team. He is famous for his *Concordance to the Greek New Testament*. See also his *Challenge of the Concordance* and *Analytical Greek Lexicon Revised*.
44. Mundhenk, "Punctuation." Mundhenk is a translations adviser with the United Bible Societies based in Papua New Guinea. Mundhenk, Moulton, Nida, and Bratcher were all from the United Bible Societies. " Editor: Translations – 1970, a Review of the Year."
45. Thang, "Eagle in the Myanmar Bible," 196.

The base text for the MCL translation was the *Good News Bible* (GNB).[46] The GNB New Testament was translated by Robert Bratcher[47] and published in 1966, which was followed by a second edition in 1967, and a third edition in 1971.[48] The Old Testament was translated by a United Bible Society committee chaired by Bratcher and published with a revised edition of the New Testament as the GNB in 1976.[49] In the 1979 edition, the Apocrypha was included, and a new edition with gender-inclusive language was published in 1992.[50]

The Greek text that Bratcher used for translating the TEV New Testament of the GNB was the 1966 United Bible Societies Greek New Testament edited by Kurt Aland, Matthew Black, Bruce Metzger, and Allen Wikgren."[51] Based on a theory of textual criticism that sees "older" texts as "better manuscripts," the editions of the UBS Greek New Testament have consulted texts that are much older than the TR text.[52]

The MCL also uses Eugene Nida's[53] principle of "dynamic equivalence."[54] Bratcher explained this principle as translating so as "to try to stimulate in the new reader in the new age the same reaction to the text as the one the original author wished to stimulate in his first and immediate readers."[55] In

---

46. Also known as Good News for Modern Man, the Today's English Version (TEV), and the Good News Translation (GNT). Bratcher, "Nature and Purpose of the New Testament." Metzger, *Bible in Translation*, 167–168.

47. Society of Biblical Literature, "Robert Galveston Bratcher 1920–2010"; Omanson, "Robert Galveston Bratcher (1920–2010)."

48. Beduhn, *Truth in Translation*, 38; Bratcher, "Nature and Purpose," 97.

49. Omanson, "Robert Galveston Bratcher," 169–175.

50. Beduhn, *Truth in Translation*, 38.

51. Bratcher, "Nature and Purpose," 39.

52. Bratcher, 39, notes that Erasmus was dependent on "late and corrupt Greek manuscripts, replete with changes, additions and deletions made by copyists during the centuries when the manuscripts were copied by hand.... British scholars, when they revised the King James New Testament in 1881, made over 5,000 changes based on the Greek text; and now even further changes must be made, as a better text is available."

53. Eugene Nida (1914–2011) was secretary of the translation department of the American Bible Society. Stine, *Let the Words Be Written*; Stine, "Eugene A. Nida."

54. Bratcher, "Nature and Purpose," 97.

55. Bratcher, 97. Porter and Boda, *Translating the New Testament*, 126, summarize Nida's understanding of dynamic equivalence: "(1) a translation must aim primarily at reproducing the message of the source language, (2) a translation is to seek equivalence of the message rather than conserving the form of the utterance, (3) the closest natural equivalent is to be used, (4) meaning is given priority over structure, and (5) style, though secondary to content, must still be preserved."

other words, translation is done by using words that best express the effect of the original Greek word . . . as naturally as possible, rather than translating the Greek word to the exact equivalent word in English.[56] This method translates "the biblical meaning into a modern cultural equivalent."[57]

A second principle adopted for the MCL was a "Common Language"[58] approach that uses "language that is common to all who read and write it, irrespective of the degree of formal education or national origin."[59] The MCL was influenced greatly by Eugene Nida himself, including from a visit he made to the Translators' Conference held in Myanmar in 1953[60] – even though that conference decided not to go ahead with a revision of the JB at that time. The MCL translation project started later in 1966.[61]

3.2 Textual Analysis of 1 Corinthians 14:34–35

3.2.1 Variances in the Judson Burmese Bible (JB)

Comparing the versions of 1 Corinthians 14:34–35 in the 1832,[62] 1837,[63] 1840,[64] 1866,[65] 1885,[66] and 2007[67] editions and reprints of Judson's Burmese Bible, the variances in Judson's usage of words are not great in number. This is seen in Table 1 (below), which provides a comparative chart of these editions and reprints. Most of the changes are suffixes that make no significant difference to the meaning of a word or words. No changes were found in the editions between 1837 and 1885.

However, some words in the 1837 edition are slightly different from the 1832 edition. This is shown in Table 2. The 1837 reprint of the JB differs from

---

56. Bratcher, "Nature and Purpose," 97.
57. Porter and Boda, *Translating the New Testament*, 179.
58. Wonderly, *Bible Translations for Popular Use*.
59. Bratcher, "Nature and Purpose," 97.
60. Willans, "Translators' Conference in Burma," 21–25.
61. Willans, 21–25; Bratcher, "Nature and Purpose," 107.
62. *New Testament in Burmese*, 1832.
63. *New Testament of our Lord and Saviour Jesus Christ*, 1837.
64. *Holy Bible: Containing the Old and New Testaments*, 1840.
65. *New Testament of Our Lord and Saviour Jesus Christ*, 1866.
66. *New Testament of Our Lord and Saviour Jesus Christ*, 1885.
67. *Holy Bible: Containing the Old and New Testaments*, 2007, (JB).

the first printing of the 1832 edition in four places. The 1837 edition replaced the word for "remain" (နေစေတော့ with နေကြစေ), the word for "preach" (ဟောပြောသော) with ဟောပြောရသော), the word for "submit" (ဝန်ခံရ၏ with ဝန်ခံရကြမည်), and the word for "should ask" (မေးမြန်းပါလေစေ with မေးမြန်းကြစေ).

In the Burmese language, these changes do not greatly alter the meaning of the words or of the sentence. For example, a suffix ကြစေ after the word "ask" (မေးမြန်း) gives a more emphatic tone to the command, but there is no change in the meaning. This is the same for "preaching," where ဟောပြောသော (*haw pyaw thaw*) changed to ဟောပြောရသော (*haw pyaw ya thaw*). Adding the suffix ရ, "*ya*," after the verb "preach" ဟောပြော (*haw pyaw*) does not alter the meaning of the word. Another variant, မိမ္မသျှင်, is a case of writing style that creates no significant change in meaning, and the suffix သျှင် is a short form of သည် only.

Table 1. Variances of the Text of 1 Corinthians 14:34–35 in Judson's Burmese Bible[68]

1885

1866

---

68. These screenshot images of versions of the Judson Bible are public materials available at www.hathitrust.org.

1840

၃၄ သင်တို့၏ မိန်းမတို့သည် အသင်းတော်၌ တိတ်ဆိတ်စွာ
နေကြစေ။ သူတို့သည် ဟောပြောရသော အခွင့်မရှိကြ။
ပညတ်တရား စီရင်သည်အတိုင်း သူတို့သည် ယောကျ်ား
၃၅ ၏ အုပ်စိုးခြင်းကိုဝန်ခံရကြမည်။ မိဿတို့သည် တစုံတခု
ကိုသင်လိုလျှင်အိမ်၌ဒီမိခင်ပွန်းကိုကိုမေးမြန်းကြစေ။
မိဿသည်အသင်းတော်၌ဟောပြောလျှင် ရှက်ဖွယ်သော
၃၆ အကြောင်းဖြစ်၏။ ဘုရားသခင်၏ နှုတ်ကပတ်တရား

1837

၃၄ သင်တို့၏မိန်းမတို့သည်အသင်းတော်၌ ထိတ်ဆိတ်စွာနေကြစေ။
သူတို့သည်ဟောပြောရသောအခွင့်မရှိကြ။ ပညတ်တရားနှင့်စီရင်သည်
၃၅ အတိုင်းသူတို့သည်ယောကျ်ား၏အုပ်စိုးခြင်းကိုဝန်ခံရကြမည်။ မိဿ
တို့သည်တစုံတခုကိုသင်လိုလျှင်အိမ်၌မိမိခင်ပွန်းတို့ကိုမေးမြန်း
ကြစေ။ မိဿသည်အသင်းတော်၌ ဟောပြောလျှင် ရှက်ဖွယ်သော
၃၆ အကြောင်းဖြစ်၏။ ဘုရားသခင်၏နှုတ်ကပတ်တရားတော်သည်သင်

1832

၃၃ ဘုရားသခင်သည်ရုန်းရင်းခတ်သောအမှုကိုပြုတော်မူသည်မဟုတ်။ သန့်ရှင်း
သူတို့၏ အသင်း တော်အား ထုံးရှိသကဲ့သို့ငြိမ်းအသင့် ညီဝပ်
၃၄ ခြင်းကိုမြတ်နိုးတော်မူ၏။ ။သင်တို့၏မိန်းမတို့သည် အသင်း
တော်၌တိတ်ဆိတ်စွာနေစေတော့။ သူတို့ဟောပြောသောအခွင့်မရှိ။
ပညတ်တရားစီရင်သည် အတိုင်းသူတို့သည် ယောကျ်ားအုပ်စိုးခြင်း
၃၅ ကိုဝန်ခံရ၏။ မိဿတို့သည်တစုံတခုကိုသင်လိုလျှင်အိမ်၌မိခင်ပွန်း
တို့ကိုမေးမြန်းပါလေစေ။ မိဿသည်အသင်းတော်၌ဟောပြောလျှင်ရှက်
၃၆ ဖွယ်အကြောင်းဖြစ်၏။ ဘုရားသခင်၏ နှုတ်ကပတ်တရားသည်

2007

၃၄ သင်တို့၏ မိန်းမတို့သည် အသင်းတော်၌ တိတ်ဆိတ်စွာ နေကြစေ။ သူတို့သည် ဟောပြောရသော အခွင့်မရှိကြ။ ပညတ်တရား စီရင်သည်အတိုင်း သူတို့သည် ယောကျ်ား၏ အုပ်စိုးခြင်းကို ဝန်ခံရကြမည်။

၃၅ မိန်းမတို့သည် တစုံတခုကို သင်လိုလျှင်၊ အိမ်၌ မိမိ ခင်ပွန်းတို့ကို မေးမြန်းကြစေ။ မိန်းမသည် အသင်းတော်၌ ဟောပြောလျှင် ရှက်ဘွယ်သော အကြောင်း ဖြစ်၏။

Table 2. Changes in the Judson Burmese Translation of 1 Corinthians 14:34–35[69]

Comparing 1832 to 1840	Comparing 1840 to 2007
သင်တို့၏ မိမ္မတို့သည် အသင်းတော်၌ တိတ်ဆိတ်စွာ နေစေတော့[နေကြစေ]။ သူတို့သည် ဟောပြော[ရ]သော အခွင့်မရှိကြ။ ပညတ်တရား စီရင်သည်အတိုင်း သူတို့သည် ယောက်ျား၏ အုပ်စိုးခြင်းကို ဝန်ခံရ၏ [ဝန်ခံရကြမည်]။ မိမ္မတို့သည် တစုံတခုကိုသင်လိုလျှင်၊ အိမ်၌ မိမိခင်ပွန်းတို့ကို မေးမြန်းပါလေစေ [မေးမြန်းကြစေ]။ မိမ္မသည် [သည်] အသင်းတော်၌ ဟောပြော လျှင် ရှက်ဖွယ်သော အကြောင်း ဖြစ်၏။	သင်တို့၏ မိမ္မ[မိန်းမ]တို့သည် အသင်းတော်၌ တိတ်ဆိတ်စွာ နေကြစေ။ သူတို့သည် ဟောပြောရသော အခွင့်မရှိကြ။ ပညတ်တရား စီရင်သည်အတိုင်း သူတို့သည် ယောက်ျား၏ အုပ်စိုးခြင်းကို ဝန်ခံရကြမည်။ မိမ္မ[မိန်းမ]တို့သည် တစုံတခုကိုသင်လိုလျှင်၊ အိမ်၌ မိမိခင်ပွန်းတို့ကို မေးမြန်းကြစေ။ မိမ္မသည်[မိန်းမသည်] အသင်းတော်၌ ဟောပြော လျှင် ရှက်ဖွယ်[ရှက်ဘွယ်]သော အကြောင်း ဖြစ်၏။

These variances raise the question of who was responsible for these changes in successive editions of the JB. For the changes between 1837 and 1840, Judson himself would have been responsible, since he was still alive during the period.[70] Between the 1840 and 2007 editions, only two words were changed. The word for "wife," မိမ္မ in the 1840 edition, was changed to မိန်းမ in 2007. While all the early editions of the JB translate "wife" as မိမ္မ, it was only changed to မိန်းမ in the 2007 reprint. Again, this change does not alter the meaning of the word. The change is due to the form of writing. In his dictionary, Judson used both မိမ္မ and မိန်းမ for woman.[71]

The following section looks at 1 Corinthians 14:34–35 in the JB. In analyzing Judson's choice of words in his translation, the Burmese text is taken from

---

69. The words in brackets are from the later editions.
70. Judson died in 1850.
71. Judson, *Dictionary of the Burman Language*, 275.

the 1885 revised edition of the JB to compare with the Greek text. The two dictionaries of Judson,[72] Burmese to English and English to Burmese, are then used to determine the meaning of the words used in his translation.

3.2.2 Analysis of 1 Corinthians 14:34–35 in the Judson Burmese Bible

To clearly identify the variances between the Judson translation and the Greek text, the verses from 1 Corinthians 14:33–35 are separated into several charts, each containing four lines. The first line gives the Elzevir edition of the TR,[73] with the KJV translation. The second line is Knapp's Greek text of 1797,[74] with the English translation given in the 1835 edition, which included the text and the various textual readings of Knapp.[75] The third line shows the NA[28] critical Greek text, with English translation in the NRSV. The fourth line gives Judson's translation from the 1885 reprint of the JB,[76] with my own English translation.

The first part of the textual analysis of 1 Corinthians 14:34–35 looks at the place of 1 Corinthians 14:33 in relation to this text. The main divide among interpreters concerns whether verse 33b is connected to verse 33a or to verse 34. Judson's translation of 1 Corinthians 14:33[77] shows that he understood verse 33b to be linked with verse 33a, rather than with verse 34. This is similar to Knapp's text that separates 33b and 33a with a semicolon, which indicates a connection rather than separation. The English translation of Knapp clarifies this further and shows verse 33b as a continuation of 33a. This is different from the NA[28] text that sees verse 33b as a separate sentence from verse 33a. Table 3 shows the differences between the Greek texts and English texts.

---

72. Judson, *Dictionary, Burmese and English*; Judson, *Dictionary of the Burman Language*.
73. Robinson, *Elzevir Textus Receptus*.
74. Knapp, *Novum Testamentum Graece*.
75. Knapp, *Holy Bible*.
76. The translation of 1 Cor 14:34–35 in this 1885 edition is the same as in the 2010 reprint by the Myanmar United Bible Society.
77. See Table 1.

Table 3. Texts of 1 Corinthians 14:33

TR	ου γαρ εστιν ακαταστασιας ο θεος αλλ ειρηνης ως εν πασαις ταις εκκλησιαις των αγιων	KJV	for God is a God not of disorder but of peace. (As in all the churches of the saints,
Knapp	οὐ γάρ ἐστιν ἀκαταστασίας ὁ θεός, ἀλλ' εἰρήνης· ὡς ἐν πάσαις ταῖς ἐκκλησίαις τῶν ἁγίων.[78]		For God is not the author of confusion, but of peace, as in all the churches of the saints.[79]
NA[28]	οὐ γάρ ἐστιν ἀκαταστασίας ὁ θεὸς ἀλλὰ εἰρήνης. Ὡς ἐν πάσαις ταῖς ἐκκλησίαις τῶν ἁγίων	NRSV	for God is a God not of disorder but of peace. (As in all the churches of the saints,
JB	ဘုရားသခင်သည် ရှုန်းရင်းခတ် သော အမှုကို ပြုစုတော်မမူ။ သ န့်ရှင်းသူ တို့၏ အသင်းတော် အပေါင်းတို့၌ ဖြစ်သကဲ့သို့ အသ င့်အတင့် ငြိမ်ဝပ် ခြင်းကို ပြုစု တော်မူ၏။		*God does not nurture a work of confusion. As happened in all the churches of the saints, [He] nurtures harmonious peace.*

In examining Judson's translation of 1 Corinthians 14:33, two things point to the role of interpretation in translation. First, this is noticeable in Judson's choice of words in translating ἀκαταστασίας.[80] He translated God as not nurturing ရှုန်းရင်းခတ်သောအမှု ("a work of confusion") rather than a literal translation ရှုန်းရင်းခတ်ခြင်း၏ ("of confusion"). In so doing, the sentence focuses on things that God does rather than on who God is. Both the KJV and NRSV focus on who God is by translating "God is a God not of disorder."

Second, Judson added the word အသင့်အတင့် ("harmonious") to ငြိမ်ဝပ် ခြင်း ("peace"). This addition is not only significant for the meaning of verse 33, but also connects well to the next verse, 34, which speaks of women's silence in the church. By adding this word, Judson connects verse 33b more strongly to verse 33a and portrays God as initiating and nurturing

---

78. Knapp, *Novum Testamentum Graece.*
79. Knapp, *Holy Bible*, 1114–1115.
80. Ἀκαταστασίας is the genitive singular feminine noun of ἀκαταστασία.

harmonious peace in the church. This connection of 33b and 33a into a sentence shows Judson following the textual decisions of Knapp, who connects the two verses with a semicolon. This is different from NA[28], which separates 33b from 33a and connects verse 33b with verse 34.

These instances challenge the general assumption that Judson's Burmese translation was a strict literal translation of Greek words to Burmese words. Rather, what we see is a high level of conscious interpretation alongside translation. From these understandings, the following section looks more closely at Judson's translation of 1 Corinthians 14:34–35.

3.2.2.1 "Silence" in Translation

Judson's translation of 1 Corinthians 13:34a highlights the role of a translator by the way in which he translated σιγάτωσαν, γυναῖκες, and ἐκκλησίαις into Burmese. This is shown in Table 4 which looks at Judson's translation of σιγάτωσαν in context. The root word for σιγάτωσαν is σιγάω,[81] which occurs ten times in the New Testament. It appears six times in Luke-Acts,[82] three times in 1 Corinthians 14,[83] and once in Romans.[84]

Table 4. The Greek, English, and JB Texts of 1 Corinthians 14:34a

TR	αι γυναικες <u>υμων</u> εν ταις εκκλησιαις σιγατωσαν	KJV	Women [ ] should be silent in the churches.
Knapp	Αἱ γυναῖκες <u>ὑμῶν</u> ἐν ταῖς ἐκκλησίαις σιγάτωσαν·		Let <u>your</u> women keep silence in the churches
NA[28]	αἱ γυναῖκες [ ] ἐν ταῖς ἐκκλησίαις σιγάτωσαν·	NRSV	women [ ] should be silent in the churches
JB	သင်တို့၏ မိန်းမတို့သည် အသင်း တော်၌ တိတ်ဆိတ်စွာ နေကြစေ။		*The wives of <u>yours</u> should stay silent in the church.*

---

81. Other words for silence in Greek are: (1) ἡσυχιά to say nothing and remain quiet, which appears four times in the New Testament: Acts 22:2; 2 Thess 3:12; 1 Tim 2:11, 12; ἡσυχάζω, Luke 4:4, 23:56; Acts 11:18, 21:14; 1 Thess 4:11; (2) σιωπάω: not be able to speak, or not having the ability to speak, Matt 20:31, 26:63; Mark 3:4, 4:39, 9:34, 10:48, 14:61; Luke 1:20, 19:40; Acts 18:9; (3) φιμόω, say nothing, muzzle (1 Cor 9:9 κημόω), put to silence, cease to make sound, Matt 22:12, 34; Mark 1:25, 4:39; Luke 4:35; 1 Tim 5:18; 1 Pet 2:15; (4) ἐπιστομίζω, to keep someone from speaking, Titus 1:11; (5) στόμα φράσσω, to silence, to remove any reason to speak, Rom 3:19.

82. Luke 9:36, 18:39, 20:26; Acts 12:17, 15:12–13.

83. 1 Cor 14:28, 30, 34.

84. Rom 16:25.

The noun form σιγή is used two times, in Acts 21:40 and Revelation 8:1. According to Balz and Schneider, in general this word σιγάω means "to keep silent or still," in the sense of holding speech and saying nothing or stopping speaking, whereas the word σιγή means silence or stillness.[85]

Judson translates this word σιγάω with four different meanings, depending on the context. In Luke-Acts,[86] he translates σιγάω as တိတ်ဆိတ် (*teih seih*), in the sense of "say nothing, keep still, keep silent . . . as to hold one's tongue."[87] However, in Luke 9:36 and also in Romans 16:25, he translates the same word as ဝှက်ထား (*whet thar*). Judson translates Luke 9:36 as တပည့်တော်တို့သည် မိမိတို့မြင်သောအရာကို ဝှက်ထား၍၊ ထိုကာလ၌ အဘယ်သူအားမျှ မကြားမပြောဘဲ နေကြ၏ ("the disciples hid all that they had seen, they told no one in those days"). He translates Romans 16:25 as ရှေးကပ်ကာလပတ်လုံး ဝှက်ထားပြီးလျှင် ယခုမှာ ထင်ရှားသည်ဖြစ်၍ ("thing that had been hidden in the old days now being revealed"). The meaning for ဝှက်ထား given in Judson's dictionary is "to hide, conceal, keep back; to be obscure ထိန် ထိန့်ဝှက် လျှို့ဝှက်."[88] This is the same as BDAG's definition, "to keep something from becoming known, keep secret, conceal."[89]

Then, in Revelation 8:1 and Acts 21:40, Judson uses တိတ်ဆိတ် for σιγάω. In Revelation 8:1, he translates it as ကောင်းကင်ဘုံ၌ နာရီဝက်မျှ တိတ်ဆိတ်စွာ နေကြ၏ ("in heaven they stayed silent for half an hour"). He translates Acts 21:40 as သူတို့သည်အလွန် တိတ်ဆိတ်စွာ နေကြသောအခါ၊ ဟေဗြဲဘာသာအားဖြင့် မြွက်ဆိုလျက်၊ ("when they became very quiet, he spoke in the Hebrew language"). Judson's Burmese dictionary gives the meaning of တိတ်ဆိတ် as "to be still, silent and quiet."[90] This meaning corresponds to BDAG's definition of σιγάω, which generally refers to "absence of all noise, whether made by speaking or by anything else, silence, quiet."[91]

In 1 Corinthians 14:28, 30, and 34, Judson uses တိတ်ဆိတ် for σιγάω in all three appearances. He translates 1 Corinthians 14:28 as စကားပြန်မရှိလျှင်၊

---

85. Balz and Schneider, *Exegetical Dictionary of the New Testament*, 242.
86. Luke 18:39; Acts 12:17; 15:12–13.
87. BDAG, 922.
88. Judson, *Dictionary of the Burman Language*, 357.
89. BDAG, 922.
90. Judson, *Dictionary of the Burman Language*, 178; Judson, *Dictionary, Burmese and English*, 481.
91. BDAG, 922.

ဟောပြောသောသူသည် အသင်းတော်၌ <u>တိတ်ဆိတ်စွာနေ၍</u> မိမိအားရင်း၊ ဘုရား သခင် အားရင်း ပြောစေ ("If no interpreter, the one who prophesied should stay silent in the church and speak only to oneself and God"). He also translates 1 Corinthians 14:30 as ထိုင်လျှက်နေသောသူအား တစုံတခုကို ဖွင့်ပြတော်မူလျှင်၊ အ ရင်ဟောပြောသောသူသည် <u>တိတ်ဆိတ်စွာနေစေ</u> ("if anything be revealed to the one sitting, the previous person that prophesied should remain silent"). First Corinthians 14:34 is translated as သင်တို့၏ မိန်းမတို့သည် အသင်းတော်၌ <u>တိတ်ဆိတ်စွာ နေကြစေ</u> ("the wives of yours should stay silent in the church"). In all of these verses, he translates σιγάω as တိတ်ဆိတ် together with a command suffix နေ (nay), since all three occurrences of σιγάω are in the imperative verb form.[92] Judson's dictionary translates နေ (nay) as "stay or remain."[93] The combined word တိတ်ဆိတ်စွာနေ (teih seih swar nay) is defined as "to prevent (one's) speaking, to still, and to put an end to."[94] This is similar to BDAG, which gives the meaning of silence in these passages as "stop speaking, become silent . . . in the sense of losing one's power of speech."[95]

In 1 Corinthians 14:34, Judson's translation adds the word ကြ (kya) to တိတ်ဆိတ်စွာနေ, resulting in တိတ်ဆိတ်စွာ နေကြစေ (teih seih swar nay kya zay), meaning "should stay silent." Judson explains the word ကြ (kya) as indicating "verb affix (suffix) of number denoting the plural,"[96] and စေ (zay) as referring to "commission, order, command."[97] Therefore, Judson's translation of σιγάω as တိတ်ဆိတ်စွာ နေကြစေ in 1 Corinthians 14:34a shows the sentence as a command or "order" from the usage of the imperative verb. However, his translation of verse 34 does not provide any hint as to whether the command to silence is referring to a temporary or a timeless silence.

---

92. All three are in the present active imperative form of σιγάω.

93. Judson, *Dictionary of the Burman Language*, 211. This first edition gave the meaning as to "stay or continue." However, to show continuance the word has to be အနေကျ or သွားနေကျ. Therefore, the word here suggests "stay" in the sense of the later edition. Judson, *Dictionary, Burmese and English*, 580.

94. Judson, *Dictionary of the Burman Language*, 465; Judson, *Dictionary, Burmese and English*, 465.

95. BDAG, 922.

96. Judson, *Dictionary of the Burman Language*, 74; Judson, *Dictionary, Burmese and English*, 225.

97. Judson, *Dictionary of the Burman Language*, 137; Judson, *Dictionary, Burmese and English*, 382.

3.2.2.2 Silence: Wives and the Church

We now examine Judson's translation of γυναῖκες and ἐκκλησίαις in verse 34a. He translates αἱ γυναῖκες as သင်တို့၏ မိန်းမတို့သည် (*thin doe eit meinma doe thi*), meaning "women of yours," and ἐν ταῖς ἐκκλησίαις as the singular အသင်းတော်၌ (*a thinn daw hnait*), meaning "in the church," rather than အသင်းတော် များ၌ (*a thinn daw myarr hnait*), meaning "in the churches."

In Table 5, both the TR and Knapp's texts use αἱ γυναῖκες with ὑμῶν, and thus we have သင်တို့၏ မိန်းမတို့သည် meaning "your women." This shows Judson agreeing with both Knapp and TR. Inserting the word ὑμῶν ("your") into αἱ γυναῖκες is supported by third to ninth century Greek manuscripts such as D F G 𝔐 (ar b) sy; Cyp (Ambst).[98]

Table 5. Women and Silence in 1 Corinthians 14:34a

TR	αι γυναικες <u>υμων</u> εν ταις εκκλησιαις σιγατωσαν	KJV	Women [ ] should be silent in the churches.
Knapp	Αἱ γυναῖκες <u>ὑμῶν</u> ἐν ταῖς ἐκκλησίαις σιγάτωσαν·		Let <u>your</u> women keep silence in the churches
NA²⁸	αἱ γυναῖκες [ ] ἐν ταῖς ἐκκλησίαις σιγάτωσαν·	NRSV	women [ ] should be silent in the churches
JB	<u>သင်တို့၏</u> မိန်းမတို့သည် အသင်း တော်၌ တိတ်ဆိတ်စွာ နေကြစေ။		<u>Your</u> wives should stay silent in the church.

However, fourth and fifth century manuscripts such as 𝔓¹²³ ℵ A B support a shorter reading of αἱ γυναῖκες without the word ὑμῶν, using only မိန်းမ တို့သည် ("women").[99] In the Burmese language, this insertion of ὑμῶν next to αἱ γυναῖκες reinforces the meaning of αἱ γυναῖκες as wives rather than women in general. It is likely that Judson chose to include "your" with "wives" based on the texts of Knapp and TR, although various interpreters conclude

---

98. ὑμῶν D F G K L 630. 1505 𝔐 ar b sy; Cyp Ambst (*cf* ᶜ). NA²⁸, 547; NA²⁷, 466.

99. 𝔓¹²³ ℵ A B Ψ 0243. 33. 81. 104. 365. 1175. 1241. 1739. 1881. 2464 lat co. NA²⁸, 547. The manuscripts D F G that support the insertion are Greek-Latin bilingual texts that have sixth and ninth century dating with Old Syriac, whereas the textual reading of "αἱ γυναῖκες" is supported by Greek witnesses like ℵ A B, which are fourth and fifth century documents. Due to the earlier date of the MSS and shorter text, many take "αἱ γυναῖκες" as the preferred reading.

that even without ὑμῶν in the sentence, the appearance of ἄνδρας together with αἱ γυναῖκες in the same context would mean "the wives."[100]

Judson's translation of ἐν ταῖς ἐκκλησίαις into the Burmese language is another indicator of the role of the translator in the process of translation. Although ἐν ταῖς ἐκκλησίαις is a plural word, he translates the phrase as အသင်းတော်၌ ("in the church") rather than အသင်းတော်များ ("in the churches"). NA[28] raises no critical points on textual issues regarding the reading, which is clearly plural. This translation into singular form suggests two possibilities. First, it could be that Judson sees this passage as an issue of the Corinthian church alone, rather than having universal application. Second, he may have chosen to translate in the singular to show agreement with verse 35, where the church is mentioned as ἐν ἐκκλησίᾳ, a singular noun. Whatever the reason may be, this variance is a reminder of the critical place of the translator in the process of translation.

3.2.2.3 Silence as No Preaching

We now highlight the textual and linguistic variances of Judson's translation of 1 Corinthians 14:34b. Table 6 (below) shows these variances. Judson's Burmese translation of the word ἐπιτρέπεται[101] shows some of the differences from the Knapp text as well. This is seen in his translation of the present passive indicative verb ἐπιτρέπω as a noun, အခွင့်, meaning "permission."[102] This translation indicates that Judson is following the perfect passive form επιτετραπται found in a number of texts[103] rather than ἐπιτρέπεται, the present passive usage of Knapp. Instead of "they are not permitted," the sentence is translated as သူတို့သည် . . . အခွင့် မရှိကြ ("they have no permission"). Further,

---

100. Various scholars such as Garland, Johnson, and Fiorenza see this word as referring to "their wives," taken from the word pair of "ἡ γυνή" to "ὁ ἀνήρ" in the same sentence. Garland points out that whenever Paul pairs the noun "ἡ γυνή" to "ὁ ἀνήρ" as in 1 Cor 7:25 and 11:3, he is making references to the relationships between wives and husbands. Garland, *1 Corinthians*, 667. See also Schüssler Fiorenza, *In Memory of Her*, and Johnson, *1 Corinthians*, 275. Others see "αἱ γυναῖκες" as referring to all women, including wives, daughters, widows, and female slaves who were considered subordinate to the man of the house. See Wire, *Corinthian Women Prophets*, 156. Chapter 4 discusses extensively the different interpretations of this word.

101. 𝔓[123] ℵ A B D F G K 0243. 33. 365. 630. 1175. 1241. 1739 lat(t). NA[28], 547.

102. Judson, *Dictionary of the Burman Language*, 7; Judson, *Dictionary, Burmese and English*, 17.

103. επιτετραπται L Ψ 81. 104. 1505. 1881. 2464 m; Mcion.[E] NA[28], 547.

although TR and Knapp use the word γάρ, Judson omits this word in his translation. Both KJV and NRSV translate this word γάρ as "for."

Table 6. Speaking in 1 Corinthians 14:34b

TR	ου γαρ επιτετραπται αυταις λαλειν	KJV	for it is not permitted unto them to speak;
Knapp	οὐ γὰρ ἐπιτρέπεται αὐταῖς λαλεῖν,		for it is not permitted unto them to speak;
NA[28]	οὐ γὰρ ἐπιτρέπεται αὐταῖς λαλεῖν,	NRSV	For they are not permitted to speak;
JB	သူတို့သည် ဟောပြောရသော အခွင့် မရှိကြ။		They have no permission to preach.

It is important to note that although TR, Knapp, and NA[28] all include the word γάρ "for" in their sentences, Judson did not include this word in his translation. This word γάρ is significant in Greek since it shows the reason for demanding women's silence. It is possible that Judson did not include the word γάρ because he ends the sentence with the word ကြ at the end of the word **အခွင့် မရှိ** "no permission." This word ကြ is generally used as a suffix at the end of a number or verb, usually denoting the plural.[104] Using this word at the end of the sentence gives a sense of connection to the previous phrase, which Judson explains as indicating "imperative affix" or "the idea of plurality left to be conveyed by the noun affix of number or gathered from the connection."[105] Therefore, omitting γάρ in translation does not significantly change the meaning of the sentence for the Burmese reader due to the way Burmese sentence is constructed with the imperative affix that shows continuity of the sentence as well as indicating the reason behind such prohibition.

Although omitting γάρ in Burmese translation does not significantly change the meaning of the sentence for the Burmese reader, the translation of λαλέω into Burmese brings a significant change to the meaning. This word λαλέω is used thirty-four times in twenty-eight verses in 1 Corinthians alone,

---

104. Judson, *Dictionary, Burmese and English*, 45.
105. Judson, *Grammar*, 43.

and it is used mostly in the context of speaking in tongues and prophesy in tongues.[106] It appears twenty-four times in 1 Corinthians 14, and is used twelve times in the context of prophesying in tongues. Judson translates these twelve usages, including λαλέω[107] in 1 Corinthians 14:34b, as ဟောပြော (*haw pyaw*). Judson also translates λαλέω in verse 35 as ဟောပြော.

In his Burmese dictionary, Judson explains this word as a combination of two separate words, ဟော and ပြော. The word ဟော means "to repeat, utter or preach, as the priests."[108] The second edition of his dictionary notes that the word ဟော means "to utter in a formal manner, as in preaching, prophesying, foretelling."[109] In both editions, the word ပြော is translated as "to say, speak, tell."[110] This usage differs from both KJV and NRSV, which translate the word literally as "speak,"[111] which is equivalent to the Burmese word စကားပြော or ပြော ("speaking"). In the New Testament, the word λαλέω is used in reference to a general sense of speaking rather than the specific form of speaking ("preaching") that Judson suggests. A number of lexical works describe the word λαλέω as referring to a general sense of speaking. Louw and Nida describe it as "speak or talk, with the possible implication of more informal usage . . . to speak, to say, to talk, to tell."[112] BDAG describes the general usage of the word λαλέω as "to make a sound," "to utter words, talk, speak."[113]

The variance between this general sense of "speak" and Judson's choice of "preach" raises again the issue of the role of interpretation in his translation. There are several interpretations of the kind of speaking that Paul would have prohibited in the context of 1 Corinthians 14:34–35. Some see the word λαλέω as referring to "frenzied shouting of tongues in the church,"[114] "inspired speech

---

106. λαλέω occurs 296 times in the New Testament, 60 times in the Pauline Epistles and 34 times in 1 Cor alone.

107. λαλεῖν is the present, active, infinitive of λαλέω.

108. Judson, *Dictionary of the Burman Language*, 411.

109. Judson, *Dictionary, Burmese and English*, 745.

110. Judson, *Dictionary of the Burman Language*, 247; Judson, *Dictionary, Burmese and English*, 469.

111. See Table 3.

112. Louw and Nida, *Greek-English Lexicon of the New Testament*, 396.

113. BDAG, 582.

114. Clark and Kroeger, "Strange Tongues or Plain Talk?" 10–13. Kittel, Friedrich, and Bromiley, *Theological Dictionary of the New Testament*, 506, define this word as "to prattle," "to babble." This view leads to the conclusion that Paul is prohibiting speaking in tongues. The

of any kind that [is] uttered in public meetings,"[115] "all kinds of speech, both inspired and uninspired,"[116] "teaching,"[117] "evaluation of prophecy by asking questions,"[118] and "chatter or disruptive form of speech."[119]

Taking these into account, there are two possible interpretations behind Judson's choice of words.

First, it is possible that Judson did see this verse as a prohibition of women "preaching," since a literal reading of the word ဟောပြော suggests such a meaning. This is a popular view in the Myanmar context, and this text is used frequently to prevent women from preaching in church. Second, it is possible that Judson viewed this passage as prohibiting wives from "prophesying" in public meetings. This view is also possible since the second edition of his dictionary defines ဟော also as "prophesying or foretelling," along with preaching.[120] It gains credence also because λαλέω is translated as ဟောပြော in the context of prophesying in tongues in 1 Corinthians 14:3, 6, 18, 23, 27–30, 39.[121] Elsewhere, in 1 Corinthians 14:2, 5–6, 9, 11, 19, 21, 26,[122] Judson translates λαλέω as ပြော (pyaw), meaning "speak," only in the context of speaking in tongues.

---

problem with this conclusion is that the word is also used for prophesying in tongues, as well as interpretation of tongues in 1 Cor 14:2–4, 27, 29.

115. Barrett, *First Epistle to the Corinthians*, 332, sees "λαλέω" referring to prohibition of inspired speech.

116. Jorunn Økland, *Women in Their Place*, 204. Økland sees Paul as prohibiting women from teaching, since female prophets were generally accepted in the culture of that time, whereas female teachers were generally banned.

117. Piper and Grudem, *Biblical Manhood and Womanhood*, 151.

118. Garland, *1 Corinthians*, 671. See also Witherington, *Conflict and Community*, 287.

119. Thiselton, *First Epistle to the Corinthians*, 1157, points out that "the use of λαλεῖν to refer to chatter in this verse ignores first-century lexicographical evidence and the context of the discussion in 14:27–40."

120. Judson, *Dictionary, Burmese and English*, 745.

121. First Corinthians 14:3–39 ပရောဖက်ပြုသောသူများကား . . . လူတို့အားဟောပြော၏၊ 6 အခြားသော ဘာသာစကားဖြင့် ဟောပြော သော်လည်း၊ 18 အခြားသော ဘာသာစကားဖြင့် ဟောပြောသောအရာကို, 23 အခြားသော ဘာသာဖြင့် ဟောပြောလျက်, 27 အခြားသော ဘာသာစကားဖြင့် ဟောပြောသော သူရှိလျှင်, 28 စကားပြန်မရှိလျှင်၊ ဟောပြောသောသူသည်, 29 ပရောဖက်နှစ်ယောက်ဖြစ်စေ သုံးယောက်ဖြစ်စေ ဟောပြော၍, 30 အရင် ဟောပြောသော သူသည် တိတ်ဆိတ် စွာနေစေ။

122. First Corinthians 14:2–26 အခြားသောဘာသာစကားအားဖြင့် ပြောသောသူသည်, 5 အခြားသော ဘာသာစကားဖြင့် ပြောစေခြင်းငှါ, 6 သင်တို့အားပြောလျှင်, 9 ကောင်းကင်ကို ပြောသောသူကဲ့သို့, 11 ဘာသာစကား၏အနက်ကို ငါနားမလည်လျှင် ပြောသော သူအားငါသည် လူရိုင်းဖြစ်လိမ့်မည်။ ပြောသောသူသည် လည်း၊, 19 စကားတသောင်းကို ပြောနိုင်သည်ထက်, 21 အခြားတပါးသောနှုတ်နှင့် ဤလူမျိုးကို ငါပြောမည်.

3.2.2.4 Silence: The Law and Consent to Man's Ruling

Table 7 shows the textual and linguistic variances of Judson's translation in 1 Corinthians 14:34c. Here, we see that Judson's translation differs from the TR, Knapp, and NA[28] Greek texts. Although these Greek texts include the word ἀλλὰ, meaning "but," Judson's translation does not include this word, which should be သို့သော်လည်း or သို့ရာတွင် in Burmese.[123] Instead, Judson translates the rest of the sentence as ပညတ်တရား စီရင်သည်အတိုင်း သူတို့သည် ယောကျ်ား၏ အုပ်စိုးခြင်းကို ဝန်ခံရကမြည် ("as the law commanded they must consent to the ruling of man"). Both the KJV and NRSV include the word "but" in their translation of the sentence. Since there is no known textual variant issue raised either by Knapp or NA[28] on the usage of ἀλλὰ,[124] the omission here once again displays an interpretive choice of the translator.

Table 7. The Greek, English, and JB Texts of 1 Corinthians 14:34c

TR	αλλ υποτασσεσθαι καθως και ο νομος λεγει	KJV	but they are commanded to be under obedience, as also saith the law
Knapp	Ἀλλ' ὑποτάσσεσθαι, καθὼς καὶ ὁ νόμος λέγει		but they are commanded to be under obedience, as also saith the law
NA[28]	ἀλλὰ ὑποτασσέσθωσαν, καθὼς καὶ ὁ νόμος λέγει	NRSV	But [ ] should be subordinate, as the law also says
JB	ပညတ်တရား စီရင်သည် အတိုင်း သူတို့သည် ယောကျ်ား၏ အုပ်စိုးခြင်းကို ဝန်ခံရကြမည်။		As the Law commanded they must **consent** to the ruling of man.

Second, the usage of the word ὑποτάσσεσθαι[125] in Burmese demonstrates that Judson was not following the textual tradition of the Greek text of Knapp, who translates ὑποτάσσεσθαι as "to obey," which is the present, passive, infinitive form of ὑποτάσσω. Griesbach's texts keep the same word, ὑποτάσσεσθαι,

---

123. Judson, *Dictionary, English and Burmese*, 63.
124. Knapp, *Novum Testamentum Graece*, 528; NA[28], 547.
125. The root word of ὑποτάσσεσθαι is ὑποτάσσω.

while noting the textual variant issue at the bottom of the page.[126] Judson's usage of the word ὑποτάσσεσθαι is closer to the critical text of NA[28], which used the present passive imperative form ὑποτασσέσθωσαν ("must obey"). Judson translates ὑποτάσσω as ဝန်ခံရကြမည် ("must consent"). Judson gives the meaning of ဝန်ခံ (*won khan*) as "to consent, agree to or comply with,"[127] the word ရ as a verb suffix meaning "must,"[128] and ကြ as a suffix sign that shows the plural number.[129] Although the word မည် would generally be used as a future suffix of the verb "shall" or "will,"[130] Judson combines ရ and မည် with the verb "go," referring to "must go" in his first Burmese dictionary.[131]

The reading of ὑποτασσέσθωσαν in NA[28] is supported by earlier manuscripts such as ℵ A B,[132] which are fourth and fifth century manuscripts. In contrast, Knapp's reading is supported by textual manuscripts such as the fifth century manuscript D and eight to ninth century manuscripts F G K L Ψ and the majority text.[133] The root word of ὑποτάσσεσθαι and ὑποτασσέσθωσαν, and the NA[28] term ὑποτάσσω, is used thirty-eight times in the New Testament,[134] with twenty-three occurrences in the Pauline Epistles alone. Throughout the New Testament, ὑποτάσσω is used mostly about relationships of God and Jesus, rulers and their subjects, and husbands and wives. The husband-and-wife relationship references are found in 1 Corinthians 14:34, Ephesians 5:21, 24, Colossians 3:18, Titus 2:5, and 1 Peter 3:1. It is only in 1 Corinthians 14:34 and Colossians 3:18 that ὑποτάσσω appears in the imperative verb form. This word appears nine times in 1 Corinthians 14–16. In these appearances,

---

126. Griesbach, *Novum Testamentum Graece*, 277.

127. Judson, *Dictionary of the Burman Language*, 348.

128. Judson, *Dictionary, Burmese and English*, 575; Judson, *Dictionary of the Burman Language*, 300.

129. Judson, *Dictionary of the Burman Language*, 74.

130. Judson, *Dictionary of the Burman Language*, 74. Also, Judson, *Dictionary, Burmese and English*, 512.

131. Judson, *Dictionary of the Burman Language*, 74.

132. ὑποτασσέσθωσαν ℵA B 33. 81. 365. 1175. 1241. 2464. Epiph. 3rd person, plural, present, passive, imperative of ὑποτάσσω. NA[28], 547.

133. υποτασσεσθαι D F G K L Ψ 0243. 104. 630. 1505. 1739. 1881 𝔐 lat(t) sy (*cf*ʳ). Present, passive, infinitive of ὑποτάσσω. NA[28], 547.

134. Luke 2:51; 10:17, 20; Rom 8:7, 20; 10:3; 13:1, 5; 1 Cor 14:32, 34, three times in 15:27, three times in 15:28; 16:16; Eph 1:22; 5:21, 24; Phil 3:21; Col 3:18; Titus 2:5, 8; 12:9; Heb 2:5, three times in 2:8 and 12:9; James 4:7; 1 Pet 2:13, 18; 3:1, 5, 22; 5:5.

ὑποτάσσω refers to the husband and wife relationship, Judson translates the word as ဝန်ခံ in the sense of consenting or agreeing to the other person.[135]

This translation of ὑποτάσσω as consenting or agreeing is significant since most of the English translations translate this word as "to obey, to submit to, obedience, submission,"[136] or "to subordinate."[137] In the Burmese language, the word for "obey or obedience" is closer to နားထောင်[138] (*nar htaung*) rather than the ဝန်ခံ that Judson uses.[139] Judson's own definition of the word "submission" is "the act of yielding to another or the act of submitting to another."[140] Therefore, Judson's translational choice of ὑποτάσσω in 1 Corinthians 14:34 as ဝန်ခံ shows that for him the concept of obedience or submission mentioned in this passage is not about subordination as suggested by the NRSV, but rather a conscientious yielding of one person to another person.

Third, Judson's translation of 1 Corinthians 14:34c includes the word ယောက်ျား၏ အုပ်စိုးခြင်းကို ("to man's ruling") after ὑποτάσσω, which neither TR nor Knapp mentions. The KJV and NRSV also do not include these words.[141] However, both Griesbach[142] and NA²⁸ mention the textual variant issues in their critical notes. They note the occurrence of textual issues in the usage of the words τοις ἀνδρασιν, and μανθανειν. The usage of τοις ἀνδρασιν is supported by fifth century manuscript A only.[143] The usage of μανθανειν is supported by fourth and fifth century scripts such as ℵ A,[144] whereas the omission of this word is supported by third to fifth century manuscripts such as 𝔓⁴⁶ ²ℵ B D

---

135. Judson, *Dictionary of the Burman Language*, 348.
136. Nida, *Greek-English Lexicon*, 467. KJV says "but they are commanded to be under obedience."
137. NRSV gives "but should be subordinate."
138. Judson, *Dictionary, Burmese and English*, 400. It gives "to listen, hearken, attend to; to mind, obey." In Judson, *Dictionary, English and Burmese*, 398, the meaning for "obey" is given as "to listen with regard and acceptance."
139. "to consent, agree to; to engage for, take the responsibility." Judson, *Dictionary, Burmese and English*, 672.
140. Judson, *Dictionary, Burmese and English*, 496.
141. See Table 7.
142. Griesbach, *Novum Testamentum Graece*, 277.
143. Both Griesbach and NA²⁸ mention only A as supporting the insertion of this word. See Griesbach, *Novum Testamentum Graece*, 277; NA²⁸, 547.
144. ℵ* Aᶜ 33. 81. 104. 365. 1241. 1505. 2464. This is mentioned in NA²⁸, 547. Griesbach mentioned the supporting textual traditions as A 17 23 26 31 and 73. Griesbach, *Novum Testamentum Graece*, 277.

and majority text 𝔐.¹⁴⁵ It is apparent that Judson followed the textual variant suggestions of Griesbach on the usage of τοις ἀνδρασιν and μανθανειν in his translation rather than the TR and Knapp textual traditions.

The role of translator in translation is also apparent in Judson's translation of τοις ἀνδρασιν, from ယောက်ျားများ ("to men") in plural form, to the singular ယောက်ျား၏ ("to man"). This translation in singular form could be for clarity, to point out that the man here refers to the husband. The women are to consent to the ruling or authority of their own husbands, but not to all men. Judson's translation of this word in 1 Corinthians 14:34 agrees with other passages that speak of the relationship of husband and wife, such as Ephesians 5:22, 24, Colossians 3:18, Titus 2:5, and 1 Peter 3:1, 5. In these verses, he uses the words "consenting to man's ruling." We also note that Judson has translated ὑποτάσσεσθαι as "consent to the ruling" because he has the translation word as အုပ်စိုးခြင်း (*oat soe chin*) in Burmese, meaning "ruling." Judson has not followed the Griesbach variant of μανθανειν. Judson gives the meaning of အုပ်စိုး as "to rule, preside over"¹⁴⁶ or "to rule, have authority over."¹⁴⁷ As mentioned above, Judson follows the textual variant that Griesbach suggests in his textual critical notes.

Judson translates ὁ νόμος¹⁴⁸ as ပညတ်တရား (*pyit nyat taya*), which is a combination of the words ပညတ် and တရား in the Burmese language. The word ပညတ် (*pyit nyat*) means "a command"¹⁴⁹ or "a prohibition or command; a name,"¹⁵⁰ and တရား (*taya*) means "moral principle or law."¹⁵¹ In two out of ten occurrences of ὁ νόμος in 1 Corinthians, in verses 9:9 and 14:21, Judson translates this word as ပညတ္တိကျမ်းစာ. The word ပညတ္တိ is a Pali form of the

---

145. 𝔓⁴⁶ ²א B D F G K L Ψ 0243. 630. 1175. 1739. 1881 𝔐 (*cf* ʳ). NA²⁸, 547.

146. Judson, *Dictionary of the Burman Language*, 39.

147. Judson, *Dictionary, Burmese and English*, 102.

148. The word "νόμος" is used 121 times in 87 verses in the Pauline epistles, 75 times in Romans, 9 times in 1 Corinthians, 32 times in Galatians, once in Ephesians, 3 times in Philippians, and 2 times in 1 Timothy. In 1 Corinthians, the word νόμος appears in 1 Cor 9:8, 9, 20 (4 times); 14:21, 34; 15:56.

149. Judson, *Dictionary of the Burman Language*, 221.

150. Judson, *Dictionary, Burmese and English*, 427.

151. Judson, 333; Judson, *Dictionary of the Burman Language*, 174. Judson describes it as "the universal, and immutable laws of the moral world, collectively considered, or any particular moral principle or law; whatever accords with the laws of the moral world, or with the established system of just retribution; justice, right."

same word in Burmese,[152] and ကျမ်းစာ means "a religious writing or book."[153] In both 1 Corinthians 9:9[154] and 1 Corinthians 14:21,[155] Judson's translation adds ကျမ်းစာ to ပညတ္တိ to differentiate the law as referring to "the Scriptures of the law."[156]

In the context of 1 Corinthians 9:8, ပညတ်တရား with မောရှေ၏ ပညတ္တိ ကျမ်းစာ ("the Scriptures of Moses' law"), supported by a quotation of Deuteronomy 25:4, ὁ νόμος clearly refers to the Pentateuch, the Torah. The law in 1 Corinthians 14:21 is referring to the Tanakh law – the whole Old Testament Scriptures – since the supporting quotation comes from Isaiah 28:11. Judson translates ὁ νόμος as ပညတ်တရား consistently in its remaining appearances in 1 Corinthians, the one exception being 1 Corinthians 15:56,[157] where the law is a reference to "the law of God" in general. The other six occurrences of ὁ νόμος in 1 Corinthians 9:20–21[158] point to the Law of Moses in the Pentateuch.

All of this leads us to ask how Judson understood the usage of ὁ νόμος in the context of 1 Corinthians 14:34. Interpreters differ greatly on what they think the reference to ὁ νόμος means in this context. Some suggest that ὁ νόμος

---

152. Judson, *Dictionary of the Burman Language*, 221; Judson, *Dictionary, Burmese and English*, 427.

153. Judson, *Dictionary of the Burman Language*, 69; Judson, *Dictionary, Burmese and English*, 168.

154. Judson's translation of 1 Cor 9:9 is မောရှေ၏ ပညတ္တိကျမ်းစာ၌လာသည်ကား၊ စပါးနင်းနယ် သော နွား၏ နှုတ်ကိုမချုပ်တည်းရဟု လာ၏။

155. Judson's translation of 1 Cor 14:21 is ပညတ္တိကျမ်းစာ၌လာသည်ကား၊ အခြားတပါးသော လျှာ၊ အခြားတပါးသောနှုတ်နှင့် ဤလူမျိုးကို ငါပြောမည်။

156. Fee, *First Epistle to the Corinthians*, 791, points out that whenever Paul appeals to the law, he always cites the text, usually to support a point he himself is making. In 1 Cor 9:8, he speaks of not muzzling an ox when it is treading out the grain, Deut 25:4; and 1 Cor 14:21 talks of God speaking to the people through strange tongues as a sign to unbelievers, quoting from Isa 28:11.

157. Judson's translation of 1 Cor 15:56 is သေမင်း၏လက်နက်ကား၊ ဒုစရိုက်အပြစ်ပေတည်း။ ဒုစရိုက်အပြစ်၏ တန်ခိုးကား၊ ပညတ်တရား ပေတည်း။

158. ယုဒလူတို့ကိုရခြင်းအလိုငှါ ယုဒလူတို့ကို ယုဒလူကဲ့သို့ဖြစ်၏။ ပညတ်တရားကိုကိုယ်တိုင် မဆည်းကပ် သော်လည်း၊ ပညတ်တရားကို ဆည်းကပ်သောသူတို့ကို ရခြင်းအလိုငှါ၊ ပညတ်တရားကို ဆည်းကပ်သောသူတို့၌ ပညတ်တရားကို ကျင့်သောသူကဲ့သို့ ဖြစ်၏။ ဘုရားသခင်ရှေ့တော်၌ တရားမဲ့မနေ၊ ခရစ်တော်၏တရားကို ကျင့် သောသူ ဖြစ်သော်လည်း၊ ပညတ်တရားမဲ့သောသူတို့ကို ရခြင်းအလိုငှါ ပညတ်တရားမဲ့သောသူတို့၌ ပညတ် တရားမဲ့သောသူကဲ့သို့ ဖြစ်၏။ Judson's translation of 1 Cor 9:20.

here refers to the secular law of the Romans,[159] others to Paul's own teaching,[160] the Jewish culture,[161] the Jewish tradition as the law,[162] the Pentateuch and the Old Testament Scriptures as law,[163] or the principle of order as law.[164]

Although Paul often used ὁ νόμος in 1 Corinthians to refer to Mosaic law, the Pentateuch, and the Old Testament Scriptures, the usage of ὁ νόμος in the context of 1 Corinthians 14:34 is difficult to determine, since there is no clear reference to specific Scriptures from which he was quoting in this context. The only clue to Judson's understanding of the law here is the translation of သူတို့သည် ယောက်ျား၏ အုပ်စိုးခြင်းကို ဝန်ခံရကြမည် ("they [women] must consent or yield to the ruling of man") after translating ပညတ်တရား စီရင်သည် အတိုင်း to mean "as the law commanded." He is referring to a law that required

---

159. Wire, *Corinthian Women Prophets*, 135, suggests that the law here refers to the Velleian decree passed by the Roman Senate during the time of Claudius to restrict the right of women to testify in court.

160. UBS⁴, 87, sees the law mentioned here as Paul's own teaching in the rabbinic tradition. This is disputed. Hiu, *Regulations Concerning Tongues and Prophecy*, 146. Hiu argues that in first century Judaism, there was usually "a reference to a prohibition, either in the Old Testament or rabbinic sources, [that] could take the negative form 'it is not permitted,' but this kind of usage is rare and Paul never refers to the rabbinic traditions with νόμος anywhere else, despite the frequent use of this word."

161. Nash, *1 Corinthians*, 382 points out that Paul may have shared the same view as Philo, who held that the law of Moses taught the subordination of wives to their husbands, and husbands' duty to teach the law to their wives. He quotes *Hypoth* 7.3.5, where Philo says that "Wives must be in servitude to their husbands, a servitude not imposed by violent ill-treatment but by promoting obedience in all things." He then continues in *Hypoth* 7.14 to say, "The husband seems competent to transmit knowledge of the laws to his wife."

162. Paul is rebuking Jewish men's attitudes. Fitzmyer, *First Corinthians*, 533, sees this as the view of Corinthian men who believe that custom derived from Jewish tradition is "the law." This law "apparently derived from it [Jewish custom] as a sort of 'unwritten law,' forbidding women to come to the synagogue (Str-B, 3:467)." He asks, "What! Did the word of God originate with you, or are you the only ones it has reached?" This double-rhetorical question formulates Paul's reaction to the attitude of Corinthian Christian men quoted in the two preceding verses. Peppiatt, *Women and Worship*, 129.

163. Barrett, *First Epistle to the Corinthians*, 330. See also Robertson and Plummer, *First Epistle of St. Paul*, 325. They see Gen 3:16, "Your desire shall be for your husband, and he shall rule over you," as the background of Paul's speech, and submission of women to their husbands as the rationale for women's silence. They also see Paul as alluding to the Genesis creation narrative in 1 Cor 11:3, 8–10, and thus the law here as referring to wives' subordination based on the Pentateuch and Old Testament Scriptures.

164. Thiselton, *First Epistle to the Corinthians*, 1153, sees the law mentioned here as the repeated emphasis of the whole Old Testament on the principle of order, where God turns chaos into order. Women are commanded to submit not to their husbands, but to the principle of order in the worship place, and this "emerges in 1 Cor 15:28." He argues that the allusion to Gen 3:16 confuses "the Christian believer's role within the created order with a role still unresolved within fallen creation, which then appears to conflict with Gal 3:28."

women to consent to the ruling of men or husbands. Given Judson's consistent usage of ὁ νόμος as ပညတ်တရား, it is likely that he sees ὁ νόμος in 1 Corinthians 14:34 as referring to the law of Moses in the Pentateuch or the Old Testament Scriptures. However, this creates a challenge in attempting to understand Judson's view of women's silence, since the law of Moses mentioned in the Pentateuch or elsewhere in the Old Testament does not mention women's silence or women preaching.

3.2.2.5 Silence and Learning

This section looks at the textual and linguistic variances of Judson's translation of 1 Corinthians 14:35a. Table 8 highlights three issues in this translation. First, he does not translate δέ although the Greek texts of TR and Knapp have the word δέ in all the texts. The word δέ is also used in Griesbach, and there is no mention of a textual variant issue.[165]

Table 8. The Greek, English, and JB Texts of 1 Corinthians 14:35a

TR	ει δε τι μαθειν θελουσιν εν οικω τους ιδιους ανδρας επερωτατωσαν	KJV	And if they will learn anything, let them ask their [ ] husbands at home:
Knapp	Εἰ δέ τι μαθεῖν θέλουσιν, ἐν οἴκῳ τοὺς ἰδίους ἄνδρας ἐπερωτάτωσαν·		And if they will learn anything let them ask their [ ] husbands at home;
NA²⁸	εἰ δέ τι μαθεῖν θέλουσιν, ἐν οἴκῳ τοὺς ἰδίους ἄνδρας ἐπερωτάτωσαν·	NRSV	If there is anything they desire to know, let them ask their [ ] husbands at home.
JB	မိန်းမတို့သည် တစ်စုံတခုကို သင်လို လျှင်၊ အိမ်၌ မိမိ ခင်ပွန်းတို့ကို မေးမြန်း ကြစေ။		*If <u>women</u> want to learn anything, let them ask their <u>own</u> husbands at home.*

Second, Judson inserts the word မိန်းမတို့သည် ("women" or "wives") into the sentence although this word is not mentioned in either the TR or the Knapp texts, and Griesbach and NA²⁸ make no mention of a textual variant issue. Although none of these Greek texts specifically use this word, the third

---

165. Griesbach, *Novum Testamentum Graece*, 277.

person plural usage of the verb θέλω, meaning "they want or desire," already points to "the women" just by looking at the context. Thus, it is likely that Judson adds this specific word မိန်းမတို့သည် into the sentence for clarification purposes, instead of using only "they."

Third, Judson keeps the aorist infinitive word μαθειν in his translation, as do the TR and Knapp Greek texts, Griesbach, and NA²⁸. A textual variant issue here concerns whether the word μανθάνω is in the aorist infinitive form μαθειν or μανθανειν in the present infinitive form. The reading of μανθανειν is supported by fourth and fifth century manuscripts ℵ* A^c[166] and the reading of μαθειν is supported by fourth and fifth century manuscripts 𝔓⁴⁶ ℵ² B D.[167] In taking the reading of μαθειν, Judson translates this word in Burmese as သင်လိုလျှင် (thinn lo hlyin), meaning "to learn or to receive instruction,"[168] rather than ဆက်လက်သင်လိုလျှင် ("to keep on learning"), which would be a translation of μανθάνω in the present infinitive to denote the action verb as "continuous or repeated."[169]

Fourth, Judson's translation includes the word ἰδίους by translating မိမိ (mi mi) as "one's own."[170] By including ἰδίους in the translation, Judson is following the textual traditions of TR and Knapp, which also use the word ἰδίους in the text (see Table 9). This is different from both the KJV and NRSV, which omit the word ἰδίους, leaving "their husbands" rather than "their own husbands." The word ἰδίους is included in the NA²⁸ and there are no textual issues.[171] It is likely that the reason for not including the word ἰδίους in the KJV and NRSV is due to the similarity of meaning between "their husbands" and "their own husbands." However, the inclusion of this word in Judson's translation gives a clearer reading of the women in this verse as "wives" rather than women in general.

---

166. The word μανθανειν is found in ℵ* A^c 33. 81. 104. 365. 1241. 1505. 2464. See NA²⁸, 547.

167. The word μαθειν is found in 𝔓⁴⁶ ℵ² B D F G K L Ψ 0243. 630. 1175. 1739. 1881 𝔪 (cf^r).

168. Judson, *Dictionary of the Burman Language*, 360.

169. Nunn, *Elements of New Testament Greek*, 49, sees in the use of the present infinitive that "the action denoted by the verb is to be regarded as continuous or repeated." The use of the aorist infinitive is "not confined to expressing action in past time."

170. Judson, *Dictionary of the Burman Language*, 275; Judson, *Dictionary, English and Burmese*, 521.

171. NA²⁸, 547.

Judson translates the word ἄνδρας into Burmese as ခင်ပွန်း (khin pun), meaning "husbands."[172] Thus, the sentence reads အိမ်၌ မိမိခင်ပွန်းတို့ကို မေးမြန်း ကြစေ ("let them ask their own husbands at home") rather than အိမ်၌ ယောက်ျား တို့ကို မေးမြန်းကြစေ ("let them ask their men at home.") The insertion of "own husbands" (မိမိခင်ပွန်း) into a sentence regarding "women" (မိန်းမတို့သည်) in Judson's translation indicates that the relationship highlighted in this verse is between husbands and wives rather than men and women in general. This translation gives us a clue to Judson's understanding of the women's silence passage as a prohibition in the context of the husband-wife relationship.

Table 9. The Greek, English, and JB Texts of 1 Corinthians 14:35b

TR	αισχρον γαρ εστιν γυναιξιν εν εκκλησια λαλειν	KJV	For it is shameful for a woman to speak in church
Knapp	αἰσχρὸν γάρ ἐστι γυναιξὶν ἐν ἐκκλησίᾳ λαλεῖν.		For it is a shame for women to speak in church
NA²⁸	αἰσχρὸν γάρ ἐστιν γυναικὶ ἐν ἐκκλησίᾳ.	NRSV	For it is shameful for a woman to speak in church
JB	မိန်းမသည် အသင်းတော်၌ ဟောပြော လျှင် ရှက်ဘွယ် သော အကြောင်း ဖြစ်၏။		It is a shameful thing for a woman to preach in the church.

It is clear from Table 9 that Judson translates γυναιξιν as မိန်းမ "woman." Judson's translation of singular "woman" is different from the plural usages of TR and Knapp, which appear as γυναιξιν, a dative plural feminine noun of the word γυνή. The difference between the usage of TR and Knapp is that TR keeps the word γυναιξιν, which is a plural form, with a singular form ἐστιν. However, Knapp keeps the word γυναιξιν in a plural form. The evidence then points to Judson following the textual guide of Griesbach, who suggests the usage of γυναικί to align with the singular verb ἐστιν in the sentence.[173] This is another example of Judson not following the TR tradition too closely.

---

172. Judson, *Dictionary of the Burman Language*, 87; Judson, *Dictionary, English and Burmese*, 196.

173. Griesbach, *Novum Testamentum Graece*, 277.

Once again, Judson translates the word λαλεῖν as ဟောပြော (*haw pyaw*) as "preach," as in 1 Corinthians 14:34b. He keeps the translation of the word ἐκκλησίᾳ in the dative singular noun form အသင်း တော် meaning "church," which he also uses in 1 Corinthians 14:34a in singular form, although the Greek texts appear in plural form. Another example of the translator's interpretive role in translation is seen in Judson's choice to omit the word γάρ here. Both the KJV and NRSV translate the conjunction word γάρ as "for." If Judson had included this word γάρ in his translation, the word would be "အဘယ် ကြောင့်နည်းဟူမူကား"[174] in the Burmese translation. In using αἰσχρὸν,[175] Judson's choice is like KJV and NRSV. He translates the adjective αἰσχρὸν as ရှက်ဘွယ် သော ("shameful"), which is like the KJV and NRSV,[176] but adds အကြောင်း, giving the sense of "an effect," "an occasion," "an event," and "a circumstance."[177] Judson thus translates 1 Corinthians 14:35b as "it is a shameful effect for a woman to preach in the church."

Analyzing these issues in 1 Corinthians 14:34–35 in Judson's Burmese Bible, several differences are discovered between Judson's translation and the Greek texts of his day, such as TR, Knapp, and Griesbach, as well as the textual critical texts of NA[28]. Most often, Judson's translation indicates that he is following the Greek texts of TR and Knapp. However, this agreement with TR and Knapp is not always consistent, as he also follows Griesbach. Overall, Judson's translation shows the influences on his interpretation of texts and this is visible in his choice of words and the meaning of those words in translation. In the same way, it was inevitable that his translation would in turn play influence the views and attitudes of readers in the Myanmar church.

Although Judson's Burmese Bible translation provides a smooth reading of the language, his translation of ဟောပြော for λαλέω as "preach" in the context of women's silence becomes more problematic than the translation of λαλέω as "speak" in KJV and NRSV. As mentioned in chapter 2, this translation had a conflicting effect on the nineteenth century women missionaries in Myanmar. Although it supported greater opportunities for women missionaries, including Judson's wives to be involved actively in the church, the

---

174. Judson, *Dictionary, English and Burmese*, 203.
175. Nominative, singular, neuter noun of αἰσχρός.
176. See Table 10.
177. Judson, *Dictionary of the Burman Language*, 4; Judson, *Dictionary, Burmese and English*, 9.

women ended up defending the preaching they did as not really constituting preaching.

Even though this translation of λαλέω as "preach" was less restrictive than the prohibition of "speak," which would have meant restriction of women from all forms of speaking in the church, it has discouraged readers in present-day Myanmar away from a critical process of textual analysis that examines the context of the biblical passage to determine the intended meaning of the original writer. In the present-day context of Myanmar, where there are a few resources other than the Bible available to believers, it is likely that a passage like 1 Corinthians 14:34–35 will be read in a way that goes beyond the intention of the original writer; a problem that will be elaborated in chapter 5.

All the above leads to our main concern: Judson's interpretive view behind the translation of the word λαλέω as ဟောပြော in the context of women's silence discussed later in this chapter. Meanwhile the following section looks at the differences and similarities of translation between the Judson Burmese Bible and the Common Language Bible, to compare their linguistic usages and highlight the influential role of the translator in the process of translating biblical texts.

3.2.3 The Translation of Silence in the Judson Burmese Bible and the Myanmar Common Language Bible

As mentioned, the Myanmar Common Language Bible closely follows the texts of the GNB or TEV. A prime example is found in the translation of the Greek word τὸ αἷμα in Matthew 27:25. The MCL translates this as ထိုသူသေရခြင်း (*tho thu thay ya chin*), meaning "this man's death," which is similar to "the death of this man" in the GNB.[178] This word is translated in

---

178. The reason for not using "the blood" in the GNB translation was explained by Bratcher: "In the Bible, both in the Hebrew Old Testament and the Greek New Testament, the word 'blood' (*dam* in Hebrew, *haima* in Greek) is often used of the violent death of animals or men, a death caused by something or someone. In Matt 27:24–25, for example, Pilate washes his hands before the crowd and says, 'I am innocent of the *haima* of this man.' The crowd answers back, 'May his *haima* be upon us and our children.' It is clear and obvious that the subject is the execution, the death, of Jesus, and in Greek it is natural and clear to speak of Jesus' execution as his *haima*. In English, however, the word 'blood' does not mean death: it means only the liquid that flows in the veins and arteries of men and animals." Bratcher, "Nature and Purpose," 99.

the KJV as "the blood of this just person," and in both the NRSV and NIV as "this man's blood."

The MCL and GNB avoid the usage of the term "the blood" in their translations.[179] This is considered problematic to many due to the important role of the blood of Christ in the doctrine of atonement. The shedding of the blood of Christ is not only redemptive but it is the power of Jesus and a significant symbol of propitiation.[180] This is one of the reasons that many conservative churches do not accept the GNB translation,[181] a decision bolstered by their rejection of the translator Robert Bratcher's critique of biblical inerrancy.[182] This resulted in a financial crisis for the American Bible Society, and Bratcher was asked to resign in 1981. Nevertheless, the GNB translation later became a model for translators around the world and it has also influenced Bible translation in Asia.[183]

Although there are several controversial issues regarding the choice of words in the GNB, Metzger notes that it "made clear some passages that are unclear in the original."[184] This underlines that "this is interpretation, not translation,"[185] though there is a measure of interpretation in any translation.

---

179. Bratcher, 106.

180. Lev 6:30 (NRSV) says, "But no sin offering shall be eaten from which any blood is brought into the tent of meeting for atonement in the holy place; it shall be burned with fire."

181. Many conservative Christians not only resented the translation because of the controversial issues, but also withdrew financial support because of Bratcher's comments about biblical authority and inspiration.

182. Martin, *Accuracy of Translation*, 15, quotes Bratcher as saying,
Only willful ignorance or intellectual dishonesty can account for the claim that the Bible is inerrant and infallible. To qualify this absurd claim by adding 'with respect to the autographs' is a bit of sophistry, a specious attempt to justify a patent error. . . . No truth-loving, God-respecting, Christ-honoring believer should be guilty of such heresy. To invest the Bible with the qualities of inerrancy and infallibility is to idolatrize it, to transform it into a false god. . . . No one seriously claims that all the words of the Bible are the very words of God. If someone does so it is only because that person is not willing thoroughly to explore its implications. Even words spoken by Jesus in Aramaic in the thirties of the first century and preserved in writing in Greek 35 to 50 years later do not necessarily wield compelling or authentic authority over us today. The locus of scriptural authority is not the words themselves. It is Jesus Christ as THE Word of God who is the authority for us to be and to do.

183. Omanson, "Robert Galveston Bratcher," 169. Bratcher later became a translation consultant with the United Bible Societies.

184. Metzger, "Recent Translations," 9.

185. Beduhn, *Truth in Translation*, 38.

A Textual Analysis of 1 Corinthians 14:34–35 in Myanmar Bibles

Bratcher highlights the role of interpretation in translation, arguing that "in trying to be clear, a modern translator avoids being vague and ambiguous, and attempts to represent the meaning of the text as simply and precisely as possible. This means that he must make more choices, and more difficult choices, than those made by traditional versions, which often are (deliberately, sometimes) ambiguous."[186] Given this situation, it was inevitable that by following the principles of the GNB, the MCL would also be influenced by the translator's own interpretations of biblical texts.

This section analyzes the command for women to be silent in 1 Corinthians 14:33–35 in the Myanmar Common Language translation, comparing it with the Judson Burmese Bible. To demonstrate the differences and similarities between the translations, the following comparison charts of 1 Corinthians 14:33–35 consist of four lines. The first line shows the Greek based texts of JB and MCL, which mention the texts of Knapp for JB and UBS for MCL. The second line gives the English translations, KJV for JB, and GNB for MCL. The third line provides the Burmese translations, JB and MCL. I then give my own translation of the Burmese texts into English.

Table 10 shows that the MCL translation differs from the JB in two places. This includes the usage of ဘုရားသခင်သည် for ὁ θεὸς ("God") in verse 34a, and နေကြစေ for ἐπιτρέπεται ("stay") in verse 35b. In the translation of 1 Corinthians 14:35, MCL is very different from JB, and they are identical in only two places where Judson uses ခင်ပွန်းများကို for ἄνδρας and အိမ်တွင် for ἐν οἴκῳ.

We will analyze the MCL text by focusing on three areas. These include the differences between the translations of MCL and JB; the translation of MCL in comparison to its base text, the GNB, to highlight differences and similarities; and the extent to which MCL applies the principle of dynamic equivalence introduced by the GNB.

---

186. Bratcher, "Nature and Purpose," 101.

Table 10. The Greek, English, JB, and MCL Texts of 1 Corinthians 14:33–34a

JB			MCL
Knapp	οὐ γάρ ἐστιν ἀκαταστασίας ὁ θεός, ἀλλ' εἰρήνης. ὡς ἐν πάσαις ταῖς ἐκκλησίαις τῶν ἁγίων. Αἱ γυναῖκες ὑμῶν ἐν ταῖς ἐκκλησίαις σιγάτωσαν.	UBS[5]	οὐ γάρ ἐστιν ἀκαταστασίας ὁ θεός ἀλλὰ εἰρήνης. Ὡς ἐν πάσαις ταῖς ἐκκλησίαις τῶν ἁγίων αἱ γυναῖκες [ ] ἐν ταῖς ἐκκλησίαις σιγάτωσαν.
KJV	For God is not the author of confusion, but of peace, as in all the churches of the saints. Let your women keep silence in the churches.	GNB	because God does not want us to be in disorder but in harmony and peace. As in all the churches of God's people, [34]the women [ ] should keep quiet in the meetings.
JB	[ ] ဘုရားသခင်သည် ရှုန်းရင်းခတ် သောအမှုကို ပြုစုတော်မမူ။ သန့်ရှင်း သူတို့၏ အသင်းတော် အပေါင်းတို့၌ ဖြစ်သကဲ့သို့ အသင့်အတင့် ငြိမ်ဝပ် ခြင်းကို ပြုစု တော် မူ၏။ သင်တို့၏ မိန်းမ တို့သည် အသင်း တော်၌ တိတ်ဆိတ်စွာ နေကြစေ။	MCL	အဘယ်ကြောင့်ဆိုသော် ဘုရားသခင်သည် စည်းမဲ့ကမ်းမဲ့ ပြုမူခြင်းကို လိုလားတော် မမူ။ ငြိမ်ဝပ် ပိပြားမှုကို လိုလားတော်မူ သောကြောင့်ဖြစ်သည်။ ဘုရားသခင်၏ အသင်းတော် အပေါင်းတို့တွင် ကျင့်သုံးသည့် မှုအတိုင်း၊ [ ] အမျိုးသမီး များသည် အစည်း အဝေးများ တွင် ဆိတ်ဆိတ် နေကြစေ။
	God does not nurture a work of confusion. As happened in all the churches of the saint, (he) nurtures peace. **Your** wives should stay silence in the church.		Because God does not want disorderly conduct. [He] wants harmony and peace. As a practice in all the churches of God, the women [ ] should keep quiet in the meetings.

The translations of 1 Corinthians 14:33–34a by MCL and JB differ on the placement of ὡς ἐν πάσαις ταῖς ἐκκλησίαις τῶν ἁγίων in the sentence. MCL places this phrase at the beginning of verse 34 rather than at the conclusion of verse 33, which was the way Judson's Burmese Bible had rendered it. By connecting this phrase with the last part of verse 33, Judson makes God the subject of administering peace in the church of Corinth as in all the other churches.

In contrast, MCL's placement of this phrase at the introduction of verse 34 presents women's silence as a regular practice in all the churches. MCL translates Ὡς ἐν πάσαις ταῖς ἐκκλησίαις τῶν ἁγίων αἱ γυναῖκες ἐν ταῖς ἐκκλησίαις σιγάτωσαν as "As a practice in all the churches of God, the women should stay quiet in the meetings." This shows that MCL is closely following the GNB translation of UBS, which starts the sentence with Ὡς, capitalized, and translates the sentence "As in all the churches of God's people, the women should keep quiet in the meetings" (see Table 11). This leads one to question how the MCL translator understands silence in relation to women in the church.

3.2.3.1 Silence as Quietness in Meetings

We now examine 1 Corinthians 14:34a to highlight differences and similarities between MCL and JB, as well as the role of the translator in the translational process. Looking at Table 11, the first visible difference between MCL and JB is that JB uses the word သင်တို့၏ whereas MCL does not include this word. The word သင်တို့၏ in Burmese refers to ὑμῶν in Greek, meaning "your." This shows that MCL is closely following the GNB, which followed the textual tradition of USB that used αἱ γυναῖκες for "the women" without ὑμῶν in the sentence.

Table 11 shows that MCL not only differs from JB, which includes the word ὑμῶν with αἱ γυναῖκες in the sentence, but also in the choice of words in translating αἱ γυναῖκες into Burmese. MCL uses အမျိုးသမီးများသည် *(a myo tha mi mya thi)* for "women" whereas JB uses မိန်းမတို့သည်. MCL continues to use အမျိုးသမီးများသည် for "women" in all three apparent usages of the word γυνή in the context of 1 Corinthians 14:34–35, where the imperative command was given on women's silence.[187] MCL keeps the translation of γυνή as အမျိုးသမီးများသည်, referring to women in general, and this is also

---

187. See Tables 11 and 13.

seen in 1 Corinthians 11:11–16. However, MCL translates the same word γυνή as မိန်းမ (*mein ma*), meaning specifically "wives," in 1 Corinthians 11:2–6. This shows that MCL is closely following the translation of GNB, which also translates "women" in 1 Corinthians 11:11–16 and "wives" in 1 Corinthians 11:2–6.

Table 11. The Greek, English, JB, and MCL Texts of 1 Corinthians 14:34a

JB		MCL	
Knapp	Αἱ γυναῖκες ὑμῶν ἐν ταῖς ἐκκλησίαις σιγάτωσαν·	UBS[5]	αἱ γυναῖκες [ ] ἐν ταῖς ἐκκλησίαις σιγάτωσαν·
KJV	Let <u>your</u> women keep silence in the churches	GNB	the women [ ] should keep quiet in the meetings.
JB	သင်တို့၏ မိန်းမတို့သည် အသင်းတော်၌ တိတ်ဆိတ်စွာ နေကြစေ။ Your wifes should stay silence <u>in the church</u>.	MCL	[ ] အမျိုးသမီးများသည် အစည်းအဝေး များတွင် ဆိတ် ဆိတ် နေကြစေ။ the women [ ] should keep quiet <u>in the meetings</u>.

In Judson's dictionaries, အမျိုးသမီး is translated "a fellow countrywoman"[188] whereas the term မိန်းမ is used for "a woman"[189] or "a female of the human race."[190] This may help to explain why Judson translates all the appearances of γυνή in 1 Corinthians as မိန်းမ. However, with the passage of time, the meaning of the Burmese word မိန်းမ used in JB later becomes "female or wife," whereas the word အမျိုးသမီး becomes a reference for "woman."[191] This explains MCL's separate usage of အမျိုးသမီးများသည် for women in general, and မိန်းမ for wives. This also shows how language and meaning have changed in the time since Judson's translation.

For the translation of σιγάτωσαν, MCL's usage does not differ greatly from Judson's translation of this word as တိတ်ဆိတ် ("silence"). MCL translates σιγάτωσαν as ဆိတ်ဆိတ် (*seit seit*). The words တိတ်ဆိတ် and ဆိတ်ဆိတ် are

---

188. Judson, *Dictionary of the Burman Language*, 24.
189. Judson, 275.
190. Judson, *Dictionary, English and Burmese*, 584.
191. Myanmar Language Commission, *Myanmar-English Dictionary*, 581.

both a combination of two words. The word တိတ်ဆိတ် is a combination of တိတ် and ဆိတ်, meaning "quiet, still, or silent,"[192] and ဆိတ်ဆိတ် is a combination of the same words, "quiet, still, silent."[193] MCL uses the same word, ဆိတ်ဆိတ်, in the context of speaking in tongues in 1 Corinthians 14:28, in the present imperative form σιγάτω.[194] However, MCL translates the same word, σιγάτω, in 1 Corinthians 14:30, in the present imperative form, to more emphatically stress ရပ်နားစေ (*yat nar say*) as "stop speaking," in the context of prophesying in tongues.[195] In the context of σιγάτωσαν in 1 Corinthians 14:34, MCL's translation is likely to have the same sense as its base text, the GNB. The GNB translates this word in the sense of "quiet," which explains the meaning of the sentence as "the women should keep quiet."[196]

However, MCL differs significantly from the JB translation of ταῖς ἐκκλησίαις in 1 Corinthians 14:34a. MCL translates ταῖς ἐκκλησίαις as အစည်းအဝေးများတွင် ("in the meetings"), whereas JB translates it as အသင်းတော်၌ ("in the church"). This indicates that MCL is closely following its base text, GNB, which translates ταῖς ἐκκλησίαις as အစည်းအဝေးများတွင် ("in the meetings"). This translation shows MCL following the dynamic equivalent principle of GNB. The translation of "in the meetings" is likely referring to worship meetings that take place in the church as it gathers, because MCL translates ταῖς ἐκκλησίαις as ဝတ်ပြုအစည်းအဝေး (*wit pyu a si a way*), a combination of the words ဝတ်ပြု ("worship") and အစည်းအဝေး ("meeting"), or worship services, in 1 Corinthians 14:19.[197]

---

192. Judson, *Dictionary of the Burman Language*, 149.

193. Myanmar Language Commission, "Myanmar-English Dictionary," 143.

194. MCL translated this as အကယ်၍ စကားပြန်မရှိပါမူ ထူးဆန်းသောဘာသာစကားဖြင့် ပြောဆိုလိုသောသူသည် ဆိတ်ဆိတ်နေ၍ မိမိတစ်ကိုယ်တည်းပြောလျက်နေစေ, meaning "But if no one is there to interpret, the one who wants to speak in strange languages must be quiet and speak only to oneself and to God."

195. MCL translates this as ဘုရားသခင် ၏ဗျာဒိတ်တော်ကိုခံယူရရှိပါကဟောပြောနေသော သူသည် ရပ်နားစေ, meaning "But if someone receives a message from God, the one who is speaking must stop speaking."

196. See Table 10.

197. ἐκκλησίᾳ is a dative singular feminine word, and MCL translates it as ပရိသတ်ဝတ်ပြုခြင်း, meaning "worship of the congregations."

3.2.3.2 Silence: Women and Speaking

Table 12 outlines the textual and linguistic variances of Judson's translation in 1 Corinthians 14:34b.

Table 12. The Greek, English, JB, and MCL Texts of 1 Corinthians 14:34b

JB			MCL		
Knapp		οὐ γὰρ ἐπιτρέπεται αὐταῖς λαλεῖν,	UBS⁵		οὐ γὰρ ἐπιτρέπεται αὐταῖς λαλεῖν,
KJV		for it is not permitted unto them to speak;	GNB		They are not allowed to speak;
JB		သူတို့သည် ဟောပြောရသော အခွင့် မရှိကြ။	MCL		သူတို့မှာ စကားပြော ပိုင်ခွင့် မရှိ။
		They are not permitted to preach.			They are not allowed to speak.

Table 12 shows that MCL does not include the word γὰρ ("for") in its translation, like Judson's Burmese translation. Here MCL is closely following the base text GNB, which translates only "they are not allowed to speak," without the word γὰρ, although UBS' Greek text includes it. The usage of သူတို့သည် in JB and သူတို့မှာ in MCL is similar in meaning. The word သူတို့ is referring to "they" in English. The Burmese word သည် is a nominative suffix to denote the agent or subject of the sentence,[198] and မှာ is a nominative suffix used interchangeably with သည်.[199] The word comes from the third person plural dative pronoun αὐταῖς[200] in the sentence. The MCL and JB translate this word as the nominative form "they" instead of "to them." This shows the role of translators in choosing terminologies as well as adjusting words to clarify the meaning of the sentence.

MCL gives ပြောပိုင်ခွင့်မရှိ for the word ἐπιτρέπεται,[201] meaning they are not "allowed," which JB translates as အခွင့်မရှိကြ, meaning they are not

---

198. Judson, *Grammar*, 16. This is a version of the Burmese and English Dictionary edited by E. O. Stevens. Everything added is indicated by the letters "st."
199. Myanmar Language Commission, "Myanmar-English Dictionary," 375, 512.
200. αὐταῖς is the third person, dative, plural, feminine pronoun of αὐτός.
201. ἐπιτρέπεται is the third person, singular, present, passive, indicative form of ἐπιτρέπω.

"permitted." MCL's usage of ပိုင် in the phrase ပြောပိုင်ခွင့်မရှိ means that women have no "right to"[202] speak, whereas JB's usage of အခွင့်မရှိကြ, means that women have no "permission" to preach.

However, MCL's translation differs significantly from JB in verse 34b in the translation of λαλεῖν, which MCL translates as စကားပြော ("speak"), whereas JB translates it as ဟောပြော "preach"). MCL translates the same word in 1 Corinthians 14:1–5 as ဟောပြော, and in 1 Corinthians 14:29–32 as ဟောပြော, meaning "preach." JB differs from MCL in translating λαλεῖν as ဟောပြော only in 1 Corinthians 14:3, 23, and in 1 Corinthians 14:27–30. This is due to MCL's understanding of the context of 1 Corinthians 14:1–5 as "preaching" and the context of 1 Corinthians 14:29–30 as "prophesying," whereas JB understands the context of 1 Corinthians 14:1–5, 23, and 1 Corinthians 14:27–30 as "prophesying in tongues."

Further, MCL's translation of λαλεῖν is slightly different from the translation of GNB, which translates it in 1 Corinthians 14:1–5 as "proclaiming" but in 1 Corinthians 14:27–30 as "speaking." This shows that MCL does not always follow the GNB. However, in 1 Corinthians 14:34b, MCL follows the translation of λαλεῖν in GNB ("speaking"). MCL's translation of λαλεῖν as စကားပြော in 1 Corinthians 14:34–35 indicates the prohibition on women "speaking" generally, rather than JB's specific form of speaking ("preaching"). MCL's view is even clearer in its translation of 1 Corinthians 14:35b, to which we will return later.

3.2.3.3 *Silence: Jewish Rabbinic Teaching and Not Leading*

We now discuss the textual and linguistic variances of the MCL translation from the JB translation of 1 Corinthians 14:34c. Table 14 shows how the MCL differs significantly from JB. First, the translation of MCL differs from JB in translating the word ὁ νόμος. MCL translates ὁ νόμος as ယုဒပညတ်ကျမ်း (*yuda panyat kyan*) as "the Jewish law," whereas JB translates it as ပညတ်တရား ("the law"). This insertion of "Jewish" before "law" implies that the command to women to be quiet in the meetings is backed by the Jewish law, whereas JB translates this term more generically as "the law." MCL also has "the book of the Jewish law." This is slightly different from MCL's base text, GNB, which

---

202. Myanmar Language Commission, "Myanmar-English Dictionary," 270.

translates it as "the Jewish law" only. The MCL reference to the Jewish law could be simply referring to the Pentateuch.[203]

Table 13. The Greek, English, JB, and MCL Texts of 1 Corinthians 14:34c

JB			MCL	
Knapp	Ἀλλ' ὑποτάσσεσθαι, καθὼς καὶ ὁ νόμος λέγει		UBS[5]	ἀλλὰ ὑποτασσέσθωσαν, καθὼς καὶ ὁ νόμος λέγει
KJV	but they are commanded to be under obedience, as also saith the law		GNB	as the Jewish Law says, they must not be in charge.
JB	ပညတ်တရား စီရင်သည် အတိုင်း သူတို့သည် ယောက်ျား၏ အုပ်စိုးခြင်းကို ဝန်ခံရကြမည်။		MCL	ယုဒပညတ်ကျမ်းတွင် ဖော်ပြသည့်အတိုင်း အမျိုးသမီးတို့သည် အစည်းအဝေးများတွင် ခေါင်းဆောင်များ မဖြစ်စေရ။
	As the Law they should consent to ruling of man.			As the book of Jewish Law mentions, women must not be leaders in the meetings.

The MCL translation explains the kind of prohibition imposed: အမျိုးသမီးတို့သည် အစည်းအဝေးများတွင် ခေါင်းဆောင်များ မဖြစ်စေရ ("women must not be leaders in the meetings"). This unique translation of MCL is derived from the word ὑποτάσσεσθαι, which MCL translates as "women must not be leaders in the meetings," rather than the JB translation, သူတို့သည် ယောက်ျား၏ အုပ်စိုးခြင်းကို ဝန်ခံရကြမည် ("they should consent to the ruling of man"). GNB, the base text of MCL, points to the prohibition imposed by Jewish law, stating "as the Jewish law says, they must not be in charge."

The MCL translation replaces GNB's translation of the word "they" with "the women." This is likely due to the intention to clarify the word "they" as referring to "women" in this context. MCL also uses the translation "women must not be leaders" rather than a literal translation of ὑποτασσέσθωσαν

---

203. Some suggest that "the Jewish law" refers here to a Jewish rabbinic tradition that prohibited women from coming to the lectern of the synagogue, mentioned in Strack and Billerbeck, *Kommentar zum neuen Testament*, 3:367. Also in Weiss, *Women at Prayer*, 71. A collection of extra-Mishnah material, Tosefta, Megillah 3:5, reads: "all are included among the seven, even a woman and even a minor. But a woman is not brought forth to read in public." Fitzmyer, *First Corinthians*, 533.

("women should submit"). Further, MCL adds the phrase "in the meetings" although both USB and GNB do not include this in their texts. By inserting "in the meetings" at the end of the sentence, MCL indicates that the place women needed to be quiet was in the "meetings" of the church, and MCL's translation of 1 Corinthians 14:35b later gave "meetings in the church." These differences are clear in Table 14. They show MCL following the principle of dynamic equivalence by inserting and changing words to give a clearer meaning of the texts. The MCL translation of this text is another example of the influence of translators in the translations of biblical texts.

3.2.3.4 Silence: Knowing and Inquiring

This leads to a discussion of the textual and linguistic variances between the MCL and JB translations of 1 Corinthians 14:35a. Looking at Table 15 below, we see that MCL omits δέ ("but") in the translation, just as JB had done. If the word δέ is translated, it would be သို့သော်လည်း in the Burmese language. MCL's omission is like its GNB base text that also omitted the word δέ.

Table 14. The Greek, English, JB, and MCL Texts of 1 Corinthians 14:35a

JB		MCL	
Knapp	Εἰ δέ τι μαθεῖν θέλουσιν, ἐν οἴκῳ τοὺς ἰδίους ἄνδρας ἐπερωτάτωσαν·	UBS⁵	εἰ δέ τι μαθεῖν θέλουσιν, ἐν οἴκῳ τοὺς ἰδίους ἄνδρας ἐπερωτάτωσαν·
KJV	And if they will learn anything let them ask their [ ] husbands at home;	GNB	If they want to find out about something, they should ask their [ ] husbands at home.
JB	မိန်းမတို့သည် တစ်စုံတစ်ခုကို သင်လိုလျှင်၊ အိမ်၌ မိမိ ခင်ပွန်းတို့ကို မေးမြန်းကြစေ။	MCL	သူတို့သည် အကြောင်း တစ်စုံတစ်ရာကို သိလိုလျှင် မိမိ တို့၏ ခင်ပွန်းများကို အိမ်တွင် မေးမြန်း စုံစမ်းကြစေ။
	If women want to learn something, let them ask their own husbands at home.		If they want to know about something they should inquire their own husbands at home.

The MCL translation gives the subject of the sentence as only သူတို့သည်, a general sense of "they," whereas JB translates it more specifically as မိန်းမတို့သည် ("women"). However, the word for εἰ ("if") appears as the suffix လျှင်[204] after the word μαθεῖν, which JB translates as သင်လိုလျှင် ("if want to learn"), while MCL translates it as သိလိုလျှင် ("if want to know"). This shows that MCL sees the word μαθεῖν as wanting "to know" whereas JB sees it as wanting "to learn." MCL further translates τι as "about something" whereas JB translates τι as just "something." Therefore, the phrase εἰ δέ τι μαθεῖν θέλουσιν in verse 35a is translated in MCL as "if they want to know about something," while JB translates it as မိန်းမတို့သည် တစုံတခုကို သင်လိုလျှင် ("if women want to learn something"). Both usages of the word show the desire in general "to come to understand as the result of a process of learning."[205]

However, MCL's "if they want to know about something" is difficult to connect with "women must not be leaders in the meetings" in the previous verse, 34c. This raises a question concerning what women leading the meetings should do with women wanting to know. Regardless of this difficulty, MCL's translation reads well. The translation of MCL includes τοὺς ἰδίους with ἄνδρας translating မိမိတို့၏ ခင်ပွန်းများကို as "their own husbands," whereas JB uses မိမိ ခင်ပွန်းတို့ကို in the sentence. The word မိမိ is in the singular and မိမိတို့ is in the plural form. Both words show one's own possession, and MCL gives the word မိမိတို့ with the possessive suffix ၏ at the end.

Although USB includes τοὺς ἰδίους with ἄνδρας, GNB does not include τοὺς ἰδίους in its translation. Here, MCL is not following GNB closely. MCL translates ἄνδρας as ခင်ပွန်းတို့ကို ("husbands"), as does JB. This usage of the word ခင်ပွန်းတို့ကို indicates the specific term for husbands, whereas အမျိုးသား could be used for "men" or "husbands."[206] In this context, MCL uses ခင်ပွန်းတို့ကို specifically to match with τοὺς ἰδίους မိမိတို့၏, meaning "their own." MCL then translates οἴκῳ as အိမ်တွင်, while JB translates it as အိမ်၌. The meaning of these words is the same since the words တွင် and ၌ are locative suffixes that indicate the same thing, "at home."[207] Further, MCL translates

---

204. Judson, *Grammar*, 31. The word လျှင် is used to denote "the completion of an action or state of being prior to another" or "supposition or conditionality."

205. Nida, *Greek-English Lexicon*, 380.

206. Myanmar Language Commission, "Myanmar-English Dictionary," 581.

207. Judson, *Grammar*, 18.

ἐπερωτάτωσαν as "inquire" or "inquiringly ask," whereas JB translates it as "ask" only. Translating the word for ἐπερωτάτωσα as မေးမြန်းစုံစမ်း in Burmese indicates a combination of two words, မေးမြန်း (*may myan*), meaning "ask," and စုံစမ်း (*song san*), meaning "investigate or inquire."[208]

It is important to note that MCL translates "the women" as အမျိုးသမီးများသည် in verse 34a, 34c, and later in 35b. Although it is possible that အမျိုးသမီးများသည် could mean both "wives" and "women,"[209] this word is used here about women. The reason is that MCL uses the term မိန်းမ in other contexts that clearly refer to wives, such as in 1 Corinthians 11:20. Although a specific term for husband (ခင်ပွန်း) is used in verse 35a instead of the generic term for man (အမျိုးသား), MCL uses အမျိုးသမီးများသည် throughout 1 Corinthians 14:34–45. If MCL intends အမျိုးသမီးများ to refer to women in general, although the word ခင်ပွန်း is used for husband in the same context, it is following the base text GNB quite closely. Another possible reason could be that MCL uses both terms interchangeably, အမျိုးသမီးများ with ခင်ပွန်း, since most of the women in that culture married early.[210]

3.2.3.5 Silence: Speaking and Shame

Finally, we examine the differences and similarities of the MCL and JB translations of 1 Corinthians 14:35a. Table 15 shows that both MCL and JB omit the Greek word γάρ in translation. Again, MCL translates γυναικὶ as အမျိုးသမီးများ, whereas JB translates it as မိန်းမသည်. It is important to note that MCL translates the singular word γυναικὶ[211] in the plural ("women"). The reason for using the plural form for a singular word could be that MCL sees this sentence as referring to all women, as in verse 34. Generally, the MCL translations closely follow the base text, GNB, by omitting γάρ in translation. However, MCL differs from GNB in translating γυναικὶ as "women," whereas GNB translates it as only "a woman."

---

208. Myanmar Language Commission, "Myanmar-English Dictionary," 357.
209. Myanmar Language Commission, 60.
210. Fee, *First Epistle to the Corinthians*, 706.
211. γυναικὶ is a noun, dative, singular, feminine form of **γυνή**.

Table 15. The Greek, English, JB, and MCL Texts of 1 Corinthians 14:35b

JB		MCL	
Knapp	αἰσχρὸν γάρ ἐστι γυναιξὶν ἐν ἐκκλησίᾳ λαλεῖν.	UBS⁵	αἰσχρὸν γάρ ἐστιν γυναικὶ λαλεῖν ἐν ἐκκλησίᾳ
KJV	For it is a shame for <u>women</u> to speak in church	GNB	It is a disgraceful thing for <u>a woman</u> to speak in a church meeting.
JB	မိန်းမသည် အသင်းတော်၌ ဟောပြော လျှင် ရှက်ဘွယ် သော အကြောင်း ဖြစ်၏။	MCL	အသင်းတော်၏ အစည်းအဝေး၌ အမျိုးသမီးများ စကားပြော ခြင်းသည် ရှက်ဖွယ်သော အမှု ဖြစ်၏။
	A <u>woman</u> to preach in the church is a shameful thing.		It is a shameful thing for <u>women</u> to speak in the meeting of the church.

MCL translates ἐν ἐκκλησίᾳ as အသင်းတော်၏ အစည်းအဝေး၌ ("in the church's meeting"). The word အသင်းတော်၏ means "of a church" and အစည်းအဝေး၌ means "in a meeting."[212] Only JB uses အသင်းတော်၌ ("in a church"). This is another example of MCL following GNB closely, because GNB translates ἐν ἐκκλησίᾳ as "in a church meeting," although a literal translation should be "in church" only. Although MCL and GNB focus on clarity of meaning for readers from the viewpoint of dynamic equivalence, this addition of အစည်းအဝေး ("meeting") to အသင်းတော်၏ ("of church") requires more explanation, since a meeting could also mean a business meeting of the local church as well as a worship meeting. If the meeting is referring to worship, then it should be translated as ဝတ်ပြုအစည်းအဝေး instead of အစည်းအဝေး in Burmese.

MCL and JB agree on the word αἰσχρὸν, but their chosen terminologies are not the same. MCL translates αἰσχρὸν as ရှက်ဖွယ်သောအမှု and JB translates this word as ရှက်ဘွယ်သောအကြောင်း. The word ရှက်ဖွယ်သော[213] means

---

212. Myanmar Language Commission, "Myanmar-English Dictionary," 553.

213. Judson, *Dictionary of the Burman Language*, 28. The range of meaning includes "modesty, shame."

"shameful" whereas အမှု means "affair,"[214] and အကြောင်း[215] means "cause, reason, or circumstance." GNB translates αἰσχρὸν as "a disgraceful thing" whereas KJV translates it as "a shame." In MCL and JB, the words အမှု and အကြောင်း appear behind the word ရှက်ဖွယ်သော to give a literal translation of αἰσχρὸν, which is a neuter adjective.[216] This is likely the reason for GNB to translate this as "a disgraceful thing" instead of "a disgrace."

Finally, in MCL, the "shameful thing" for women to do in church meetings is စကားပြောခြင်းသည် ("speaking"), whereas in JB the shameful thing for women to do in the church is ဟောပြောလျှင် ("preaching"). Both translations, speaking and preaching, come from the word λαλεῖν in Greek. This shows that MCL is again closely following the translation of GNB, which says that for a woman "to speak" in a church meeting is a disgraceful thing. This also shows GNB following a literal reading of λαλεῖν by translating it as "speak." In the context of "in the meeting of the church," MCL's use of "speaking" is likely about the prohibition of women from all forms of speaking rather than a specific form of speaking ("preaching") in JB's translation.

Comparing the MCL and JB translations, it is noticeable that they are relatively different from each other. The differences are expected since MCL started with the view that the terminologies used in the JB translation were distant from modern-day usages. One difference in terminology in 1 Corinthians 14:34–35 occurs with JB's translation of γυναιξὶ as မိန်းမ for women, which changes to အမျိုးသမီးများ in more modern usage. The other differences are basically due to the translator's understanding of the passage rather than terminological changes. Regardless of these differences, both translations read well.

The MCL and JB translations show the influence of the translators' understanding of the passages and their interpretive role in the process of translation, such as choosing what they believe to be appropriate terminologies and adding as well as omitting words in the sentence. In comparing these two translations, JB stays closer to the base Greek texts, whereas MCL differs more from its base text, the GNB. This is likely due to MCL's claim to be following a meaning-based translation that allows for adding words to give a

---

214. Judson, 25. The range of meaning includes "business, work, affair, a process in law."
215. Judson, *Grammar*, 18.
216. αἰσχρὸν is an adjective, nominative, singular neuter form of αἰσχρός.

clearer meaning of the text, taking into account the context of the readers. However, as noted above, the MCL translation of အသင်းတော်၏ အစည်းအဝေး၌ ("in the church's meeting") especially raises more questions than the literal translation of JB that gives အသင်းတော်၌ as "in a church."

However, although MCL's literal translation of λαλεῖν as "speaking" puts forward the notion that women are prohibited from all forms of speaking, rather than JB's specific form of speaking, the MCL translation is helpful in raising critical questions about the text and the context of its contemporary readers, which will be discussed in chapter 6. In the JB translation, this critical questioning process is missing in the process of interpreting, since the translation already indicates the kind of prohibition as preaching. The literal translation of λαλεῖν as "speaking" not only occurs in the MCL, but in most English versions, such as NIV, ESV, NRSV, KJV, NLT, NKJV, and RSV. This further explains the lack of critical engagement with the Judson translation in Myanmar, because its translation of λαλεῖν already provides an answer to the kind of silence that is required of women in the context of 1 Corinthians 14:34–35.

All the above findings show the important role of interpretation in the process of translation. This leads to the raising of further interpretive issues in translation. Here, we examine the kinds of influences that lie behind Judson's decision to interpret women's silence as women's silence in preaching. This involves looking at the "culture attitudes, education, and experience" of the translator, which influence "personal predispositions" and "theological assumptions."[217] These issues are elaborated in the following section.

3.3 Historical Influences Affecting Judson's Translation

Adoniram Judson's view of women preaching was influenced by the understanding of women's role in church and society prevalent in nineteenth-century America. The view that women should not preach was observable in denominational teachings and commentaries in this period. In a study on women and preaching in the early nineteenth century in America, Catherine Brekus notes that during this period most mainline American Protestant

---

217. Smalley, "Language and Culture," 61.

churches including Presbyterians, Episcopalians, and Congregationalists, strongly opposed women preaching. Alongside the command for women's silence in 1 Corinthians 14:34–35, they used passages such as 1 Corinthians 11:3 that refer to the headship of man, and 1 Timothy 2:11–12, that commands women not to usurp authority over men by teaching.[218]

Among the biblical commentaries available in Judson's day, the six-volume work of Matthew Henry[219] had a significant influence on the Protestant churches, from the printing of the first volume in 1710. The fifth volume, including 1 Corinthians, was printed in 1806,[220] a few years before Judson left for Burma. It is likely that Judson was familiar with the work of Matthew Henry, although he did not specifically mention him. In Henry's comments on 1 Corinthians 14:34–35, he described women's silence as a prohibition of women's speech in the limited sense of "preaching, or interpreting scripture by inspiration."[221] He added that for "a woman to prophesy in this sense was to teach, which does not so well befit her state of subjection. A teacher of others has in that respect a superiority over them, which is not allowed the woman over the man, nor must she therefore be allowed to teach in a congregation."

This understanding about women preaching was common among early nineteenth-century Protestant churches. Rosemary Skinner Keller notes that although there were "Reformed women who felt called to preach," the churches "tended to take Paul's admonitions about women's silence literally, [and] women's preaching was not always welcome."[222] Restrictions on women preaching and speaking in the church were spelled out in formal declarations. For instance, in 1832 the Presbyterian General Assembly stated that "to teach and exhort, or to lead in prayer, in public and promiscuous assemblies, is clearly forbidden to women in the Holy Oracles."[223]

---

218. Brekus, *Female Preaching*, 22.

219. Matthew Henry (1662–1714). The first volume was published in 1708, and other volumes in 1710. Acts was included in 1811. Williams, *Memoirs of the Life*.

220. Henry, *Exposition*, 342.

221. Henry, 342.

222. Brekus, *Female Preaching*, 22.

223. Matthew Henry (1662–1714). The first volume was published in 1708, and other volumes in 1710. Acts was included in 1811. Williams, *Memoirs of the Life*.

Another American church historian, Clare Midgley, mentions the Baptist church along with the Congregational church as prominent among the denominations that opposed women preaching based on 1 Corinthians 14:34–35. Through denominational views and popular teaching on women's position in the family and church, as helper and supporter of men, the interpretation of this women's silence passage also led the foreign missionary societies of the early nineteenth century to avoid recruiting women as missionaries.[224] As a result, the only opportunity for women to go into missionary service was to go as wives of the male missionaries.

Since preaching the gospel was considered the primary work of missionaries and the other aspects of ministry were considered secondary, the involvement of missionary wives in Bible translation and schools was considered acceptable, along with their primary vocation of helping and supporting their husbands. This explains why Ann Judson, as well as other women missionaries mentioned in chapter 2, claimed that their preaching, or what we today would regard as preaching, was not actually doing the work of preaching. The prohibition of women from preaching persisted in all the mainstream churches until the latter part of the nineteenth century.[225]

Judson was born into a Congregational minister's family,[226] and became an ordained minister as well as a missionary, first in the Congregational church and later in the Baptist church, both of which opposed women preaching based on their interpretation of 1 Corinthians 14:34–35. Before becoming a minister, he studied theology, beginning in 1808,[227] at Andover Theological Seminary,[228] which was known as a conservative Calvinist school.[229] All of these experiences undoubtedly influenced Judson's attitudes[230] and helped form the theological assumptions behind his translational work.[231] Judson's

---

224. Henry, *Exposition*, 342.
225. Henry, 342.
226. Keller et al., *Encyclopedia of Women and Religion*, 347.
227. Brekus, *Female Preaching*, 21.
228. Midgley, "Can Women Be Missionaries?" 338.
229. Midgley, 338.
230. Wayland, *Memoir of the Life*, vol. 1, 24–25.
231. Wayland, 27–28. He was admitted to Andover on 12 October 1806 though he had not yet made a public profession of faith. By 2 December, Judson had made a solemn declaration of himself to God and joined the Third Congregational Church in Plymouth, where his father was the pastor.

writings and preaching notes[232] reveal his high regard for the Bible as God's inspired word[233] which underlay his theology of ministry and his sense of strategy for missionary work.[234]

Judson would have been well acquainted with the prevailing views of women preaching, since discussion of these issues had been commonplace in the mainline churches since the seventeenth century.[235] According to Kim, these churches prohibited women from preaching by adopting Luther's view of women's inferiority to men in voice, eloquence, memory, and other natural gifts, and Calvin's view of social inequality between men and women. Thus, the possibility of women being allowed to preach in this period was "nearly unthinkable."[236]

Despite all these restrictions on women preaching in the church, questions were raised in some Puritan churches about the appropriate status of women in church and society in America.[237] Ann Hutchinson (1591–1643) was a prominent voice among those who raised such questions in the seventeenth century.[238] Although the Puritans did not allow women to preach or speak

---

232. Rowe, *History of Andover Theological Seminary*, 9. Andover was founded in 1807.

233. Rowe, 14. The purpose of Andover Seminary was to increase "the number of learned and able defenders of the Gospel of Christ, as well as of orthodox, pious, and zealous ministers of the New Testament; being moved, as we hope, by a principle of gratitude to God and benevolence to man."

234. Wayland, *Memoir of the Life*, vol. 1, 37, notes that Judson read Claudius Buchanan's *Star in the East*, which appealed for missions in India, and in 1809 he began to consider missions as his calling. He became interested in Burma when he read Symes's *Embassy to Ava*.

235. Wayland, 155, notes Judson's Calvinist belief in God's "irresistible grace" which prompts the elect to respond to the electing love of God.

236. Wayland, 154. Judson believed that because of Adam and Eve's sin, their descendants "became sinners" and "in consequence of the sin of each individual, every descendant of Adam is deserving of eternal banishment from God." As a result, the race of man must be "doomed to misery temporal and eternal." Wayland, 136. However, "in consequence of the incarnation, obedience, and sufferings of Christ, a free and full pardon is now offered to all the race of man, who, in sincere repentance for sin, commits themselves, in humble trust, to the mercy of God through the . . . proclamation of the Gospel, the good news of salvation, . . . [and that the] "Holy Spirit should with irresistible energy accompany the proclamation of the message of salvation." Calvinist teachings are also evident in the only English sermon Judson ever preached in Burma, and in the Confession of Faith he wrote for the Burmese in 1829. Hulse, *Adoniram Judson*, 13.

237. Anderson, *To the Golden Shore*, 411. After finishing his translation, Judson prayed that God would make "his own inspired word, now complete in Burman tongue, the grand instrument of filling all Burmah with songs of praise to our Great God and Saviour Jesus Christ."

238. Wayland, *Memoir of the Life*, vol. 1, 157. Ann Judson captured what they hoped to accomplish through translating the Bible: "O, that the time may soon come, when this people

in the church or in society, the Quakers[239] allowed them to do so during this period. For this reason, some of the sympathizers of Anne Hutchinson left Puritan churches and joined the Quakers.[240]

Broader changes regarding the role of women in the church began to occur in the eighteenth century[241] influenced by two major revivals, the First Great Awakening (1740–1770) and the Second Great Awakening (1790–1850).[242] During the First Great Awakening, all the churches in the northern and middle colonies of America, regardless of denomination, experienced revivals that reflected the Wesleyan revivals in England and Scotland.[243] Many new members were drawn into the churches, especially women.[244] These mass conversions marked the beginning of the Great Awakening and changed many aspects of church life during this period, including marking it as the beginning stage for the greater involvement of women in the church.

During this time, several laywomen, alongside laymen, became itinerant preachers in churches due to the revivalists' view of the authority of preaching being the "preacher's experience of conversion and inner regeneration,"[245] rather than formal theological training or social status. Several women

---

will be able to read the scriptures of truth in their own language and believe in that Savior." Judson, *Letters*, 83–84.

239. In the seventeenth century, Puritans generally saw women as "the daughters of Eve," and inferior to men, and held that "they should subordinate to male authority at home, at church, and in society at large." However not all women were daughters of Eve, and some "good wives" who were "pious and obedient to the norms of social order, are spiritually equal to men." See Kim, *Women Preaching*, 91.

240. Kim, 85.

241. MacHaffie, *Her Story*, 134.

242. Keller et al., *Encyclopedia of Women and Religion*, 347. Ann Hutchinson was a Puritan from Boston who felt called to teach and preach. Despite strong opposition, she continued to teach and preach to mixed audiences in her own home. She was accused of teaching false doctrine and exercising authority over men in public gatherings, and was exiled to Rhode Island. Kim, *Women Preaching*, 91.

243. Kim, 85. Quakers allowed women to preach.

244. Kim, 85. Quakers used references such as Acts 2:17–18; 21:9; 1 Cor 11:5, and Joel 2:28–29 to support the legitimacy of women in ministry. They believed that the Pauline prohibitions in 1 Cor 14 should be understood as "local temporary conditions which have passed away." They emphasized the direct inspiration of the Holy Spirit and a personal relationship with God as qualifications for being a preacher, rather than theological education. So, even in the seventeenth century, some women could engage in preaching and receive ordination to various ministerial offices.

245. Tucker and Liefeld, *Daughters of the Church*, 247; Keller et al., *Encyclopedia of Women and Religion*, 347.

became itinerant preachers in the Methodist churches through the encouragement of John Wesley,[246] who believed the Awakening was an extraordinary time in which "exceptions to the biblical command of silence [for women] could be made."[247] Others shared the view of Jonathan Edwards that the occurrence of mass conversion and women preaching in the Great Awakening were signs of the "the Latter-day Glory."[248]

However, Judson's Congregational church, like the Reformed and Presbyterian churches, was among those that retained the conservative views of the Puritans. Their emphasis on orthodox theology rather than on spiritual gifts, as well as their insistence on an educated clergy, did not permit lay ministry in their churches during the First Great Awakening. They did not allow women to preach during this period, "since women did not have access to Seminary education at that time, and [the churches] encouraged women to follow traditional gender roles and expectations of women in the church."[249]

Although the First Great Awakening brought religious passions and enthusiasm into the churches, it also resulted in divisions.[250] This led some churches that had been open to women preaching to prohibit women from speaking and preaching. Among the Baptist churches, Brekus notes that the northern Separate Baptist congregations began to ban women from praying aloud in public as early as 1750.[251] The role of deaconess, once enjoyed by the women of the southern Separate Baptist congregations, which was a role of care for the poor and the sick (a pastoral role except for preaching), ended when the Separate Baptists merged with other Baptists in 1787.

Among the Wesleyan churches, the acceptance of women preaching began to fade with the death of Wesley in 1791, and they began to restrict women's preaching to only women's groups by 1803.[252] Although the influence of the First Great Awakening on the role of women lasted only a short time, due to

---

246. Brekus, *Strangers and Pilgrims*, 466.

247. Noll, *History of Christianity*, 91.

248. Noll, 91.

249. Kim, *Women Preaching*, 92–93. Brekus, *Strangers and Pilgrims*, 466, notes that women, regardless of race or age, were "praying aloud, testifying, and ecstatically responding to the guidance of the Spirit during worship services. Women even began acting as exhorters, informal evangelists who from their pews encouraged others to repent.

250. Rack, *Reasonable Enthusiast*, 244.

251. MacHaffie, *Her Story*, 136.

252. Kim, *Women Preaching*, 93.

the rising conservatism across the churches, the spiritual enthusiasm and conversion experiences did pave the way for a greater involvement of women in the Second Great Awakening.

In the Second Great Awakening (1790–1850), the subject of women preaching intensified as women's participation in evangelism grew. As in the First Awakening, the evangelistic nature of preaching during this revival again contributed to massive conversions across denominational lines, including Presbyterians, Methodists, Congregationalists, and Baptists. Due to female conversions outnumbering those of men, women started to gain more active roles in the leadership of the church as well. Some revivalists[253] encouraged women to lead public prayers and to preach, even to gender-mixed audiences, to promote revival.[254] Through the encouragement of male leaders of the revivals, women began to stand behind the pulpit in those churches that were open to women preaching.

The churches that allowed women to preach and who challenged the restrictions on women's preaching in the early nineteenth century included the Freewill Baptists, the Christian Connection, the northern Methodists, the African Methodists, and the Millerites (predecessors of the Seventh-day Adventists).[255] These churches allowed female preaching, first, for a practical reason, since they lacked male ministers to keep pace with their fast growth in the early nineteenth century revival.[256] Second, women preachers were allowed based on theological considerations that interpreted Paul's teaching as only against the "ruling" of women over men despite their rightful authority in the church, but not prohibiting women to pray, sing, witness, exhort, or preach in public; thus, women were allowed to help save souls.[257]

Those who supported women preaching during this period were likely sourcing the commentary of Adam Clarke (1760–1832).[258] The silence of women in 1 Corinthians 14:34 was explained by Clarke as referring to the Jewish law that forbade women from teaching and asking questions in the

---

253. Keller et al., *Encyclopedia of Women and Religion*, 347.
254. Keller et al., 226. New Lights supported revivalists and Old Lights did not.
255. Brekus, *Strangers and Pilgrims*, 466.
256. Kim, *Women Preaching*, 88.
257. The revivalist Charles Finney encouraged women in public ministry. Hambrick-Stowe, *Charles G. Finney*, 84.
258. Kim, *Women Preaching*, 95.

assembly until the time of the gospel. He linked 1 Corinthians 11:5 with women's prophecy and the teaching of Joel's prophecy mentioned in Acts 2, and concluded that women are liberated to prophesy and to teach since the Spirit of God was poured out on women as well as on men. He maintained the view that the wife was subordinate in marriage but emphasized that a woman who was gifted and enabled by God should not remain silent in the church.[259]

In the Second Great Awakening, Baptist churches remained divided on women preaching. Resolutions opposing women speaking publicly were adopted around 1756 and again in 1785, but the Freewill Baptists allowed women to preach and began licensing women preachers in 1815. However, the mainline Baptists did not allow women to preach even in the earlier part of the nineteenth century. The Freewill Baptist churches began opening theological departments for women in 1878 and began to ordain women in 1886.[260] The American Baptists began to ordain women preachers only at the end of the nineteenth century from 1894.[261]

Congregational churches did not allow women to preach even in the Second Great Awakening period due to their focus on traditional theology and a theologically trained clergy. However, their theological institutions began to open doors for women to study around the middle of the nineteenth century. Thus, the role of women began to change, and the Congregational church in 1853 became the first denomination to ordain women to pastoral leadership.[262] Although Judson witnessed single women being appointed as missionaries in his lifetime, he died three years before the first woman was ordained in the Congregational church.

Congregationalists, as well as many Baptists, were among those who strongly prohibited women from preaching based on their interpretation of 1 Corinthians 14:34–35. They affirmed the view of the place of women in the home and the role of women in the church as helpmeet to men, and prohibited women from speaking or preaching in public. Since Judson was an ordained minister and missionary first in the Congregational church, and later in the

---

259. Brekus, *Female Preaching*, 22.
260. Kim, *Women Preaching*, 94.
261. Brekus, *Strangers and Pilgrims*, 217–219.
262. Adam Clarke was converted through Methodist preaching in 1782 and was commissioned by Wesley as an itinerant preacher. Hassey, *No Time for Silence*, 120.

Baptist church, it is reasonable to conclude that Judson's translation of λαλεῖν as ဟောပြော, meaning "preach," in 1 Corinthians 14:34–35 was influenced by the dominant interpretation of his day and his church affiliations.

3.4 Conclusion

After examining the two major Bible translations in Myanmar, the role of a translator is clear in both the Judson Burmese Bible and the Myanmar Common Language Bible. Historical as well as textual analysis shows that the translators' interpretations of 1 Corinthians 14:34–35 influenced their choice of words and structures in translation. A prime example is the usage of "wives" as opposed to "women" in Judson's translation. This shows the need for interpreters today to look carefully at the Judson Bible in its own historical context. The analysis of the MCL text shows that the meaning of words has sometimes changed since the time of Judson.

The comparative analysis of the JB and MCL translations provides further insight into the major concern of this thesis, which is the influence of Judson's unique translation of λαλεῖν as ဟောပြော in 1 Corinthians 14:34–35. In the context of Myanmar, which has had limited access to biblical resources other than the Bible itself, this translation as well as a literal approach to interpretation, would see the meaning of women's silence as a prohibition of women from preaching. Comparing the JB and MCL texts with Greek texts reveals several critical issues within the text and highlights the need for critical scrutiny of the translator's usage of words by considering the historical context of the translator, along with critical analysis of the biblical text in its own historical context, to understand the intended meaning of the original author.

This highlights the importance of critical approaches for present-day interpreters in Myanmar, especially in interpreting difficult passages like 1 Corinthians 14:34–35. It is essential to recognize the influential role of an individual's theological views and cultural perception of words in interpretation. As Judson was influenced by his own cultural and theological context, interpreters today are likewise influenced by the prevailing understanding of the present time. In his paper on Judson's translation of βαπτίζω, and the changes and comments made by other translators since, Khoi Lam Thang highlights the role of the translator in the translation process. He notes how the "personal theological concept of translator can influence on his or her product and at the same time the theological bias of the readers can also create a similar reaction on the existing translation."[263] From this understanding, the following chapter examines several contemporary interpreters of 1 Corinthians 14:34–35 in order to critically assess their interpretations.

---

263. Clarke, *New Testament*, 278.

Part Two

Hermeneutics and Context

CHAPTER 4

Silence in Contemporary Scholarship

Hermeneutics has a vital role to play in analyzing how the command for women to be silent in 1 Corinthians 14:34–35 has been understood in different periods and contexts. It provides analytical tools for critical analysis to bridge the gap between the world of the text and the world of the interpreter, which can be thought of as "two horizons."[1] Academic and popular biblical scholarship has produced quite different readings of 1 Corinthians 14:34–35, reflecting not only the complexity of interpreting the Bible generally, but also the different ways in which this text appears to resonate with or challenge social values and situations. In the context of Myanmar, the translational issues in Judson's translation noted in the previous chapter add to the complexity. This also reflects the role of interpreters in constructing the meaning of the text, and their conceptual understanding of silence as influencing the hermeneutical process.[2]

From the interpreters' understanding of silence, this chapter looks at three different hermeneutical schools of thought from Western biblical scholarship to identify appropriate hermeneutical tools to help resolve interpretational issues that Judson's Burmese translation raises concerning the texts that command women to be silent. These contemporary interpretations are chosen due to their influential place in Myanmar's hermeneutics around women's role in the church, along with their ways of doing theology and approaches to biblical texts. Therefore, the chapter seeks to identify relevant

---

1. Thiselton, *Two Horizons*, 10.
2. Thiselton, 16.

hermeneutical principles that are appropriate for the Myanmar context in interpreting difficult texts like 1 Corinthians 14:34–35.

The first part of the analysis focuses on the interpretations of the three schools of contemporary scholarship on 1 Corinthians 14:34–35. This section focuses in particular on the interpretive decisions of these interpreters regarding crucial terminology that provides interpretive meaning within the texts that command women to be silent. This is done to highlight the process and the approach of each individual school of thought to this text.

The second part of the analysis focuses on two hermeneutical issues affecting these three schools of thought. The first hermeneutical issue is the role of presuppositions in interpretation, which includes interpreters' view of the Bible, their choice of starting point in interpretation, their sociological perspective, and their theoretical framework behind interpretation. The second hermeneutical issue looks at the interpreters' approach to the historical setting of the 1 Corinthians context. This includes their view of Paul's overall attitude toward women, and how they deal with 1 Corinthians in the context of Pauline literature. These issues are approached with a consciousness of how they interact with the context of the original writer and their own contemporary context.

4.1 The Hermeneutics of Contemporary Scholarship

The following analysis of contemporary scholarship focuses on one contemporary scholar from each contemporary hermeneutical school of thought. For a literal-traditional hermeneutic, the complementarian scholarship of Wayne Grudem is chosen for analysis. The work of Elisabeth Schüssler Fiorenza is analyzed as a representative of feminist scholarship, and the work of Ben Witherington III is analyzed in terms of an egalitarian evangelical feminist interpretation.

Wayne Grudem taught at Trinity Evangelical Divinity School and was research professor of Bible and Theology at Phoenix Seminary in Scottsdale,

Arizona.³ He received his PhD from the University of Cambridge, England.⁴ He was president of the Evangelical Theological Society in 1999, and a co-founder and president of the Council on Biblical Manhood and Womanhood.⁵ This was founded in 1987 to represent a complementarian view⁶ of women and men which sees them as equal in value and worth but having gender-differentiated roles and functions in marriage and ministry in the church.⁷ He was a member of the Translation Oversight Committee and also served as general editor of the English Standard Version of the Bible from 2005 to 2008. His published works include systematic theology, prophecy, politics, business, biblical doctrines, and the role of women in the church.⁸

For a feminist interpretation, the work of Elisabeth Schüssler Fiorenza⁹ is analyzed. She was the first Krister Stendahl Professor of Scripture and Interpretation at Harvard Divinity School, and co-founder and co-editor of the *Journal of Feminist Studies in Religion*. She earned her PhD at the University of Münster.¹⁰ In 1970, she moved to the United States and taught at the Catholic University of Notre Dame for fifteen years.¹¹ She then moved to the Episcopal Divinity School in Cambridge Massachusetts, and then in

---

3. Grudem, *Biblical Foundations*, 9. Grudem was born in 1948 in Wisconsin. After teaching at Trinity Evangelical Divinity School, he became research professor of Theology and Biblical Studies at Phoenix Seminary in 2001.

4. Flemming, *Contextualization*; Grudem, *Biblical Foundations*, 9.

5. Baker, "Analysis of the Leadership Challenges," 8.

6. Grudem, *Countering the Claims*, 5.

7. Baker, "Analysis of the Leadership Challenges," 17.

8. See Bibliography.

9. Matthews, Kittredge, and Johnson-Debaufre, *Walk in the Ways of Wisdom*, 2. Elisabeth Schüssler was born into a Roman Catholic family in Romania, and grew up in Germany where her family fled in 1944. She received her Licentiate of Theology from the University of Würzburg in 1963. She married Francis Fiorenza in 1967. See also Shepherd, *Feminist Theologies*, 13; Milhaven, *Inside Stories*, 43–46; Ng, *Reconstructing Christian Origins?* 7.

10. Schüssler Fiorenza, *Discipleship of Equals*, 39. Opportunities for ministry within the Roman Catholic church were closed because of her gender and she was refused a scholarship because a woman "had no future in the academy." These experiences and her training in German philosophy (including Bultmann's emphasis on the interpreter's pre-understanding in the hermeneutical process), shaped her feminist hermeneutics. Schüssler Fiorenza, "Changing the Paradigms," 54, and *Bread Not Stone*, 160.

11. Ng, *Reconstructing Christian Origins?* 8. Schüssler Fiorenza again experienced alienation from male colleagues just as she had in Germany. She was also unhappy with official Roman Catholic statements opposed to women's leadership and ordination. Schüssler Fiorenza, *Bread Not Stone*, 159.

1988, to Harvard.[12] She became the first female president of the Society of Biblical Literature in 1987.[13]

At the center of her work is her concept of the "discipleship of equals," which is also known as "ekklesia of wo/men," which expresses an egalitarian vision of discipleship of both men and women together and opposes "hierarchical structures of domination both within the church and in society at large."[14] Schüssler Fiorenza has emerged as a major feminist biblical interpreter. She has written and edited more than twenty-five books on biblical studies.[15] Her writing ranges from biblical studies to hermeneutics, ecclesiology, and theology.

For egalitarian hermeneutics, the interpretation of Ben Witherington III is analyzed. Witherington completed his PhD on the topic, "Women and Their Roles in the Gospels and Acts" from the University of Durham, England in 1981.[16] He then taught at High Point College, North Carolina from 1982–1983, Duke Divinity School from 1982–1983, and at Ashland Theological Seminary from 1984–1995.[17] He has been professor of New Testament for Doctoral Studies at Asbury Theological Seminary since 1995. He has been a member of the Society for the Study of the New Testament since 1989[18] and has written over forty books, a number of commentaries,[19] and many works on the subject of women in the New Testament, and on other topics.[20] He represents a school of interpretation which believes that "women [should]

---

12. Ng, 8.

13. Ng, 9; Matthews, Kittredge, and Johnson-Debaufre, *Walk in the Ways of Wisdom*, 2.

14. Matthews, Kittredge, and Johnson-Debaufre, 24–31.

15. Some of her works include: *In Memory of Her*; *Discipleship of Equals*; *Bread Not Stone*; *Jesus: Miriam's Child*; *Rhetoric and Ethics*; *Wisdom Ways*; *Power of the Word: Scripture*.

16. His advisor was C. K. Barrett.

17. Asbury Theological Seminary. "Dr. Ben Witherington III." http://asburyseminary.edu/person/dr-ben-witherington-iii/.

18. http://www.benwitherington.com/cv.html. Studiorum Novi Testamenti Societas.

19. For example, *Acts of the Apostles*, *Paul's Letter to the Romans*, *Conflict and Community*, and *Grace in Galatia*.

20. Other topics include: (1) the Historical Jesus: *Jesus the Sage*, *Gospel Code*. (2) Christology of the New Testament: *Christology of Jesus*, *Many Faces of the Christ*, *Christologies of the New Testament*. (3) Pauline exegesis and theology: *Paul's Narrative Thought World*, *Paul Quest*. (4) Johannine exegesis and theology: *John's Wisdom*. (5) Women in Ministry: *Women in the Ministry*, *Women in the Earliest Churches*, *Women and the Genesis*. (6) The Jesus Seminar: *Jesus Quest*. He also writes for many church and scholarly publications, and is a contributor to the website, http://www.patheos.com.

function within the church based upon character, qualifications, gifts, and theological education, not on the basis of gender restrictions."[21] A major organization representing this view is Christians for Biblical Equality (CBE).[22]

4.2 Points of Comparison

In analyzing the silence passage of 1 Corinthians 14:34–35, it is helpful to focus on differences and similarities of these scholars' interpretations of the text. Points of comparison include their understanding of authorship, the context of the text that commands women to be silent, and decisions about key terms such as σιγάτωσαν, γυναῖκες, ἐκκλησίαις, λαλειν, ὑποτάσσεσθαι, and νόμος.

4.2.1 Pauline Authorship

Many of the interpretive differences among the three interpreters regarding 1 Corinthians 14:34–35 are concentrated around the question of authorship, namely, whether Paul is the author of the passage that commands women to be silent. This question arises out of an occurrence of textual transposition in which 1 Corinthians 14:34–35 is moved after verse 40. This transposition is found in Western manuscripts such as uncials D (06),[23] F (010),[24] G (012),[25] a b,[26] vg^{ms},[27] and the fourth-century church father Ambrosiaster.[28] However, the very early papyrus **P**^{46} together with uncials ℵ (01), B (03), Ψ (044), and most of the 𝔐 manuscripts[29] read these verses in their traditionally accepted order.

The occurrence of a textual transposition of verses 34–35 after verse 40 in some manuscripts and peculiarities of linguistic usages viewed as being unlike Paul have led some interpreters, including Gordon Fee, to conclude that these verses were not authored by Paul. Their arguments are based on

---

21. Baker, "Analysis of the Leadership Challenges," 17.
22. Baker, 9.
23. Codex Claromontanus. For an introduction to early manuscripts, see Metzger and Ehrman, *The Text of the New Testament*.
24. Codex Augiensis. See Metzger and Ehrman.
25. Codex Boernerianus. See Metzger and Ehrman.
26. Old Latin manuscripts Armachanus and Veronensis from the fourth and fifth centuries. See Metzger and Ehrman.
27. Codex Fuldensis. Vulgate manuscript. See Metzger and Ehrman.
28. NA^{28}, 466.
29. NA^{28}, 466.

verses 34–35 being words of the Corinthian men,[30] or that these verses were an interpolation.[31] However, Grudem, Schüssler Fiorenza, and Witherington, all argue for the Pauline authorship of 1 Corinthians 14:34–35 as well as the placement of verses 34–35 in the traditionally accepted order before verse 40.[32] At the same time, each points out aspects different from the others.

While acknowledging a textual transposition issue in which verses 34–35 are placed after verse 40 in some texts, Grudem notes that these verses are mentioned in all the known Greek manuscripts and sees this as affirming Pauline authorship of the text. He then argues for the traditional accepted order of verses 34–35.[33] According to Grudem, the traditionally accepted order of verses 34–35 is supported by two arguments. First, the fact that the transposition of these verses is found in the Western manuscripts strengthens the traditionally accepted order (or vv. 34–35 after v. 33), because the Western texts are "unreliable elsewhere."[34] Second, the traditionally accepted order of these verses is supported by UBS[4] which gave the "B" rating of "almost certain" for the placement of these verses in the traditionally accepted order.[35]

Schüssler Fiorenza agrees with Grudem's view of Pauline authorship, and her method is in line with the structural analysis of Grudem, although from a different perspective. However, she considers that Paul's injunction to silence is because of the context. She does not think there are any text-critical grounds

---

30. Peppiatt, *Women and Worship*, 9; Flanagan and Snyder, "Let the Women Speak," 90–93.

31. Gordon Fee sees this text as interpolation arguing that "although these two verses are found in all known manuscripts, either here or at the end of the chapter, the two text-critical criteria of transcriptional and intrinsic probability combine to cast considerable doubt on their authenticity." Despite their being present in all known manuscripts, Fee considers these verses as inauthentic of Paul for three reasons: linguistic usages, such as speaking, silence, and submission are used differently from other usages of Paul; the seeming contradiction of 1 Cor 11:2–16 and 1 Cor 14:34; and usages such as "the law" which are foreign to Paul. Fee, *First Epistle to the Corinthians*, 699. Payne also sees this text as interpolation. Payne, *Man and Woman*, 246; Payne, "Vaticanus Distigme-obelos Symbols," 604–625; Payne, "Is 1 Corinthians 14:34–35 a Marginal Comment?" 24–30. This is also the view of Epp, *Junia*, 15–20. Munro regards both 1 Cor 11:2–16 and 14:33b–36 verses as post-Pauline "pastoral insertions." Munro, *Authority in Paul and Peter*, 67–82.

32. Grudem, *Gift of Prophecy*, 224; Schüssler Fiorenza, *In Memory of Her*, 230; Witherington, *Conflict and Community*, 288.

33. Grudem, *Evangelical Feminism*, 236.

34. Grudem, 236.

35. A "B" rating is an assessment that the text is "almost certain." See UBS[4], 3.

for these verses being an interpolation.[36] Thus, she approaches these verses as "original Pauline statements" and contends that explaining these verses "within their present context" is a better approach.[37]

Like Grudem and Schüssler Fiorenza, Witherington also sees the textual issue of the displacement of verses 34–35 to the end of verse 40 as not a significant "argument for interpolation."[38] In his view, the displacement probably occurred due to scribes,[39] who assumed that these passages were about "household order, not order in worship," based on their own context "when there were church buildings separate from private homes."[40] However, he rejects the view of verses 34–35 as an edited work by scribes using 1 Timothy 2:11 as a base text,[41] because he sees the issues in 1 Timothy and 1 Corinthians as divergent from one another, since the first one deals with "teaching and authority" whereas the latter deals with "asking questions and learning."[42] Witherington sees a consistent usage of four key terms found in both places, verses 34–35 and the whole context of 1 Corinthians 14, as validating Pauline authorship of these verses. These terms include "λαλέω (repeatedly from 14:14 to 35), σιγάω (14:28, 30, 34), ἐν ἐκκλησίᾳ (14:28, 35; cf. 34), and ὑποτάσσω (14:32, 34)."[43]

Looking at the explanations of these three contemporary interpreters, their decision on the Pauline authorship of verses 34–35 centers on the fact that these verses appear in all the known Greek manuscripts, even though some placed them in different locations. Agreeing with this view, I argue for Pauline authorship and the traditionally accepted order of 1 Corinthians 14:34–35.[44] From their understanding of Pauline authorship of verses 34–35 as well as establishing the place of these verses in the traditionally accepted order, these three contemporary interpreters approach the texts that

---

36. Schüssler Fiorenza, *In Memory of Her*, 230.
37. Schüssler Fiorenza, 230.
38. Witherington, *Conflict and Community*, 288.
39. "Such scribal alterations represent attempts to find a more appropriate location in the context for Paul's directive concerning women." Metzger, *Textual Commentary*, 565.
40. Witherington, *Conflict and Community*, 288.
41. Witherington, 288.
42. Witherington, 288; Thiselton, *First Epistle to the Corinthians*, 1152.
43. Witherington, *Women in the Earliest Churches*, 91; Thiselton, 1152.
44. See chapter 7.

command women to be silent from a contextual analysis of the text within their immediate historical context. The following section looks at how they see verses 34–35 within the context of 1 Corinthians 14 and read the overall context of 1 Corinthians.

4.2.2 The Corinthian Context

The exegetical decisions of Grudem, Schüssler Fiorenza, and Witherington on 1 Corinthians 14:34–35 revolve around how they see these verses fitting into the overall context of 1 Corinthians as well as the immediate context of 1 Corinthians 14. For the immediate context of 1 Corinthians 14:34–35, 1 Corinthians 14 is analyzed to determine the context. For the overall context of 1 Corinthians, the passage that apparently allows women to pray and prophesy in 1 Corinthians 11:2–16 is compared with the passage of 1 Corinthians 14:34–35 that commands women to be silent, in order to determine whether Paul gave conflicting commands in the same book.

Grudem, Schüssler Fiorenza, and Witherington all see the immediate context of 1 Corinthians 14:34–35 as restricting women to the context of prophecy.[45] However, they disagree on the kind of event that Paul is restricting. Grudem sees Paul as restricting all women from evaluating and judging men in the context of prophecy.[46] Schüssler Fiorenza sees Paul as instructing Corinthian wives to embody decency and order in the practice of spiritual gifts in the context of prophecy.[47] Witherington sees Paul as commanding Corinthian prophetesses to ask questions in an appropriate manner without disrupting worship services.[48] This section looks at how these interpreters deal with the peculiarities of linguistic usages and the flow of the sentence in explaining their understanding of the context.

First, the three interpreters take note of the linguistic usages and the flow of the sentences from 1 Corinthians 12–14 in explaining the context of the text that commands women to be silent. Grudem points out that Paul mentions prophecy in twelve verses and tongue-speaking in thirteen verses in

---

45. Wire and Thiselton also understand this passage in the context of prophecy. Wire, *Corinthian Women Prophets*; Thiselton, *First Epistle to the Corinthians*.

46. Grudem, *Gift of Prophecy*, 224.

47. Schüssler Fiorenza, *In Memory of Her*, 230.

48. Witherington, *Conflict and Community*, 287.

1 Corinthians 14 alone.⁴⁹ He sees Paul as following procedure in writing 1 Corinthians 14:29–33, which is an evaluation of prophecy. Then, as he notes, "the closest contextual material to the verses about women being silent, verses 29–33a, does not refer to tongues, but it does contain a discussion of prophecy."⁵⁰ Therefore, Grudem believes that approaching 1 Corinthians 14:33b-35 from the context of prophecy fits well with a "consistent Pauline advocacy of women's participation without governing authority in the assembled church."⁵¹

Describing 1 Corinthians 14:26–36 as being about "church order" in the context of prophecy, Schüssler Fiorenza notes a structural pattern in 1 Corinthians 14 as important in determining the context of 1 Corinthians 14:34–35. She points out the pattern as containing dialogues on tongue speakers in verse 27, prophets in verses 29–33, and wives in verses 34–36.⁵² She sees these passages that command women to be silent in verses 27, 29, and 34 as general statements on regulations in the texts that command women to be silent, and then verses 28, 30, and 35 as describing ways to apply this command for women to be silent.

Agreeing with Grudem and Schüssler Fiorenza about 1 Corinthians 14:34–35 being in the context of prophecy, Witherington notes two areas in particular that support these verses in the context of prophecy. First, he sees the appearances of the word σιγάω in verses 28, 30, and 34 of 1 Corinthians 14 as a "catch-word connection,"⁵³ indicating that these verses follow the same flow of arguments.⁵⁴ Second, he sees 1 Corinthians 14:34–35 as following Paul's pattern of "ethical exhortation," as in the structure mentioned in 1 Corinthians 14:27, Ephesians 5:19, and Colossians 3:18. In these passages, Paul mentions women in relation to ὑποτάσσω ("submission") regularly after mentioning forms of inspired speech, which include prophecy, tongues, and

---

49. Grudem, *Gift of Prophecy*, 220.
50. Grudem, 224.
51. Grudem, 224.
52. Schüssler Fiorenza, *In Memory of Her*, 230.
53. Ellis, *Prophecy and Hermeneutic*, 27, fn 25.
54. Witherington, *Women in the Earliest Churches*, 91.

spiritual songs. He sees this same pattern of exhortation appearing in 1 Corinthians 14:34–35.[55]

Second, the three interpreters pay close attention to the place of verse 33b in analyzing the context of 1 Corinthians 14:34–35. Both Grudem and Witherington agree that verse 33b is linked logically with verse 34. Grudem explains 1 Corinthians 14:33b, ὡς ἐν πάσαις ταῖς ἐκκλησίαις τῶν ἁγίων ("as in all the churches of the saints"), as connecting to verse 34, which is different from those who see verse 33b as linked with 33a.[56] Grudem argues that if verse 33b goes with verse 33a, "for God is not a God of confusion but of peace," this would suggest God as being God of peace in some churches but not in others.[57] For this reason, verse 33b makes better sense with verse 34a in the context of instructions on behavior in the worship setting, as it reads, "as in all the churches, women should keep silence."[58] In this view, women should keep silence not just in the Corinth church but also in all the churches of Paul's time. He reasons that Paul's rule cannot be restricted to "one local church where there supposedly were problems," and that Paul directs the Corinthians to "conform to a practice that was universal in the early church."[59] Thus, he sees verse 33b as fitting well with what Paul is attempting to prohibit in the following verses on the "weighing of prophecies."[60]

For the immediate context, Witherington sees "as in all the churches" in 1 Corinthians 14:33b as the beginning of verses 34–35, and the reason is that he sees the whole context of chapter 14 as instruction for orderly worship. In other words, "worship should be undertaken with the same orderliness in Corinth as elsewhere, since God is the same everywhere."[61] According to Witherington, whenever this phrase "as in all the churches" is used, such as in 1 Corinthians 4:17; 7:17; and 11:16, Paul is referring to a rule of behavior – "his rule, or the rule of all the Christian churches" – but not to the rule "of

---

55. Witherington, 91, quotes from J. M. Robinson, "Die Hodajot-Formel in Gebet und Hymnus des Fruhchristentums," 224.

56. NA[28]; Ellingworth and Hatton, *Handbook on Paul's First Letter*, 324; Ciampa and Rosner, *First Letter to the Corinthians*, 717. Bible translations such as KJV, RV, NBV, LB, and *The Message* attach 33b to 33a, as does JB.

57. Grudem, *Evangelical Feminism*, 234.

58. Grudem, 234.

59. Grudem, 245.

60. Grudem, *Gift of Prophecy*, 219.

61. Witherington, *Conflict and Community*, 287.

God in all the churches."[62] Thus, in this context also, Paul is setting forth a "general rule in his congregations or in all early Christian congregations," describing how the Corinthians should "conform to the practice elsewhere in the Body of Christ."[63]

Schüssler Fiorenza does not explain clearly the place of 1 Corinthians 14:33b in the context of 1 Corinthians 14. This is likely due to her feminist method that is concerned with uncovering ideologies and structures that restrict women's role in the church rather than textual issues.[64] However, she mentions "1 Cor 14:33b-36" as a title in her notes on the debate about whether these verses are an authentic Pauline injunction or added later by a Pauline school. This would seem to indicate that Schüssler Fiorenza accepts the place of verse 33b with verse 34. She notes that "it is exegetically more sound to accept" the 1 Corinthians 14:33b-36 verses as "original Pauline statements and then explain them within their present context."[65]

Third, the three interpreters also look at Paul's attitudes toward women in setting the context of 1 Corinthians 14:34–35. Acknowledging that Paul sees women as prophesying in the New Testament churches, Grudem gives two examples: Acts 21:9, in which the four unmarried daughters of Philip prophesy in the assembly of Christians; and 1 Corinthians 11:5, where women were praying and prophesying with a head covering.[66] From that understanding, Grudem notes that the silence command for women in 1 Corinthians 14:34–35 is not about stopping women from praying or prophesying, but rather prohibiting women from evaluating prophesies given by men.[67]

Regarding Paul's attitudes toward women in the setting of the context of 1 Corinthians 14:34–35, Schüssler Fiorenza sees Paul's view on women's role in the church as conflicting. While women, including married women such

---

62. Witherington, *Women in the Earliest Churches*, 96.
63. Witherington, *Conflict and Community*, 287.
64. Schüssler Fiorenza, *Jesus: Miriam's Child*, 12.
65. Schüssler Fiorenza, *In Memory of Her*, 230.
66. Grudem, *Gift of Prophecy*, 215, mentions that Luke wrote about these women when he reported that Paul and his companions came to Caesarea near the end of Paul's third missionary journey. The fact that Luke reported it strongly suggests that "Paul and those with him were present while these women were prophesying." He also points out that the present participle usage for prophesying, προφητεύουσα (present, active, plural, feminine, participle) suggests that the prophesying was "a regular or continuing occurrence with these daughters."
67. Grudem, 222.

as "Prisca, Junia," and "Apphia" were leaders, apostles, and missionaries, she sees Paul as prohibiting women from leadership in specific situations, such as the "speaking and questioning of wives in the public worship assembly." This is due to his concern for preserving "order and propriety" in the church, "so that an outsider cannot accuse the Christians of religious madness."[68] However, she sees Paul as not expecting "his regulation to be accepted without protest by the Corinthian community which knows of wives as leading Christian apostles and missionaries,"[69] and thus he asks a rhetorical question in 1 Corinthians 14:36. Therefore, she concludes that verses 14:37–40 are the concluding statement of the whole context of order, showing how serious the issue is "for Paul and how much he expects resistance to his viewpoint."

Fourth, the three interpreters also look at 1 Corinthians 11:2–16 in setting the context of 1 Corinthians 14:34–35. They see the women's silence passage in 1 Corinthians 14:34–35 as not conflicting with 1 Corinthians 11:2–16, where he encouraged women's praying and prophesying without a gender specification. Grudem sees 1 Corinthians 14:34–35 in the same context as not only 1 Corinthians 11 but also as 1 Timothy 2, where women are prohibited from teaching in the church.[70] He explains that the silence in 1 Corinthians 14 does not mean that women were to keep silence always, but that "women could not give spoken criticism of the prophecies which were made during a church service."[71] He sees the underlying theme of Paul, which is role distinctions between men and women, in all three passages. His explanation of the usage of the law in 1 Corinthians 14 sums up his view:

> Paul elsewhere appeals to the Old Testament to establish the idea of male headship and female submission to male leadership (see 1 Cor 11:8–9 and 1 Tim 2:13), and it is certainly possible, therefore, to see him as appealing to the Old Testament to support a distinction in authority of judging prophecies as well. But it would be difficult to derive from the Old Testament any

---

68. Schüssler Fiorenza, *In Memory of Her*, 232.
69. Schüssler Fiorenza, 232.
70. Schüssler Fiorenza, 233.
71. Grudem, *Gift of Prophecy*, 224.

prohibition against noisy women in church or against women speaking in tongues.⁷²

According to Schüssler Fiorenza, 1 Corinthians 14:34–35 is in the same context as chapter 11, and 1 Corinthians 12–14 is about Paul seeking "to persuade the Corinthians that decency and order⁷³ should be more highly esteemed than the spiritual status and exercise of individual pneumatic inspiration."⁷⁴ Schüssler Fiorenza's view of the context of 1 Corinthians 14 derives from her understanding of what Paul meant in the context of 1 Corinthians 7,⁷⁵ where he addresses problems related to the relationship between the sexes, and 1 Corinthians 11:2–16, where he talks about head-covering.⁷⁶ Thus, she sees the continuation of the missionary intention of Paul in 1 Corinthians 11:2–16 and 14:33b–36, and points out that these verses cohere with the overall argument in chapter 14. She views 1 Corinthians 11:2–16 as in "the ring composition" with 14:33b-36, "beginning and ending

---

72. Grudem, 223.

73. Schüssler Fiorenza, *In Memory of Her*, 230, reasons that Paul here is persuading the Corinthians to prioritize decency and order. To Paul, the Corinthians seem to value speaking in tongues, which is individual pneumatic inspiration, more than the gift of prophecy and interpretation, which Paul favors in terms of "order and mission (14:4, 5, 19)." Thus, Paul is reminding the Corinthian pneumatics of their main mission, which is not being concerned just with exercising of their spiritual gifts but also "with the building up of the community and with the impression they make on interested outsiders (14:16, 17, 23ff)."

74. Schüssler Fiorenza, 230.

75. Schüssler Fiorenza, 221. In the context of 1 Cor 7, Schüssler Fiorenza explains that Paul had the baptismal declaration of Gal 3:28, which is equality in Christ, in mind when he was addressing the problems of the relationship between the sexes in chapter 7. She sees Paul as maintaining marriage as a calling and gift of God, and even insisting on equality and mutuality in sexual relationships between husbands and wives as well as promoting celibacy as "the higher calling."

76. Schüssler Fiorenza, 227–230, sees the traditional interpretation, in which Paul insists that pneumatic women leaders wear the veil according to Jewish custom, is incorrect. She states that since v. 15 maintains that women do not need a head-covering, Paul is likely speaking about the way "women and men should wear their hair praying and prophesying." Thus, she points out that the practices of unbound hair and head thrown back were typical in "the cult of Dionysos, in that of Cybele, the Pythia at Delphi, the Sibyl, and unbound hair was necessary for a woman to produce an effective magical incantation," and this was also found in the "Isis cult, which had a major center in Corinth." She thinks that the Corinthian pneumatics copied those practices, because they understood them as "a mark of true prophetic behaviour," but for Paul "building up of the community and intelligible missionary, proclamation, not orgiastic behaviour, are the true signs of the spirit," and women should "keep their hair bound up."

with a discussion of women's role" in the worship of the Christian assembly.[77]

Like Grudem and Schüssler Fiorenza, Witherington sees 1 Corinthians 14:34–35 in the context of prophecy, as a continuation of 1 Corinthians 11:25–33. He points out that this passage must be explained in terms of two contexts, the immediate and the larger context. He sees the discussion of prophecy and judging of the prophecies in chapter 14 as the immediate context and chapters 11–14 as the larger context. He explains that chapters 11–14 are about the "discussion of abuses in Corinthian worship caused by *pneumatikoi*," who are women prophetesses, and that they seem to have been "imitating some of the practices of women involved in the mysteries" that resulted in "significant disorder."[78]

Looking at the three interpreters' approaches to the contextual background of 1 Corinthians 14:34–35, all three look carefully at the immediate context of the text, as well as the overall context of Paul, to determine the meaning of the text. Their analyses of the context center on how they deal with the flow of the sentences from 1 Corinthians 12–14, how they deal with verse 33b in the context of 1 Corinthians 14:34–35, how they reconcile the verses with Paul's attitudes toward women in general, and how they connect 1 Corinthians 11:2–16 and 1 Corinthians 14 in terms of women's silence.

4.2.3 Silence: Women and the Church

This section examines how Grudem, Schüssler Fiorenza, Witherington, and several other commentators make exegetical decisions on the meaning of the terms γυναῖκες and ἐκκλησίαις in 1 Corinthians 14:34a. The text αἱ γυναῖκες ὑμῶν ἐν ταῖς ἐκκλησίαις σιγάτωσαν is translated by the NRSV as "women should be silent in the churches."[79] Grudem, Schüssler Fiorenza, and Witherington all disagree on who αἱ γυναῖκες is referring to in 1 Corinthians 14:34a. Grudem sees "αἱ γυναῖκες" in this context as referring to all women, including unmarried women.[80] Schüssler Fiorenza sees αἱ γυναῖκες as refer-

---

77. Schüssler Fiorenza, "Rhetorical Situation," 395.
78. Witherington, *Women in the Earliest Churches*, 92.
79. NRSV.
80. Grudem, *Gift of Prophecy*, 222.

ring to "wives,"[81] and Witherington sees αἱ γυναῖκες as referring to Christian "women prophetesses" who are married.[82] Looking at their decisions about who αἱ γυναῖκες is referring to hinges on their understanding of the textual variant issue concerning the omission of ὑμῶν in verse 34 following αἱ γυναῖκες,[83] and their understanding of τοὺς ἰδίους ἄνδρας in verse 35.

Agreeing with Grudem, other interpreters such as Wire and Fitzmyer also see αἱ γυναῖκες as referring to all women, including daughters, widows, and women slaves, who are all subordinate to the man of the house.[84] They explain the meaning of "αἱ γυναῖκες" in 1 Corinthians 14:34 in connection to "αἱ γυναῖκες" in verse 35, where the context is about women asking questions in order to learn. Grudem explains women here as including the unmarried women since they would be required to ask "other men within their family circles, or within the fellowship of the church, with whom they could discuss the content of the prophecies."[85] Grudem argues that if only "married women" are being restricted in this passage, then the proposal is guilty of "making Paul's command nonsensical. For it would allow very young and immature girls to speak in church while denying that privilege to all married [women], even those who were much older and wiser and thereby much more qualified to speak."[86]

Although the word γυναῖκες here could refer to "all the women [including the very young]," the definition of BDAG does not allow this interpretation, since it gives the meaning of γυναῖκες as including "young woman," meaning an adult female person, including virgins, "a wife" meaning a married woman, and a "bride" referring to a newly married woman.[87] Therefore, the "immature girls" that Grudem has suggested would not be counted among the γυναῖκες mentioned in the BDAG. Furthermore, it is also not all clear whether "very

---

81. Schüssler Fiorenza, *In Memory of Her*, 230–231.

82. Witherington, *Conflict and Community*, 287.

83. As noted in Chapter 3.2.2.2, inserting the word ὑμῶν, meaning "your," into αἱ γυναῖκες is supported by sixth to seventh century Greek manuscripts such as D F G 𝔐 (a b) sy; Cyp (Ambst). Inserting the word ὑμῶν is also supported by K L 630. 1505 𝔐 ar b sy; Cyp Ambst (*cf* ʳ) NA²⁸, 547; NA²⁷, 466.

84. Wire, *Corinthian Women Prophets*, 156; Fitzmyer, *First Corinthians*, 531–532.

85. Grudem, *Gift of Prophecy*, 222.

86. Grudem, 248.

87. BDAG, 208–209.

young and immature girls would have been permitted to speak in the church at all."[88]

Grudem does not mention the textual variant issue regarding the omission of ὑμῶν in verse 34 following αἱ γυναῖκες, and he gives his translation of the verse without mentioning the word ὑμῶν for "your." Grudem's choice of interpreting the word "αἱ γυναῖκες" as "all women" has more to do with aligning his interpretation of silence with τοὺς ἰδίους ἄνδρας in verse 35. This could be due to his understanding that the translation of the word as "wives" would omit all the other women who can exercise the gifts of prophecy in 1 Corinthians 11. This is contested by Garland,[89] who sees "αἱ γυναῖκες" here as referring to the wives only, given the relationship of "ὁ ἀνήρ" with "ἡ γυνή" in this context, and contends that "Paul is not laying down rules for women in general for women prophets," but rather, he is laying down rules for the wives.[90] Agreeing with Garland, Johnson also points out that whenever Paul pairs the noun "ἡ γυνή" to "ὁ ἀνήρ" elsewhere, as in 1 Corinthians 7:25 and 11:3, he is making references to the relationship between wives and husbands.[91]

For Schüssler Fiorenza, "αἱ γυναῖκες" must be interpreted in 1 Corinthians 14:33–36 as wives in order to avoid a contradiction with 1 Corinthians 11:5,[92] since 1 Corinthians 11:5 already recognized women as spiritually gifted and permitted to pray and prophesy with tongues within the worship of the community. Thus, she sees 1 Corinthians 7:32–35 mentioning "wives" as a clear indicator that 1 Corinthians 14:33–36 is referring to the "wives of Christians" rather than women in general, since "not all women in the community were married or had Christian spouses" and therefore they could not ask "their husbands at home."[93]

---

88. Rosner, *First Letter to the Corinthians*, 722.

89. Garland, *1 Corinthians*, 667. See also Johnson, *1 Corinthians*, 275; Schüssler Fiorenza, *In Memory of Her*, 230–231.

90. Garland, 667.

91. Johnson, *1 Corinthians*, 275. Johnson also points out in the same way that whenever "ἡ γυνή" is used in the same context with "ὁ ἀνήρ," "wife" is the "correct translation (1 Cor 7:14; Eph 5:22; 1 Tim 3:2; 1 Pet 3:1)," but adds that "on the other hand, there are places such as in this context where 'woman' and 'man' may be more appropriate (Acts 5:14; 8:12; 22:4; 1 Cor 11:11–12)."

92. Schüssler Fiorenza, *In Memory of Her*, 230–231.

93. Schüssler Fiorenza, 231.

Also, Schüssler Fiorenza argues that Paul is only prohibiting participation of wives in the worship of the community, but not prohibiting the pneumatic participation of the "holy" women who are unmarried women and virgins because of their special holiness status mentioned in 1 Corinthians 7.[94] She sees Paul as acknowledging the equality of husband and wife even though Paul makes clear his preference for the unmarried state by arguing that the married person is "divided and concerned with the issues of marriage and family, while the unmarried person is completely dedicated to the affairs of the Lord."[95] She sees Paul's concern here as in line with traditional Roman sentiment against wives speaking in public and questioning other women's husbands.[96]

Schüssler Fiorenza argues that "the women" refers to "wives" especially in verse 14:35b, which says "Let them ask their husbands at home." She points out that the community rule of 1 Corinthians 14:34–36 presupposes that, "within the Christian worship assembly, wives had dared to question other women's husbands or point out some mistakes of their own during congregational interpretational custom and law."[97] Thus, the restriction imposed by

---

94. Schüssler Fiorenza, 231, notes that "Paul here ascribes a special holiness to the unmarried woman and virgin, apparently because she is not touched by a man (cf. 7:1)." She sees Paul as further qualifying the single-minded dedication of the unmarried woman and virgin in 1 Cor 7:34, with a subordinate clause that "she may be holy in body and spirit." Paul then gives "his injunction by invoking propriety" to the wives in verse 14:35b, saying "it is shameful for a woman to speak in church."

95. Schüssler Fiorenza, 231.

96. Schüssler Fiorenza, 231–232. However, Antoinette Wire, who, like Fiorenza, sees Paul being against women's involvement in the church, differs from her on whether the women here means "wives" or "all women," and points out that Paul is referring here to women in general rather than wives. Wire agrees that "αἱ γυναῖκες" could mean "wives" in other contexts, but points out that this is not so in this context. She explains that in this context the women are "women in general, or at least women of various stations." She points out that Paul's reference to women in plural form, as well as his earlier instruction in 11: 5 to "any woman who prays and prophesies," his repeated statements that all can prophesy in 14:5, 24, 31, and his admonishment to all to be zealous for the higher gift in 12:21; 14:1, 12, 39, are good indicators that Paul is referring to women at large who are prophesying "as the spirit moves them." She also points out that τοὺς ἰδίους ἄνδρας which is often read as "their own husbands," appears in a separate sentence six clauses later, and that this could be translated as "their own men," because of the cultural context of the time in which all women in the Hellenistic world were subject to the dominant male of their extended family. Thus, to her the phrase is "appropriate not only for wives, since daughters, widows, and women slaves are just as subordinate to the man of the house." Wire, *Corinthian Women Prophets*, 156.

97. Schüssler Fiorenza, *In Memory of Her*, 232.

Paul is only for the wives, with a missional concern for the appearance of the Christian community to outsiders.

Like Schüssler Fiorenza, Witherington contends that "αἱ γυναῖκες" in 1 Corinthians 14:34 is referring to "married women."[98] At the same time, he acknowledges that it could also refer to "all women," since the phrase "their own men" in verse 35 could also be referring to "the male head" of a household, although "husbands" is more likely what Paul has in mind in this context.[99] Like Grudem, Witherington does not mention the textual variant issue of the omission of ὑμῶν in verse 34 following αἱ γυναῖκες. He differs from Grudem and Schüssler Fiorenza in what he thinks Paul is referring to as "the women," and explains that those women are not only wives, they are prophetesses who prophesied and who were also "entitled to weigh" what was being prophesied.[100]

Witherington points out that it seems to have been assumed that Christian prophets and prophetesses functioned much like the oracle at Delphi, who only prophesied in response to questions, including questions about purely personal matters.[101] These women were asking questions, perhaps inappropriate questions, that caused disruption in the worship service.[102] In response to this situation, he sees Paul as explaining to the Corinthians that "Christian prophecy is different: Prophets and prophetesses speak in response to the prompting of the Holy Spirit, without any human priming of the pump."[103]

Given the decisions of these interpreters on who αἱ γυναῖκες refers to, it is possible to conclude that their decisions hinge mostly on their understanding of τοὺς ἰδίους ἄνδρας in verse 35, rather than any textual variant issue. Since a critical text of NA[28] raises no critical notes on textual issues on the usage of ἐκκλησίαις, whether it is plural or singular, all the contemporary interpreters keep the reading of ἐκκλησίαις in the plural – "churches"[104] or "congregations."[105]

---

98. Witherington, *Conflict and Community*, 287.
99. Witherington, 287.
100. Witherington, 287.
101. Witherington, 287.
102. Witherington, 287.
103. Witherington, 287.
104. Grudem, *Gift of Prophecy*, 225; Schüssler Fiorenza, *In Memory of Her*, 232.
105. Witherington, *Conflict and Community*, 287.

4.2.4 Speaking

The exegetical decisions of Grudem, Schüssler Fiorenza, and Witherington on the meaning of the word σιγάω are linked to how they understand the word λαλέω in the text. Although all three interpreters see this verse in the context of prophecy, they differ on their understanding of λαλέω in relation to σιγάω. Grudem sees λαλέω as referring to the "judging or evaluation" of an inspired form of speech.[106] For Schüssler Fiorenza and Witherington, the word λαλέω conveys the informal sense of speak, talk, or question.[107]

According to Grudem, Paul is not requiring women to keep silent (σιγάω) from praying or prophesying, but rather to be silent by not asking (λαλέω) evaluative questions about prophesies given by men during a worship service.[108] Grudem interprets the common term λαλέω ("speak") here as "judging" or "evaluating," since he sees the context as suggesting such a meaning, and thus notes that "women shouldn't speak out and judge these prophecies; they should be subordinate."[109] Grudem links the concept of "silence" to "submission" in verse 34b, and notes λαλέω in this context as involving judging prophecies. The evaluation of prophecies is a "governing" or "ruling" function in the congregation, "the opposite of being submissive to male leadership in the church."[110]

Grudem's view derives from his understanding that women can prophesy but not teach. He sees prophecy as different from teaching and the authority of a prophet as unlike the authority of a teacher. He gives Romans 12:6–7, 1 Corinthians 12:28–29, and Ephesians 4:11 as examples to show that prophecy and teaching are separate gifts. In his analysis, prophecy is always "reporting something God spontaneously brings to mind" whereas teaching is the "explanation and application of Scripture."[111] He sees elders as the ones who do the teaching, and eldership as reserved only for males. Thus, he notes that

---

106. Grudem, *Gift of Prophecy*, 225. Barrett, *First Epistle to the Corinthians*, 332, understands λαλέω as referring to a form of inspired speech, "speaking in tongues." Matthew Henry understands λαλέω as referring to "preaching, or interpreting scripture by inspiration." *Matthew Henry's Commentary*, 2271.

107. Schüssler Fiorenza, *In Memory of Her*, 232; Witherington, *Conflict and Community*, 287.

108. Grudem, *Gift of Prophecy*, 225.

109. Grudem, 221.

110. Grudem, *Evangelical Feminism*, 234.

111. Grudem, 229.

in the context of teaching in 1 Timothy 2:11, "doctrinal guardianship" and "eldership" are already reserved for men in 1 Timothy 3:3 and Titus 1:6.[112] Therefore, he sees Paul as saying that "only men can give spoken correction to prophecies," since correction is part of the task of "teaching and having authority" over the congregation. He sees this prohibition as fitting with the subordination passage in 1 Corinthians 14:34, since evaluating "involves assuming the possession of superior authority in matters of doctrinal or ethical instruction."[113]

Schüssler Fiorenza sees Paul as using σιγάω to prohibit only the wives of men in the church from λαλέω in the general sense of "speaking to and questioning."[114] She sees the wives' behavior in 1 Corinthians 14:34–35 as causing offense to all traditional custom and law, because they were either questioning other women's husbands or pointing out the mistakes of their own husbands during the congregational interpretation of the Scriptures and of prophecy.[115] She sees Paul's main concern in this prohibition as protecting the image of the Christian community from looking like "religious madness" to outsiders.[116] She notes that Paul does not want the Christian community to be "mistaken for one of the orgiastic, secret, oriental cults that undermined public order and decency."[117] In this light, Paul is not denying women the right to prophesy and pray in the worship assembly, since he already allowed them to do so, with the proviso of having a proper hairstyle, in 1 Corinthians 11:2–16.[118] She sees Paul as having a specific situation in mind, namely, "the speaking and the questioning of wives in the public worship assembly."[119]

---

112. Grudem, 234.

113. Grudem, *Gift of Prophecy*, 222. See also Grudem, *Evangelical Feminism*, 232.

114. Schüssler Fiorenza, *In Memory of Her*, 228.

115. Schüssler Fiorenza, 230.

116. Schüssler Fiorenza, 233.

117. Schüssler Fiorenza, 230, notes that oriental cults were widespread in the second or third century BC and that there was a public law prohibiting women from participating in these secret cults, particularly those which encouraged drunkenness and ecstasy.

118. Schüssler Fiorenza, 228, adds that in Paul's day loose hair was the mark of a woman accused of adultery, as in Num 5:18 (LXX), and the sign of the uncleanness of a leper, as in Lev 13:45 (LXX). Thus, she sees Paul as arguing that "women should not worship as cultically unclean persons by letting their hair down but should pin it up as a sign of their spiritual power and of control over their heads" since "the angels are present in the pneumatic worship service of a community that speaks the 'tongues of angels.'"

119. Schüssler Fiorenza, 233.

Hence, she sees Paul as suggesting that wives in this context keep silent from speaking and questioning in the public assembly, and "remain subdued" in the assembly of the community.[120]

Although Witherington shares Grudem's view of λαλέω in the context of evaluating prophecies, he differs on who can evaluate the gifts of prophecy, and on what kind of speech is being prohibited. The difference hinges on the identity of the οἱ ἄλλοι ("others") in 1 Corinthians 14:29.[121] Grudem sees οἱ ἄλλοι referring to those who can evaluate in 1 Corinthians 14:29, that is male prophets.[122] Witherington sees οἱ ἄλλοι referring to both male and female prophets.[123] Although Witherington does not believe that the οἱ ἄλλοι here means "the whole congregation," he accepts that this view cannot be ruled out.[124]

Witherington shares Grudem's view that the prophets in 1 Corinthians 12:29 are not like those in the Old Testament,[125] but adds that in the Corinthian context a prophet was "an individual who perceived him or herself as a prophet," rather than "an appointed office of prophet."[126] This required "an evaluation, an investigation, a testing" of such individuals' prophecies in order "to check the abuse of the gift of prophecy," since these prophecies would include "a mixture of God's words and human words."[127] Christian prophecy is also different from the oracles of the Pythia at Delphi who spoke in a state of "trance or possession by the god" which led to "utterances including moans, cries and phrases to be interpreted by a prophet."[128] Witherington sees Paul as already defining Christian prophecy as "an intelligible communication" that even non-believers can hear and be convicted by, as in 1 Corinthians

---

120. Schüssler Fiorenza, 232.

121. προφῆται δὲ δύο ἢ τρεῖς λαλείτωσαν καὶ οἱ ἄλλοι διακρινέτωσαν. The NRSV translates this as "Let two or three prophets speak, and let the others weigh what is said."

122. Grudem, *Gift of Prophecy*, 238.

123. Witherington, *Women in the Earliest Churches*, 94.

124. Witherington, 95.

125. Grudem, *Gift of Prophecy*, 238.

126. Witherington, *Women in the Earliest Churches*, 94.

127. Witherington, 95, sees the gift of prophecy as different from weighing prophecy, though both gifts were exercised by prophets. It is also different from teaching and preaching, though there may be some overlap in the function, because they all are "gifts of the word" and "gifts of the spirit."

128. Witherington, 93.

14:19 and 1 Corinthians 14:24–25.[129] Since Christian prophecy was different from the oracles at Delphi, and λαλέω referred to the general sense of asking questions, Witherington argues that Paul was using σιγάω to silence wives who were asking disruptive questions during the prophetic worship service.[130]

Witherington argues that λαλέω in this context could not be referring to feminine chatter or "disruptive chatters,"[131] including gossiping during the service, since λαλέω does not "normally have this meaning when Paul uses it." He points out the usages of λαλέω in chapter 11 as praying and prophesying in church.[132]

Witherington agrees that the women asking questions might "not yet [be] educated enough in the school of Christ to know what was and was not appropriate in Christian worship."[133] The main point is that whatever the women asked may have been considered "disrespectful" or asked in "a disrespectful manner," and thus the result was chaos, such that Paul has to rule that "questions should not be asked in worship. The wives should ask their husbands at home. Worship was not to be turned into a question-and-answer session."[134] Therefore, Witherington sees the word λαλέω in this context as a reference to uninspired speech in the form of questions, where women were asking questions that were disrupting the worship service.[135]

Witherington concludes that evaluating prophecies is not a gender-specific gift since there is nothing in 1 Corinthians 12–14 that suggests that prophecy (or preaching or teaching) is gender-specific.[136] Like Grudem and Schüssler

---

129. Witherington, 92–93. In response to Grudem's view that the gift of teaching is higher than the gift of prophecy, Witherington notes that Paul lists the gift of prophecy ahead of glossolalia in Rom 12:6 and 1 Cor 12:10, and in 1 Cor 12:29 (cf. Rom 12:1–7) prophets rank after apostles but before teachers. James Dunn, *Jesus and the Spirit*, 227, notes that "In all various lists and discussions of charismata in Paul's letters the only constant member is 'prophecy' or 'prophet' (Rom 12:6–8; 1 Cor 12:8–10, 28ff., 13:1–3, 8ff., 14:1–5, 6ff., 26–32; Eph 4:11; 1 Thess 5:11–12)."

130. Witherington, 102.

131. Witherington, *Conflict and Community*, 287. Keener sees Paul in the context of 1 Cor 14:34–35 as silencing women from "disruptive chatters." Keener, *Paul, Women and Wives*, 81.

132. Witherington, *Women in the Earliest Churches*, 99.

133. Witherington, *Conflict and Community*, 287.

134. Witherington, *Women in the Earliest Churches*, 103.

135. Witherington, 102.

136. Witherington, 96. Thiselton agrees: "The speaking in question denotes the activity of sifting or weighing the words of prophets, especially by asking probing questions about the

Fiorenza, Witherington also sees silence in this context not as total silence, which would prevent a person from ever speaking in the church or being involved in a worship service. He explains the silence here as like that in 1 Corinthians 14:28 and 30, where a prophet or a tongue speaker is to be silent while the other is speaking in the context of prophecy.[137] He sees verse 35 as indicating that the reason for women asking questions was their desire to learn since "they were not yet educated enough in the school of Christ to know what was and was not appropriate in Christian worship."[138] He therefore sees verse 35 as indicating that Paul is affirming the right of women to learn, but also suggesting that women learn from their husbands at home.[139]

In summary, in their interpretations of the text, Grudem and Witherington render the word σιγάω as "keep silent,"[140] and Schüssler Fiorenza as "remain silent."[141] Schüssler Fiorenza and Witherington see the word λαλέω as conveying the informal sense of speak, talk, or question.[142] Grudem sees it as referring to an inspired form of speech "judging or evaluation,"[143] which is similar

---

prophet's theology or even the prophet's lifestyle in public. This would become especially sensitive and problematic if wives were cross-examining their husbands about the speech and conduct which supported or undermined the authenticity of a claim to utter a prophetic message and would readily introduce Paul's allusion to reserving questions of a certain kind at home. The women would in this case (i) be acting as judges over their husbands in public; (ii) risk turning worship into an extended discussion session with perhaps private interests; (iii) militate against the ethics of controlled and restrained speech in the context of which the congregation should be silently listening to God rather than eager to address one another, and (iv) disrupt the sense of respect for the orderliness of God's agency in creation and in the world as against the confusion which pre-existed the creative activity of God's Spirit." *First Epistle to the Corinthians*, 1158.

137. Witherington, *Women in the Earliest Churches*, 103.

138. Witherington, *Conflict and Community*, 287, notes that Keener sees the pedagogical problem involved as the limitation of education for women at that time. Keener, *Paul, Women and Wives*, 81.

139. Witherington, *Women in the Earliest Churches*, 103.

140. Grudem, *Gift of Prophecy*, 222; Witherington, *Women in the Earliest Churches*, 102.

141. Schüssler Fiorenza, *In Memory of Her*, 232.

142. Nida, *Greek-English Lexicon*, 396. See also "λαλεῖν," in BDAG, 582. Barrett, *First Epistle to the Corinthians*, 332, sees the speaking here as referring to inspired speech.

143. Barrett, 332, understands λαλέω as referring to a form of inspired speech, "speaking in tongues." Matthew Henry notes that women "are not permitted to speak (v. 34) in the church, neither in praying nor prophesying. The connection seems plainly to include the latter, in the limited sense in which it is taken in this chapter, namely, for preaching, or interpreting scripture by inspiration. And, indeed, for a woman to prophesy in this sense were to teach, which does not so well befit her state of subjection. A teacher of others has in that respect a superiority over them, which is not allowed the woman over the man, nor must she therefore be allowed to teach in a congregation: I suffer them not to teach. But praying, and uttering hymns inspired,

to Adoniram Judson, who interprets it as "preaching." Their interpretation of the word σιγάω is connected to their understanding of the word λαλέω in the overall context of 1 Corinthians 14. Furthermore, their interpretation of the word σιγάω and λαλέω correlate with how they understand the word ὑποτασσέσθωσαν, which comes from the root word ὑποτάσσω ("submission"). This leads to the next section, which focuses on how these contemporary interpreters make exegetical decisions on the term ὑποτασσέσθωσαν.

4.2.5 Silence and Submission

The exegetical decisions about the word ὑποτασσέσθωσ differ based on the interpreter's understanding of who it is the women should submit to, and the context in which they should submit. Grudem sees ὑποτασσέσθωσαν as referring to the submission of all women to "male leadership in the church."[144] Schüssler Fiorenza interprets this word as referring to the submission of wives to their husbands.[145] Witherington sees it as referring to the submission of wives to the principle of order in worship services.[146]

Both Grudem and Witherington consider the usage of ἀλλὰ ("but") important for understanding the kind of speaking that Paul has in mind. Both see ἀλλὰ as indicating a strong contrast to λαλέω ("speaking") and ὑποτάσσω ("subordination"), and thus providing the rationale for women to be silent.[147] However, they see the silence required of women as backed up by different principles and Scriptures. Grudem sees the main concern of Paul regarding silence backed by the "principle of submission" that covers family as well as church relations,[148] whereas Witherington sees Paul's main concern here as

---

were not teaching." *Commentary*, 2271, https://www.biblestudytools.com/commentaries/matthew-henry-complete/1-corinthians/14.html.

144. Grudem, *Evangelical Feminism*, 247. Grudem objects to the idea that Paul's main concern is with order in the church, noting that "Paul himself says that his concern is the principle of submission." The problem is, however, that although Paul does mention submission, he does not actually say it is his main concern.

145. Schüssler Fiorenza, *In Memory of Her*, 232, reasons from "Greco-Roman exhortations for the subordination of wives as part of the law."

146. Witherington, *Women in the Earliest Churches*, 100.

147. Grudem, *Gift of Prophecy*, 222; Witherington, *Women in the Earliest Churches*, 100.

148. Grudem, *Evangelical Feminism*, 247.

the "principle of order" in the worship service, not disorder in family relations.[149]

In identifying the kind of speaking that Paul intended to stop, Grudem argues that the clause beginning with ἀλλά indicates that Paul is concerned about an insubordinate form of speech.[150] He notes that the Corinthian women's "speaking aloud to judge prophecies" is problematic since "it would involve assuming the possession of superior authority in matters of doctrinal or ethical instruction, especially when it included criticism of the prophecy."[151] In this sense, women's evaluation of prophecies is the opposite of "being submissive to male leadership in the church."[152] Grudem supports this view of male authority over women by referring to Genesis 2,[153] where he sees Adam being the firstborn as giving him "headship in the family," further validated by his being given authority by God to name Eve, and being given Eve as a suitable helper.[154] He sees this concept of male headship as the rationale behind the governing and teaching authority of the elders in the early churches.[155] From this understanding of eldership in the church as belonging only to male leaders,[156] Grudem views Paul as establishing the idea of male

---

149. Witherington, *Women in the Earliest Churches*, 102.

150. Grudem, *Gift of Prophecy*, 222.

151. Grudem, 222.

152. Grudem, *Evangelical Feminism*, 230.

153. Although Grudem connects his view of male leadership with Genesis 2, he does not give a specific verse. However, Carson, who shares the same view as Grudem, refers to Gen 2:20b-24. Grudem and Carson both admit that the passage in Gen 2 does not mention "silence," but insist that Gen 2 does suggest that because "man was made first and woman was made for man, some kind of pattern has been laid down regarding the roles the two play." Carson, "'Silent in the Churches,'" in Piper and Grudem, *Biblical Manhood and Womanhood*, 152.

154. Grudem, *Gift of Prophecy*, 223.

155. Grudem mentions the following passages (NRSV): Heb 13:17: "Obey your leaders and submit to them, for they are keeping watch over your souls and will give an account."; 1 Pet 5:5: "In the same way, you who are younger must accept the authority of the elders."; 1 Tim 5:17: "Let the elders who rule well be considered worthy of double honor, especially those who labor in preaching and teaching."

156. Grudem, *Evangelical Feminism*, 230.

headship, and female submission to male leadership in 1 Corinthians 11:8–9[157] and 1 Timothy 2:13[158] as well.[159]

Witherington notes that the word ὑποτασσέσθωσαν is used to describe several relationships, including relationships between husband and wife, child and parents, slaves and masters, all men and women to secular authority, Christians to church officials, all people in relation to God, and believers in relation to Christ.[160] However, he points out that interpreting ὑποτασσέσθωσαν to mean subordination of wives requires clarification about why Paul tells women to keep silent in the worship service. Like Grudem, Witherington sees 1 Corinthians 14:34–35 as not mentioning to whom the women should show subordination.[161] He sees the silence Paul enjoins here as indicating the fact that women were "speaking in some sense in the church" and that they are "to be silent because (causal γὰρ) it is not permitted them to speak."[162] He reasons that since Paul's command to silence and submission is "caused by disorder in the worship service, not disorder in family relations," ὑποτασσέσθωσαν here refers to subordination of wives to the principle of order in the worship service.[163] In other words, "women are not being commanded to submit to their husbands, but to the principle of order in the worship service, the principle of silence and respect shown when another is speaking."[164]

Schüssler Fiorenza sees ὑποτασσέσθωσαν here as referring to the submission of wives to their husbands rather than to the community leadership.[165] Acknowledging that the 1 Corinthians 14:34–36 text does not clearly explain to whom the wives should be subordinate, she sees the issue as the behavior of wives who question "other women's husbands or point out some mistakes of their own during the congregational interpreting of the Scriptures and of prophecy," behavior which was considered going "against all traditional

---

157. First Corinthians 11:8–9 (NRSV) says, "Indeed, man was not made from woman, but woman from man. Neither was man created for the sake of woman, but woman for the sake of man."

158. 1 Tim 2:13 (NRSV) says, "For Adam was formed first, then Eve."

159. Grudem, *Gift of Prophecy*, 223.

160. Witherington, *Women in the Earliest Churches*, 101.

161. Witherington, 101.

162. Witherington, 100.

163. Witherington, 101.

164. Witherington, 102.

165. Schüssler Fiorenza, *In Memory of Her*, 231.

custom and law."¹⁶⁶ In particular, she sees the wives here as violating the "Jewish-Hellenistic missionary tradition" that derived from the "Greco-Roman exhortations for the subordination of wives as part of the law."¹⁶⁷

To summarize, Schüssler Fiorenza sees the term ὑποτασσέσθωσαν here as submission of wives to their husbands, Grudem understands it as referring to submission of wives to the principle of male headship, and Witherington understands it as the submission of wives to the principle of order in the worship service. Since none of them mention a textual issue concerning a reading of ὑποτασσέσθωσαν with τοῖς ἀνδράσιν, their exegetical decisions on the meaning of ὑποτασσέσθωσαν are linked to their understanding of the context rather than to a textual variant reading. (The alternative reading of ὑποτασσέσθωσαν with τοῖς ἀνδράσιν is mentioned in one manuscript, codex A.¹⁶⁸ The preferred reading given by NA²⁸ is ὑποτασσέσθωσαν without τοῖς ἀνδράσιν ("to the husbands") rather than ὑποτασσέσθωσαν τοῖς ἀνδράσιν ("submit to the husbands").¹⁶⁹

Furthermore, these interpreters do not mention another textual issue, namely, whether the usage of ὑποτάσσω is in the infinitive verb form ὑποτάσσεσθαι or the imperative ὑποτασσέσθωσαν. Their explanations indicate that they see ὑποτάσσω here as taking the imperative verb form. This is seen in Grudem's quote from the RSV translation of "should be subordinate," which shows the imperative form,¹⁷⁰ and Witherington's usage of the word ὑποτασσέσθωσαν, which is in the imperative form.¹⁷¹

Looking at the exegetical decisions of Grudem, Schüssler Fiorenza, and Witherington on ὑποτασσέσθωσαν, their decisions not only hinge on how they see the word σιγάω in connection to the word λαλέω, but also how they see the word σιγάτωσαν (v. 34) being measured by the word ὑποτασσέσθωσαν, in contrast with λαλεῖν in the same verse.¹⁷² This influences how they understand the word ὁ νόμος in the context of 1 Corinthians 14:34–35. With this

---

166. Schüssler Fiorenza, 232.
167. Schüssler Fiorenza, 231.
168. 'A' refers to Codex Alexandrinus. NA²⁸ 1 Cor 14:34–35. See also Metzger and Ehrman. *The Text of the New Testament.*
169. NA²⁸.
170. Grudem, *Gift of Prophecy*, 222.
171. Witherington, *Women in the Earliest Churches*, 100.
172. Witherington, 100.

in mind, the following section looks at how these interpreters make decisions regarding the word ὁ νόμος.

4.2.6 Silence and the Law

The exegetical decisions of Grudem, Schüssler Fiorenza, and Witherington on the word ὁ νόμος revolve around how they see Paul using this word in the overall context of the New Testament. The fact that Paul did not specify which law he is referring to when he used ὁ νόμος in the context of 1 Corinthians 14:34–35 contributes to differing interpretations. Grudem sees ὁ νόμος as referring to the Old Testament in general in terms of its views on men and women.[173] Schüssler Fiorenza sees ὁ νόμος as referring to "Greco-Roman exhortations for the subordination of wives,"[174] and Witherington sees ὁ νόμος as referring to Old Testament understanding of silence in terms of respect of a student for a teacher.[175] The fact that Paul does not specify the object of the women's submission in the text raises questions as to whether ὁ νόμος is talking about ὑποτάσσω ("submission") or αἰσχρὸν ("shame"). All three interpreters link ὁ νόμος to ὑποτάσσω in the context of prophecy.

Grudem sees ὁ νόμος in the context of 1 Corinthians 14:34–35 as referring to the teaching of the Old Testament regarding submission to male leadership. Acknowledging that Paul does not quote any specific Old Testament passage, he cites Romans 3:19 and 1 Corinthians 9:8 as instances when Paul mentions "as the law says" with reference to Old Testament passages.[176] From that understanding, he sees ὁ νόμος in this context as referring to an Old Testament passage, but not to "Roman law or to Jewish oral traditions," for "Paul does not elsewhere use *nomos* in those ways."[177] Thus, he sees ὁ νόμος in this context as referring to Genesis 2,[178] "where Adam is the 'firstborn' (with the

---

173. Grudem, *Evangelical Feminism*, 246.
174. Schüssler Fiorenza, *In Memory of Her*, 231.
175. Witherington, *Women in the Earliest Churches*, 100.
176. Grudem, *Evangelical Feminism*, 246.
177. Grudem, 246; Grudem, *Gift of Prophecy*, 223. Grudem notes that out of 119 usages of ὁ νόμος, Paul never uses the law in reference to either Roman law or rabbinic law. Although this is true, the fact that Paul writes in the context of a missionary church suggests that Paul may be referencing the law that was familiar in the Corinthian context. I will show this in my interpretation of the text in chapter 7.
178. Barrett, Robertson, and Plummer see "ὁ νόμος" as referring to Gen 3:16: "Your desire shall be for your husband, and he shall rule over you." Barrett, *First Epistle to the Corinthians*, 330. Robertson and Plummer, *First Epistle of St. Paul*, 325. They see the background of Paul's

concomitant headship in the family which that status implied), where he also has the authority from God to name Eve, and where Eve is made as helper suitable for Adam."[179] He sees Paul as alluding to the subordination of the wife already in the Genesis creation narrative of 1 Corinthians 11:3, 8–10. The fact that submission is already alluded to in the creation narrative provides a reason for Paul not to repeat the theme of subordination in the context of 1 Corinthians 14.

As mentioned, Schüssler Fiorenza sees ὁ νόμος in the context of 1 Corinthians 14:34–35 referring to Roman law against wives speaking in public and gathering for public demonstrations.[180] This is rejected by Grudem because "Paul does not elsewhere use *nomos* in those ways."[181] However, Schüssler Fiorenza sees Paul as deriving his theological argument from "Jewish-Hellenistic missionary tradition," which adopted the "Greco-Roman exhortations for the subordination of wives as part of the 'law.'"[182] These sentiments were famously expressed in 195 BC by the Roman Consul Cato.[183]

> If each man of us fellow citizens had established that the right and authority of the husband should be held over the mother of his own family, we should have less difficulty with women in general; now at home is conquered by female fury, here in the Forum it is bruised and trampled upon. . . . What kind of behavior is this? Running around in public, blocking streets, and speaking to other women's husbands! Could you not have asked your husband the same thing at home? . . . Give the reins

---

speech as submission of women to their husbands in the way of silence. Garland says the problem with seeing Gen 3:16 as a background to Paul's thought is that the passage is "predictive, not prescriptive," because the condition required in that passage is the domination resulting from the curse of the fall. See Garland, *1 Corinthians*, 672. Also, F. F. Bruce comments that referring to Gen 3:16 "is unlikely, since MT and LXX Gen 3:16 speaks of a woman's instinctive inclination . . . towards her husband, of which he takes advantage to dominate her. The reference is more probably to the creation narratives." He suggests that the Pentateuch or Gen 1:26–28 and 2:21–24 might be what Paul is alluding to. F. F. Bruce, *1 and 2 Corinthians*, 135–136.

179. Grudem, *Gift of Prophecy*, 223.
180. Schüssler Fiorenza, *In Memory of Her*, 231.
181. Grudem, *Evangelical Feminism*, 246.
182. Schüssler Fiorenza, *In Memory of Her*, 231.
183. In the face of women demonstrating in the streets, Cato spoke (unsuccessfully) against the repeal of laws (the Lex Oppia) which had been passed in 215 BC restricting what women could own and wear.

to their unbridled nature and this unmastered creature, and hope that they will put limits on their own freedom? Unless you do something yourselves, this is the least among the things imposed upon them either by custom or by law which they endure with hurt feelings. They want freedom, nay license (if we are to speak the truth) in all things. . . . As soon as they begin to be your equals, they will have become your superiors.[184]

Schüssler Fiorenza's decision on the meaning of ὁ νόμος in the context of 1 Corinthians 14:34–35 is an example not only of an interpreter being influenced by their understanding of the text in the context of prophecy, but also by their understanding of Corinth in a context of mission where new believers are learning to live together in the community of faith. She sees ὁ νόμος referring to community law, which derives from Roman law. Thus, she sees Paul as encouraging the Christian wives of Corinth to keep quiet in the assembly of the community in order to "prevent the Christian community from being mistaken for one of the orgiastic, secret, oriental cults that undermined public order and decency."[185]

Witherington's exegetical choice regarding ὁ νόμος hinges on his understanding of σιγάω in connection to ὑποτασσέσθωσαν. Witherington sees ὁ νόμος here as probably referring to the "respectful silence when a word of counsel is spoken" as in Job 29:21.[186] He reasons that this concept of respectful silence mentioned in the Old Testament should be a familiar subject among the Corinthians.[187] He points out that silence is associated with submission in the Old Testament only in the contexts of respect for "God,"[188] for "one in position of authority,"[189] for "wise men noted for their knowledge and counsel,"[190] and silence imposed by God on "someone who speaks insolently to a righteous person."[191] Witherington sees the concept of respectful silence

---

184. Schüssler Fiorenza, *In Memory of Her*, 231–232, quoting Lefkowitz and Fant, *Women in Greece and Rome*, 135.

185. Schüssler Fiorenza, *In Memory of Her*, 232.

186. Witherington, *Women in the Earliest Churches*, 103.

187. Witherington, 103.

188. Hab 2:20; Isa 46:1; and Zech 2:13.

189. Judg 3:19.

190. Job 29:21.

191. Ps 31:17; Witherington, *Women in the Earliest Churches*, 102.

of a student for a teacher when a word of counsel is spoken as perfectly fitting to the context of the church in Corinth, which is troubled with disorderliness in the worship service.[192]

Looking at the exegetical decisions of Grudem, Schüssler Fiorenza, and Witherington on ὑποτασσέσθωσαν, σιγάω, λαλέω, and ὁ νόμος in the context of 1 Corinthians 14:34–35, it is significant that their decisions on these words correlate with each other and their exegetical choices on the usage of σιγάω in the context of 1 Corinthians 14:34–35 correlate with how they understand λαλέω, ὑποτασσέσθωσαν, and ὁ νόμος in the same context. Furthermore, their understanding of these words influence how they interpret Paul's expectation in verses 35–36.

4.2.7 Paul's Expectations

As mentioned, the exegetical decisions of Grudem, Schüssler Fiorenza, and Witherington on 1 Corinthians 14:34 revolve around how they see these verses fitting into the overall context of 1 Corinthians. This dynamic happens in their interpretation of verses 35 and 36 as well. All three see the sentence in verse 35, εἰ δέ τι μαθεῖν θέλουσιν, ἐν οἴκῳ τοὺς ἰδίους ἄνδρας ἐπερωτάτωσαν·αἰσχρὸν γάρ ἐστιν γυναικὶ λαλεῖν ἐν ἐκκλησίᾳ, as providing an additional rationale for Paul's usage of σιγάω in verse 34.[193]

According to Grudem, Paul in this context of verse 35 is anticipating evasion from some women in Corinth concerning his teaching about silence in verse 34. Grudem sees Paul as expecting some women to say, "Okay, we won't stand up and pass judgment on any prophecies. But we just want to ask a few questions. What's wrong with that?" Anticipating such evasion, Grudem sees Paul in verse 35 as telling the women to ask their husbands at home.[194] He quotes from the RSV translation of verse 35, "If there is anything they desire to know, let them ask their husbands at home,"[195] which omits the word ἰδίους ("one's own") in translation. This might be due to his view of ἄνδρας as referring not only to "husbands" but also to "other men within their family circles,

---

192. Witherington, 102.
193. Grudem, *Gift of Prophecy*, 222; Schüssler Fiorenza, *In Memory of Her*, 230; Witherington, *Women in the Earliest Churches*, 102.
194. Grudem, *Evangelical Feminism*, 234.
195. Grudem, *Gift of Prophecy*, 222.

or within the fellowship of the church" to ask about the prophecies.[196] Although Grudem raises the possibility of Paul's expectation of Corinthian women's evasion, he does not discuss the context of shame in asking questions as a subordinate, whether it is shameful for a husband when his wife questions him publicly or any other form of shame that might relate to a woman.[197]

Like Grudem, Witherington sees Paul as providing an additional reason in verse 35 for Paul's usage of σιγάω in verse 34. He sees Paul as appealing to "shame" as a "secondary argument"[198] to help correct the problem of disorderliness, as in 1 Corinthians 11:4–5. The fact that Paul commands the wives to ask these questions at home in verse 35, ἐν οἴκῳ τοὺς ἰδίους ἄνδρας ἐπερωτάτωσαν ("let them ask their husbands at home"), supports the view that Paul's primary concern here is "the *manner* in which the wives ask, not the fact of their asking."[199] He stresses that Paul sees disruptive manner as shameful, and thus the command of silence is "correcting an abuse of a privilege, not taking back a woman's right to speak in the assembly," which he had already granted in 1 Corinthians 11.[200]

In short, Grudem, Schüssler Fiorenza, and Witherington all see verse 36 as Paul's refutation of the expected argument of the Corinthians on Paul's command in verses 34–35. Grudem explains the usage of particle ἤ here as a disjunctive referring to a "rebuttal" of the Corinthians' view.[201] He agrees with Carson in saying, "In every instance in the New Testament where the disjunctive particle in question is used in a construction analogous to the passage at hand, its effect is to reinforce the truth of the clause or verse that precedes it."[202] Grudem points out that Paul is insisting here that the Corinthian church return to the "common practice and perspective of the

---

196. Grudem, 222.

197. Garland, *1 Corinthians*, 668.

198. As Witherington notes, "In both 1 Cor 11:2ff. and 14:33bff., Paul first plays his theological trump card (11:7ff., 14:34) and then backs it up by arguing by what was considered at that time natural, normal, or honorable for Christian women (11:13ff., 14:35)." *Women in the Earliest Churches*, 100.

199. Witherington, 102; Thiselton, *First Epistle to the Corinthians*, 1159; Wire, *Corinthian Women Prophets*, 152–158. Keener, *Paul, Women and Wives*, 70–100, suggests that the reason women asked irrelevant questions during the assembly was that they were uneducated and wanted to learn.

200. Witherington, 287.

201. Gilbert Bilezikian, *Beyond Sex Roles*, 186.

202. Carson, "'Silent in the Churches,'" 150–151.

churches (1:2; 4:17; 7:17; 11:16; 14:33) and to wholehearted submission to apostolic authority (14:37–38)."

Schüssler Fiorenza also argues that Paul realizes that this instruction for women to be silent "goes against the accepted practice of the missionary churches in the Hellenistic urban centers," since "wives were called to missionary preaching and were founders of house churches."[203] These women included married women such as "Prisca," "Junia," and "Apphia."[204] Paul's injunction for women to be silent in the church and ask their husbands questions at home would sound "preposterous" to the Corinthians' ears, since these women were already considered prominent leaders in the church.[205] For that reason, she sees Paul as expecting counter-arguments from the Corinthian community. This is the reason she sees Paul claiming in verse 37 that his regulation has "the authority of the Lord." It is also why she sees Paul reaffirming in verse 40 that his command to be silent is not from "theology," but from "concern for decency and order" in the "behavior of pneumatic women and men in the worship service of the community."[206]

Witherington sees verse 36 as Paul's reaction to the abuses he had been dealing with in 1 Corinthians 11–14.[207] After ruling out the view that advocates verse 36 as a Pauline forceful rhetorical response to the Corinthians' views on verses 34–35,[208] Witherington points out that it is contextually more probable to see 1 Corinthians 14:36–40 as the conclusion to the whole section of chapters 11 to 14. He sees Paul as revealing his "frustrations with the whole mess he had been dealing with" since 1 Corinthians 11:2, and thus concludes that Paul is "anticipating the response he expected to get (v. 36) when the Corinthians read his argument (vv. 34–35)."[209]

---

203. Schüssler Fiorenza, *In Memory of Her*, 232.
204. Schüssler Fiorenza, 232.
205. Schüssler Fiorenza, 232.
206. Schüssler Fiorenza, 233.
207. Witherington, *Women in the Earliest Churches*, 98; Witherington, *Conflict and Community*, 287.
208. Odell-Scott, "Let the Women Speak in Church," 90–93, sees 1 Cor 14:34–35 as the "Corinthian's view" and verse 36 as Pauline rhetorical questions over the Corinthian's view. Witherington sees this as making sense "if the Corinthians were appealing to their own inspired utterances alone, but not if they were appealing to: (a) conventional church practice; (b) the law; and (c) what was shameful." Witherington, *Women in the Earliest Churches*, 98.
209. Witherington, 99.

In summary, Grudem sees the command of σιγάω here as meaning that "the women should keep silence during the evaluation of prophecies."[210] He sees Paul as arguing from a "larger conviction about an abiding distinction between the roles appropriate to males and those appropriate to females in the Christian church."[211] Therefore, commanding women to be silent fits well "with a consistent Pauline advocacy of women's participation without governing authority in the assembled church."[212]

Schüssler Fiorenza sees the command of σιγάω as meaning that the Christian "wives" of Corinth should "keep quiet and remain subdued in the assembly of the community,"[213] so that "an outsider cannot accuse the Christians of religious madness."[214] She sees Paul's intention as not to exclude women from active participation of ministry, but to place "a limit and qualification on the pneumatic participation of women in the worship service of the community."[215] She concludes that this restriction has a "double-edged" impact on women's leadership in the church, which further develops into the gradual exclusion of "all women from ecclesial office and to the gradual patriarchalization of the whole church."[216]

Witherington sees the command of σιγάω as "silencing" the Corinthian women from "their particular abuse of speech and redirecting their questions to another time and place," because Paul wishes the "women to learn the answers to their questions."[217] Witherington notes that women alone are mentioned in this context since they were "the cause of the problem," and as such they are the "ones needing correction."[218] The problem addressed by the texts that command women to be silent is not "a creation order or family order problem," but "rather a church order problem caused by some women in the congregation." He therefore concludes that this interpretation in "no way

---

210. Grudem, *Gift of Prophecy*, 224.
211. Grudem, 224.
212. Grudem, 224.
213. Schüssler Fiorenza, *In Memory of Her*, 232.
214. Schüssler Fiorenza, 233.
215. Schüssler Fiorenza, 233.
216. Schüssler Fiorenza, 236.
217. Witherington, *Women in the Earliest Churches*, 104.
218. Witherington, 104.

contradicts 1 Cor 11.5, nor any other passage which suggests that women can teach, preach, pray, or prophesy in or outside the churches."[219]

Concluding their interpretations on 1 Corinthians 14:34–35, Grudem and Witherington give what they believe is a relevant application of this text for the contemporary setting. Due to his understanding of the authority of the Bible, Grudem finds the texts that command women to be silent as normative for today's churches.[220] From the same understanding of the authority of the Bible, Witherington also finds the texts that command women to be silent as normative for today's churches, but only in similar situations in worship services.[221] Schüssler Fiorenza does not offer any application.

Given their interpretations of 1 Corinthians 14:34–35, it is reasonable to conclude that the exegetical decisions of Grudem, Schüssler Fiorenza, and Witherington, depend mainly on how they understand σιγάω in connection to words like γυναῖκες, ὑποτασσέσθωσαν, λαλέω, and ὁ νόμος in the context. This further influences how they interpret Paul's expectations of reactions from the Corinthians, and how they arrive at the meaning of this passage that commands women to be silent. The question then is, how did they end up with different meanings of the text even though all three were looking at the text using traditional hermeneutical tools that include exegetical and historical studies? The fact that these three contemporary interpreters arrive at quite different conclusions regarding the meaning of the text indicates an issue of interpretation beyond methodology and suggests the influence of their different commitments as complementarian traditionalist, feminist, and egalitarian interpreters.

In the past, the historical-critical approach was predominantly focused on understanding the world of the biblical text. It paid attention to the study of the linguistic and historical context so that, "through rationally defensible modes of analysis, the reader as investigator seeks to reconstruct the meanings of the text objectively within the time of its origins."[222] An example from the history of biblical interpretation is Ferdinand Christian Baur, who said in 1853 that his "standpoint in one word is historical. This alone is the basis

---

219. Witherington, 104.
220. Grudem, *Evangelical Feminism*, 245.
221. Witherington, *Conflict and Community*, 274.
222. Yarchin, *History of Biblical Interpretation*, xxiv.

on which to set forth a given fact in so far as it is overall possible to be understood in its pure objectivity."[223] This method suggests a starting point in which there is an assumption of "separation and distance between subject (reader) and object (text) by virtue of the recognition that the text originated in an ancient world and was written to speak to that world."[224] Thus, the reader approaches and examines from outside the text as a "neutral observer"[225] who is "unencumbered by contemporary questions, values and interests,"[226] in order to achieve the objectivity in interpretation that uncovers the original intention of the author.

However, over time, biblical interpreters began to acknowledge difficulties with the assumption that objective interpretations could be so readily achieved. Recognizing this, many interpreters began to refer to "the myth of interpretive objectivity,"[227] acknowledging that however objective they might seek to be, the interpreters still had views and assumptions which shaped their understanding of "the text," and influenced their understanding of "the assumption behind the text,"[228] and the "exegetical questions" that they sought to address."[229] Yarchin notes that "just as the biblical text was created within a historical and cultural situation that affects the way it was written," readers of the Bible are themselves "situated within a cultural situation that cannot but affect the way they read."[230]

This leads us to ask questions about the influence of the views and assumptions behind the exegetical decisions of the three contemporary interpreters. As Crocker asserts, knowing the background of the interpreter is important because it helps determine "how historical-critical methods are applied to various passages, and . . . what should be considered as central evidence and what can be discarded as unimportant."[231] Therefore, the following section explores the hermeneutical keys of the three contemporary

---

223. Reventlow, *History of Biblical Interpretation*, 277.
224. Yarchin, *History of Biblical Interpretation*, xxiv.
225. Yarchin, xxvii.
226. Schüssler Fiorenza, "Ethics of Biblical Interpretation," 11.
227. Scholer, "Feminist Hermeneutics," 412.
228. Scholer, 409.
229. Scholer, 412.
230. Yarchin, *History of Biblical Interpretation*, xxvii.
231. Crocker, *Reading First Corinthians*, 35.

interpreters that guided their interpretations of the passage that commands women to be silent. This includes looking at their presuppositions, commitments, and ideologies to identify their role in the hermeneutical process.

4.3 Hermeneutical Keys of Contemporary Interpreters

On examining the hermeneutics of the three contemporary interpreters, three keys can be identified: methodologies, presuppositions, and interpretational approach.

The first part of this section investigates the methodologies of the interpreters. The second section then looks at the hermeneutical presuppositions which influence their approach to interpreting 1 Corinthians 14:34–35. This focuses on the interpreter's view of the locus of authority in interpretation, which includes attitudes toward the Bible and the role of interpreter. This section also looks at the sociological perspectives and theoretical framework behind the hermeneutical presuppositions. The final section identifies the hermeneutical approaches of the interpreters, which include their starting point and other factors that influence their interpretive choices.

4.3.1 Hermeneutical Methodology

There are significant differences in the hermeneutics of these three interpreters which can be discussed around three principles – the principle of analogy, the principle of determining meaning, and the principle of application.

Grudem believes that much of the controversy over the role of men and women in marriage and the church has to do with how one interprets the Bible.[232] His complementarian hermeneutical method arises out of his literal-traditional hermeneutics. This method hinges on the principle of the analogy of faith, the belief that "since God is the author of Holy Scripture, what is taught in one Scripture cannot contradict what is taught in another Scripture on the same subject," and thus, "an obscure text or passage may be illumined by other texts of Scripture whose meaning is clear."[233] This principle takes the

---

232. Grudem, *Evangelical Feminism*, 329.

233. Elwell, *Evangelical Dictionary of Theology*, 58. Grudem's usage of the principle of analogy of faith is based on the premise that Scriptures' meanings are clear.

authority of Scripture seriously and is committed to the grammatical and historical method of exegesis.

According to Grudem, the interpreter's acceptance of the authority of Scripture is the most important part of interpretation.[234] He argues that since "all the words in the Bible are God's words" and "Scripture cannot contradict Scripture,"[235] to disbelieve or disobey them is "to disbelieve or disobey God himself."[236] His involvement in translating the English Standard Version of the Bible (ESV), as a literal word for word translation, gives an example of this approach. This literal translation is different from dynamic equivalent translation that translates thoughts for thoughts.[237] Thus, from his view of the authority of Scripture, Grudem sees the locus of authority in interpretation as resting on the Scripture texts themselves.

Schüssler Fiorenza describes her method as a "hermeneutic of suspicion,"[238] "a feminist critical theology of liberation,"[239] or "a critical feminist rhetorical interpretation of liberation."[240] Describing the method of interpreters like Grudem as a hermeneutic of "respect, acceptance, consent, and obedience"[241] or "hermeneutics of affirmation,"[242] she notes that her method is significantly different. Identifying biblical interpretation as a political act, she argues that "a feminist reconstitution of the world requires a feminist hermeneutic that shares in critical methods and impulses of historical scholarship on the one hand and in the theological goals of liberation theologies on the other hand."[243]

---

234. Grudem, *Evangelical Feminism*, 23.

235. Grudem, 362. From this understanding of the internal agreement of Scripture, Grudem considers that 1 Tim 2:12 is not isolated from the rest of Scripture that speaks about church office and about conduct in public worship.

236. Grudem, *Christian Beliefs*; Grudem, *Systematic Theology*, 73.

237. Grudem, "Are Only Some Words?" 29. He argues that the translator should ask not only "Have I rendered the main idea of this sentence correctly?" but, "Have I represented correctly the meaning that each word contributes to this sentence?"

238. Schüssler Fiorenza, *Wisdom Ways*, 175.

239. Schüssler Fiorenza, *Bread Not Stone*, xvi.

240. Schüssler Fiorenza, *But She Said*, 47, describes this as a method that examines "not only the rhetorical aims of biblical texts but also the rhetorical interests emerging in the history of interpretation or in contemporary scholarship."

241. Schüssler Fiorenza, *Wisdom Ways*, 175.

242. This term was first introduced by Paul Ricoeur, "The Critique of Religion," 213–222.

243. Schüssler Fiorenza, *In Memory of Her*, 29. Schüssler Fiorenza regards critical analysis as essential in a critical feminist theology of "liberation committed to transformation." See Schüssler Fiorenza, *Jesus: Miriam's Child*, 13.

She uses the term "critical" to show that the first part of her methodology is a critical theology that uncovers Christian traditions and theologies that have preserved alienation, domination, and oppression which are multiple structures of oppression that control "wo/men's lives."[244] Her method thus analyzes patriarchal elements both in the context of the texts themselves and the context of the interpreter.[245]

Witherington calls his methodology "socio-rhetorical criticism"[246] or "historical rhetorical criticism."[247] This focuses on sociological insights that examine the "behavior and social forms of the society"[248] surrounding the texts in their historical context, and on exegetical insights derived from the "ideas and images, the communication and form, of the texts."[249] Like Grudem, his hermeneutical principles are rooted in the authority of Scripture and a commitment to the grammatical and historical method of exegesis. He notes that the interpreter "ought to begin with a posture of trust," in contrast to Schüssler

---

244. Schüssler Fiorenza, *Jesus: Miriam's Child*, 12, sees this approach as investigating contradictions and silences inscribed in the text to reconstruct the world of the biblical text by using "persuasive power and literary strategies of a text which has a communicative function in a concrete situation" and invite a "response." See also Schüssler Fiorenza, "Rhetorical Situation," 387.

245. Schüssler Fiorenza, *In Memory of Her*, 108–109. Schüssler Fiorenza notes that this method is based on four presuppositions: "(1) Texts and historical sources must be read as androcentric texts. (2) The glorification, denigration and marginalization of women must be read as patriarchal social construction or projection. (3) Formal patriarchal laws are generally more restrictive than the actual interaction of men and women. (4) Women's actual social-religious status must be determined by their economic autonomy and social roles rather than any ideological or prescriptive statements."

246. Witherington, *What's in the Word*, 1; Witherington, *Conflict and Community*, xii–xiii. Witherington's approach includes the study of historical Greco-Roman rhetoric, which is "the art of persuasion, and particular literary devices and forms [that] were used in antiquity to persuade a hearer or reader to some position regarding the issue that the speaker or writer was addressing." He sees this combination of sociology and rhetorical study as "historical discipline," since he seeks to develop a "historical understanding of what the 'authors' of the New Testament were doing using the art of persuasion and what their social worlds were like." See also Witherington, *What's in the Word*, 2.

247. Witherington, *What's in the Word*, 1. In applying this method to the study of Paul's letters, he notes, "The rhetorical dimension of Paul's letters has revealed how certain forms of argument or exhortation function in his letters, and thus how those forms ought to be interpreted." See also Witherington, *Conflict and Community*, xii.

248. Witherington, *Conflict and Community*, xi.

249. Witherington, xi, sees studying theological intentions of the New Testament writers alone as "traditional concerns" of the historical context. He sees socio-rhetorical criticism as a solution to bridge the gap between sociological and exegetical study, because "there is much to be learned about the text itself by allowing sociological insights to inform, reform, and expand traditional historical study of the text."

Fiorenza's stance which includes "a posture of distrust," "doubt," or "suspicion"[250] in approaching a historical subject. He reasons that "ancient texts deserve the same respect and benefit of the doubt and willingness to trust and listen to."[251]

Regarding the principle of determining meaning, the hermeneutical methods of the three interpreters influence how they approach the biblical texts, whether from faith or from suspicion. Grudem sees the role of the interpreter as important for discovering a "single meaning"[252] in a Scripture text. From this view of the principle of determining meaning, Grudem concludes that even ordinary believers can understand[253] as well as discover "the plain meaning of the text of Scripture" due to the "clarity of Scripture," also known as "the Perspicuity of Scriptures."[254] Admitting that some passages are easier to understand than others, Grudem nonetheless claims that "the Scripture is written in such a way that its teaching is able to be understood by ordinary believers."[255] In his view, a denial of the discoverability of the meaning of Scripture would be "an attack on the character of God – his goodness, his power, and his ability to communicate clearly to his people."[256] The meaning from the texts must be discovered through objective interpretation, not just from "some person's subjective experience."[257]

---

250. Witherington, *Living Word of God*, 87. Witherington here is referring to the "hermeneutics of suspicion" of Schüssler Fiorenza. See Schüssler Fiorenza, *Wisdom Ways*, 175.

251. Witherington, *Living Word of God*, 87.

252. Grudem, "Perspicuity of Scripture."

253. Grudem sees the understandability of Scripture "in Deuteronomy's instructions to parents, in the Psalmist's exhortations to meditate daily on Scripture, in Jesus' repeated expectations that his hearers should know and understand Scripture, and in the willingness of Paul and Peter to address entire congregations with the expectation of being rightly understood." Grudem, 303.

254. Grudem, 307. Grudem explains "perspicuity" as "an older term for the clarity of Scripture." See also Grudem, *Systematic Theology*, 108. The idea of perspicuity was made famous by Martin Luther, and is considered an important principle of Protestant hermeneutics. Melton, *Encyclopedia of Protestantism*, 266; Couch, *Dictionary of Premillennial Theology*, 164.

255. Grudem, "Perspicuity of Scripture," 307.

256. Grudem, 303. Grudem's belief that the meaning of Scripture is discoverable is linked to his rejection of postmodern hermeneutics and the idea that "there is no absolute truth, nor is there any single meaning in a text – meaning depends on the assumptions and purposes that an interpreter brings to a text. Therefore, claims to know what Scripture means on any topic are just disguised attempts to exert power over others."

257. Grudem, *Evangelical Feminism*, 481. "God never calls people to disobey His word. Our decision on this matter must be based on objective teaching of the Bible, not on some person's subjective experience, no matter how godly or sincere that person is."

Grudem's method relies on the clarity of Scripture along with the analogy of faith, which have long been important principles of Protestant hermeneutics.[258] It is also important that Grudem acknowledges, as Scripture does itself, that not everything is easy to understand. A valid question then concerns Grudem's understanding of which category women's silence belongs to – is it clear or unclear? Grudem does not answer this question in terms of 1 Corinthians 14:34–35, but he notes that commands for women's silence, along with passages that prohibit women from being elders and from teaching, are "not isolated passages."[259] He reasons from their appearances in "the heart of the main New Testament teachings about church office and about conduct in public worship."[260] Thus, he notes that the "obscurity" or difficulty in understanding these texts on the restriction of women in church leadership throughout church history is not the problem of "the text of Scripture but in the eye of the beholder."[261]

Like Grudem, Witherington sees the interpreter as having an important role in discovering the meaning of the Scripture.[262] He argues that "meaning resides in the text and is placed there by the author by means of his or her configuration of its words and phrases." He points out that "though the writer may be deceased, his or her words and meaning can still live on without our trying to impose a modern meaning on the text that violates the author's intended sense." Therefore, the main task of the interpreter is to "interpret and apply God's Word, not to create a personal canon within the larger canon."[263] Like Grudem, he sees the goal as the discoverability of the original meaning, the intent of the original author. Thus, the first step in discovering the original meaning intended by the original author is attending to the original historical setting and context of the text.[264]

---

258. Melton, *Encyclopedia of Protestantism*, 266.
259. Grudem, *Evangelical Feminism*, 263.
260. Grudem, 263.
261. Grudem, 263.
262. Witherington, *Conflict and Community*, xiv.
263. Witherington, xiv.
264. Witherington, *Living Word of God*, 165, notes, "Understand as much as possible about the original historical setting and context of the text, remembering that the true meaning of the text must be something the human author and/or God would have wanted to say or allude to, to that original author and audience (e.g. 1 Cor 13, 'when the perfect comes' refers

In response to Grudem's view of the "clarity of Scripture," Witherington notes that clarity is only possible for the original hearer of the words.[265] He points out that the difficulty of gaining clarity today is the "considerable cultural distance from the book and the literary conventions used to compose it."[266] In contrast to Grudem's views of the discoverability of a "single meaning"[267] in the text,[268] he points out that "an author can say more than he realizes under inspiration."[269] He does not however suggest that "the whole Bible" has multivalent meanings.[270] He sees a trajectory that can lead a text to have several meanings, "more than its original historical intent."[271] According to Witherington, the "fundamental principle of the interpretation of the Bible is that a document cannot mean something today that would contradict the thrust or trajectory of meaning that was originally intended by the writer."[272] This meaning has "to be consistent with the literal sense of the text, and had to be intelligible to its original audiences."[273] From his view of the principle of analogy, Scripture must be interpreted in a manner consistent with the theme of redemption.[274]

The second step in gaining the meaning of the text is the need to "hear the word as it is addressed to that original situation" in the context of the original audience.[275] For difficult passages, he points out that the problem is

---

to what happens at the eschaton). Failure to attend to this rule leads to numerous errors and especially to anachronistic misreadings of the NT."

265. Witherington, *Living Word of God*, 16. Grudem rejects this view. He gives the example of Jesus, who "held people responsible for understanding the Old Testament writings, though many of which were written more than 1000 years in the past, and the New Testament writers similarly expected their readers to know and to be able to understand the Old Testament rightly. Therefore, I think that the perspicuity or clarity of Scripture requires us to believe that it is still able to be understood rightly by readers today." Grudem, "Perspicuity of Scripture," 293.

266. Witherington, *Living Word of God*, 81.

267. Grudem, "Perspicuity of Scripture," 302.

268. Witherington, *Living Word of God*, 187, points out that although "the text can mean more than its original historical intent," it cannot mean other than "its original meaning," which is "what the original author had in mind."

269. Witherington, 158.

270. Witherington, 183.

271. Witherington, 158.

272. Witherington, *Conflict and Community*, xiii.

273. Witherington, *Living Word of God*, 158.

274. Witherington, 156.

275. Witherington, 165.

not discoverability of original meaning. He sees jumping "straight for application without properly understanding the meaning of the text" as one of the problems in the "misuse of 1 Cor 14:33b-36 and 1 Tim 2:8-15" to prevent women from pastoral ministry. He concludes that there is "no purely objective, value-free scholarship," and hence suggests interpreters should admit their own presuppositions and inclinations.[276]

Unlike Grudem and Witherington, Schüssler Fiorenza locates "meaning" within texts themselves as less important. Determining the ideological constructs of texts that silence others is more important than determining a text's meaning and how the text operates within its historical contexts.[277] She sees a hermeneutic of suspicion as a method that investigates how ideology functions "in the interest of domination."[278] Since she regards all biblical scholarship as advocacy scholarship and identifies one's method with one's interest,[279] she claims that a text can have multiple meanings depending on interpreters' varying frameworks.[280] Therefore, "intellectual neutrality is not possible in a historical world of exploitation and oppression."[281]

Regarding the principle of application, Grudem applies the principle of the analogy of faith and the clarity of Scripture to the principle of application, claiming that all the teachings of the Bible are relevant for today and thus the duty of the reader is to obey.[282] In his view, the Bible has only to say something once for it to be true and God's word to us, which the reader is obligated to obey.[283] In this framework all the teaching of the Bible is normative, with application to Christians in all times and places, unless Scripture itself

---

276. Witherington, 86–87.
277. Schüssler Fiorenza, "Biblical Interpretation," 11.
278. Schüssler Fiorenza, *Wisdom Ways*, 175.
279. Schüssler Fiorenza, *Rhetoric and Ethics*, 8.
280. Schüssler Fiorenza, "Biblical Interpretation," 11.
281. Schüssler Fiorenza, *Bread Not Stone*, 45.
282. Grudem, *Evangelical Feminism*, 331.
283. Grudem, 362, gives examples of matters he considers as valid practice in the church even if they appear only once, such as taking the Lord's Supper in 1 Cor 11:27–32, the value of being single in ministry in 1 Cor 7, and the characteristics of deacons in 1 Tim 3:8–13.

indicates otherwise.[284] Even isolated passages must not be dismissed.[285] Grudem suggests that since God would not ask people to disobey his word, therefore, everything in the Scriptures must be consistently followed through obedience. However, although this sounds compelling, it raises more questions about whether all the teachings of the Bible are timeless, constantly binding on all people, especially as both the New Testament and the Old Testament show God requiring different things of different people at different times.

Regarding the application of the text, Grudem follows the principle of identifying cultural relativity which may allow a different application of the same principle in a contemporary situation.[286] He admits emphasizing some texts over others on the ground of applicability to the contemporary situation, but he argues that this is not the same as choosing to be subject to some parts of Scripture and not others, which would be a "canon within the canon."[287]

Regarding the principle of application, Witherington believes that "the basic rule of thumb is that while principles remain the same, practices often do not and should change with the differing cultural situations," since the transition between two very different cultures in different historical periods is not a simple task.[288] Therefore, he explains the third step in his methodology as hearing "the word as it addresses our situation." Here Witherington looks at the text from the principle of differentiation, which recognizes that the context of the interpreter is very different from the "original situation in

---

284. Grudem, 368, reasons that even the so called "egalitarian texts" of Gal 3:28 opposite the "complementarian texts" of 1 Tim 2:12 "would not lead us to affirm that because they do not teach that."

285. So Grudem, 362, argues that the fact that "the restriction of some governing and teaching roles to men occurs in only a few passages, or in one passage" still means "we are still obligated to obey it." They cannot be disregarded as "isolated" passages. On the issue of head covering in 1 Cor 11, he believes that Paul's concern was over what a head covering symbolized and not its outward form, and so he teaches that women do not have to cover their heads anymore. He considers that it is better to ask married women to wear "whatever symbolizes being married in their own cultures" instead of saying "we don't have to obey today." Grudem, 338.

286. Grudem, 402. Grudem explains that "culturally relative" commands concerning physical action that carry symbolic meaning (the holy kiss, head covering, foot washing, short hair for men, and lifting hands in prayer) must still be obeyed but may be applied in different forms today.

287. Grudem, *Evangelical Feminism*, 369.

288. Witherington, *Living Word of God*, 169.

the context of the original audience."[289] In other words, this principle asks "what the text meant in its first-century context" and "what it might mean for us here and now."[290] The interpreter must "be faithful to the text and be guided and guarded by what it excludes and what it allows."[291] This leads Witherington to the fourth step in his hermeneutical methodology, which applies "the original meaning to new situations that are analogous and appropriate."[292]

Schüssler Fiorenza sees the Bible as historically conditioned as well as "ideologically determined" by the patriarchal attitudes of the biblical authors and editors.[293] Hence, interpreters should critically examine the text with suspicion and then "reject all religious texts and traditions" as authoritative that contribute to women's oppression.[294]

Given their hermeneutical principles and methods, all the three interpreters deal seriously with the historical aspects of the biblical texts. However, their approaches and commitments vary markedly. While Schüssler Fiorenza's approach differs significantly from Grudem, Witherington shares some similarities with Grudem, such as the importance of approaching biblical texts from the perspective of faith and locating their meaning within the historical setting, with the aim of applying them to contemporary settings. These interpretive and methodological differences and similarities suggest the importance of presuppositions for hermeneutics, which is the focus of the next section.

4.3.2 Hermeneutical Presuppositions

There are four hermeneutical presuppositions in particular that influence Grudem, Schüssler Fiorenza, and Witherington in their interpretation of

---

289. Witherington, 165.
290. Witherington, *Conflict and Community*, xiii.
291. Witherington, xiii-xiv.
292. Witherington, *Living Word of God*, 165. Drawing from difficult texts of Paul as an example, Witherington points out that a letter of Paul may have "significance" in terms of "different applications today," but it should not be "applied in a way that violates the apostle's intended sense and meaning." Recognizing that "Paul addressed specific people at a specific time" is important so that interpreters can understand that what Paul intended as the meaning of the text "must be the starting point for all responsible uses of the text today." See Witherington, *Conflict and Community*, xiii.
293. Schüssler Fiorenza, *Power of the Word: Scripture*, 64.
294. Schüssler Fiorenza, *Bread Not Stone*, xvi.

1 Corinthians 14:34–35. These are the interpreter's view of the locus of authority in interpretation, the interpreter's understanding of the role of interpreter, the sociological perspective of the interpreter, and the theoretical framework of the interpreter.

4.3.2.1 *The Locus of Authority*

The interpreters' views of the locus of authority are linked to their views of the Bible. As we have seen, Grudem and Witherington view the Bible in the traditional sense of the Scriptures as the word of God, whereas Schüssler Fiorenza sees it as the written works mostly of elite men.[295] Given their views of the Bible, Grudem and Witherington see the Bible as the locus of authority in interpretation, while Schüssler Fiorenza sees women's experiences as the locus of authority. Arguing "for the authority of the Bible,"[296] Grudem sees the texts themselves as the locus of authority for interpretation and affirms that "the Bible, as originally given, is the inspired and infallible Word of God. It is the supreme authority in all matters of belief and behavior."[297] He sees all sixty-six books of the Bible[298] as both human words and the words of God.[299] God does not dictate every word of Scripture to the human authors, but God influenced and directed the life of each author such that "the words were fully their own words but also fully the words that God wanted them to write, words that God would also claim as his own."[300] Grudem notes that

---

295. Schüssler Fiorenza, *Power of the Word: Scripture*, 64.

296. Grudem, *Systematic Theology*, 79.

297. Grudem, " Perspicuity of Scripture," 288, note 4. This is the declaration of the Tyndale Fellowship doctrinal basis, which Grudem affirms.

298. Grudem, *Systematic Theology*, 55–68. Grudem sees the formation of the biblical canon as God at work in the "preservation and assembling together of the books of the Scripture for the benefit of his people for the entire church."

299. Grudem, *Systematic Theology*, 81; Grudem, *Bible Doctrine*, 33.

300. Grudem, *Systematic Theology*, 81.

the Bible itself claims to be authoritative and demands obedience, providing examples such as "thus says the Lord,"[301] and the "commands of the Lord."[302]

In Grudem's view, then, making anything other than the Bible the locus of authority is only a human construction of "logic, reason, sense experience," and "scientific methodology."[303] This is dangerous due to flaws in human reasoning, and Grudem points out that human deductions drawn from the statements of Scripture are not equal to the statements of Scripture themselves.[304] He does believe that asking about the words and situations that lie behind the text of Scripture may at times be helpful in understanding what the text means, but he also warns that these reconstructions should "never replace or compete with Scripture itself as the final authority."[305] Grudem differentiates himself from non-evangelical theologians who are not convinced that the Bible is God's word or absolutely authoritative.[306] Unfortunately, Grudem's position fails to address the fact that all perceptions of truth are mediated by interpretation.

In contrast to Grudem, Schüssler Fiorenza's understanding of the locus of authority lies in the experiences of women.[307] Her approach to hermeneutics hinges on her understanding of the Bible. In her view, the Bible "contains the word of God" or "becomes the word of God" when the reader encounters

---

301. Grudem, *Bible Doctrine*, 33; Grudem, *Systematic Theology*, 73. Grudem notes that "thus says the Lord" appears hundreds of times in the Old Testament and whenever the prophet says "thus says the Lord" the words which follow are "the absolutely authoritative words of God." He cites passages from the New Testament such as in 2 Tim 3:16 and 2 Pet 1:21, that declare that all the Old Testament writings are thought of as God's word. In showing the New Testament writings as also God's word and authoritative, he notes that 2 Pet 3:15–16 and 1 Tim 5:18 indicate an awareness that additions were being made to this special category of writings called "Scripture."

302. Grudem, *Bible Doctrine*, 36; Grudem, *Christian Beliefs*, 13–15. Grudem notes Paul's usage of "commands of the Lord" to the Corinthians, which he sees Paul as using "to imply" "that his own judgments were to be considered as authoritative as the commands of Jesus!"

303. Grudem, *Systematic Theology*, 79.

304. Grudem, *Countering the Claims*, 25. He believes that our human "ability to reason and draw conclusions is not the ultimate standard of truth – only Scripture is."

305. Grudem, *Systematic Theology*, 85. Affirming the prophetic gift for today, Grudem points out that although God at times uses subjective impressions of his will to "remind us of moral commands that are already in Scripture" and suggest facts that we "could have known or did not know," they are not to replace Scripture. Grudem, 128.

306. Grudem, 129.

307. Schüssler Fiorenza, *Bread Not Stone*, xvi.

it.[308] She sees the Bible as a collection of texts written mostly by elite men in "androcentric-kyriocentric language,"[309] a work that arose out of "patriarchal/kyriarchal societies, cultures, and religions," and that "serves patriarchal . . . kyriarchal interests."[310] Therefore, the emphasis on "scripture alone" (*sola scriptura* and *claritas scriptura*) is problematic since it has not only been written by humans but by elite men.[311] Such androcentric ideologies distorted not only the writing but also the canonical formation of the Bible, since it was the winners of the debates who determined the canon.[312] This is why there is less mention of the contributions of women than men in the Bible.[313] Thus, the Bible is historically conditioned as well as "ideologically determined,"[314] and the Bible within the Christian tradition is the source of abuse and the silencing of women by elite men with kyriarchal interests.[315]

From her understanding of the locus of authority in biblical interpretation in the experiences of women,[316] Schüssler Fiorenza identifies these as including the experiences of women who were part of the historical Jesus movement, as well as others throughout history who have worked for justice.[317] In this light, theological statements such as "the Bible is the revealed Word of God" have been used as "norms for judging wo/men's experience."[318] There is thus a need for women to become subjects in the hermeneutical process, arriving

---

308. Schüssler Fiorenza, *Power of the Word: Scripture*, 64; Schüssler Fiorenza, *Bread Not Stone*, 10.

309. Schüssler Fiorenza, *Wisdom Ways*, 117. The word "androcentric" refers to "male-centeredness." Schüssler Fiorenza derives "kyriocentric" from the word kyriarchy, meaning "master-centered." She argues that structures of domination matter and suggests that "we replace the dualistic notions of patriarchy and androcentrism with the intersectional analytic of kyriarchy that is emperor, lord, slave-master, father, husband, elite educated male structures of domination and focus on its ideological kyriocentric discursive formation." This is a pyramidal system of domination in which women are at the bottom of the sociopolitical and religious pyramid. Schüssler Fiorenza, *"Power of the Word: Charting,"* 46; Schüssler Fiorenza, *But She Said*, 104–125; Schüssler Fiorenza, *Rhetoric and Ethics*, 5–6.

310. Schüssler Fiorenza, *Wisdom Ways*, 9.

311. Schüssler Fiorenza, *Power of the Word: Scripture*, 64.

312. Schüssler Fiorenza, *In Memory of Her*, 53. Schüssler Fiorenza argues that books such as *The Acts of Paul and Thecla* were not included in the canon for androcentric reasons.

313. Schüssler Fiorenza, *In Memory of Her*, 48.

314. Schüssler Fiorenza, *Power of the Word: Scripture*, 64.

315. Schüssler Fiorenza, *Bread Not Stone*, x.

316. Schüssler Fiorenza, xvi.

317. Schüssler Fiorenza, xvi.

318. Schüssler Fiorenza, *Wisdom Ways*, 168.

at meaning through the hermeneutical framework of the "discipleship of equals."[319] This can be accomplished by approaching the Bible as a historical "prototype"[320] of Christian community and life rather than as an unchanging "archetype."[321]

Although she views the Bible through its patriarchal lens, she finds signs of hope within the Bible and Christian tradition which resist the patriarchal overlay of the texts. She therefore suggests interpreting the Bible from a "critical commitment to the Christian community and tradition," since the Bible continues to influence and empower the lives of women around the world.[322]

Like Grudem, understanding the Bible is crucially important for Witherington given his view of the Bible as "the living Word."[323] He sees "Scripture as divine inspiration"[324] that claims "to be and is a word from, not merely about, God."[325] The source of the Bible is "God who inspires, speaks, and empowers the words with qualities that reflect the divine character."[326] He also shares Grudem's view of the Bible as both the words of God while being composed of human words.[327] However, he rejects the mechanical dictation view that sees God as dictating every word of Scripture to the human authors.[328] On the basis of his view of the Bible as the living word of God, he also rejects two claims of Schüssler Fiorenza that view the Bible as

---

319. Schüssler Fiorenza, *In Memory of Her*, 33.

320. Schüssler Fiorenza notes that seeing the Bible as a prototype allows women to reclaim the whole Bible as an "enabling resource, as bread not stone, as legacy and heritage, not only of patriarchal religion but also of women-church as the discipleship of equals." Schüssler Fiorenza, *Bread Not Stone*, xvii.

321. "Archetype" refers to an unchanging pattern and ideal form to be received as a universal principle and authoritative for all cultures and times. Schüssler Fiorenza, *Power of the Word: Scripture*, 67; Schüssler Fiorenza, *In Memory of Her*, 33; Schüssler Fiorenza, "Feminist Theology and New Testament," 44; and Schüssler Fiorenza, *Bread Not Stone*, 10.

322. Schüssler Fiorenza, *But She Said*, 137.

323. Witherington, *Living Word of God*, 13. Witherington sees the living word as including "an oral message," "an Incarnate person" who is Jesus himself, and finally "a text," particularly the Old Testament (the only Scripture in the time of the New Testament authors), which was certainly regarded as the inspired word of God in 2 Tim 3:16–17.

324. Witherington, xiii.

325. Witherington, xiv.

326. Witherington, 13.

327. Witherington, 36, explains the Bible as "always the word of God in human words whether it involves oracles where God speaks directly or some more indirect means of communication."

328. Witherington, *Living Word of God*, 21.

"containing the word of God" or "becoming the word of God."[329] These are problematic since the interpreter becomes the final authority. He sees the Bible as "making not only a truth claim but an objective claim on human beings in general, whether they are aware of it or respond to it or not."[330]

This understanding of the Bible leads Witherington to see the locus of meaning as residing in the text.[331] He also recognizes the important role of personal experiences, which he views as "windows into the Scripture,"[332] but warns that these experiences "must be normed by the Scriptures."[333] In his view, to suggest that reason, tradition, or experience has equal authority with the Bible or even higher authority is problematic, because even a genuine experience "does not in itself tell us the ethical or spiritual quality of the experience, or whether in the end it is good or bad for the person."[334] Thus, he points out the importance of keeping the Bible as the locus of authority in biblical interpretation.[335]

Against the backdrop of this discussion, we now turn our attention to the question of how they understand the role of the interpreter in the hermeneutical process.

4.3.2.2 *The Role of the Interpreter*

As mentioned in our discussion of the methodology of the selected contemporary interpreters, all three are aware of the subjective participation of the interpreter in determining meaning, and all agree on the existence of interpreters' biases in interpretation. However, some of them also see the possibility of being able to exclude, or at least minimize, those biases.

---

329. Schüssler Fiorenza, *Power of the Word: Scripture*, 64; Schüssler Fiorenza, *Bread Not Stone*, 10. Witherington sees such claims of Schüssler Fiorenza as "far from the claim made in 2 Timothy 3:16 that every Scripture is God-breathed," because "the very character of the document itself" is "truthful as God is truthful." Witherington, *Living Word of God*, 16.

330. Witherington, 16.

331. Witherington, *Conflict and Community*, xiv.

332. Witherington, *Living Word of God*, 160.

333. Witherington, 160.

334. Witherington, 160.

335. "Without the final objective norm of Scripture, it becomes difficult if not impossible to tell the difference between a heart-warming experience brought about by the work of the Spirit, and some sort of emotive 'spiritual' experience that is neither edifying for the person in question nor glorifying to God." Witherington, 160–161.

Grudem acknowledges the role of "culture, tradition, personal inclination . . . [and] personal predispositions" in influencing past and present interpretations,[336] but sees the possibility of interpreters excluding their subconscious influences, biases, and prejudices from the hermeneutical process. He advocates the careful consideration of other Bible passages as one way of keeping the influence of the interpreter's own biases to a minimum.[337] He also believes interpreters can keep the influence of their own biases to a minimum by searching their "motives and seek[ing] to empty self of that [which] would tarnish true perception of reality;" by praying "to God for humility, teachability, wisdom, insight, fairness and honesty," by making "every effort to submit one's mind to the unbending grammatical and historical reality of the biblical texts in Greek and Hebrew, using the best methods of study available to get as close as possible to the intentions of the biblical writers;" by testing "conclusions by history of exegesis to reveal any chronological snobbery or cultural myopia;" and by testing "conclusions in the real world of contemporary ministry and look[ing] for resonance from mature and godly people."[338]

Schüssler Fiorenza's view of the role of the interpreter in the hermeneutical processes is quite the opposite. She argues that every interpretation of the Bible has elements of bias, since all biblical interpretations are conditioned by the interpreter's present political interests which lead to selectively focusing on the "life setting"[339] of the biblical text. She thus rejects the historical-critical claim of "objectivist-factual understanding of biblical texts,"[340] which assumes a value-neutral approach to historical inquiry that insists that interpreters stand somehow outside of their own time. She sees such approaches as "radical detachment, emotional, intellectual and political distancing," a kind of "disinterested and dispassionate scholarship" which is unconstrained by "contemporary questions, values and interests."[341] A neutral approach is impossible for it is also filled with "presuppositions, commitments, beliefs, or cultural and institutional structures influencing the questions they raise

---

336. Piper and Grudem, "Overview of Central Concerns," 84.
337. Piper and Grudem, 90.
338. Piper and Grudem, 84.
339. Schüssler Fiorenza, *In Memory of Her*, xv.
340. Schüssler Fiorenza, 5.
341. Schüssler Fiorenza, "Biblical Interpretation," 387.

and the models they choose for interpreting their data."[342] The fact that the biblical exegete and theologian of today searches the Bible not "solely for the historical meaning of a passage, but also rais[ing] the question of the Bible's meaning and authority for today," also makes a neutral approach impossible.[343] Therefore, she considers the best approach to historical inquiry as requiring "reflecting critically on and naming one's theoretical presuppositions and political allegiances."[344]

Like Grudem and Schüssler Fiorenza, Witherington is aware of the role of presuppositions and biases that the interpreter brings into the interpretational process. He acknowledges that so often an interpreter comes to the biblical text with their own agenda, and so by partially clarifying and partially obscuring "the truth," "catches what it is intended to catch."[345] This is the link to "our presuppositions about the text, our ways of handling it, [which] dictate what sort of results we harvest."[346] Hence, he warns interpreters to recognize and admit their own faith postures, inclinations, or predispositions "before approaching the biblical text."[347] He sees the only way around the problems of the intrusion of the interpreter's agenda into the text is that of "careful, comprehensive, historical study of the relevant material," where one should first examine "what it meant to its author and audience in its original historical setting."[348] This involves the interpreters being aware of their own commitments and taking them into account in the interpretational process, even being open to correction. He sees such persons as "critical scholars" who are "capable of being self-critical and self-corrective, as well as being able to cast a discerning eye on this or that biblical text."[349]

All three interpreters acknowledge the role of the interpreter's presuppositions in the process of interpretation, and they agree also that there is no such thing as "purely objective" and "value-free" scholarship. However, Grudem sees a possibility for interpreters to exclude those influences through methods

---

342. Schüssler Fiorenza, *In Memory of Her*, xxii.
343. Schüssler Fiorenza, *Bread Not Stone*, 46.
344. Schüssler Fiorenza, *In Memory of Her*, xvii.
345. Witherington, *Women in the Ministry*, 22.
346. Witherington, 22.
347. Witherington, *Living Word of God*, 86–87.
348. Witherington, *Women in the Ministry*, 22.
349. Witherington, *Living Word of God*, 86–87.

that he has suggested, which I will show later as unsuccessful.[350] Schüssler Fiorenza maintains it is impossible to eliminate biases and thus sees hermeneutics as "reflecting critically on and naming one's theoretical presuppositions and political allegiances."[351] Although Witherington agrees with Grudem's view of the authority of the Bible, his understanding of the interpreter's role is closer to Schüssler Fiorenza's view that sees the impossibility of excluding one's presuppositions in the process of interpretation. These viewpoints lead to the next question, the influence of these three interpreters' sociological perspectives on their approach to biblical passages that command women to be silent.

4.3.2.3 Sociological Perspectives

The interpretations of the three contemporary interpreters not only hinge on how they see the locus of authority and the role of the interpreter, but also depend on their sociological perspectives. Grudem's sociological perspective centers on his views of patriarchy and hierarchy given a "complementarian" orientation.[352] Grudem disapproves of being called a "traditionalist" or "hierarchicalist."[353] He reasons that "traditionalist" implies "an unwillingness to let Scripture challenge traditional patterns of behavior" and "hierarchicalist" overemphasizes "structured authority while giving no suggestion of equality or the beauty of mutual interdependence."[354] He argues for a complementary view that sees men and women as being created "equal before God as persons and distinct in their manhood and womanhood," and believes that distinctions in the masculine and feminine roles are "ordained by God as part of the created order."[355]

Although he sees male dominance and male superiority as the result of sins "that have been seen in nearly all cultures in the history of the world,"[356]

---

350. Piper and Grudem, "Overview of Central Concerns," 84.
351. Schüssler Fiorenza, *In Memory of Her*, xvii.
352. See the history of this term in Grudem, *Evangelical Feminism*, 23–32.
353. Piper and Grudem, "Overview of Central Concerns," xiv.
354. Piper and Grudem, xiv.
355. Piper and Grudem, "The Danvers Statement," in *Biblical Manhood and Womanhood*, 470. The statement was prepared by the Council of Biblical Manhood and Womanhood meeting in Danvers, Massachusetts, in December 1988.
356. Grudem, *Evangelical Feminism*, 26.

he argues that the leadership of man is affirmed by God. God does this by creating role distinctions as part of the created order, such that male headship[357] in marriage was ordained before the fall.[358] He sees the headship of man as derived from the created order of Adam, the representation of Adam as the human race, who names woman, has a primary accountability role, and finds Eve created as his helper[359] before the fall.[360] He sees the salvation of Christ in the New Testament as reaffirming the order of male headship. Therefore, he believes that the Bible affirms the patriarchal nature of the family, where the father is responsible for leading, providing for, and protecting.[361] Acknowledging the problems in patriarchal cultures, Grudem finds that these evils are the result of sin and the abuse of male leadership, while patriarchy itself, its views and values, are not the problem.[362] In his view, the Bible affirms the wife's responsibility to respect her husband and serve as his helper in managing the home and nurturing children.[363]

Schüssler Fiorenza's sociological perspective derives from her view of the Bible as being deeply enmeshed not only in patriarchy but also in the structures of what she has termed "kyriarchy,"[364] a combination of patriarchy and androcentrism, highlighting the structures of power and domination of the "master."[365] In her view, speaking against the patriarchal power of the father alone is problematic, since this only focuses on exploitation and victimization of women by men based on gender and sex while ignoring the fact that women can be agents of domination over other women.[366] She argues that some women of elite status or some educated women have "mediated and

---

357. Grudem, "The Meaning of Kephalē ('Head')."

358. Grudem, *Evangelical Feminism*, 38.

359. Grudem, *Systematic Theology*, 462. Grudem agrees with Raymond Ortlund that "helper" here means that whenever someone helps someone else the person who is helping is occupying a subordinate or inferior position in relation to the person being helped. This implies that God is taking an inferior role as helper. See Ortlund, "Male-Female Equality," in Piper and Grudem, *Biblical Manhood and Womanhood*, 104.

360. Grudem, *Evangelical Feminism*, 30–40.

361. Grudem, 44.

362. Grudem, 147.

363. Grudem, 44.

364. As noted, Schüssler Fiorenza sees kyriarchy as a pyramidal system of domination, in which women are at the bottom of the sociopolitical and religious pyramid.

365. Schüssler Fiorenza, "Power of the Word: Charting," 46.

366. Schüssler Fiorenza, *Wisdom Ways*, 115.

supported prejudices and structures of domination in and through education and 'missionary' work."[367] Likewise, she sees speaking against the androcentric nature of biblical texts as problematic since it also only deals with "the power relation between the sexes."[368]

Schüssler Fiorenza sees the structures of kyriarchy or "kyriocentrism" inscribed in Christian Scriptures in and through household "codes of submission," just as in androcentrism.[369] She views this kyriocentric nature of Christian tradition as guilty of oppression, subordination, and injustice, and burdensome to women. It must be contested through ideological "kyriocentric discursive formation,"[370] which looks at the "socio-cultural, religious, and political system of elite male power, which does not only perpetrate the dehumanization of sexism, heterosexism, and gender stereotypes but also engenders other structures of women's oppression, such as racism, poverty, colonialism, and religious exclusivism."[371] Thus, she asks women not to leave the Christian tradition, but rather that "this tradition must be critically exorcised and rejected, wherever it is necessary."[372]

Like Grudem and Schüssler Fiorenza, Witherington's sociological perspective of patriarchy and hierarchy is important for understanding the influences behind his interpretation. Witherington describes his view as "the reformed patriarchal view,"[373] where he argues for a reaffirmation of the traditional concept of headship in the family and introducing new roles in the community of faith. He explains this as centering on "the concept of the *imago dei*"[374] in Genesis and "its renewal in Christ."[375] He notes that the relationship between male and female was broken after the fall, such that "to love and

---

367. Schüssler Fiorenza, 117. Schüssler Fiorenza gives black women's experience of slavery as an example. She notes that these women were abused not only by male masters but also by female masters.

368. Schüssler Fiorenza, 117.

369. Schüssler Fiorenza, 123.

370. Schüssler Fiorenza, 123.

371. Schüssler Fiorenza, *Power of Naming*, xxi; Schüssler Fiorenza, "Power of the Word: Charting," 47; Schüssler Fiorenza, *Wisdom Ways*, 121.

372. Schüssler Fiorenza, *Power of Naming*, 118.

373. Witherington, *Women in the Ministry*, 25.

374. Witherington, *Indelible Image*, 10. Witherington highlights the *imago dei* in Genesis as showing that "all human beings are created in God's image."

375. Witherington, 10.

cherish was turned into the curse to desire and to dominate ('Your desire will be for your husband, and he will lord it over you' [Gen 3:16]).["]376 Therefore, he sees the effects of this sin on the relationship between men and women as the ideology of domination and male superiority known as "patriarchy,"377 which is different from the "origin and purpose" of God's design for men and women that rested on "mutual dependency."378

Although his view shares some similarities with Grudem's complementarian view, Witherington considers Grudem's view of headship as God-ordained, permanent, male leadership over woman as problematic, since it leads to the permanent subordination of women and it also leads to the suggestion of the eternal subordination of Christ in the Godhead.379 He sees Grudem's view as guilty of following the pattern of the fall rather than the original design of God. What is needed is restoration from the "sporadic and broken relationship" between God and humankind, as well as the relationship between male and female "in order to have an ongoing positive relationship with God" and renew "human character so that the relationship can be both ongoing and positive."380 Thus, salvation should serve "not merely to restart a relationship, but to conform a group of people to the image of God's Son, who is the ultimate image of God ever to grace the earth with his presence."381 For Witherington, the story of Christ is "the hinge, crucial turning point, and climax of the entire larger drama."382 The story of Christ is the example to follow in dealing with patriarchy.

Witherington believes that Jesus did two things about patriarchy. First, "by not rejecting the traditional concept of headship,"383 Jesus did not reject the patriarchal framework of culture. In Witherington's view, Jesus came into a patriarchal cultural setting where "males, by nature of the culture, assume

---

376. Witherington, 317–318. Witherington argues that in the original creation order, with its distinctions that are God-ordained, "men are still men and women are still women," differentiated in "origin and purpose" that rest on "mutual dependency." See also Witherington, *Women and the Genesis*, 170.

377. Witherington, "Why Arguments against Women."

378. Witherington, *Women and the Genesis*, 170.

379. Witherington, "Eternal Subordination of Christ," quoting writings by Kevin Giles.

380. Witherington, *Indelible Image*, 10.

381. Witherington, 10.

382. Witherington, *Paul's Narrative Thought World*, 5.

383. Witherington, *Women in the Ministry*, 25.

the basic leadership role," and where they were "the heads of tribes, judges in the courts of law, heads of families and leaders in religious observances."[384] Since patriarchy was already normative in that time and place, Witherington believes that Jesus was attempting to reform patriarchal culture but not to reject the patriarchal framework of his culture.[385]

Second, Witherington sees Jesus as reforming the patriarchal culture by redefining the concept of headship and the leadership model of his kingdom into a model of "servants of all," where the headship takes the initiative in serving.[386] He sees Jesus as breaking both "biblical and rabbinic traditions that restricted women's roles in religious practices, and that He rejected attempts to devalue the worth of a woman, or her word of witness."[387] Furthermore, Jesus's willingness to accept women as disciples and traveling companions[388] and his teaching on the eunuchs and what defiled a person "effectively pave the way for women to play a vital part in His community. Anyone could have faith in and follow Jesus – He did not insist on any other requirements for entrance into His family of faith."[389] For Witherington, this possibility of new status and new roles being available for anyone who has faith in and follows Jesus influenced the influx of women into the community of Jesus, which continued even after Easter.[390]

Witherington sees Jesus as promoting a "balance between the old and the new" consistently throughout his teachings.[391] He argues that Jesus allowed women to have a significant place and status in ministry by combatting prejudice and double-standards, while at the same time trying to "strengthen

---

384. Witherington, "Women in Ministry," *The Asbury Herald* 108, no. 1 (Winter 1997).

385. "Jesus [sic] choice of and commissioning of the Twelve men both before and after His resurrection makes quite clear that Jesus was concerned about reformation, not rejection of the traditional concept of headship." Also, Witherington sees his teaching on marriage, family, and divorce as "views [that] remain within a patriarchal framework," showing the unfair treatment of women in adultery in Matt 19:9, showing his intolerance of the double standard of Jewish leaders in responding to a woman caught in adultery in John 7:53, and reaffirming male leadership in teaching on males taking responsibility for their own actions in Matt 5:27–28 and John 7:53. Witherington, *Women in the Ministry*, 25, 27; Witherington, *Women and the Genesis*, 49.

386. Witherington, *Women in the Ministry*, 25.

387. Witherington, 29.

388. Luke 8:1–3; 10:38–42.

389. Witherington, 29.

390. Witherington, 29.

391. Witherington, *Women and the Genesis*, 48.

women's traditional roles in the family."³⁹² Witherington finds Jesus's approach to be one of preserving a "healthy balance," an approach that is neither "feminist" nor "traditionalist."³⁹³

To summarize, the influence of the sociological perspectives of Grudem, Schüssler Fiorenza, and Witherington is noticeable in each of their interpretations. For example, the male headship concept of Grudem is consistently found in his explanation of 1 Corinthians 14:34–35. The tone of contestation is noticeable in Schüssler Fiorenza's interpretations.³⁹⁴ The concept of reforming the old is clearly visible in the interpretations of Witherington.³⁹⁵ Furthermore, these sociological perspectives not only serve as presuppositions that influence their interpretations, but they also provide the framework within which they approach the text. The following section looks at how the sociological perspectives of the interpreters are situated in their theoretical framework.

4.3.2.4 *Theoretical Frameworks*

Grudem admits that his complementarian position is guided by the "principle of male headship" as well as the "principle of male-female equality in the image of God."³⁹⁶ In response to the egalitarian critique that complementarianism is inconsistent when it applies the principle of male headship only to the home and the church, Grudem points out that "the principle of male headship is not the only principle in the Bible," and that "the principle of male-female equality in the image of God" is also included.³⁹⁷ He therefore concludes, "We are simply to obey the Bible in the specific application of these principles. What we find in the Bible is that God has given commands

---

392. Witherington, *Women in the Ministry*, 30, sees Jesus's teaching on male headship as entailing "extra responsibility not extra liberty" (Matt 5:27–32) and that it is also strengthening a woman's stature and security within the family. Jesus's teaching on men taking responsibility for their own lust as well as his teaching on divorce and marriage liberates women from a social stereotype of common Jewish teaching while reaffirming the traditional family structure. From that perspective, Witherington sees Jesus's teaching on singleness as a viable option since Jesus does not see a "conflict between the demands of [the] family of faith and of the physical family." Witherington, *Women and the Genesis*, 49–50.

393. Witherington, *Women in the Ministry*, 30.
394. Witherington, 30.
395. Witherington, 30.
396. Grudem, *Evangelical Feminism*, 392.
397. Grudem, 392.

that establish male leadership in the home and in the church, but that other teachings in His Word give considerable freedom in other areas of life. We should not try to require either more or less than Scripture itself requires."[398]

From this understanding, Grudem sees the teaching of manhood and womanhood as God's design applicable to the practical details of church life, which is the family of God. He notes that just as "in the home, the husband's loving, humble headship tends to be replaced by domination or passivity... in the church, sin inclines men toward a worldly love of power or an abdication of spiritual responsibility."[399] Grudem explains that while man and woman are "equally valuable to God and equally important to God's work in the church,"[400] they do not have "equality in functions."[401] He believes that these functional differences between men and women were clearly pointed out by Jesus. Examples include Jesus's choosing of twelve men as apostles in the Gospels, and also passages such as 1 Corinthians 14:33b–36, 1 Timothy 2:11–15, 1 Timothy 3:2, and Titus 1:5 where teaching and governing are roles or functions reserved for males.[402] He sees this male leadership as a consistent pattern in Scripture since creation and that it has been practiced consistently in the history of the church. He thus concludes that "some governing and teaching roles within the church are restricted to men."[403]

Schüssler Fiorenza's theoretical framework for feminist interpretation is her understanding of the *ekklesia* of women, which refers to a "democratic assembly/ congress."[404] She adds the phrase "of women" to *ekklesia* to indicate that the church will never be a complete democratic assembly without

---

398. Grudem, 393.

399. Piper and Grudem, *Biblical Manhood and Womanhood*, 470.

400. Grudem, *Evangelical Feminism*, 62, notes passages such as Acts 2:17–18 and Gal 3:28 as showing the biblical view of equality of value in the body of Christ.

401. Grudem, 63.

402. Grudem, 81–82.

403. Grudem, 98. For more detail, see the Danvers Statement of the Council on Biblical Manhood and Womanhood; affirmation 6 in Piper and Grudem, *Biblical Manhood and Womanhood*, 470.

404. Schüssler Fiorenza, *Wisdom Ways*, 128.

including women.[405] She notes that the *ekklesia* of women[406] includes the female disciples in Jesus's movement, where women were both disciples of Jesus and leading members of the early Christian communities.[407]

Applying historical criticism to the Gospels, she points out that Jesus of the Gospels is against the marginalization of women and that, therefore, female subordination is not part of the original gospel.[408] To the contrary, she sees Jesus as calling forth the discipleship of women as equally as men.[409] She describes the early Christian movement as a community that practiced equal discipleship where women were as actively engaged in leadership in the church as men. However, women's engagement in leadership created tension with "the patriarchal ethos of the Greco-Roman world."[410] This resulted in female subordination in the church. To restore Jesus's vision of a discipleship of equality, she seeks to restore the women's liberation movement that began during the early years of the church as a "Jesus movement."[411] This movement believes that the disciples of Jesus are called to "one and the same praxis of

---

405. Schüssler Fiorenza, *Discipleship of Equals*, 196. Although Schüssler Fiorenza originally saw the "ekklesia of women" exclusive of men, she later included men who identify with women's struggle for equality, authority, and citizenship in the church. See also Schüssler Fiorenza, *Discipleship of Equals*, 293, and *Jesus: Miriam's Child*, 27.

406. Schüssler Fiorenza created the inclusive word "wo/men" to refer to "the movement of self-identified women and self-identified men," and describe the identities of women as well as oppressed men in the church in this struggle of liberation. Schüssler Fiorenza, *Power of the Word: Scripture*, 6. See also *Bread Not Stone*, xiv; *But She Said*, 127; *Jesus: Miriam's Child*, 24–31. Also Matthews, Kittredge, and Johnson-Debaufre, *Walk in the Ways of Wisdom*, 5.

407. Schüssler Fiorenza, *In Memory of Her*, xx.

408. Schüssler Fiorenza, xx. She explains that this subordination happened later, since "the story of Jesus movement as an emancipatory *basileia tou theou* movement is told in different ways in the canonical and extra canonical Gospel accounts, which have undergone a lengthy process of rhetorical transmission and theological editing. The gospel writers did not simply write down what Jesus said and did. Rather, they utilized the Jesus tradition shaped by Jesus' first followers, women and men, or their own rhetorical interests and molded them in light of the political-theological debates of their own day." Schüssler Fiorenza, *Jesus: Miriam's Child*, 94; Schüssler Fiorenza, "Feminist Theology and New Testament," 37.

409. Schüssler Fiorenza, *In Memory of Her*, 34; Schüssler Fiorenza, "Feminist Theology and New Testament," 38. She adds, "the *basileia* [kingdom] vision of Jesus calls all women without exception to wholeness and selfhood, as well as to solidarity with those women who are impoverished, the maimed, and outcasts of our society and church." See also *In Memory of Her*, 153; *Discipleship of Equals*, 174–179.

410. Schüssler Fiorenza, *In Memory of Her*, 35; *Jesus: Miriam's Child*, 93.

411. Schüssler Fiorenza, *In Memory of Her*, 107; "Feminist Theology and New Testament," 38.

inclusiveness and equality lived by Jesus-Sophia," which means becoming a "discipleship of equals."[412]

Within this framework, feminist interpretation centers on correcting this lapse of memory by reconstructing "early Christian history as women's history . . . not only to restore women's stories to early Christian history but also to reclaim this story as the history of women and men."[413] She explains that women's struggle for liberation is not to become masculine or like men, but "to achieve the rights, benefits, and privileges and equal authorities and citizenship which are legitimately theirs but which are denied to them by the kyriarchal regimes of most societies and the major world religions."[414] This reconstructing of "women's heritage as church," a discipleship of equals as part of the *basileia* of God,[415] is at the heart of the theoretical framework that shapes her hermeneutical approach.

Witherington's understanding of the role of male and female in creation is important for his theoretical framework of a conservative egalitarian view. As mentioned, he frames his egalitarian view on "the concept of the *imago dei*" in Genesis and "its renewal in Christ."[416] From this understanding of Jesus reforming the patriarchal culture of his day as his theoretical framework, Witherington sees Paul as redefining the patriarchal culture, and thus argues that Paul is neither feminist nor patriarchal.[417]

Recognizing the aim of Jesus in redemption as the restoration of relationships between God and humankind as well as between male and female, Witherington views Paul's perspective as a "kingdom or eschatological orientation," which places emphasis not on "what men and women are by way of the creation order, but rather on what they now are in Christ."[418] Thus, Paul

---

412. Schüssler Fiorenza, *In Memory of Her*, 135.

413. Schüssler Fiorenza, xiv.

414. Schüssler Fiorenza, *Wisdom Ways*, 128.

415. Schüssler Fiorenza, *Discipleship of Equals*, 229–230, sees the *basileia* of God as a "political symbol that appealed to the oppositional imagination of people victimized by an imperial system [Roman Empire]." See also Schüssler Fiorenza, *Jesus: Miriam's Child*, 93.

416. Witherington, *Indelible Image*, 10.

417. Witherington, *Women in the Ministry*, 30.

418. Witherington, *Indelible Image*, 317. Witherington sees that this "already-not yet" eschatological perspective, "holds that God in Christ has already acted in history and has begun to transform humanity, a process that is not yet completed but will be completed at the end time." He sees Paul as focusing "on the final state of affairs breaking into human story, and this

was not only drawing from Jesus's teaching, but also working from this eschatological outlook of Jesus[419] and the transformed vision of Jesus which affirms new roles for women in the community of faith.[420] From this perspective, Paul allows women to take up new roles in the church as long as the creation order of male headship in the physical family is recognized and affirmed.[421] Witherington therefore sees Paul's writings as redefining, not rejecting, "the concept of male headship and leadership in light of Christian or biblical ideas."[422]

Within this theoretical framework, Witherington views Paul as encouraging women to exercise their spiritual gifts in "a way that did not involve the violation of their husband's headship" in their physical family setting and thus permitting women to be involved in new roles in the religious context, where he considered several women as his co-workers.[423] Like Jesus, Paul affirmed a transformed vision of the patriarchy in the physical family setting, while also affirming women's new roles in the community of faith. Witherington admits that Paul also "walked a difficult line between reaffirmation and reformation of the good that was part of the creation order, and the affirmation of new possibilities in Christ."[424] Hence, he argues that Paul is neither feminist nor patriarchal, but a balance between the two.[425]

The interpretational differences between these three interpreters can be traced to their presuppositions. Like Grudem, Witherington's view can be traced back to his understanding of the distinctive functions of man and woman in creation.[426] He shares Grudem's view of Jesus's choice of male disciples as staying within the ideology of patriarchy. However, his view also differs significantly from Grudem in his explanation of headship, where Grudem sees headship in creation as a validation of universal male leadership

---

relativizes all worldly institutions, including marriage" for "the form of this world is passing away" (1 Cor 7:31)." Witherington, *Indelible Image*, 317–318.

419. Witherington, *Paul's Narrative Thought World*, 153.
420. Witherington, *Indelible Image*, 317–318; Witherington, *Women and the Genesis*, 238.
421. Witherington, *Women and the Genesis*, 179.
422. Witherington, 248.
423. Witherington, 248.
424. Witherington, 179.
425. Witherington, *Women in the Ministry*, 30.
426. Grudem, *Evangelical Feminism*, 63.

in the church,[427] but Witherington sees this as the headship of man over his own family, in the sense that "headship comes to mean head servant, or taking the lead in serving."[428] Like Schüssler Fiorenza, Witherington sees Jesus as the center for changing the role of women in the church. However, he disagrees with Schüssler Fiorenza's view of Jesus as the liberator of women from their patriarchal and hierarchical context, for he sees Jesus as neither feminist nor patriarchal. Witherington shares her view of women as actively engaged in leadership in the early church, just as men were during and after Jesus's time, and that Jesus's attitude toward women helped change the roles of women in the emerging church.[429]

This discussion also reveals that interpreters' presuppositions influence not only the meaning they discern in texts but also the whole hermeneutical process. The hermeneutical presuppositions of the three contemporary interpreters highlight their views on the locus of authority in interpretation and their understanding of their own role as interpreters in the hermeneutical process. Further, we have seen how their sociological perspectives provide a foundation for their theoretical framework in approaching the biblical texts. All of these hermeneutical presuppositions provide insights into their interpretation of the passages in the Bible that command women to be silent. The following section looks at how these presuppositions further influence their choice of a starting point in the hermeneutical process related to 1 Corinthians 14:34–35.

4.3.3 Hermeneutical Processes Relating to 1 Corinthians 14:34–35

In examining the hermeneutical process of Grudem, Schüssler Fiorenza, and Witherington in relation to 1 Corinthians 14:34–35, it was inevitable that their hermeneutical presuppositions influenced how they interpreted the texts that command women to be silent. In particular, their presuppositions influenced their choice of starting point for interpreting these texts. This choosing or prioritizing of a text, namely a starting point, likewise influenced their hermeneutical results. We begin, therefore, by identifying the starting

---

427. Piper and Grudem, *Biblical Manhood and Womanhood*, 470.
428. Witherington, *Women and the Genesis*, 245.
429. Schüssler Fiorenza, *In Memory of Her*, 135.

points of each of the interpreters in approaching 1 Corinthians 14:34–35 and then investigate how this continues to influence these interpreters as they analyze Paul's overall attitude to women in connection to the passages that command women to be silent.

4.3.3.1 Starting Points in the Interpretational Process

Looking at the hermeneutical processes of Grudem, Schüssler Fiorenza, and Witherington regarding 1 Corinthians 14:34–35, two Scripture passages are often mentioned in their interpretation of the texts that command women to be silent. These texts are Galatians 3:28 and 1 Timothy 2:11–14. Although they warn that choosing another text as a starting point is problematic, their interpretations of 1 Corinthians 14:34–35 indicate that they have done so. Possibly due to the influences of their sociological perspectives and theoretical frameworks, their interpretations mention or emphasize some Scripture texts more than others. These texts are emphasized to the point that they become central to their interpretation of the texts that command women to be silent. This section evaluates the three interpreters' usage of these texts in interpreting 1 Corinthians 14:34–35.

Grudem considers that choosing one text as a "hermeneutical priority" or starting point weakens the authority of Scripture, because it suggests being subject to "some parts of Scripture and not others."[430] However, he acknowledges some texts do receive more emphasis than others,[431] and perhaps this is the case with respect to his usage of 1 Timothy 2:11–14. Acknowledging that his hermeneutics is guided by "the principle of male leadership," and highlighting 1 Timothy 2:12 as a "complementarian text,"[432] Grudem finds the male leadership in the church mentioned in 1 Timothy 2:12 important for understanding the 1 Corinthians 14:34–35 text.

According to Grudem, among the biblical passages that address restricting "some governing and teaching roles in the church to men," 1 Timothy 2:11–15 is the most directly relevant passage.[433] He points out that this passage appears in the context of "the assembled church" (1 Tim 2:8–10), and that "Paul does

---

430. Grudem, *Evangelical Feminism*, 368.
431. Grudem, 369.
432. Grudem, 369.
433. Grudem, 65.

not allow a woman to teach and have authority[434] over a man in the assembled church, where Bible teaching takes place." He believes that the kind of teaching Paul has in mind is "Bible teaching," or "preaching and teaching the word of the Lord, which is reserved for male leaders only."[435] He reasons that Paul in these verses is affirming male leadership by arguing from the creation story where Adam was formed first, meaning that "God was giving a leadership role to Adam."[436] Since Eve was deceived first, he sees Paul as highlighting the "differences in preferences and inclinations" of men and women.[437] In this framework, God gave men a "rational" disposition toward "teaching and governing in the church"[438] and women a "relational" disposition that inclines toward "nurturing" in the church. From this understanding, Grudem concludes that this command for women is not a specific instruction only for Ephesus[439] nor a temporary command.[440] He sees male leadership as transcending "cultures and societies."[441]

Given this understanding of male leadership, Grudem argues that 1 Corinthians 14:33b–36 "is consistent with the teachings of the rest of the New Testament on appropriate roles for women in the church," and that "speaking out and judging prophecies before the assembled congregation is a governing role over the assembled church, and Paul reserves that role for men."[442] He adds, "as in 1 Tim 2:11–15, this distinction comes to focus in the

---

434. Grudem, 306. According to Grudem, this usage of "αὐθεντεῖν" is in the sense of the normal, neutral exercise of authority, meaning to "have authority." He sees this authority as not in the sense of wrongful practice, abuse of authority, or a domineering use of authority in the negative sense.

435. Grudem, 66, mentions Acts 15:35; 18:11; 1 Cor 14:47; 1 Tim 4:11; 6:2; 2 Tim 2:2; 3:16 to support his argument.

436. Grudem, 67.

437. Grudem, 70, 298. He does not see the usage of "ἀνήρ" and "γυνή" as referring to husband and wife here since the context is not that of marriage. He also does not think that Paul's reference to Eve being deceived first shows the "intellectual inferiority of women."

438. "A disposition that is better suited to teaching and governing in the church, a disposition that inclines more to rational, logical analysis of doctrine and a desire to protect the doctrinal purity of the church." Grudem, 72.

439. Grudem, *Evangelical Feminism*, 280. He notes that the false teachers named at Ephesus are men, not women. No clear proof of women teaching false doctrine at Ephesus has been found either in or outside the Bible.

440. Grudem, 301. He also explains that the present indicative tense in the command "ἐπιτρέπεται" in the phrase "I do not permit" means it "cannot be . . . a temporary command."

441. Grudem, 69.

442. Grudem, 79, 235.

prohibition of women from exercising doctrinal and ethical governance, even from time to time, over the congregation."[443] He concludes that 1 Corinthians 14:33b–35 "fits well with a consistent Pauline advocacy of women's participation without governing authority in the assembled church."[444]

Schüssler Fiorenza believes it is important to state one's assumptions upfront. She admits that her feminist hermeneutics, like other approaches to biblical interpretation, represents "a political act."[445] Hence, the starting point for her feminist critical interpretation must begin with "women's experience in their struggle for liberation,"[446] but not with "certain biblical texts."[447] She argues that using a certain biblical text to interpret another is a "canon within the canon," meaning "a theological criterion and measuring rod with which to assess the truth and authority of the various biblical texts and traditions."[448] That said, the issues concerning women presented in the whole Corinthians context must be viewed as a modification of women's self-understanding in Galatians 3:28.

Schüssler Fiorenza finds that women's self-understanding in Galatians 3:28 comes from the believers' realization of their received status of equality in Christ through their baptismal declaration, being "the new creation."[449] Baptism in Christ initiates a believer into a new creation, in which all distinctions of status between Jews and Greeks, free and slave, male and female are abolished, thus giving them all "religious equality."[450] She sees this religious equality in Christ generating changes in social roles and the ecclesiastical status of the women, "because in Judaism religious differences according to the law were to [be] expressed in communal behavior and social practice."[451] This concept of a new creation creates opportunities for women to become "full members of the people of God with the same rights and duties" as men.[452]

---

443. Grudem, *Gift of Prophecy*, 224.
444. Grudem, 224.
445. Schüssler Fiorenza, *In Memory of Her*, 32.
446. Schüssler Fiorenza, *Bread Not Stone*, 13.
447. Schüssler Fiorenza, 14.
448. Schüssler Fiorenza, *Bread Not Stone*, 12; Schüssler Fiorenza, *But She Said*, 142, and "Power of the Word: Charting," 64.
449. Schüssler Fiorenza, *In Memory of Her*, 210.
450. Schüssler Fiorenza, 210.
451. Schüssler Fiorenza, 210.
452. Schüssler Fiorenza, 210.

In this new creation, women's role are no longer determined by "family and kinship"[453] or "sexual dimorphism," which is socializing people "into sex and gender roles as soon as they are born according to their biological differentiation as male and female as well as cultural, racial and social differences."[454]

Thus, for Schüssler Fiorenza, "there is no male and female" in Galatians 3:28 refers to the equality of "the social roles" between men and women in the sight of God, but is not "a denial of biological sex differences."[455] In other words, oneness in Christian baptism is not "anthropological oneness but ecclesiological oneness or unity in Christ Jesus."[456] The usage of "there is no male and female" also refers to "marriage and gender relationships," such that patriarchal marriage and sexual relationships between male and female are "no longer constitutive of the new community in Christ."[457] This new creation in Christ gives women a new identity, which is defined by "discipleship and empowering with the Spirit."[458] This will bring forth an inescapable change for women in their ecclesial-social status and function, just as it did for Jewish and Gentile Christians.

Schüssler Fiorenza regards Galatians 3:28 not as "a Pauline 'peak formulation' or a theological breakthrough achieved by Paul," but belonging to the pre-Pauline "theological self-understanding of the Christian missionary movement."[459] She traces this understanding of egalitarian leadership as

---

453. Schüssler Fiorenza, 210.

454. Schüssler Fiorenza, 213, explains, "Sexual dimorphism and strictly defined gender roles are products of a patriarchal culture, which maintain and legitimize structures of control and domination – the exploitation of women by men. Gal 3:28 not only advocates the abolition of the religious-cultural divisions and of the domination and exploitation wrought by institutional slavery but also of domination based on sexual divisions. It repeats with different categories and words that within the Christian community no structures of dominance can be tolerated. Gal 3:28 is therefore best understood as a communal Christian self-definition rather than a statement about the baptized individual. It proclaims that in the Christian community all distinctions of religion, race, class, nationality and gender are insignificant. All the baptized are equal, they are one in Christ."

455. Schüssler Fiorenza, 211. She sees the main issue here as the Galatians' view that male and female must marry and have children to be truly in Christ, which is the traditional way of reading the creation story in Genesis 1–2, with its command, "be fruitful and multiply."

456. Schüssler Fiorenza, 214.

457. Schüssler Fiorenza, 211. Schüssler Fiorenza argues that this usage of "male and female" as a pair is alluding to Gen 1:27, where "humanity [was] created in the image of God as 'male and female' in order to introduce the theme of procreation and fertility."

458. Schüssler Fiorenza, 213.

459. Schüssler Fiorenza, 199.

originating from two groups of women prior to Paul, one of which worshipped the goddess Sophia as an aspect of the godhead and the other which followed Jesus-Sophia as Messiah and in both groups, women held important leadership roles.[460] She sees Paul's acceptance of these women leaders arising from a sense of obligation and says, "he probably has no other choice than to do so," because these women already "occupied leadership functions and were on his level in the early Christian Missionary movement."[461] Thus, Paul's command for women to be silent in 1 Corinthians 14:34–35 shows the problems among family relationships in the church caused by a new religious vision that denied all male "religious prerogatives in the Christian community based on gender roles. Just as born Jews had to abandon the privileged notion that they alone were the chosen people of God, so masters had to relinquish their power over slaves, and husbands that over wives and children."[462]

Schüssler Fiorenza sees that this new understanding among the Corinthian women created tension in family relationships and brought disorder into the church. For that reason, Paul, having a missionary concern about order in the church, and given the danger of misunderstanding by outsiders, asks the Corinthian "wives" to be silent in the church by appealing to them to undertake culturally appropriate behavior.[463] Although she sees Paul as not restricting women's involvement in the church, she notes that the command in 1 Corinthians 14:34–35 paves the way for students of Paul to later impose strict restrictions on women's leadership in the church.[464]

Like Schüssler Fiorenza, Witherington's understanding of Galatians 3:28 is important in explaining his view of the role of women in 1 Corinthians 14 and 1 Timothy 2. He sees Galatians 3:28 as the "Magna Carta[465] not only of

---

460. Schüssler Fiorenza, 130–140.

461. Schüssler Fiorenza, 50.

462. Schüssler Fiorenza, 218.

463. Schüssler Fiorenza, 218, notes that it was "this egalitarian ethos of 'oneness in Christ' preached by the pre-Pauline and Pauline Christian missionary movement provided the occasion for Paul's injunction concerning the behavior of women prophets in the Christian community."

464. Schüssler Fiorenza, 220.

465. Stendahl, *Bible and the Role of Women*; Scanzoni and Hardesty, *All We're Meant to Be*; Russell, *Human Liberation*; Jewett, *Man as Male and Female*; Mollenkott, *Women, Men, and the Bible*.

true humanity but of Christian freedom,"[466] and refers to it as the "Emancipation Proclamation for Women."[467] Unlike Grudem, who sees the Galatians 3:28 passage as having spiritual implications for an individual's access only into the body of Christ, Witherington asserts that Paul's statement is not "merely about the believer's position," but that "it has social implications for the covenant community and women's status in *ekklesia*."[468] This is also the view of Schüssler Fiorenza. Witherington sees Paul's declaration as meaning that a female does not have to be linked to a male to have a place in the church community, so that the door to ministry is being opened to women, including the ministry of single men and women.[469]

Like Schüssler Fiorenza, Witherington also sees Paul's declaration that there is no longer Jew or Gentile, slave or free, and male or female having clear social implications,[470] and considers that Paul knew that social implications for males and females were inevitable "in the light of being one in Christ and being in the light of new creation."[471] However, Witherington warns that these implications do not mean that ethnic, social, and sexual distinctions simply disappear in Christ, rather that "in the new creation the old is transformed and transfigured."[472] This transformation means that although the ethnic, social, and sexual distinctions continue to exist, in Christ "they do not determine one's soteriological, spiritual, or social standing in the body of Christ, nor do they determine the ministerial roles one can play in Christ. That is a matter of who is called and who is gifted by the Spirit to do certain tasks in the church."[473] In other words, the leadership structures in the church

---

466. Witherington, *What's in the Word*, 120. Also Witherington, "Rite and Rights for Women." Witherington also mentions the opposite view from Magna Carta of humanity or emancipation proclamation for women as *coram Deo*, which sees that there is no implications for social relations within the body of Christ.

467. Witherington, "Rite and Rights for Women," 593.

468. Witherington, 600.

469. Witherington, 600.

470. Schüssler Fiorenza, *In Memory of Her*, 213. Witherington, *What's in the Word*, 120, points out that Paul affirms the social implications of being neither Jew nor Gentile in Christ when he says that he can be a Jew to the Jew and a Gentile to the Gentile in 1 Cor 9 and Phil 3:4–9, and when he asks Onesimus to treat Philemon "no longer as a slave, but as a brother in Christ."

471. Witherington, 120.

472. Witherington, 120.

473. Witherington, 120.

for Paul are not based on gender but rather on individual gifting and the graces of the Holy Spirit.

Unlike Grudem,[474] Witherington sees 1 Timothy 2:11–14 as Paul writing to correct "specific problems affecting worship" where some women's behavior had taken on the negative sense of "*authenteo*," which means to "usurp authority," in the sense of domineering.[475] He sees the usage of Genesis texts in 1 Timothy 2:11–14 as indicating that these women were not properly instructed just as Eve was not properly instructed.[476] Therefore, he interprets this text as Paul saying that he was "currently not allowing" these women to teach since they "need to be learning,"[477] which is quite different from Grudem's interpretation that women should not teach since they are more susceptible to deception, as was Eve. Witherington characterizes this passage as "situation-specific advice," not a universal prohibition of women teaching, since Priscilla and Aquila were mentioned in this role in 2 Timothy 4:19.[478]

Witherington's understanding of headship in Ephesians 5:22 is also important in his interpretation of 1 Corinthians 14. As mentioned, his theoretical framework in interpreting Paul's passages on women is "the concept of the *imago dei*" and "its renewal in Christ."[479] He sees Paul working from a trajectory in which the image of God is being renewed through the redemptive work of Christ. This renewal in Christ does not eliminate the headship of man found in the order of creation, but transforms it to the concept of Christ's headship, where headship means taking responsibility as the head servant. He sees the term "head" as meaning "one's role and behavior in an

---

474. Grudem, *Evangelical Feminism*, 317. This view is shared by Schreiner, "Interpretation of 1 Timothy 2:9–15," 102–104.

475. Witherington, *Women and the Genesis*, 192; Witherington, *Women in the Ministry*. He sees 1 Tim 2:11-14 in the context of grumbling men in 1 Tim 2:8 and certain women in 1 Tim 2:8-15. He suggests the passage should be understood from the larger context of 1 Timothy, where Paul wants the older women to instruct the young women, which is an indication that Paul is not prohibiting women from all kinds of teaching.

476. Witherington, *Letters and Homilies*, 231. Witherington believes Paul is saying, "Eve is like these women, inadequately instructed and therefore not prepared for the confrontation she has."

477. Witherington, 232.

478. Witherington, *Women and the Genesis*, 196.

479. Witherington, *Indelible Image*, 10; Witherington, *Women and the Genesis*, 248.

ongoing relationship," rather than "source, as in the source of a river,"[480] and "more responsibility" but not "more privilege" or "authority."[481] Therefore, he sees Paul as writing here to the husband to say that headship means "to take initiative in active loving and self-sacrificial serving as Christ has done for the Church. Head would then mean head servant, and we are reminded that the definition of 'the one who would be greatest' is the one who serves (Luke 22:24–27)."[482] His explanation of headship is thus different from Grudem's literal meaning that sees head as the authority of the one taking the lead.

Given this understanding, Witherington sees Paul in Ephesians 5:21 as calling "for mutual submission of all Christians to each other which includes, of course, marital partners. This does not lead the author to speak of totally interchangeable roles."[483] For Witherington, Paul not only wants the headship pattern to be maintained in the physical family, as mentioned above, but also wants this headship pattern to be expressed when "the family of faith meets in worship."[484] He sees Paul as asserting the headship pattern in two ways: first, "with the head coverings in 1 Corinthians 11,"[485] and second, "by a command to silence in 1 Corinthians 14 and an insistence that one direct one's questions to husbands at home."[486] He sees Paul as reminding the Corinthians that new creation does not obliterate the original creation order distinctions in 1 Corinthians 11, and that men are still men and women are still women,

---

480. Witherington, *Women and the Genesis*, 158. Witherington reasons that whenever Paul wishes to talk about the roles or functions, "he speaks of headship and submission," and that Eph 5 is written in the context of Christ's headship over the church.

481. Witherington, *Paul's Narrative Thought World*, 310.

482. Witherington, *Women and the Genesis*, 158.

483. Witherington, 156.

484. Witherington, *Paul's Narrative Thought World*, 310.

485. Witherington, *Women and the Genesis*, 167–170. Regarding the headship pattern in 1 Cor 11, Witherington sees "head" in Eph 5:22 as a reference to "one's role and behavior in an ongoing relationship," and "head" in 1 Cor 11 as "source or origin." He reasons that "head" in 1 Cor 11 is metaphorically talking about "Christ as the source of all men," "God being the origin or source of Christ," and "the source of man and women in verses 8–9," which would mean that man (not her husband but Adam) is the ultimate source of woman. He follows the traditional interpretation of 1 Cor 11 regarding the creation order, where man was not created for the sake of woman but was made before her in Gen 2, and that woman is made for the sake of man. Woman is the glory of man and woman's hair is her own glory. The phrase "to have an *exousia* on/over her head" is translated here as meaning "an authority which women had to have to do what they were apparently doing which she would otherwise not be able to do."

486. Witherington, *Paul's Narrative Thought World*, 310.

by asking them to wear "a head covering in worship."[487] Again, he points out that Paul is both reaffirming the creation order, which is of the old, and establishing something new, which is women praying and prophesying in worship.[488]

Witherington understands Paul's concept of headship as the climax of the redemption narrative which leads to an ethic that focuses on the imitation of Christ's servant leadership.[489] Paul is seen as reaffirming the role of man in creation, a leadership role within the physical family, while introducing the greater involvement of women in the church.[490] In other words, he sees Paul as affirming the traditional patriarchal obligations for women while instilling the concept of freedom for women in a way that does not "involve the violation of their husband's headship."[491] From this perspective, Witherington sees Paul as addressing women and men "both in 1 Cor 11 and 1 Cor 14," who thought their new status in Christ through baptism (Gal 3:28) obliterated "such distinctions and ordering patterns."[492]

The interpretations of all three interpreters are guided by their presuppositions, which in turn influenced their choosing and emphasizing particular Scripture texts to support their interpretation of 1 Corinthians 14:34–35. Although some of them refer to choosing a Scripture text as "emphasizing," the above analysis of their interpretations demonstrates that those selected texts influenced their interpretations. It is reasonable to conclude that their presuppositions, including their sociological perspectives and theoretical frameworks, influence their starting point in interpreting 1 Corinthians 14:24–35. In short, their presuppositions play an influential role in their hermeneutical processes. This leads to a question concerning how these three interpreters understand Paul's relationship with several women mentioned in his writings as co-workers and leaders in the church. Thus, the following section examines how these interpreters address Paul's overall attitudes

---

487. Witherington, *Women and the Genesis*, 169–170. Witherington sees the value of head covering in this way: "(1) it preserves the order in worship – only God's glory is to be revealed there, and (2) it authorizes women to pray and prophesy without denying the creation order distinctions."

488. Witherington, *Women and the Genesis*, 171.

489. Witherington, *Paul Quest*, 111.

490. Witherington, *Paul's Narrative Thought World*, 310.

491. Witherington, *Women and the Genesis*, 248.

492. Witherington, *Paul's Narrative Thought World*, 310.

toward women in their hermeneutical process regarding 1 Corinthians 14:34–35.

4.3.3.2 Paul's Overall Attitudes toward Women and the Interpretational Process

Grudem, Schüssler Fiorenza, and Witherington all agree that Paul allowed the Corinthian women to pray and prophesy in public, as 1 Corinthians 11 shows. But although they agree that Paul recognized women's involvement in the church and offered words of appreciation to these women, they differ on the level of women's involvement in the church and Paul's attitude toward these women. This shows how the interpreters' presuppositions influence their view of Paul and his attitudes toward women. In this section, we will see how Grudem, Schüssler Fiorenza, and Witherington understand the extent of women's involvement in the early churches and how they interpret Paul's attitude toward women in 1 Corinthians 14:34–35, based on their understanding of Paul's overall attitudes toward women in the church.

According to Grudem, women's involvement in the early church did not include authoritative speaking.[493] Grudem's hermeneutical assumption of the principle of male leadership influences his view of Pauline attitude toward women and their role, and this is found in his interpretations of women's involvement in the church as deacons, apostles, teachers, and prophets. Concerning the role of women as deacons, Grudem considers that Paul accepted women as deacons in Romans 16, because "the office of deacons in the New Testament does not include the governing and teaching authority that is reserved for elders."[494] He points out that although there were women deacons in some parts of the early church, " they did not have teaching in the churches."[495] He explains the deacons' tasks mentioned in Acts 20:17 and 1 Timothy 5:17 as "practical service to the needs of the congregation," whereas elders teach (1 Tim 3:2) and govern (1 Tim 3:5).[496] Concerning the role of apostle for women in the church, Grudem notes that the role of Junia in

---

493. Grudem, "Prophecy – Yes,," 18.
494. Grudem, *Evangelical Feminism*, 263.
495. Grudem, 266.
496. Grudem, 266.

Romans 16 was not the same as "apostles in the sense of the Twelve or Paul."[497] While admitting that Junia could be a woman,[498] the "apostle" reference for her carries only the sense of "church messenger," "one who is sent," which Paul uses elsewhere in his writings, as in 2 Corinthians 8:23, "referring to the men who were accompanying Paul in bringing money to Jerusalem," or Philippians 2:25, where Paul tells the Philippians that Epaphroditus is "your messenger and minister[ed] to my need."[499]

Concerning the teaching role of women in the church, Grudem regards the teaching of Priscilla, who taught Apollos in Acts 18:26, as private teaching that includes "private discussion and in small group Bible studies, as Christians everywhere have done for centuries."[500] Although the same word, ἐκτίθημι "explain or expound," also appears in Acts 28:23, where Paul was expounding the kingdom of God, Grudem sees Paul's teaching in Acts 28 as public teaching.[501] He differentiated the teaching of Priscilla as less authoritative than Paul. For women like Euodia and Syntyche in Philippians 4:2, where Paul calls them "co-workers," Grudem argues that Paul's naming them as such does not imply that they had "equal authority to Paul, or that they had the office of elder or that they taught or governed in any New Testament churches."[502] Grudem points out that since teaching provided the doctrinal and ethical guidance for the New Testament church, there is a close connection "between the role of elder," and "the role of teacher" (1 Tim 3:2; 5:17; Titus 1:9) where authoritative teaching is reserved only for male leadership.[503]

---

497. Grudem, 227.

498. Grudem mentions that the name Junia (Ἰουνίαν in Greek) could be either a man's name or a woman's name, because in Greek "this could be either masculine of feminine." He lists differences in translations: "Junias" is used in NIV, NASB, RSV, ASV, and "Junia" in KJV, NJKV, NRSV, NLT, ESV. Grudem also argues that οἵτινές εἰσιν ἐπίσημοι ἐν τοῖς ἀποστόλοις means "well-known to the apostles," not "well-known among the apostles," from the usage of the dative case with ἐν. Thus, he sees that whether Junia is man or woman is not significant for it "does not even name Junia (Junias) as an apostle." See Grudem, 224–225. Witherington also refers to Junia as a woman. See Witherington, *Women in the Earliest Churches*, 115.

499. Grudem, *Evangelical Feminism*, 226.
500. Grudem, 178.
501. Grudem, 179.
502. Grudem, 248.
503. Grudem, "Prophecy – Yes," 18.

Concerning the prophetic role of women in the church, Grudem believes that Paul allows this role for women because prophecy does not require the same authority as scriptural or apostolic teaching. He argues that Paul sees prophecies in the New Testament as unlike prophecies in the Old Testament,[504] because the prophecies in the Old Testament were "based on something that God had brought to mind or 'revealed,' something that was then reported in the prophet's own words" and "did not consist of the interpretation and application of Scripture."[505] Such prophecies are different from teaching, which is "an explanation or application of Scripture" that is "equal to Scripture in authority."[506] The activity of New Testament prophets does not consist of teaching or the interpretation and application of Scripture. Thus, Grudem sees the prophetic role of Philip's four unmarried daughters in Acts 21:9 as not problematic for Paul.

Based on these understandings, Grudem concludes that 1 Corinthians 14:34–35 does not contradict 1 Corinthians 11, because Paul is not prohibiting women from prophesying. He sees Paul as affirming an abiding principle of male headship or male leadership in 1 Corinthians 14:34–35, as Paul prohibits women from "speaking aloud to judge prophecies," which would indicate a "'governing' or 'ruling' function in the congregation."[507]

According to Schüssler Fiorenza, as I have noted, women's extensive involvement in the various expressions of ministry in the early church occurred before Paul and Paul accepted these women leaders since they were already active in the church before him.[508] However, overall, she finds Paul's view of women puzzling. She reasons that Paul accepted women as leaders in the church, valued them as co-workers, and even expressed his gratitude for them by listing several names of women as leading missionaries and respected heads of churches in Romans 16 and 1 Corinthians.[509] At the same time, Paul then restricts the ministry involvement of wives on the grounds of holiness,

---

504. Grudem, *Gift of Prophecy*, 25.
505. Grudem, "Prophecy – Yes," 17; Also in Grudem, *Gift of Prophecy*, 67.
506. Grudem, "Prophecy – Yes," 17.
507. Grudem, *Gift of Prophecy*, 223.
508. Schüssler Fiorenza, *In Memory of Her*, 50.
509. Schüssler Fiorenza, 47–50.

mentioning virgins as holy in 1 Corinthians 7 and thus suggesting that wives were less pure and holy.[510]

This apparent contradiction makes Schüssler Fiorenza wonder how Paul could have made "such a theological point when he had Prisca as his friend and knew other missionary couples who were living examples [that] his theology was wrong."[511] She concludes that Paul's previous expression of appreciation for women as co-workers was out of obligation, since women like Junia and Prisca had already occupied leadership positions before him and were "on his level in the early Christian missionary movement."[512]

As a result, Schüssler Fiorenza assesses Paul as being among those who hold patriarchal views and values. She sees evidence of this in Paul's referring to himself as a "father of the community."[513] It is because of his patriarchal views and values that he restricts the active participation of wives in the "affairs of the Lord" in 1 Corinthians 7:34 and 9:5,[514] and then limits the pneumatic participation of women in worship in 1 Corinthians 11 and 14.[515] Thus, Paul's expressed appreciation of women in ministry mentioned in Romans 16 is less important than his restrictions on women elsewhere. Schüssler Fiorenza's view of Paul as a person steeped in patriarchy influences her interpretive choices.

According to Witherington, Paul recognizes the ministries of women not out of obligation but in genuine appreciation.[516] He notes that Paul does not prohibit women from any sort of teaching ministry but, rather, values them and relies on them to help him continue his ministry to the Gentiles. This makes his view of Paul's attitude toward women a contrast to Grudem's view. Although Grudem sees the usage of the word "co-worker" as not referring to someone of equal authority as Paul, Witherington understands this term "co-worker" in 1 Corinthians 16:16 and 1 Thessalonians 5:12 as Paul's favorite description for one who aided him in his ministry, meaning someone who

---

510. Schüssler Fiorenza, 235.
511. Schüssler Fiorenza, 226.
512. Schüssler Fiorenza, 50.
513. Schüssler Fiorenza, 234.
514. Schüssler Fiorenza, 233.
515. Schüssler Fiorenza, 233.
516. Witherington, *Women in the Earliest Churches*, 116.

has a "leadership" role "involving some form of authoritative speech."[517] This term is used with reference to women in 1 Corinthians 11:14 and in Philippians 4:2–3 to refer to the two women, Euodia and Syntyche, who worked together with Paul in the spreading of the gospel.[518]

Witherington also points out that Paul mentions several women in Romans 16:1–16 as co-workers, including Phoebe, and the husband-and-wife team of Priscilla and Aquila. Paul further mentions Mary as a hard worker, another Christian husband-and-wife ministry team Andronicus and Junia – as "outstanding" and "among the apostles,"[519] Tryphaena and Tryphosa, probably two sisters, as workers in the Lord, and Persis as someone beloved and who labored hard "in the Lord."[520] Regarding Junia mentioned in Romans 16, he takes the term "apostle" here as meaning "itinerant missionary," since Andronicus and Junia were engaged in evangelism and church planting.[521]

Witherington rejects Grudem's view that Priscilla's teaching of Apollos was only "instructing" in private, and refers to Priscilla's "teaching" in Romans 16 and Acts 18:24–26.[522] He also differs from Grudem in pointing out that 1 Timothy 3:11 refers only to what character a "deacon or deaconess" must have, but not to what they did, whereas Grudem insists that the tasks of deacon do not include a governing or teaching authority. Witherington understands the terms co-worker, deacon, and apostle in Philippians 4 and Romans 16 as an indication that "Paul was receiving assistance from women in ministry not only in practical ways, but also in the ministry of the word."[523] He therefore concludes that "there is certainly nothing in the undisputed Pauline texts that would rule out a woman from teaching and preaching," although at times Paul "did apply restrictions when new roles . . . were taken

---

517. Witherington, *Women and the Genesis*, 185.
518. Witherington, 186.
519. Witherington, 186. This differs from Grudem, *Evangelical Feminism*, 226.
520. Witherington, *Women and the Genesis*, 186.
521. Witherington, 188; Witherington, *Women in the Earliest Churches*, 115. He notes four ways the term apostle was used in the New Testament: (1) the original twelve apostles, (2) a person who had seen Jesus and was commissioned by him, (3) an emissary (messenger) sent out by a particular church to perform particular tasks, and (4) a missionary.
522. Witherington, *Letters and Homilies*, 387; Witherington, *Women and the Genesis*, 196.
523. Witherington, *Women and the Genesis*, 190.

to imply the repudiation of women's traditional roles and the importance of maintaining sexual distinctions."[524]

In analyzing the views of Grudem, Schüssler Fiorenza, and Witherington on Paul's attitudes toward women in the church, it is apparent that their interactions with various biblical texts concerning women's involvement in the church are influenced by their presuppositions regarding authority, their sociological perspectives, and their theoretical frameworks. The examples we have provided affirm the important role of the interpreter in the hermeneutical process, including approaches, choice of terminologies, and decisions regarding the meaning of texts. Whether the interpreters admit their biases and influences or not, our analysis has clearly demonstrated the role of presuppositions in their interpretations.

4.4 Conclusion

The divergent approaches of Grudem, Schüssler Fiorenza, and Witherington have highlighted the challenges involved in interpreting 1 Corinthians 14:34–35. They demonstrate the complex nature of biblical interpretation, where the interpreter's presuppositions and expectations of the text influence the hermeneutical outcome. Since the purpose of analyzing these interpreters is to learn how to best interpret 1 Corinthians 14:34–35 in the context of Myanmar, the following principles may be drawn from their hermeneutical processes.

First, the interpretations of Grudem, Schüssler Fiorenza, and Witherington are helpful in identifying the textual problems and interpretational issues raised in the 1 Corinthians 14:34–35 text. Their diverse interpretations highlight the importance of exegetical studies as well as historical studies. Their exegetical studies point out the importance of linguistic and textual structures and their historical studies point out contextual issues surrounding the text. Thus, the principle here is to commit to serious textual studies and historical studies.

Second, they are also helpful in raising the crucial issue of the role of the interpreter in the hermeneutical process. This is also useful in understanding how the interpreter's sociological perspective, whether complementarian or feminist or egalitarian, influences one's theoretical framework in approaching

---

524. Witherington, 190.

the text. This highlights again the importance of the interpreters' conscious awareness of influences and of their own theological and ideological commitments. Thus, the principle here is to know one's own theological and ideological commitments.

Third, the approaches of the three interpreters clarify the importance of the locus of authority in interpretation. For interpreters who approach Scripture from the analogy of faith, Grudem and Witherington provide hermeneutical principles that are helpful. Their method provides the principle of the analogy of faith, the principle of determining meaning, and the principle of application. Schüssler Fiorenza's principle of identifying factors contributing to the meaning of silence in the texts is helpful in identifying the factors impinging on Myanmar Bible translation.

Fourth, the interpretation of Schüssler Fiorenza provides a hermeneutical principle that is helpful for interpreters whose approach tackles contextual questions. This principle is a recognition that one's presuppositions derive from experiences that affect the process of interpretation even before starting the hermeneutical process. Although Grudem and Witherington did not identify their hermeneutical questions in approaching the text, Schüssler Fiorenza indicates that her approach arises from the feminist concern for women's experience. Since the concern of this thesis derives from a Burmese Bible translation of 1 Corinthians 14:34–35 on the role of women in the church, our approach to the text will be different from an abstract search of history.

Fifth, our understanding of the interpreter's role in the hermeneutical process leads us to one of the most important factors for consideration in doing hermeneutics in the Myanmar context, namely, identifying the contextual background that informs presuppositions and influences in the hermeneutical process. Looking at Adoniram Judson's interpretation of 1 Corinthians 14:34–35 in chapter 3, I have shown that his interpretation was influenced by certain presuppositions and interpretations of his time. Likewise, concerning the interpretations of the three contemporary interpreters, it is clear that their presuppositions have influenced their interpretations. Given all of the insights derived from Judson's Bible translation and these three contemporary interpreters, the challenge for Myanmar interpreters is to recognize that our own presuppositions will inevitably influence our interpretations.

The question here is whether we should attempt to interpret the Bible in Myanmar knowing that "all interpretations of texts depend upon the presuppositions, intellectual concepts, politics, or prejudices of the interpreter or historian."[525] In approaching the translation of Judson, Flemming's advice clarifies the need to interpret in the light of these challenges. He says, "the gospel must challenge the presuppositions of the missionary's culture if it has any hope of speaking prophetically to the new culture in which it is being contextualized."[526]

This means allowing the gospel to challenge one's own presuppositions. Flemming gives Paul as an example of someone whose old views were challenged by the gospel of Christ. Although Paul's interpretations of the meaning of the gospel for the emerging church were influenced by three cultures (Jewish, Greek, and Roman), he also challenged those worldviews, values, and practices of Greco-Roman society which were normative in Corinth. Paul challenges "the culture of status, power and self-promotion" that characterized Roman Corinth in light of the cross.[527]

Finally, our analysis of the three contemporary interpreters' interpretations of 1 Corinthians 14:34–35 and their hermeneutical assumptions raises the question of the appropriate method for Myanmar interpreters in interpreting biblical texts on women. Although these interpreters clarify the abovementioned principles, they do not give a satisfactory answer regarding how to deal with the pertinent contextual questions. Since the concern of this thesis is how to approach biblical texts that concern women from the perspective of questions raised within the experiences of individuals or groups in the context of Myanmar, the following chapter looks at a new hermeneutical method that addresses contextual questions raised within a given culture, in this case Myanmar.

---

525. Schüssler Fiorenza, "Feminist Theology," 613.
526. Flemming, *Contextualization*, 140.
527. Flemming, 171.

CHAPTER 5

A Critical Contextual Hermeneutic for Myanmar

The critical analysis undertaken so far has revealed the need to develop hermeneutical principles which consider the context of Myanmar as a valid source in the task of interpretation. The aim is to faithfully interpret the meaning of biblical texts in dialogue with the Myanmar context. This chapter therefore focuses on what a satisfactory hermeneutic in Myanmar would look like, specifically as it interprets biblical passages that concern women.

The first section of the chapter identifies and explains the criteria for a satisfactory hermeneutic in Myanmar. It looks for principles of hermeneutics that reflect critical contextualization. It draws upon insights from the examination and comparison of three contemporary schools of interpretation, together with a contextual theology orientation and an understanding of critical contextualization. Considering the principles gleaned from these sources, this chapter then constructs a critical contextual hermeneutic for Myanmar.

This method provides analytical tools and a framework for evaluating Christian traditions and interpretations that affect the role of women in the church in Myanmar. The analytical tools focus on three contexts – the Myanmar context, the Bible translator's context, and the historical context of the Bible – and include guidelines for contextually relevant applications of biblical texts. Finally, there is a description of a "dynamic interaction process" which is the centerpiece of a critical contextual hermeneutic for Myanmar.

Drawing on these principles and methodology for a critical contextual hermeneutic for Myanmar, chapter 7 revisits 1 Corinthians 14:34b-36 in order to show that analyzing biblical texts by means of the suggested principles and process is an effective way to address contextual questions in biblical interpretation, thereby contributing to a contextually appropriate application of biblical texts in Myanmar.

5.1 Hermeneutical Schools

Three representative schools of interpretation and contextual theology provide points of reference in the quest to develop relevant principles for a Myanmar hermeneutic. These principles derive from an evaluation of the three hermeneutical schools and the principles of contextual theology. We begin with summaries and evaluation of the guiding hermeneutical principles of the three schools.

5.1.1 Evaluation of Three Hermeneutical Schools

The hermeneutical principles that underlie much of Western biblical scholarship have greatly influenced contemporary ways of doing theology and approaches to biblical texts in Myanmar. Among them, three hermeneutical approaches in particular – literal-traditional, feminist, and egalitarian – have relevance for our concern to construct a hermeneutic for Myanmar.

Beginning with the feminist hermeneutics of Elisabeth Schüssler Fiorenza, three aspects are relevant. First, she asserts the importance of recognizing the interpreter's role and honestly stating one's presuppositions before approaching the text.[1] This is where her approach differs from literalist and evangelical feminist approaches, which fail to acknowledge the significance of one's presuppositions. This recognition is important for Myanmar contextual hermeneutics, where such self-awareness has until now been largely missing. Feminist hermeneutics, like contextual hermeneutics generally, acknowledges the subjective elements of the interpretive process. Both appreciate the importance of experience and focus on the relevance of biblical texts for contemporary local social contexts.

---

1. Schüssler Fiorenza, "Feminist Theology," 613.

According to Gordon Fee, any interpretive method that focuses mainly on relevance is subjective.[2] He explains this with reference to the two tasks of biblical studies: understanding the intended meaning of the biblical authors in their historical context and finding relevant applications for today. In terms of the first task, he argues that the interpreter must carefully examine word usage, syntax, and the literary forms to understand the intended meaning of the biblical authors. He sees this as the place where interpreters can engage the text with "a relative degree of objectivity," despite the "cultural baggage and personal bias" that interpreters bring to a text.[3] He then notes the difficulty of upholding objectivity in hermeneutics when it moves to the second task of biblical studies, which focuses on the relevance of the intended meaning of the biblical text for today. As Fee notes,

> What does the biblical author's intended meaning, as expressed in these ancient texts, mean for us today? At this point much depends on the presuppositions of the interpreter. Here is where evangelical and liberal divide, where Pentecostal and dispensationalist, or Baptist and Presbyterian, part company.[4]

The question is whether the subjective nature of such an analysis is more a negative or a positive thing. Many see the inevitably influential role of the interpreter and the context in biblical studies as negative precisely because it colors the interpretive process with subjectivity. However, a contextual theologian like Stephen Bevans sees subjectivity as an unavoidable feature of all theology. He calls on Christians to accept and even affirm that the interpreter's "cultural and historical context plays a part in the construction of the reality in which we live, so our context influences our understanding of God and the expression of our faith."[5] Hence, all theologies are contextual in one way or another. Angie Pears likewise recognizes the contextual nature of all theologizing, and notes that feminist theology, along with other contextual theologies, is "influenced and indeed determined by the context of those engaged in the theological enterprise."[6]

---

2. Fee, "Hermeneutics," 365.
3. Fee, 365.
4. Fee, 365.
5. Bevans, *Models of Contextual Theology*, 4.
6. Pears, *Doing Contextual Theology*, 1.

Second, Schüssler Fiorenza's method of a "critical" approach is also potentially helpful for the construction of a hermeneutic for Myanmar. Her critical method provides some insights which other viewpoints miss. Her emphasis on critical analysis not only offers helpful insights regarding the influence of patriarchy in the culture(s) of the Bible, but also points out patriarchal influences in the writing of biblical texts and also in the canonization process. These insights derive from her understanding of the Bible as largely the work of human authorship. As noted in chapter 4, Schüssler Fiorenza sees the androcentric ideologies[7] associated with the male authorship of the Bible as the reason why the contributions of women were included less often than those of men. She claims that such androcentric ideologies must be contested.

This approach differs from the literal-traditional and egalitarian interpreters who mainly focus on divine authorship, even though they also acknowledge the human authorship of the Bible. Although I do not share Schüssler Fiorenza's view of the Bible as the product of androcentric ideologies and human constructions alone, her insights on the patriarchal culture of the Bible and patriarchy's influence on interpretations of the Bible throughout church history help clarify the historical context of the Bible.

Third, Schüssler Fiorenza's feminist hermeneutics not only provide insights that other readings miss, but it also asks questions that are relevant for the situation of women in church and society. Like liberationist hermeneutics, Schüssler Fiorenza's method calls for reading the Bible from the "underside,"[8] which allows the experiences and perspectives of oppressed or marginalized people to be heard and highlighted. Like other feminist hermeneutics, her method focuses on identity, and thus asks important questions that concern women in the church. For example, as mentioned in chapter 5, she focuses on analyzing the ways in which Christian traditions and theologies of the past have perpetuated women's alienation, domination, and oppression over many centuries of church history. She describes this domination and oppression as the direct result of the attitudes of "patriarchy" and "kyriarchy"[9] in the church and society. She explains how these attitudes have influenced the

---

7. Schüssler Fiorenza, *In Memory of Her*, 48.
8. Scholer, "Evangelical Feminist Hermeneutics," 2.
9. Schüssler Fiorenza, *Wisdom Ways*, 9.

interpretive process and the construal of meaning in the history of interpretation. In this sense, her approach is helpful for my study as it poses questions that are relevant to the situation of women in church and society within the context of Myanmar.

However, Schüssler Fiorenza moves beyond liberationist hermeneutics, which is mostly concerned with liberating themes in the Bible. From her view of the Bible as written mostly by elite men conditioned historically and ideologically by patriarchy,[10] she insists on not regarding as normative Scripture passages that restrict or denigrate women. She concludes that the central authority for interpretation is the experience of women, not the Bible, and thus insists on a critical reconstruction of the Bible.[11] This raises a question regarding the validity of relying on the Bible at all. Although historical truthfulness is one of Schüssler Fiorenza's goals in interpretation, the difficulty of her method lies in its evaluation of texts relying mostly on external evidence and judged by the "experiences" of women and "historical imagination."

For these reasons, Grudem and Witherington regard Schüssler Fiorenza's view of the Bible as questionable. Not all experiences of women are the same around the world, as cultures and societies differ greatly and continually evolve. Not even all feminist viewpoints concur in every respect, as they are as diverse as the times and places in which they emerge. Therefore, grounding the interpretations of biblical texts in the sphere of experiential relativity allows them to end up wherever the interpreter desires.

Additionally, there is the difficulty in Schüssler Fiorenza's hermeneutics of locating God in the story. Jesus is revealed as only human, not God incarnate who came to save sinners. Instead of God being the one who brings liberation and wholeness throughout history to free the oppressed, her view suggests that humans are their own liberators and Jesus is merely an exemplar for those who initiate women's liberation. In a context like Myanmar, where most Christians hold a high view of Scripture that accepts the Bible as the very word of God, the approaches of Grudem and Witherington will be more widely accepted than that of Schüssler Fiorenza, given her view of the Bible.

In evaluating the literal-traditional hermeneutics of Wayne Grudem, a positive feature is his affirmation of biblical authority and the Bible as both

---

10. Schüssler Fiorenza, *Power of the Word: Scripture*, 64.
11. Schüssler Fiorenza, *In Memory of Her*, 34.

human words and the word of God.¹² Witherington shares this view which moves both him and Grudem to accept the Bible as the locus of authority, rather than human experience. They approach biblical texts from the perspective of faith rather than a hermeneutic of suspicion. Additionally, they focus on discovering authorial intent, that is, the intended meaning of the biblical texts.

However, although Grudem and Witherington share a similar view of the Bible and its authority in interpretation, they approach texts differently. These differences start from their acknowledgment of the interpreter's role in interpretation and continue to the application of biblical texts in contemporary contexts. Although Grudem acknowledges the influence of his presuppositions in interpretation, he sees the possibility of keeping the influence of the interpreter's own biases to a minimum.¹³ However, he fails to show how such biases can be minimized and his method shows the influence of his own religious, political, and cultural presuppositions in the interpretational process.

Although Witherington believes that all the interpreter's presuppositions "must be normed by the Scriptures,"¹⁴ his view of presuppositions gives interpreters more freedom to engage with the texts from their contextual setting. He describes the presuppositions of the interpreters as "windows into the Scripture" and "good things."¹⁵ This approach provides helpful guidelines for contextual hermeneutics that seeks to take Scripture, culture, and theology seriously. It also views the questions and presuppositions of interpreters as a valid starting point for the theological and hermeneutical process. This approach highlights the failure of the literal-traditionalist view to take the context of the reader seriously.

One of the positive features that all three methods – literal-traditionalist, feminist, and egalitarian – share is an insistence on serious exegesis of the historical aspects of biblical texts. Literal-traditionalists and egalitarians recognize the importance of discovering meaning within the historical context in order to apply insights to the present day. Schüssler Fiorenza is more

---

12. Grudem, *Systematic Theology*, 81; Grudem, *Bible Doctrine*, 33.
13. Piper and Grudem, "Overview of Central Concerns," 90.
14. Witherington, *Living Word of God*, 160.
15. Witherington, 160.

interested in determining the ideological constructs of the text and how they operate within the historical contexts than in determining meaning.

Given his commitment to biblical authority, Grudem seeks to discover a "single meaning,"[16] but this approach fails to allow for changes in understanding how the historical biblical context has influenced interpretation. Witherington seeks to discover both "the [original] meaning and the trajectory of the advice given."[17] He sees a trajectory that can lead to the text meaning "more than its original historical intent,"[18] and he proposes that texts be interpreted through the lens of the theme of redemption.[19] Witherington uses an interdisciplinary approach, incorporating sociorhetorical studies, for example, to engage with the texts in the broadest possible way.

Grudem and Witherington also differ in how they apply the meanings of the texts to the contemporary context. Grudem argues that because the Bible is transcultural and normative for all times, unless Scripture itself indicates otherwise,[20] all the teachings of the Bible are relevant for today and all readers should obey them.[21] The "culturally relative" commands in Scripture must also still be obeyed though applied in different forms today.[22] A questionable feature of this approach is its uncritical determination of relevance. Grudem's assumption of "clear texts" also fails to take the context and culture of the reader seriously and he fails to allow that not all teachings of the Bible are in fact clear in their instructions for today.

I find that Witherington's method applies the meaning of texts to the contemporary context more thoughtfully than Grudem's literal-traditionalist approach. Witherington sees that making a transition or connection between two very different cultures in different historical periods is not a simple task. He cautions the interpreter to remember that "the past [the historical context] is like a foreign country, for they do things differently there."[23] In this sense, he seeks to differentiate between principles and practices, where "the basic

---

16. Grudem, "Perspicuity of Scripture," 302.
17. Witherington, *Letters and Homilies*, 383.
18. Witherington, *Living Word of God*, 158.
19. Witherington, 156.
20. Grudem, *Evangelical Feminism*, 362.
21. Grudem, 331.
22. Grudem, 402.
23. Witherington, *Living Word of God*, 162.

rule of thumb is that while principles remain the same, practices often do and should change with differing cultural situations."[24] He then insists on asking both "what the text meant in its first-century context" and "what it might mean for us here and now."[25] Only in so doing will the interpreter "be faithful to the text and be guided and guarded by what it excludes and what it allows."[26]

Witherington's approach to hermeneutics not only takes culture seriously alongside Scripture and theology, it is also aware of the diversity of cultures. His keen awareness of cultural differences, and differences between historical contexts and contemporary contexts, is a positive aspect of his approach. In addition, Witherington's method deals with contextual issues more appropriately than the literal-traditionalist view because he recognizes the nature of culture as dynamic and evolving. This leads him to propose biblical applications only "where the situation is clearly analogous today."[27] This also focuses on the missionary concern for applying biblical texts both faithfully and effectively in differing cultures and contexts.

The three hermeneutical schools of thought all deal with contextual issues in their interpretive approaches. Feminist interpretation views women's experiences as a central authority and values the importance of "social location."[28] From this perspective, Schüssler Fiorenza approaches biblical texts with suspicion. The literalist school approaches Scripture based on the centrality of biblical authority, and thus considers authorial intent in historical context and the perspective of faith, to be of fundamental importance. Evangelical feminist interpretation takes seriously the experiences of contemporary individuals in the process of interpretation, more so than the literal-traditionalists. Evangelical feminist application principles consider differences between cultures, and thus this method is more missional and contextual than the literal-traditionalist. However, along with the literal-traditionalist approach, this method argues that the process of interpretation should take as its starting point the historical-critical research of the biblical texts and only move

---

24. Witherington, 169.
25. Witherington, *Conflict and Community*, xiii.
26. Witherington, xiii–xiv.
27. Witherington, *Letters and Homilies*, 383.
28. Bevans, *Models of Contextual Theology*, 6.

to their application as a secondary task. In my view, this overlooks the key role of the interpreter in forming theological meaning throughout the hermeneutical process.

The approaches of all three hermeneutical schools are somewhat abstract. I do find feminist hermeneutics to be helpful in elevating the role of experience in the hermeneutical process. I also find that both literal-traditionalist and evangelical feminist methods clarify the importance of the Bible as the locus of authority. However, since the concern of this thesis is how to approach biblical texts from the perspective of questions raised by the experiences of Myanmar Christians, I find that none of these three hermeneutical schools offers satisfactory strategies for addressing contextual questions raised within a given culture. Even though all three hermeneutical methods acknowledge to some degree that their own North American context influenced their questions and approaches, they do not spell out or grapple with the contextual factors that have influenced their interpretations. Therefore, to better address contextual questions within the contemporary culture in Myanmar, the next section explores contextual theology for helpful principles of interpretation.

5.1.2 Evaluation of Contextual Theology

The role of interpreter in the interpretive process and understanding the context of the interpreter are the two most important features of contextual hermeneutics. These highlight the relationship between theology and context. When forming a hermeneutical methodology for Myanmar, the role of the interpreter's context cannot be overlooked since the interpreter plays a key role in interpreting the meanings of biblical texts. Contextual theologians around the world have highlighted the importance of the interpreter's context. Among the most significant work is that of two Catholic contextual theologians, Stephen Bevans[29] and Robert Schreiter.[30] Both have contributed significantly to defining the criteria for a satisfactory contextual hermeneutic. Bevans's work is helpful in aiding our understanding of the role of context in hermeneutics, and Schreiter's work contributes to an understanding of how the process of listening to both contemporary culture and the Bible works.

---

29. Bevans, *Models of Contextual Theology*.
30. Schreiter, *Constructing Local Theologies*.

Stephen Bevans's contextual theology developed out of his experiences as a missionary in the Philippines. He came to believe that there is no such thing as a universal theology, but "only contextual theology, feminist theology, black theology, liberation theology, Filipino theology, Asian-American theology, African theology, and so forth."[31] He concluded that "doing theology contextually is not an option, nor is it something that should only interest people from the Third World, missionaries who work there, or ethnic communities within dominant cultures."[32] In other words, contextualization is a "theological imperative."[33]

From this perspective, Bevans argues that contemporary human experience, or a people's context, should be considered as an essential source for theology, along with Scripture and tradition.[34] This does not mean ignoring past traditions or approaches to interpretation, but he argues that although "we can certainly learn from others (synchronically from other cultures and diachronically from history)" without taking into account the contextual nature of all theology, "the theology of others can never be our own."[35]

Bevans further claims that an acknowledgment of the significance of context for theology is essential. He sees that not only are Scripture and tradition inevitably contextual, since they were "developed by human beings, written and conceived in human terms, and conditioned by human personality and human circumstances," but they are also studied and interpreted today "within our own context as well."[36] From this perspective, doing theology contextually necessarily entails two elements: first, "the faith experience of the past that is recorded in scripture and kept alive, preserved, defended, and perhaps even neglected or suppressed-in-tradition,"[37] and; second, "the experience of the present, the context."[38]

Bevans notes that in order for theology to be authentically one's own, "the received tradition must of course pass through the sieve of our own individual

---

31. Bevans, *Models of Contextual Theology*, 3.
32. Bevans, 3.
33. Bevans, 3.
34. Bevans, 3.
35. Bevans, 5.
36. Bevans, 5
37. Bevans quotes Rosemary Radford Reuther, *Sexism and God-Talk*, 12–16. Bevans, 5.
38. Bevans, 5.

and contemporary-collective experience,"[39] which includes "experiences of a person's or group's personal life," the system of inherited ideas in the communal experience called "culture," and our own "social location."[40] He suggests therefore a dialectical reading between human experiences and the Christian tradition.[41] He then identifies six models of doing theology that focus on context: translation, anthropological, praxis, synthetic, transcendental, and countercultural.[42]

Bevans's explanation of the role of context in doing theology, and the interrelatedness of contextual theology and hermeneutics, leads to the conclusion that the experiences of a person or group within a given context are vitally important in contextual hermeneutics. What does this mean for contextual hermeneutics in Myanmar? First, hermeneutics in the Myanmar context cannot rest solely on the inherited methodologies of missionaries from the past. Their hermeneutical approach was embedded in the faith experiences of the past, recorded in Scripture and in church tradition. It was also itself a product of their own Eurocentric context. This acknowledgment does not mean that the old approach of the missionaries must be completely discarded, but rather that the present experiences of the people of Myanmar are also valid sources for theological reflection. For Myanmar hermeneutics, both past and present experiences are important for theological reflection today.

Bevans's explanation of context in theology shares some similarities with the feminist hermeneutical methodology in that it places emphasis on the importance of experience in hermeneutical formation and the process of interpretation. One difference is that the feminist hermeneutical approach focuses on the experiences of women, whereas contextual theology focuses on the experiences of people groups in a cultural context. Like the feminist hermeneutical methodology, contextual hermeneutics considers one's presuppositions before the interpretational process begins. Both approaches see the role of experience as essential for the theological task.

---

39. Bevans quotes Douglas John Hall, *Professing the Faith*, 33. Bevans, 5.

40. Bevans explains that social location "makes a difference, both feminist and liberation theologians have insisted, whether one is male or female, rich or poor, from North America or Latin America, at the center or at the margins of power."

41. de Mesa and Wostyn, *Doing Theology*, 14–18.

42. Bevans uses only five models in the first edition.

I find Bevans most helpful in understanding how context influences interpretation, and Robert Schreiter is particularly helpful in understanding how the process of constructing theology takes place in contextual theology. Like Bevans, Schreiter stresses the importance of context in theology. He points out that people who raise concerns related to context often do so because of the inability of the "traditional frameworks of theology" to respond to the questions and issues that arise in local cultures and social settings.[43]

Also, like Bevans, Schreiter argues that these questions about the role of context in theology have often arisen out of the experience of colonialism and dissatisfaction with colonial interpretations. He sees the main questions confronting many of today's Christians as: "How can one be faithful both to the contemporary experience of the gospel and to the tradition of Christian life that has been received? How is a community to go about bringing to expression its own experience of Christ in its concrete situation? And how is this to be related to a tradition that is often expressed in language and concepts vastly different from anything in the current situation?"[44]

Schreiter points out that the fact that such questions arise out of discontent often leads to new ways of doing theology particularly concerned with "context, procedure, and history."[45] Among these, he sees context as most critical for theological reflection, and therefore focuses on the context first before constructing a theology. For postcolonial Christians, this differs from the approach inherited from missionaries, which focuses first on an assumed "universal theology," out of which theological principles are "applied" to a given context. He notes that, without the analysis of context as part of the theological process, theology can "become either irrelevant or a subtle tool of ideological manipulation."[46]

According to Schreiter, there are three ways of doing local theology – translation, adaptation, and contextualization. He sees translation as a model which missionaries in the past often employed when they saw what they considered to be parallel cultural situations from one context to the next. Schreiter describes this as "dynamic equivalence," which he analyzes as

---

43. Schreiter, *Constructing Local Theologies*, 3.
44. Schreiter, xi.
45. Schreiter, 3.
46. Schreiter, 4.

problematic in that it assumes that "there is a direct equivalent in the local culture for the cultural pattern coming from another church setting."[47] However, this approach ignores the complexity of culture.

Schreiter sees the adaptation approach as a development of the translation model, with a more inclusive approach to the interplay between Christianity and local culture. However, he notes that this model still uses Western methods, if somewhat in dialogue with local contextual needs. This has limited value since the Western perspective is still prioritized over that of the local culture.[48] He therefore argues for a third model, the contextual approach, which takes the local context seriously as it begins theological reflection with the cultural context. He notes two types of contextual theology – the "ethnographic approach" and the "liberation approach."[49]

Within the contextual approach to interpretation, which takes the cultural context very seriously, Schreiter highlights the process of analysis as "listening" to contemporary culture and the Bible. In order to begin to articulate a local theology, he argues, the theological process must begin with "the opening of culture," which includes an uncovering of a culture's "principal values, needs, interests, directions and symbols."[50] Out of this listening to culture as a starting point in the interpretive process, he suggests a method called *dynamic interaction*, which is a dialectical study that moves "back and forth among the various aspects of gospel, church and culture."[51] He notes that this dialectical movement "raises questions that need to be addressed if local theology is to become an authentic and compelling voice in local churches."[52] He demonstrates how this dialectic works in what he calls a *local theology map*.

Schreiter's approach sheds further light on Bevans's view of context in the interpretive process. Schreiter addresses head-on the inability of the "traditional frameworks of theology" to answer the questions and issues arising within local cultures and situations – a central concern of this thesis. Therefore, I find that his explanation of ways of listening to culture and his

---

47. Schreiter, 8.
48. Schreiter, 9.
49. Schreiter, 13.
50. Schreiter, 28.
51. Schreiter, 22.
52. Schreiter, 22.

highlighting of the influential role of context in theological reflection are helpful for constructing a Myanmar hermeneutic.

I also find particularly helpful the "semiotic analysis"[53] which Schreiter proposes for the process of listening to culture in forming local theologies. According to Schreiter, this analysis is "the study of signs (from the Greek *semeion* = sign)" in culture, which examines "the apparent differences in understanding the meanings of the signs or symbols from one culture to another due to 'artificial, or assigned, meanings' attached to their cultural system."[54] This is a study of signs in the "forms of words, images, sounds, gestures and objects" in cultural systems.[55] These signs appear linguistically as well as in "painting, sculpture, music, dance, modes of exchange, dress, and family structure."[56]

This analysis takes into account the complexity of language and signs in a culture. Recognizing that semiotics is an enormous field which cannot be fully explored here,[57] I will focus on only one aspect of Schreiter's semiotic analysis that is particularly helpful for understanding the Myanmar context. This aspect analyzes the sign systems of a culture to aid understanding of the meaning of linguistic usages in interpretations of biblical texts.

The linguistic usages of Adoniram Judson in his Burmese translation of the Bible are a valid example of Schreiter's concern, especially his use of the word "silence" in 1 Corinthians 14:34–36, given the contextual understanding of this word in Myanmar. As noted in chapter 2, the word "silence" in Burmese signifies much more than the general meaning of "not speaking," because of the signs, codes, and messages attached to the sign systems of Myanmar culture. In Myanmar culture, the word "silence" also suggests patriarchy and therefore a dictatorial authoritarianism which renders women silent – an

---

53. Schreiter, 56.
54. Schreiter, 50.
55. Vanhoozer, *Dictionary for Theological Interpretation*, 735.
56. Vanhoozer, 736. James Barr has criticized traditional methods of interpretation for ignoring this aspect of language in biblical studies in his book, *Semantics of Biblical Language*.
57. Vanhoozer, 734. Semiotics involves "the study not only of what we refer to as 'signs' in everyday speech, but of everything which 'stands for' something else. In a semiotic sense, signs take the form of words, images, sounds, gestures and objects." According to this definition, semiotics makes use of three disciplines: the study of signs, or semantics; the study of relationships between signs, or syntax, and; the study of relating signs to their users, or pragmatics. These fields of study take account of "the effects of sociocultural and linguistic contexts."

association that then became associated with biblical authority because of Judson's translation. This cultural understanding of "silence" has influenced how a biblical text like 1 Corinthians 14:34–36 has been interpreted in Myanmar.

To summarize, Schreiter's focus on cultural influences in interpreting the meaning of biblical texts is particularly helpful for constructing a hermeneutic for Myanmar. This analysis sees culture as a "complex whole," describing "a society's beliefs and values, behavioral norms, institutions and artifacts."[58] It therefore takes cultural influences very seriously in determining the meanings of biblical texts. In the Myanmar context, such analysis would need to examine the language usages which missionaries adopted in Burmese Bible translations. It would also need to analyze the implications of language usages for a local context by identifying influences behind interpreters' assumptions in the hermeneutical process and the results of such assumptions. Our discussions in chapters 1, 2, and 3 demonstrate this form of analysis. Chapter 8 will explore how this analysis adds to a contextual understanding and exegesis of 1 Corinthians 14:34b-36.

The question here is how an interpreter does contextual hermeneutics with an acute awareness of the context while also holding on to a commitment to the authority of the Bible.

I find the approach of the evangelical contextual theologian Larry Caldwell to be particularly useful in this regard.[59] His method evolved during thirty years of teaching in the Philippines, and his experience of frustration with the uncritical adaptation of Western curriculum and methodologies in Asian seminaries. He came to see that the Western model of theological education was irrelevant for the Asian context because it did not address contemporary issues, concerns, and values in that context. Further, he saw the lack of acknowledgment by Western-modeled theological educators of local people's cognitive environment and the role of contextually informed assumptions in the interpretive process, resulting in an uncritical adaptation of imported theology and methodologies. This is an accurate depiction of the environment in Myanmar seminaries as well.

---

58. Vanhoozer, *Dictionary for Theological Interpretation*, 151.
59. Caldwell, "Scripture in Context Part 1," 92.

Caldwell contends that most practitioners of Western evangelical hermeneutics who claim to value contextualization in the mission of the church tend to follow two steps in their hermeneutical process. The first step is to analyze the original context of the biblical text to find out what the text meant to its original hearers. The question asked is, "How is a particular Bible passage best interpreted in light of its original context?" The second step is to ask, "How can the meaning of the text in its original context be best interpreted and applied today?"[60] According to Caldwell, while this method attempts to engage the Bible contextually, the social location of the reader only becomes relevant in the second stage of inquiry, after the so-called "objective" exegetical work is complete. He sees this as problematic, since such interpreters are not challenged to become aware of their own "cultural influences" which shape their "hermeneutical orientations"[61] and "hermeneutical assumptions."[62]

Caldwell concludes that this two-step approach to hermeneutics is flawed, primarily because it does not recognize that meaning is "shaped by the cognitive environment of the reader/hearer/interpreter."[63] He thus finds that this methodology has questionable relevance for the non-Western world, arguing that "any hermeneutical method must pay attention to both the interpreter's own cognitive environment and its influence on the interpretation of a biblical text, as well as to the [original] reader/hearer and his/her interpretation of that same text."[64] He insists that this recognition of the interpreter's role in forming meaning does not imply that the interpreter's interpretation takes precedence over what the biblical text is saying. Rather, taking the interpreters' and readers' contexts into account will help the interpreters to understand their own cognitive environment, as well as that of "the audience."[65] Since he sees that the context of interpreters does in fact shape their interpretation

---

60. Caldwell, 92.
61. Caldwell, 91.
62. Caldwell, 93.
63. Caldwell, 92.
64. Caldwell, 92.
65. Caldwell, 93.

of texts, he calls for a hermeneutical methodology that reflects the relevance of their cultural context and cognitive environment.[66]

These approaches of contextual theologians can contribute to a new way of doing hermeneutics in Myanmar. Based on my evaluation of these contextual approaches to interpretation – two Catholics and an evangelical – I conclude that a satisfactory contextual hermeneutic for Myanmar cannot rely only on traditional methods of interpretation used in the past. Although these imported hermeneutical methods may have made positive contributions to the Myanmar church and theological education in the past, they cannot provide adequate answers to contextual questions raised within our present-day context. Therefore, there is a need for a new methodology that appreciates the methods of the past while exploring new ways of doing hermeneutics today. Contextual hermeneutics has much to offer to a new way of reading, interpreting, and applying biblical texts in Myanmar.

This need for constructing such contextual hermeneutics is explained by Walter Dietrich and Ulrich Luz in their preface to *The Bible in a World Context: An Experiment in Contextual Hermeneutics*.

> When our own ways of understanding no longer work, it is essential to listen to others and learn from them. It seems to us that Western biblical scholarship suffers most from being "without context." It is carried out abstractly and therefore leads to abstract results and truths, which are not related to any context. "Abstract" is not only understood in the usual sense of being opposed to "concrete." "Abstract" also means: unattached to the life and reading of "ordinary" people, far away from their questions, developed in the ivory tower of the university. "Abstract" means: detached from the present and from its problems, concerned only with the reconstruction of a past with all its problems. Finally, another way of scholarly, "abstract" reading that is disconnected from the real concerns of present-day readers is to flee into an imaginary "text world" – imaginary, because it is entirely created by scholars. "Abstract" in the widest sense

---

66. Caldwell, "Scripture in Context Part 2," 120. See also his "Interpreting the Bible"; "How Asian?", and; "Towards the New Discipline."

means: without context. All this does not contribute to understanding, which is related to our own context.[67]

In Myanmar, as elsewhere, reading the Bible is always contextual, because people approach the texts in relation to personal and coextensive communal issues. Due to prolonged economic, social, and political problems within the country, the abstract, academic study of theology has been a luxury that only a very few could enjoy. Hermeneutics in Myanmar now requires the participation of the laity in the hermeneutical process, as they reflect on interpretations and traditions of the past in conversation with the contemporary context of Myanmar. Including the laity as well as the clergy and theological "experts" in the hermeneutical process would aid the process of claiming interpretation, and theology in general, as our own. A new way of approaching biblical texts in Myanmar must include looking at the texts with an awareness of the contextually informed assumptions and experiences of the interpreters, while at the same time being willing to be corrected by the biblical texts. Grounded in this understanding, the following section introduces a new way of interpreting biblical texts in Myanmar.

5.2 Toward a Satisfactory Contextual Hermeneutic
5.2.1 The "Critical Contextualization" of Paul Hiebert

In constructing a satisfactory contextual hermeneutic for Myanmar, Paul Hiebert's explication of "critical contextualization"[68] is particularly helpful, since he confronts the challenge of grappling with questions of value that arise within particular contexts. He notes that contextualization has both positive as well as problematic implications for the church's mission. In a positive sense, contextualization helps local theologies to avoid "the foreignness of a gospel dressed in Western clothes" by taking cultural worldviews and social realities seriously. He sees this as helping biblical interpreters avoid a "monocultural approach"[69] and affirms "the right of Christians in every country" to

---

67. Dietrich and Luz, ed., *Bible in a World Context*, ix-x.
68. Hiebert, "Critical Contextualization."
69. Hiebert, 108.

be "cognitively free from Western domination," and the right of every church "to develop its own theology,"[70] institutions, and traditions.

However, Hiebert points out that an over-reliance on contextualization in theology and hermeneutics carries with it several potential shortcomings. First, he sees that it can run "counter to the core Christian claims about the truth of the gospel and the uniqueness of Christ,"[71] since contextualization may view all local cultural forms and systems of belief as inherently good. He calls this "uncritical contextualization" and points out the need to evaluate every culture critically, considering the truth claims of the gospel.

Second, he sees the tendency to separate form and meaning in contextualization as problematic, since they are "inextricably linked."[72] He gives as an example of this linkage the fact that names are often inseparable from larger religiocultural identities in most tribal societies. In Myanmar, some terminologies are inseparable from ideologies of the Buddhist religion. Adopting such terminologies without analyzing the meaning critically could lead to an undermining of the message of the gospel.

Third, Hiebert sees that contextualization often places emphasis on "accurate communication of meaning" while ignoring "the emotional and volitional dimension of the gospel."[73] Fourth, in contextualization "contemporary cultural contexts are taken seriously, but historical contexts are largely ignored."[74] He argues that there is still much to be learned from church history. As Christians face new questions in each cultural and societal setting, they will need to draw on the rich heritage of Christian traditions and biblical insights. Fifth, Hiebert points out that the extreme form of uncritical contextualization leaves no common ground between the theologies of one culture versus another, creating theological relativism. Finally, he notes that uncritical contextualization has a weak view of sin since it affirms that "human social organizations and cultures are essentially good," which can undermine the gospel and lead to syncretism.

---

70. Hiebert, 108.
71. Hiebert, 108.
72. Hiebert, 108.
73. Hiebert, 108.
74. Hiebert, 108.

Despite these challenges entailed in doing theology contextually, Hiebert proposes a "critical contextualization" theological method that takes "the Bible seriously as the rule of faith and life."[75] He bases this critical method on an understanding that views "all human knowledge as a combination of objective and subjective elements" and "as partial but increasingly closer approximations of truth."[76] His critical method takes "both historical and cultural context seriously." It looks critically at the "relationship between form and meaning in symbols such as words and rituals."

Hiebert's views have affinities with those of Bevans and Schreiter, in that they all see the need for studying the historical context dialectically with the present context. He emphasizes the need to compare the messages and ritual practices of a given culture with the original intended messages of biblical texts, through a process of mutual and analytic dialogue. This way of studying takes the perspective of faith very seriously, while at the same time freeing local theology from Western presuppositions, and from the need to do theology only by blaming colonialism or responding with a reactionary attitude of "anti-colonialism."[77]

In sum, in his response to the question of how non-Western Christians should appropriate traditional cultural beliefs and practices, Hiebert argues that a critical contextual analysis must include "exegesis of the culture," "exegesis of Scripture and the hermeneutical bridge," "critical response," "new contextualized practices," and "checking against syncretism."

Drawing on all of the above perspectives, a critical contextual hermeneutic is proposed as a fitting method for Myanmar Christians to adopt in order to interpret the Bible faithfully and effectively. This method considers key contextual questions. It also critically evaluates historical Christian traditions and, specifically in terms of the theme of this thesis, biblical interpretations affecting the role of women in the Myanmar church today. The following section elaborates the principles of such a critical contextual hermeneutic for Myanmar.

---

75. Hiebert, 110.
76. Hiebert, 111.
77. Hiebert, 109.

5.2.2 The Components of a Critical Contextual Hermeneutic

Following Hiebert's exposition of critical contextualization, a satisfactory hermeneutical method for Myanmar comprises three main components: *critical, contextual,* and *feminist*. The first component of this hermeneutical method, critical analysis, examines two contexts in Myanmar. It begins with the interpreters' context – the cultural presuppositions and worldviews that influence how they interpret biblical texts. The purpose here is to understand the contextual influences behind such interpretations.

This analysis includes looking critically at Bible translations in Myanmar considering the original languages of the Bible as well as local influences, which vary in different regions of Myanmar, thus affecting translation preferences. For the purposes of this thesis, the critical analysis focuses on the Judson Burmese Bible translation, and evaluates the impact this translation has had on the role of women in the Myanmar church. The critical contextual analysis also examines the historical context of the biblical texts, which influences the intended meanings of texts in specific times and circumstances.

The third component of this methodology draws on feminist analysis. Like liberationist hermeneutics, this method insists on reading the Bible from the "underside,"[78] which is the perspective of the oppressed or marginalized. However, the commitment to feminist analysis is nuanced by an evangelical underpinning, which means that it accepts the Bible as the authority for faith and life. It is in this light that this method attempts to interpret and reevaluate biblical texts that concern the role and status of women in the church and society.

This method identifies the effects of patriarchy in the traditional interpretation of biblical texts as well as in the translation of biblical texts. It thus challenges traditional interpretations of the Bible in Myanmar which have been conditioned by interpreters' patriarchal presuppositions. From the perspective of feminist hermeneutics, this work not only identifies issues surrounding the roles and status of women, but also reviews patriarchy based on the theme of liberation within the Bible. Thus, there is a reassessment of biblical texts considering their historical setting and the liberationist thrust of the gospel.

---

78. Scholer, "Evangelical Feminist Hermeneutics," 2.

To summarize, critical contextual hermeneutics is a critical analysis of the Myanmar context, biblical translations, and the historical and theological contexts of the Bible. This method looks at these contexts dialogically, linking key themes by means of a hermeneutical bridge to arrive at appropriate applications for women in the contemporary Myanmar church. The following section explains the presuppositions behind this approach to interpretation.

5.2.3 The Presuppositions of a Critical Contextual Hermeneutic

Two main presuppositions undergird a critical contextual hermeneutic for Myanmar. First, there is the affirmation of Hiebert's view of the Bible as the rule of faith and life. This is also the view of Grudem and Witherington, who see the Bible as claiming "to be and is a word from, not merely a word about, God."[79] Drawing on their principle of situating oneself within an acceptance of the authority of the Bible, this method understands the Bible as the locus of authority in interpretation. In this sense, it differs from the approach of Schüssler Fiorenza, who sees the experience of women as the locus of authority. At the same time, it does take the contemporary experience of women as a valid source for critical reflection in the process of interpretation. This derives from the views of contextual theologians Bevans and Schreiter, who see the "the present human experiences" of any local community as a valid source for *"loci theologici,"* alongside Scripture and tradition.[80] Within this framework of biblical authority alongside recognition of the role of the contemporary context, this method focuses on discovering how to interpret the Bible faithfully in the local context, and on relevant ways of presenting the gospel in the context.

It is important to reiterate that, although this method does not consider the experiences of women or the context as the locus of authority, it does consider the experiences of women as a valid starting point for a reevaluation of biblical texts that concern women's role in the church. This method understands that although the Bible emerged out of a context of patriarchy, patriarchy is not part of God's original creation, because God created all

---

79. Witherington, *Living Word of God*, xiv.
80. Bevans, *Models of Contextual Theology*, 4; Schreiter, *Constructing Local Theologies*, 19.

human beings in his image with equal worth and dignity.[81] Patriarchy is the effect of sin on relationships and is revealed in form and substance as the domination and assumed superiority of men over women.[82] In this sense, this method shares Witherington's theological grounding in "the concept of the *imago dei*" in Genesis and "its renewal in Christ."[83]

These presuppositions need to be stated at the beginning of the interpretation process since this method recognizes that "all interpretations are influenced and conditioned by the interpreter and the interpreter's context and viewpoint,"[84] regardless of one's commitment to biblical authority and view of the location of meaning in the text. This method acknowledges the interpreter's presuppositions at the outset of interpretation to minimize bias.

An important critical tool of this method is examination of the historical context of biblical texts through careful exegesis. This critical tool is important not only in discovering the intended meanings of the texts, but also in minimizing bias in interpretation. Hence, this method acknowledges the importance of experiential questions arising within the interpreter's context with sensitivity to hermeneutical issues surrounding biblical passages. In addition, it dialogues critically with the historical contexts of the Bible with an awareness of the interpreter's biases in the hermeneutical process, to generate contextually appropriate responses.

5.2.4 Criteria for a Satisfactory Hermeneutic for Myanmar

Criteria for a satisfactory hermeneutic for Myanmar include three elements: attention to comparative analysis, application analysis, and procedure. First, the comparative analysis includes an analysis of the present context of Myanmar and exegesis of two historical contexts – the translator's context and the scriptural context. The second area is concerned with an analysis of the contextual applicability of the meaning discovered within the biblical text. The final function, procedure, explains how the abovementioned contexts interact in the proposed contextual hermeneutic for Myanmar.

---

81. Witherington, *Indelible Image*, 10.
82. Witherington, "Why Arguments against Women."
83. Witherington, *Indelible Image*, 10.
84. Scholer, "Evangelical Feminist Hermeneutics," 2.

5.2.4.1 Comparative Analysis of Three Contexts

Having evaluated the contemporary schools of interpretation and contextual theology, my method focuses on three contexts which have relevance for Myanmar hermeneutics: the present context of the interpreter, the Bible translator's context, and the historical context of the Scriptures.

The context of the interpreter in this case is the context of Myanmar. The translator's context is that of Adoniram Judson, who translated the Burmese Bible and whose historical influences have informed the teachings of the church in Myanmar. The historical context of the Scriptures includes the sociohistorical setting of the biblical texts and the literary context, both of which influence the meaning of the texts. This critical contextual hermeneutic for Myanmar looks critically at all three contexts by means of comparative analysis. The following subsections elaborate on these contexts in detail.

Analysis of the Myanmar context

Drawing on the perspectives of Witherington, who sees experience as a "window into the Scripture,"[85] and contextual theology, which views experience as a starting point of interpretation, my critical contextual hermeneutic understands the analysis of the Myanmar context to be crucial for biblical interpretation. This analysis of the Myanmar context includes an examination of cultural influences that have shaped theological and biblical interpretations, as well as the cultural symbols and values embedded in the language.

Bevans addresses the importance of symbols in his explanation of culture, which he describes as the "system of inherited conceptions expressed in symbolic forms by means of which people communicate, perpetuate, and develop their knowledge about and attitudes toward life."[86] In this light, the analysis of Myanmar culture requires not only a critical examination of values and worldviews, but also the meanings of words and symbols within the local context.

For Myanmar Christians, symbols clearly influence the meaning of words in biblical texts. These cultural symbols derive from a collective religious and cultural history. They inform the meanings of words for interpreters, and interpreters in turn form the meanings of words in the biblical texts for other

---

85. Witherington, *Living Word of God*, 160.
86. Bevans, *Models of Contextual Theology*, 6.

readers. Schreiter highlights this informing and forming nature of language in his discussion of semiotic analysis,[87] referenced earlier. From this understanding of culture as informing and forming meanings embedded in language, he suggests a "holistic"[88] approach between religion and culture. The reason for this is that he sees that one aspect of culture cannot be separated from other aspects, as they are all interconnected.

In the Myanmar context, religion and culture are connected to political history as well. Thus, any analysis of the Myanmar context in relation to hermeneutics needs to include all these three aspects of cultural analysis. A focus of cultural analysis related to our theme is how Myanmar culture influences the meanings of biblical texts. Such knowledge leads to a deeper understanding of how these contextualized meanings inform Burmese Christians' understanding of Scripture.

This cultural analysis also helps to identify contextual questions raised by the text. Kevin Higgins' work is helpful in this regard. Referring to how the recipients of a translated Bible respond to it, he notes that the cultural context of the recipient greatly influences how biblical texts are understood. In other words, "a person's current and potential matrix of ideas, memories, experiences, and perceptions"[89] determines "what the recipient [of the Bible translation] will assume to be the meaning of the text," as well as framing "questions that are brought to the text."[90] This is important in any analysis of the Myanmar context, because many of the questions raised in relation to Bible translation in Myanmar highlight the role of the recipient in assuming the meaning of the text.

The final focus area in critical cultural analysis entails an examination of contemporary interpretations of biblical texts. This is important because contemporary interpretations also greatly influence how the local community understands the meaning of biblical texts. As noted in chapter 4, current biblical interpretation in Myanmar owes an intellectual debt to Western scholarship. It plays an influential role since biblical interpretations in Myanmar depend greatly on the doctrinal teachings of the respective denominations,

---

87. Schreiter, *Constructing Local Theologies*, 56.
88. Schreiter, 43.
89. Higgins, "Biblical Interpretation," 190.
90. Higgins, 195.

which came about through the efforts of missionaries from Western countries. As noted, their interpretations have generally been adopted uncritically, without people realizing that these interpretations were influenced by the foreign interpreters' own context. Therefore, the need in Myanmar is to evaluate the strengths and weaknesses of these Western interpretations to address contextual questions more effectively.

Analysis of the translator's context

As mentioned in chapter 3, the Judson Burmese translation is, for some, viewed as a product of colonialism since it emerged during that period, even though the translator was from America. This view may also be related to Judson's role as an interpreter for the British colonialists for a period of time. In analyzing this translator's context, I support Hiebert's statement that interpreters from that era must not be evaluated solely by blaming colonialism or responding with a reactionary attitude of anti-colonialism.

John de Jong concurs with this view. Although he agrees that Judson was certainly influenced by the prevailing assumptions of his time, he concludes that "the point is not to blame him for this, but rather that we too are all affected in the same way. There are areas of our interpretation and understanding of the Bible that may also not stand the test of time. We are thus called to humility and openness to other views with which we may not agree. The Word of God is infallible, but our interpretations are not!"[91] This is valuable advice when analyzing the translator's context.

However, as I have argued, the challenge in Myanmar is more that the translation of Judson is unquestioned than that he is blamed for any outdated approach to translation. This makes it even more important that the translator's role in forming local theology is not ignored in developing a hermeneutic for Myanmar. Considering the translator's role in determining the meaning of texts and applying such meanings in each context, this role must be viewed as being as important as other aspects of contextualization. A critical approach insists on approaching translations of the Bible as interpretations of the translators, who were influenced by the worldview of their time and the presuppositions which flowed from it.

---

91. De Jong, "'Sin Offering'?" 91.

Given this perspective, my analysis focuses on the following questions in the Judson Burmese translation of the Bible (although this principle is valid in relation to other Bible translations as well): What are the distinctive vocabularies that Judson used? Are these different from other Bible translations in Myanmar? Are they different from the original languages of the Bible? What are the influential factors predisposing Judson to translate in the way he did? Is there any sign of patriarchal and androcentric ideologies and theologies behind the terminologies he used? What is the impact of his translation choices on the church?

These questions are asked from the assumption that "every translation is already an interpretation."[92] Given an understanding of the intermediary role of scholarship, one must conclude that the analysis of the translator's context is critical in Myanmar biblical studies.

Exegesis of the historical context of Scripture

The critical contextual hermeneutic I am proposing differs in certain key respects from feminist and non-evangelical contextual theology approaches to exegesis of the historical context of Scripture. It approaches the historical context of the Bible from the perspective of faith, drawing on a high view of the Bible that sees biblical texts as the inspired word of God. This method concurs with Witherington that all contextual presuppositions are to be normed by the Scriptures.[93]

Given this understanding, my method focuses, first, on determining the intended meaning of the biblical texts in their historical context. This differs from the feminist view of Schüssler Fiorenza and non-evangelical contextual theologians who view the Bible as mostly the work of men. Feminist and non-evangelical contextual theologians focus on discovering how the texts operate within the historical context and how these texts influence the present day.[94] They look at the ideological constructs of the text that silence others and seek a historical reconstruction.

Critical contextual hermeneutics focuses on the historical context of the biblical texts to discover the intended meaning of the texts, that is, the

---

92. Witherington, *Living Word of God*, 16.
93. Witherington, 160.
94. Schüssler Fiorenza, "Biblical Interpretation," 11.

meaning that the original recipients of the texts would have taken for granted in their historical setting. This method takes seriously Witherington's view of context as "king"[95] in determining meaning, and thus analyzes a text in relation to both its immediate historical context and the overall context of the Bible.

Joel Green in *Dictionary of Theological Interpretation of the Bible* describes this aspect of interpretation as "context as cotext," which refers to "the location of an utterance within a string of linguistic data, the sentences, paragraphs, and chapters surrounding and related to a text and within which an utterance finds its meaning."[96] This historical analysis of biblical passages includes linguistic data, literary forms, grammar, and critical analysis of the cultural and historical backgrounds of the text. Here, the historical context is the dynamic element in determining the meaning of the text.

5.2.4.2 Analysis of the Contextual Application of the Text

The primary concern of critical contextual hermeneutics differs from that of Schüssler Fiorenza. She sees any quest for "normativeness"[97] in a biblical text as another influence of patriarchal ideology and thus to be rejected. Critical contextual hermeneutics, in contrast, seeks to identify an appropriate application of the biblical text to the present context from the perspective of faith and the authority of the Bible. It focuses on "discerning between the permanent, universal, normative teaching of Scripture on the one hand and, on the other hand, that which is transient, not applicable to every person in every culture, not intended to function as a mandate for normative behavior."[98] This has affinities with both Grudem and Witherington's appeal to faith as a principle for application.

A question raised here is the criteria for deciding whether a text is normative. As mentioned in the beginning of the chapter, Grudem sees all teachings of the Bible as normative, with applications for Christians in all times and places, unless Scripture itself indicates otherwise. According to Grudem, even regarding the teaching of isolated passages, Christians are "still obligated to

---

95. Witherington, "Hermeneutics."
96. Vanhoozer, *Dictionary for Theological Interpretation*, 132.
97. Schüssler Fiorenza, *But She Said*, 138.
98. McQuilkin, "Problems of Normativeness," 409.

obey it,"⁹⁹ although the application may assume different forms today than in the original context.

Generally, Witherington agrees with Grudem that, although the principles remain unchangeable, practical applications often do and should change with differing historical and cultural situations.¹⁰⁰ He reminds interpreters of the importance of applying the texts only "where the situation is clearly analogous today."¹⁰¹ As mentioned in my evaluation of his approach, Witherington adds that any application must consider not only the original meaning of the text, but also the trajectory of the advice given.

Witherington's caution to consider the overall trajectory of New Testament theology is important for critical contextual hermeneutics in Myanmar. My approach takes seriously both the historical setting of texts, the theological trajectory of the New Testament, and the influences that have guided interpreters, whether in the past or the present. From their position of looking back into historical texts – rereading through the lens of the present – interpreters today are taking note of patriarchy and other contextual issues in the Bible. Also, from this position of looking back, interpreters can see the direction in which the New Testament is moving, which can stimulate attitude changes today.

One of the examples that Witherington gives to illustrate the notion of trajectory is that of New Testament teaching on slavery. Rather than simply condoning the practice of slavery that existed in the world of the New Testament, the broader underlying liberating thrust of New Testament theology helped to bring about a change of attitudes about slavery among Christians later in the history of the church.¹⁰² He sees the same kind of attitude change occurring today regarding the role of women in the church, since the liberating thrust of New Testament theology is pushing believers today toward "the reformation of patriarchy coupled with affirmation of women's new role."¹⁰³

This focus on the theological trajectory of the Bible forces us to think critically about how issues such as patriarchy, violence, and other problems

---

99. Grudem, *Evangelical Feminism*, 362.
100. Witherington, *Living Word of God*, 169.
101. Witherington, *Letters and Homilies*, 383.
102. Witherington, *Women in the Earliest Churches*, 220.
103. Witherington, 220.

of inequality which can be observed in the Bible should be interpreted and responded to today. The analysis of critical contextual hermeneutics considers the broad trajectory of the Bible in the direction of inclusion and "oneness in Christ" in determining appropriate applications of biblical texts in present-day Myanmar.

5.2.4.3 Procedure: The Dynamic Interaction Process

My critical contextual hermeneutic process is a modification of the "dynamic interaction"[104] process outlined by Robert Schreiter in contextual theology. Instead of the two contexts which Schreiter compares (the biblical context and the interpreter context), my method focuses on the relationships between three contexts – the Myanmar context, the translation context, and the biblical context – to evaluate their importance in the development of a critical contextual hermeneutics.

This can also be explained by means of mapping. The flow chart of the critical contextual hermeneutics map (Chart 2) is a modification of Schreiter's local theology map (Chart 1). Although some elements are adopted from Schreiter, most of my mapping differs from his. The main components are identified in numbered boxes. The arrows indicate a possible flow of thoughts in the process of contextual hermeneutics.

Schreiter's mapping of the construction of local theology and the dynamic interaction process between the three contexts of critical contextual hermeneutics are outlined below. He notes that this process occurs "especially when a community has wrapped up its identity in one particular theological expression."[105]

---

104. Schreiter, *Constructing Local Theologies*, 22.
105. Schreiter, 26.

A Critical Contextual Hermeneutic for Myanmar

Spirit and Spirit and Gospel: Shaping the Community Context

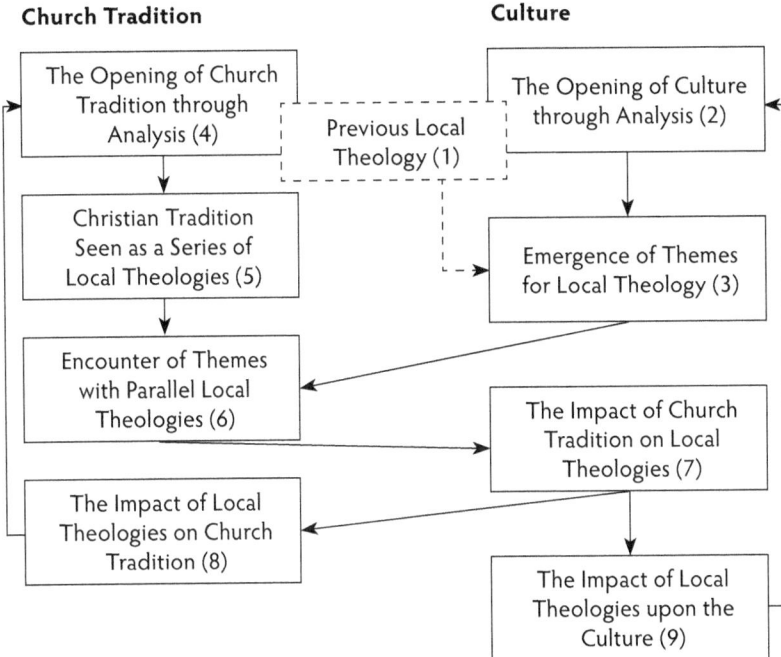

Chart 1. Robert Schreiter's Map of Constructing a Local Theology[106]

In my hermeneutical flow chart, Chart 2, the boxes that overlap show the link between previous local interpretations and other influences. A dotted line from the contemporary interpretations to the previous interpretations shows the influences of these interpretations on different local understandings. In short, this first step of critical contextual hermeneutics identifies the problematic nature of previous local interpretations. This process then leads to the next step, which seeks to ascertain the appropriate starting point of interaction in response to the issues identified in previous local interpretations. In the context of Myanmar, interpreters' cultural worldviews have guided their interpretive assumptions, as well as those of the missionaries' Bible translations and denominational teachings, and even contemporary interpretations that have come from other cultural contexts outside of Myanmar.

---

106. Schreiter, 25.

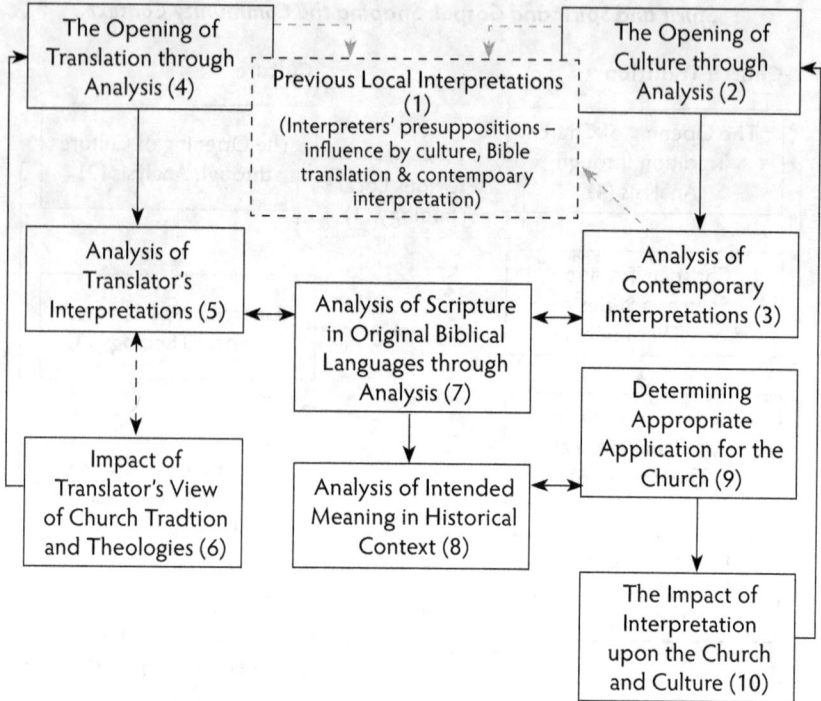

Chart 2. Flow Chart of a Critical Contextual Hermeneutics[107]

Previous local interpretation (1)

Like Schreiter's map, critical contextual hermeneutics begins with analyzing previous local interpretations. This step deals with questions of interpretation arising from the community of believers. These local questions arise when previous interpretations are no longer satisfactory for the local context in answering questions regarding biblical texts. According to Schreiter, these local questions, raised within a community to begin the theological process, indicate that the community is "coming to a certain maturity" and assume that "it has been fed by other local theologies up to that time."[108] This first stage in the process examines previous local interpretations of scriptural passages to answer questions about why a former interpretation is no longer satisfactory or is now problematic.

---

107. Based on Schreiter's local theology map, *Constructing Local Theologies*, 25. Only nos. 1, 2, and 10 are taken directly from Schreiter.

108. Schreiter, *Constructing Local Theologies*, 26.

The opening of culture (2)

Following Schreiter, this area starts with "the opening of culture through analysis."[109] For Schreiter, cultural analysis is generally regarded as an ideal place to begin the process of analyzing previous local theologies. In contextual hermeneutics, the process can begin either with cultural analysis (Area 2) or with analysis of biblical texts (Area 4) considering Bible translation issues. Irrespective of where one begins, both areas must be in dialogue with the original biblical language texts (Area 7). The double-headed arrow illustrates the back-and-forth nature of this dialogue and interrelationship.

The opening of the cultural process entails analysis of cultural influences that shape theological and biblical meanings. This area first analyzes values and worldviews found in Myanmar cultural and religious experience. As a part of this analysis, it evaluates the significance of religiocultural symbols and meanings embedded in the language, and the influential factors behind such meanings. These symbols found within the language influence how one understands the meaning of words in biblical texts. Chapters 2 and 3 demonstrated how certain key words and symbols are understood in Myanmar and how they have influenced interpretations of biblical texts.

Analysis of contemporary interpretations (3)

Differing from Schreiter's map, the next area analyzes contemporary interpretations of biblical texts by considering their influential role in determining how the local community interprets and forms the meanings of biblical texts. It is important to examine contemporary interpretations, including considering how they have been influenced by the prior interpretations analyzed in the first stage of the method.

As noted earlier, current biblical interpretations in Myanmar owe an intellectual debt to outside scholarship, mainly Western scholarship. Christians in Myanmar adopted Western interpretations without an awareness of how the interpreters' Eurocentric worldview had influenced these interpretations. Because these interpretations are still normative for most Myanmar Christians today, it is essential to study them through critical analysis rather than uncritical adaptation. Hence our analysis of three contemporary schools of interpretation to show their influences on Myanmar interpretations, and

---

109. Schreiter, 25.

highlight the presuppositions behind their interpretations which influenced their interpretation of 1 Corinthians 14:34b-36.

The opening of Scripture through analysis (4)

The primary concern of a critical contextual hermeneutics is its relevance for the local context. This area therefore unfolds through analysis of local Bible translations, which are used regularly to interpret meanings in the local context. Looking critically at local Bible translations involves paying close attention to the usages of terminologies and linguistic structures in translation. It also involves uncovering differences from and similarities with other Bible translations.

The opening of Scripture through analysis differs from Schreiter's "opening of Church tradition through analysis."[110] In his concern for forming a relevant local theology, Schreiter mainly analyzes church traditions so that they may dialogue with local cultures.

The purpose of the opening of Scripture through analysis is to gain an understanding of contemporary local questions by critically revisiting the choices made by the translator in question. As mentioned in Area (2), the opening of dialogue with previous local interpretations can begin either with the opening of culture through analysis (Area 2) or with the opening of Scripture (Area 4). One example of the link between local questions and local translations of Scripture can be found in Judson's translation of 1 Corinthians 14:34b-36, as was explored in chapter 2.

Analysis of translator's interpretations (5)

This area diverges significantly from Schreiter. After critically analyzing the language usages in translations, the process moves to the translator's interpretations, where the focal point is the context of the translator-as-interpreter. Investigating the context of the translator includes looking at the historical setting and prevailing interpretations in the translator's time and place. This is done from the perspective that translation *is* interpretation; in other words, the act of translating the Bible is a process of interpretation by the translator. It is a product of the translator's context, and this influences interpretation.

---

110. Schreiter, 25.

The way this analysis of translation operates in the critical contextual hermeneutics process was explained in chapters 2 and 3. Chapter 2 focused on the influence of the Judson Bible translation in Myanmar. Chapter 3 examined his translation of 1 Corinthians 13:34b-36 by comparing it with the Greek texts. Chapter 3 also included a comparative analysis between Judson's translation and another Burmese translation to show differences in the use of the Burmese language. As explained in chapter 5, such analysis of a translator's interpretations has occurred very infrequently in Myanmar due to respect for the translator.

The impact of translator's interpretations on church traditions and theologies (6)

After analyzing the context of translations and translators, the process then seeks to discover the impact of the translator's interpretation on church tradition and theology. This diverges from Schreiter (Area 8), where he focused on "the impact of local theologies on church tradition."[111] The impact of the translator's interpretation is the main concern here, since the translator significantly influences local understanding of Scripture. Local understanding came about through reading translations, which has shaped the theology of the church.

As mentioned in chapter 2, the translator's usage of language and their choice of terminology also reflect their views of the text. These views are products of the translator's theology and culture, which in turn influence local theologies and church traditions. Therefore, this area focuses on discovering the nature and extent of the influence which the translator's views have had on church tradition and theology in Myanmar. In the case of 1 Corinthians 14:34b-36, chapter 2 revealed the impact of the translator's interpretation on the role of women in the church. It is important to note that Area 6 feeds back into Area 4, the opening of Scripture through analysis. This shows the circle of influence that Bible translation has on local interpretation.

---

111. Schreiter, 25.

Analysis of Scripture in original Biblical languages (7)

As mentioned, the opening of interaction can begin either with the local culture or with the local translation of the Bible. Regardless of where one starts the process, there must be interaction with the historical context of the Bible. In order to analyze the historical context of biblical texts, it is necessary to analyze the texts in their original language. In the context of Myanmar, this step is especially crucial since local interpretations have rested on imported theological traditions and, particularly, the Bible translation of Adoniram Judson. The analysis of biblical texts in their original language contributes to the interpreter's awareness of problematic areas in local interpretations.

This step is of central importance to the critical contextual hermeneutics process, because contextual hermeneutics as I practice it is committed to scriptural authority. Grounded in this commitment, contextual hermeneutics seeks to discover the intended meanings in the historical biblical context to apply them in a contextually appropriate manner. Therefore, this area examines the terminology usages, grammar and structural features of the original biblical language, and compares them with local Bible translations, pinpointing similarities and differences. Chapter 3 employed this analysis and pointed out similarities and differences between the original biblical language and Judson's translation of the text in question.

Analysis of intended meaning in historical context (8)

After analyzing biblical texts in their original languages, we proceed to an analysis of the meaning of the biblical texts. Due to time and cultural distance between the biblical authors and the present day, careful exegesis of the biblical texts in their own setting is crucial in critical contextualization. To this end, this process begins by examining the sociohistorical backgrounds of the texts. The process then explores the theology and teachings of the biblical author elsewhere on similar issues. In addition, it looks critically at the author's usage of words, syntax, and literary forms. All of this is done to discover the intended meaning of the original author of the text. Chapter 7 will demonstrate this process of critical contextual hermeneutics.

Determining appropriate application for the church (9)

The next important component of critical contextual hermeneutics is identifying appropriate applications for the church in Myanmar today. This entails linking the original meaning of the biblical texts to the contemporary situation. In other words, the process of critical contextual hermeneutics moves from determining the original meaning of the texts to discovering their contemporary significance.

The principles related to analysis of the contextual application of the text are as follows: The first principle of application looks at whether the text is restricted to its original historical context or is broadly applicable in the present context. The second principle of application analyzes cultural relativity as applied to the present context. These principles also consider the theological trajectory of the New Testament to determine whether the text is applicable to the present-day context.

Impact of local interpretation on the church and culture (10)

The final process of critical contextual hermeneutics is like Schreiter's local theology map (Area 9), where he looks at "the impact of local theologies upon the culture."[112] Critical contextual hermeneutics examines the impact of local interpretations on the church and culture. This is approached from the perspective that the contestation related to previous local interpretations, which involves critically reflecting on inherited local interpretations of biblical texts, will contribute positive results for the church and the culture. Schreiter's summary is helpful:

> Like contextual theology, any reading of the context affects local theology, the traditions of the local church, and the local culture. Thus, this process looks at the contributions of new interpretations to local theology and church traditions. This process also investigates the impact of local interpretations in light of new understandings of the texts in local settings – that is, the extent to which the Bible affirms or challenges the local culture. This area feeds back into the cultural setting which is the focus of Area 2. This demonstrates the "dialectical cycle" of influence that local interpretation has on the local church and culture.[113]

---

112. Schreiter, 25.
113. Schreiter, 36.

5.3 Conclusion

Drawing on the issues raised in the earlier chapters, this chapter has outlined a critical contextual hermeneutic for Myanmar. Three contemporary schools of interpretation, together with an appropriation of contextual theology and a hermeneutic of critical contextualization, have contributed to an articulation of principles of interpretation for Myanmar. This analysis has highlighted criteria for a Myanmar hermeneutic, incorporating dialectical analysis of three contexts, analysis of the contextual application of the texts, and a dynamic interaction process. Together, these provide a framework for evaluating traditional interpretations affecting the role and status of women, while retaining a high view of the authority of Scripture and its role in the church. From these understandings, the next section revisits the context of Myanmar and also the 1 Corinthians 14:34b-36 text.

Part Three

Revisiting the Context and the Text

CHAPTER 6

Revisiting the Context

This chapter looks at the problematic nature of Myanmar hermeneutics in engaging critically with the 1 Corinthians 14:34–35 text. They are vital for understanding obstacles that interpreters encounter in approaching the text and how these obstacles hinder interpreters when analyzing the Bible translation of Adoniram Judson. The chapter examines some of the obstacles to doing contextual hermeneutics in Myanmar and highlights aspects of interpretation that require rethinking. This is followed by specific suggestions to overcome these obstacles through the application of contextual hermeneutical principles. These involve using step 2 ("The Opening of Culture") from Chart 2 (see page @@). Then chapter 7 uses step 4 ("The Opening of Scripture through Analysis," see page @@), revisiting the 1 Corinthians 14:34–35 text through principles learned from the context-sensitive hermeneutics outline proposed in chapter 5.

6.1 An Interplay of Contexts

Since the movement toward church independence after the repatriation of missionaries by the authorities in the 1960s,[1] some Christian scholars in Myanmar have begun to address the need to develop a contextual theology relevant to the Myanmar setting. However, since Christians are a small minority in Myanmar facing difficult challenges in terms of co-existence with

---

1. England, Kuttianimattathil, and Prior, eds., *Asian Christian Theologies*, 56. Following military rule in 1962 and the expatriation of missionaries in 1966, Burmese churches became self-reliant indigenous churches and began to address contextual theology, if only in private publications and the private circulation of theological reflections.

or evangelization of the dominant Buddhists, their focus has primarily been on understanding the Buddhist worldview. They have devoted much less attention to the influence of the Myanmar context on interpreters' approach to biblical texts.

As explained in chapter 2, the Myanmar worldview is deeply rooted in a complex and overlapping cultural, religious, and political framework. These elements play influential roles in interpreters' "hermeneutical orientations"[2] or "hermeneutical assumptions,"[3] which determine the kinds of questions that are raised about the text and the presuppositions one has about the meanings of words in the text. Recognition of these influences on the formation of theological meaning becomes an important focal point in developing a contextual hermeneutical method that is relevant for Myanmar. This is particularly pertinent for understanding biblical passages concerning women, as interpretations of these passages have a bearing on how the church perceives the role of women in the church.

Given my concern to construct a hermeneutical methodology that has relevance for the Myanmar cultural context or "cognitive environment,"[4] I identified in chapter 3 the context of Bible translation as another important influence on the interpretations of passages about women's silence, along with the context of the interpreter and the context of the text. In chapter 4, I also evaluated three contemporary hermeneutical approaches from Western interpreters, whose views represent popular approaches to interpretation in Myanmar, to show "the function and place of the interpreter,"[5] and how the interpreter's context influences assumptions and theological meanings.

In evaluating three contemporary hermeneutical approaches to determine the meaning of 1 Corinthians 14:34–35, it became clear that all three are influenced by two contexts: the context of the Bible and the context of the interpreter. All three hermeneutical methodologies show the overlap between the biblical context and the interpreter's context, whereby "a fusion of the horizons"[6] occurs as their cultural backgrounds dialogue with the text. None

---

2. Caldwell, "Scripture in Context Part 1," 91.

3. Caldwell, 93.

4. Caldwell, "Scripture in Context Part 2," 120. See also Caldwell, "Interpreting the Bible"; "How Asian?"; and "Towards the New Discipline."

5. Sugirtharajah, "Introduction, and Some Thoughts," 258.

6. Osborne, *Hermeneutical Spiral*, 334.

of these scholars mention the translator's context, since they worked directly with the original biblical languages, Greek and Hebrew. However, as I have argued previously, Bible translation must be included as another key context for interpretation in Myanmar, alongside the interpreter's context and the historical context of the text, for translation has played a crucial role in biblical studies in Myanmar. Since a Bible translation is the interpretation of the translator, a careful consideration of the translator's worldview and contextual setting is an important dynamic in Myanmar contextual hermeneutics. Considering the importance of these three contexts, the following section will examine some of the obstacles to doing contextual hermeneutics in Myanmar.

6.2 Cultural Obstacles to Developing a Myanmar Contextual Hermeneutic

In Myanmar, there are several obstacles which arise in reading biblical passages that command women to be silent in the church. As mentioned previously, the most obvious obstacles are the personal biases and assumptions that interpreters bring to the text. However, the obstacles I wish to highlight here are more to do with cultural roadblocks that make it difficult to move beyond the common hermeneutical practices in Myanmar which prevent interpreters from reading biblical texts with critical eyes. We will consider several of these obstacles in turn.

6.2.1 Problems with the Culture of Obedience

The culture of obedience is a major obstacle to doing critical analysis of biblical texts in Myanmar. Since the concept of silent obedience to authority is deeply rooted in culture, religion, and history in Myanmar, biblical passages concerning women's silence in 1 Corinthians 14:34–35 and 1 Timothy 2:11–12 have been accepted without critical analysis. There are strong similarities between the cultural worldview revealed in these texts and that which predominates in Myanmar, and this contributes to an uncritical and literal appropriation of the texts.

In writing about the parallels between the patriarchal cultures of the Bible and Myanmar, Anna May Chain's comments can aid our understanding of why there is such an uncritical approach to biblical interpretation in Myanmar.

In her research among Myanmar women interpreters, she found that women in Myanmar generally see the Bible as affirming their traditional female role as wife and mother, whose sphere is confined to the home. As she notes:

> The stories of Sarah, Rebekah, Rachel, Naomi and Ruth, among others, resonate in their lives. They identify closely with these women as they lived in cultures and societies very similar to their own. They suffer together with Sarah in Pharaoh's harem, they are angry with Lot who was willing for his daughters to be raped in place of his guests, and they sympathize with Naomi and Ruth as they struggle for survival in a man's world. These biblical women's stories are their stories.[7]

Many Myanmar Christian women do indeed see the lives of ancient Israelite women, who lived in a thoroughly patriarchal system, as like their own lives. Like these biblical women, Burmese women see themselves, in Chain's words, as having "to work hard to put food on the table, working outside in the fields, factories, and offices; at the same time, they must fulfil the traditional roles of wife and mother by caring for the children, doing household chores, and pleasing their husband." It is thus understandable that they would view biblical women as "circumscribed by customs and traditions that are so familiar to Burmese women. They must act within the boundaries set for them. They have been taught since childhood to be obedient and passive daughters, wives, and mothers."[8]

A male contextual theologian, Peter Thein Nyunt, has also affirmed this circumscribed image of women in Myanmar's patriarchal system. As he points out, "concerning women's role, mothers, being submissive to fathers . . . are strictly bounded by patriarchal traditions and cultures, not only to bear and care for children, but also to control the purse, prepare food, keep order and discipline, to be responsible for the general wellbeing of the whole family, and to share what she can with her husband's relations and her own."[9]

Myanmar Christians often reference the Genesis 2 creation narrative to reinforce the view that, because Eve was created second, and from Adam's

---

7. Chain, "Wives, Warriors and Leaders," online.
8. Chain, "Wives, Warriors and Leaders," online.
9. Nyunt, "Toward a Paradigm," 105. See also Ling, "Burmese Christian's Responses," 68.

rib, women are meant to be subordinate and therefore obedient to men. Aye Aye Win points out that in Myanmar churches, the traditional interpretation of "Genesis 2 is especially used to show how the Bible complements the Bamar Buddhist cultural heritage,"[10] which is similarly patriarchal. Anna May Chain suggests that this literal reading of Scripture leads both men and women to believe that "the Bible affirms the traditional woman's role as wife and mother, her sphere confined to the house," because such patriarchal stories in the Bible resonate with their own lives; "they identify closely with these women, as they lived in cultures and societies very similar to their own."[11]

The postcolonial feminist biblical scholar Eh Tar Gay links this uncritical correlation between biblical and Myanmar patriarchy to the fact that most churches in Myanmar are fundamentalist, and thus their approach to biblical interpretation is literal. She sees this literal approach as contributing greatly to the blind acceptance of less than flattering passages about women, whereby interpreters conclude that the "stories of Eve, Potiphar's wife, Lot's daughters, Moabite women, Delilah, Jezebel, Herodias, and Salome, show women as weak, prone to temptation, and as seducers of men."[12] This view is backed up by Myanmar churches' teachings that Eve's disobedience to God and God's subsequent punishment of all women was a "divine injunction for perpetuity so that women should always accept the power and authority of men over them. Therefore, they must resign themselves to this inferior position and not attempt to take positions of leadership in the home, church, or public affairs."[13] Given this perspective, it is inevitable that such interpretations will reaffirm the ideology of patriarchy, and thereby reinforce the subordination of women in church and society.

To summarize, there is a clear link between the Myanmar culture of obedience to patriarchal traditions and interpreters' literalist acceptance of biblical texts that appear to support patriarchy. This way of reading the Bible leads to accepting such texts without question. It is because of this culture of obedience that interpreters in Myanmar often conclude that the Bible confirms the subordinate role of women.

---

10. Win, "Women in Creation," 55.
11. Chain, "Wives, Warriors and Leaders."
12. Gay, "Authority and Submission," 49.
13. She also cites Pa, "Because of Eve."

6.2.2 Problems with the Virtue of Submission

Some interpreters in Myanmar have highlighted the similarities between the biblical and Myanmar virtue of female submission, and its other side, the culture of shame. Eh Tar Gay points out, for example, that the apparent inference in some New Testament texts that long hair represents the glory of women (feminine virtue rooted in modesty and submission) finds resonance with "the concepts of *eindaray, theika* and *hpon*" in Myanmar culture.[14]

In Myanmar culture, long hair is considered not only a proper hairstyle for women but also a symbol of their feminine virtue. A famous saying in Myanmar describes men's *hpon* (glory) as their *letyone* (strength), while women's glory is their *san htoone* (a hair bun that requires having long hair). This long hair symbolizes a key virtue ascribed only for women, *eindaray*, which Eh Tar Gay defines as "decent, silent and submissive behaviour."[15] Possessing this virtue means that a woman must speak softly, never shout, have a submissive attitude to the "control and protection of a father or a brother or a husband," and avoid "a job involving contact with or leading many men, having more than one partner, [or] turning to prostitution."[16] The Burmese saying, "women's *eindaray* cannot be bought with gold," is widely used in Myanmar to reinforce women's submission. Shame occurs when this virtue of submission is not practiced. If a woman does not exhibit the virtue of *eindaray*, she is described as someone who does not possess *theikha*, meaning dignity or reverence, and the absence of *theikha* is the epitome of shame.

Given this cultural orientation, Myanmar interpreters often see 1 Corinthians 11 as affirming not only a proper hairstyle for women (long hair), but also their submissive role. Eh Tar Gay notes that since this virtue of submission does not allow women "to have equal status with men or participate in many spheres of social, political and religious affairs," women in Myanmar accept such biblical texts as affirming that their virtue consists in "modesty . . . silence, submissiveness, bearing children, faith, love and holiness."[17] Since this understanding of virtue creates in women a sense of "timidity, lack of self-confidence and other constraints of culture," Anna May

---

14. Gay, "Authority and Submission," 316.
15. Gay, 300.
16. Gay, 301.
17. Gay, 301.

Say Pa refers to such submission and shame as "dragons" that create obstacles to Myanmar women's quest for wholeness, including for those attempting to do theology.[18] Since Judson's rendering of 1 Timothy 2:9–15 translates the term for women's propriety and decency as *eindaray* ("decent, silent and obedient behaviour"), interpreters in Myanmar have seen this text as reinforcing women's submissive role. Later in this chapter, I will elaborate on Judson's usage of this word *eindaray* as one of the problematic aspects of his translation.

In sum, since women's silent submission, and shame if this virtue is violated, are accepted as cultural norms in Myanmar, the tendency in Myanmar has been to internalize biblical passages that appear to validate this virtue, without critically analyzing these texts. This understanding of women's virtue is taught from the earliest age and is reinforced by the culture of shame in the socialization process. For this reason, biblical passages that indicate a submissive and silent role for women are accepted at face value, because they echo what people already accept about women.

6.2.3 Problems with the Passive Acceptance of Biblical Texts

As we have seen, the stranglehold of patriarchy in Myanmar, whether in society or in the church, forces women into obedient and submissive roles. Many women in Myanmar therefore approach biblical texts from the perspective of passive acceptance, which does not permit questioning or scrutiny. This leads to a literal acceptance of the words they read in Scripture, which creates a significant obstacle to interpreting a passage such as 1 Corinthians 14, with its reference to women remaining silent in church.

Samuel Ngun Ling sees a sign of this pattern of passive acceptance of whatever is authoritative, whether the words of Scripture or cultural norms, in Myanmar women's passive response to violence. He argues that women tend to accept the violence they suffer at the hands of men because they have internalized patriarchal assumptions. As he observes, "Myanmar women were for many centuries acculturated to subjugate their roles as inferior to men," and "these submissive roles of Myanmar women have much to do with the imposition of their religion and culture."[19] Given this religiocultural

---

18. Pa, "Asian Feminist Theology."
19. Ling, "Violence, Poverty, Justice," 52.

worldview, which views one's present condition as the direct result of one's deeds in past lives, women in Myanmar often find themselves accepting their low status as the result of bad *karma*, or fate. Consequently, "even educated women will support a view that they are less worthy than men and that they do not need liberation from male dominance."[20]

Feminist theologians in Myanmar such as Anna May Say Pa[21] and Anna May Chain[22] have addressed this reality of women's passive acceptance of male authority and their own inferiority. They also link women's passive acceptance of patriarchal assumptions in Scripture to the concept of *karma*, such that they accept their subordinate role as foreordained. This predisposes Christian women not to question or "dig deeper" into biblical passages that appear to support the patriarchal authority that silences them. This passive acceptance is a major obstacle to doing contextual hermeneutics in Myanmar.

6.3 Rethinking Our Approaches to Interpretation

All the abovementioned obstacles to doing contextual hermeneutics in Myanmar show the need to rethink our approaches to interpretation. This includes rethinking the influence of the culture of respect in interpretation (particularly regarding translation), our approaches to language study, comparative biblical studies and hermeneutical methods, and our theology of leadership.

As just one example of the need to rethink our approaches to interpretation, it is worth considering Myanmar Christians' approach to polygamy in the Bible. The practice of polygamy was noted by one of the earliest Catholic missionaries in Myanmar, Father Vincentius Sangermano, who observed that although "the Law of Gautama forbids polygamy, still the Bamar people, besides their lawful wife, have two or three concubines."[23] The practice of polygamy is also mentioned in the report of the United Nations Convention on the Elimination of All Forms of Discrimination against Women (CEDAW), as being permitted by Buddhist customary law under the condition that the

---

20. Ling, 52.
21. Pa, "Asian Feminist Theology," 21.
22. Chain, "Wives, Warriors and Leaders."
23. Sangermano, *Description of the Burmese Empire*, 159.

second wife must be given an equal social status with the first wife.[24] However, this practice of polygamy is no longer legal in Myanmar since 30 March 2015, when the parliament passed a monogamy bill.[25]

The fact that polygamy was practiced in Myanmar's historical past and until recently does raise interpretational challenges for Christians. The apparent similarities between the patriarchal cultures of Myanmar and the Bible mean that non-Christians in Myanmar have at times labelled the Bible as "affirming violence such as tribal conflicts, family conflicts (in the case of polygamy) . . . and many other forms of oppression of one group over another."[26] However, polygamy has never been practiced among Christians in Myanmar. The fact that Myanmar Christians have rejected polygamy shows a selective literalism in their approach to biblical texts that accept polygamy. These passages are conveniently ignored, despite the general support for literalism. This raises the need for critical analysis between the culture of Myanmar and that of the Bible.

Another example of selective literalism is the fact that interpreters in Myanmar typically view the biblical prohibition against "wearing jewelries and braiding hair" (1 Tim 2:9) as a cultural practice which was relevant to biblical times but is not binding for Myanmar today. However, when it comes to women's silence, the same interpreters view these biblical injunctions as a literal command that is binding forever and in all contexts.

The challenge, then, for Myanmar hermeneutics is to reread biblical texts with a critical eye. Since culture is a lens through which interpreters approach the text, interpreters in Myanmar need to acknowledge and analyze the

---

24. Gender Equality Network, "Myanmar Laws and CEDAW."

25. "Law on the Practice of Polygamy." Also in Richard Horsey, "New Religious Legislation." The monogamy law was passed under the umbrella of "race and religion" bills that included a Buddhist women's special marriage bill, a religious conversion bill, and a birth control bill. Horsey translates the monogamy law from Burmese to English and notes, "The law applies to all people living in Myanmar, Myanmar citizens living abroad, and foreigners who married Myanmar citizens while living in Myanmar. A marriage contracted in accordance with an existing law or religious or customary practice shall be deemed legitimate only if it is solemnized in accordance with monogamy. Any man or woman who has married one spouse or more, under any relevant law or religious or customary practice, shall not marry again or unofficially live together with another person as long as the earlier marriage remains valid. Lawful marriages contracted prior to this law coming into force shall remain valid." Violation of this law is committing a family crime, punishable up to "seven years' imprisonment under section 494 of the Penal Code, and shall also be liable to a fine."

26. Ling, "Violence, Poverty, Justice," 45.

influential role of their own cultural lens in their reading of texts. Reading the text with a critical eye would also include analyzing the differences between biblical culture and Myanmar culture. This enables the interpreter to discern whether a text is situational or normative. This would in turn assist the interpreter in addressing the issue of selectivity in biblical interpretation, whereby interpreters claim neutrality in their reading of texts but are guilty of selective interpretations, as seen in the examples of polygamy and feminine adornment. Against this backdrop, we now consider several aspects of interpretation which require rethinking.

6.3.1 Rethinking the Culture of Respect in Interpretation

The culture of respect in Myanmar, wherein younger persons must always show respect to older persons, from more junior in rank to more senior in rank: students to teachers, lower classes to higher classes, and, of course, women to men, forms a major hindrance to reading biblical texts with a critical eye. An Indian biblical scholar, who shares this same culture of respect, clarifies the impact of this attitude of respect on biblical studies. Monica Melanchthon points out that, in this kind of culture, "the teacher is the expert, with ascribed authority as well as achieved authority," and students expect teachers to transmit knowledge to the students in the form of a 'banking system,'[27] in which students' brains are the passive "banks" into which teachers deposit knowledge. This means that students are not prepared to ask questions or think critically and are often "unprepared and ill equipped to handle research which requires skill, individual initiative, evaluation of sources, and the identification of a hermeneutical framework."

From the perspective of this culture of respect that has taught us never to question teachers, theological education in Myanmar in the past did not encourage critical thinking. Due to government restrictions, seminaries have focused on practical training and indoctrinating denominational leaders. One theologian in Myanmar links this to the traditional Buddhist monastery teaching method "known in Burmese as *kyet-thu-yueh sa-an* (parrot learning method),"[28] which requires a student to recite back exactly what the monks say. He argues that this kind of teaching methodology also influenced

---

27. Melanchthon, "Graduate Biblical Studies," 127.
28. Ling, "Challenges, Problems, and Prospects," 7.

Christian theological education in Myanmar, and consequently, "most teachers of seminaries and Bible schools also became accustomed to the depository or banking method rather than participatory methods. The net result is that these traditional teaching methods do not seem to help students to be critical and creative."

Another perspective on the culture of respect is raised by Aye Nwe, a feminist theologian and lecturer at the Myanmar Institute of Theology in Yangon. She notes that the famous Burmese expression *lah na dei*, meaning "a desire not to impose on others or reluctance to impose on others,"[29] which places the highest value on considering others' feelings and avoiding upsetting the other, has greatly influenced the behavior of the people of Myanmar. From this perspective of respect for others, students will always obey the teacher and accept what the teacher says, even if the teacher is demonstrably in error. Students would rather keep quiet than challenge the teacher. Nwe believes this culture of respect is particularly strong among Myanmar women, and notes that "most women in society do not speak out or critique others."[30]

Given this culture of respect, it is important to note its impact on biblical studies. The following subsections will show how significantly this attitude impacts Myanmar interpreters' attitude toward the Bible, and toward translation issues. I argue that these two ramifications of the culture of respect prevent interpreters from critically examining biblical texts.

6.3.1.1 *Respect for the Bible in General*

The respect that Myanmar interpreters have for the Bible leads them to accept whatever they read at face value, without critically considering possible nuances of meaning. Aye Nwe has noted the link between this culture of respect and the common practice of a literal reading of biblical texts in Myanmar. Such respect demands blind obedience and precludes questioning.

Nwe argues that "uncritical interpretation of the Bible" makes it difficult for the church to recognize "its patriarchal domination that engenders women's exclusion and oppression, as well as its negative consequence of the church being alienated from its democratic ideals of equality, freedom, rights

---

29. Nwe, "Empowerment as Constructive Power."
30. Nwe, 1.

and justice."[31] She charges her own denomination, the Myanmar Baptist Church, to move away from their traditional "respectful" reading of the Bible because it makes them "gender blind," in the sense that they ignore the harmful effects of the patriarchal elements of the Bible on women. She calls for a transformation in approaches to reading and applying the Bible in Myanmar, such that the Bible can be read from "social, political and gender perspectives," "through the lens of Myanmar women's 'redemptive body' or liberation."[32] She advocates Jesus's model of church, which Schüssler Fiorenza describes as being a "discipleship of equals." This is a direct challenge to the "culture of respect" orientation which blocks any critical or questioning approach to reading biblical texts.

6.3.1.2 Respect for the Translation

The culture of respect for the translation work of Adoniram Judson is another challenge for biblical interpreters in Myanmar. Given the culture of respect for teachers, and Myanmar Christians' widespread respect for Judson as the most revered missionary in Myanmar's history, until very recently his translation has been accepted uncritically. Even when Judson's work has been questioned, it is mostly concerned with his mission strategies, specifically his communication strategy related to evangelization of Buddhists.

Among the books and articles written about Judson are publications by Samuel Ngun Ling,[33] Tha Din,[34] Cung Nawl,[35] Cung Lian Hup,[36] Aung Mang,[37] Simon Pau Khan En,[38] La Seng Dingrin,[39] and Peter Thein Nyunt.[40] These scholars see the positive aspects of Judson's work but also raise some critiques of his mission strategy. Dingrin deals extensively with Judson's borrowing of Buddhist terminology from sacred literature, particularly Judson's

---

31. Nwe, "Women's Roles, Rights," 32.
32. Nwe, 33.
33. Ling, *Communicating Christ in Myanmar*. See also his "Doing Theology," and "Challenges, Problems, and Prospects."
34. Din, *Comparative Study*.
35. Nawl, *Why Myanmar Church Fails*.
36. Hup, "Brief Survey of Mission."
37. Mang, "Training to Effectively Communicate."
38. En, "*Nat* Worship."
39. Dingrin, "Adoniram Judson's Tracts."
40. Nyunt, *Missions amidst Pagodas*.

language for God and theological concepts borrowed from Buddhism. He acknowledges Judson's sincere efforts to achieve translatability between Buddhist and Christian concepts, but also points out that Judson's negative attitude toward Buddhism contributed to his failure to win over the Burmese Buddhists to Christianity.

To my knowledge, only a very few Christian scholars have ever questioned the work of Judson in terms of his word usage in his Bible translation. Khoi Lam Thang[41] is one who has addressed some problematic aspects of Judson's translation. For example, he highlights what he sees as Judson's unfortunate choice of the term *shwe lin ta* ("golden vulture") rather than *lin yung* ("eagle") in Isaiah 40:31. He notes that a new translation of this passage by unknown authors, called the Eagle Edition, came out in 2006 and revised this word usage in Judson's translation. Thang agrees that, in the context of Isaiah 40, "it is appropriate to translate *nesher* as 'eagle' rather than 'vulture,' because although both birds are noted for their ability to soar upwards, the vulture has many more negative associations because of its carrion-eating, and is therefore a less suitable translation."[42] In response to the argument that Judson might not have known the term for "eagle" in Burmese, he notes Judson's usage of both *lin yung* and *shwe lin ta* in Leviticus 11.13 and Deuteronomy 14.12. However, he acknowledges that critics of Judson question his usage in Isaiah due to "a very strong negative connotation" associated with vultures in Myanmar, and that even the positive term "golden" before "vulture" "cannot supersede the negative connotations of vulture."[43]

The fact that the authors of the revised translation remain anonymous, and that so few have questioned Judson's translation, can be linked to Myanmar's culture of respect. Adoniram Judson is not only respected among Christians but also by other religious groups in Myanmar, because of his contributions to the Burmese language. U Pe Maung Tin noted this widespread respect in relation to the legacy of Judson College. This widely acclaimed institution was founded in 1920, but it was closed by the authorities in 1948. In lamenting this closure, Maung Tin noted that "the Judson Bible was a welcome contribution to Burmese literature and the Buddhists would

---

41. Thang, "Eagle in the Myanmar Bible," 195.
42. Thang, 195.
43. Thang, 195.

never dream of burning it, but Judson College, with its fine academic record, was closed down"[44] nonetheless, because it was a foreign (American) missionary college. The point is that, because of the culture of respect, the people of Myanmar have found it extremely difficult to critique the work of someone as highly respected as Judson.

The challenge for Myanmar biblical interpreters is to understand the difference between constructive criticism and negative, disrespectful criticism. The need to reexamine Judson's Burmese translation is an important task for biblical studies in Myanmar. As a case in point, let us return to a concern, from our earlier discussion of the virtue of submission, about the use of the word *eindaray* ("decent, silent, submissive behavior") in Judson's translation of 1 Timothy 2:9–15. His choice of *eindaray* rather than other terms for modesty and self-restraint indicates the need for a critical revisiting of this translation decision.

Eh Tar Gay has commented on the usage of this word *eindaray* in Judson's translation of 1 Timothy 2:9[45] and 15,[46] rather than other words for feminine virtue.[47] But she does not mention the conceptual distance between the word that Judson used and the actual context of the texts. For example, in 1 Timothy 2:9 and 15, the Greek word used is σωφροσύνη, "decently" or "modestly." Louw and Nida define this word as "to have understanding about practical matters and thus be able to act sensibly – to have sound judgment, to be sensible, to use good sense, sound judgment."[48] In contrast, as noted earlier, the word *eindaray* refers to a distinctively feminine understanding of decency which includes "having long hair," "speaking softly, not shouting," "having a submissive attitude to the control and protection of a father or a brother or a husband," and avoiding "a job involving contact with or leading many men, having more than one partner, turning to prostitution."[49] The difference in meaning between σωφροσύνη and *eindaray* shows the problematic nature of

---

44. U, "Professor U Pe Maung Tin," 40.

45. "Also that the women should dress themselves modestly and *decently* (σωφροσύνης) in suitable clothing, not with their hair braided, or with gold, pearls, or expensive clothes." (NRSV)

46. "Yet she will be saved through childbearing, provided they continue in faith and love and holiness, with *modesty* (σωφροσύνης)." (NRSV)

47. Gay, "Authority and Submission," 304.

48. Nida, *Greek-English Lexicon*, 383.

49. Gay, "Authority and Submission," 301.

Judson's translation choice in this instance. Judson's choice of *eindaray* has consequences in terms of Myanmar women's understanding of what it means to have the virtue of submission. Critical analysis is likewise needed in relation to Judson's word choices in 1 Corinthians 14:34–35 regarding women and silence.

To summarize, there is a need for biblical interpreters in Myanmar to come to a new understanding that rereading the Judson translation with a critical eye does not mean disrespecting the translator. Without liberating the Myanmar culture of respect from its most extreme constraints, it will be impossible for interpreters to fully understand how the translator's context-influenced choices play such an important role in translation. The need in Myanmar is to understand Judson's translation as an interpretation of the translator, influenced by the translator's context as well as the receptor's context. This understanding will help us both to appreciate the depth of Judson's scholarship as well as to open space for critical inquiry that will aid Myanmar scholars in constructing adequate hermeneutics.

6.3.2 Rethinking Language Study

The need for Myanmar interpreters to develop some critical contextual hermeneutics also surfaces around language study, which includes original biblical languages and Burmese Buddhist terminologies in Judson's Bible translation. Although the biblical languages, Greek and Hebrew, are taught in Bible colleges and seminaries in Myanmar, they are taught in dialogue with English texts rather than the Burmese Bible translation. From my personal experience of teaching Greek language courses in Myanmar, I have found that this process of translating Greek into English prevents interpreters from examining biblical texts in Burmese with a critical eye.

This deficiency in language training in biblical studies highlights a more general need to revisit the standard curriculum in Myanmar theological institutions. Since Christianity came to Myanmar from the West, our theological education was also imported from the West, and Western curricular models are still being used, even though the missionaries have been gone for many years. This uncritical acceptance of imported models of theological education is a serious weakness. This has been noted by Thein Nyunt in his comment that Myanmar theologians and biblical interpreters are "venerating the imported mission outreach or strategy inherited from the past centuries and eras without critical appraisal of their relevancy and empowering vitality," and that this results in "weaknesses in mission strategy, ineffective Christian communication, and lack of indigeneity in particular."[50] This has created a Myanmar church that "looks like an imported monstrosity. Its buildings, forms, music, and methods are often so different from those of the Bamar Buddhist society."[51] Samuel Ngun Ling also notes the dependency patterns of theological formation in Myanmar, which continue to rely on the missionaries' teaching and imported theologies, and which are still seen in "the textbooks, curricula, and teaching methodologies used in Bible Schools and theological institutes of Myanmar."[52]

Recognizing the need to transform these patterns, some of the theologians in Myanmar referenced earlier in this chapter have sought to construct a contextual theology that addresses the contextual concerns of the people of Myanmar. Among these scholars, La Seng Dingrin has drawn attention to the important role of Adoniram Judson in forming Christian terminologies by borrowing Pali words in his translation of the Bible. He notes that Judson borrowed at least eighty principal Burmese Buddhist terms in his construction of Christian terminologies. Some examples include the usage of *bhura* (God or god), *tara* (law), *kusala* (merit), *kye ju to* (grace), and many more.[53] La Seng Dingrin argues that "Judson would not have been able to communicate the Christian concept of God without borrowing, and then Christianizing, the term *bhura* (God or god) from Burmese Buddhism." Because these Burmese Buddhist concepts are so prominent in Judson's Bible translation, dialectical studies of Buddhism and Christianity are now finally beginning to be taught in some seminaries that are attempting to take context seriously. The serious study of all relevant languages is essential if we are to construct a relevant hermeneutical methodology for Myanmar.

---

50. Nyunt, "Toward a Paradigm," 4.
51. Nyunt, 5.
52. Ling, "Challenges, Problems, and Prospects," 3.
53. Dingrin, "Conflicting Legacy."

6.3.3 Rethinking Comparative Studies

A common practice in Myanmar hermeneutical approaches is to compare the texts of several English translations, at times with the text in its original language for those who have some knowledge of the original biblical languages. The most popular English translations used in Myanmar for comparative study are the New International Version (NIV) and the King James Version (KJV). The problem with comparing these English translations is that they are, of course, their translators' understandings of the text. Without understanding the translator's role as interpreter, interpreters today often end up with different meanings than what the text originally said, and this is especially so in the case of 1 Corinthians 14:34–35.

As discussed in chapter 3, the Judson Burmese translation of 1 Corinthians 14:34–35 has significantly influenced the role of women in the church. Given the propensity of the culture of obedience to take a literal approach to reading the Bible, it is understandable that interpreters who have only used Judson's translation take this passage as a prohibition of women preaching in the church. However, surprisingly, many of the interpreters who do comparative studies with English versions often end up with even stricter restrictions on women. This will be demonstrated in the following chart, which compares the Judson Burmese Translation with the KJV and NIV English versions.

We see here that although the KJV and NIV translate σιγάω (silence) as applying to "speak," the Judson Burmese translation has silence being applied to "preach." Instead of considering these differences that highlight problematic aspects of the text, Myanmar interpreters often take this prohibition in English translations as applying to all kinds of speech, as well as preaching. Thus, the English translation becomes more restrictive for women than the Burmese translation would indicate. This shows the weakness in comparing translations without critical analysis and in limiting the translations under comparison.

Table 16. A Comparison of the JB, KJV, and NIV
Translations of 1 Corinthians 14:34a

Judson Burmese Translation	Literal Translation of Judson Burmese Bible	King James Version	New International Version
သင်တို့၏ မိန်းမတို့သည် အသင်းတော်၌ တိတ်ဆိတ်စွာ နေကြစေ။	Your wives should remain silent in the church.	³⁴ Let your women keep silence in the churches:	³⁴ Women should remain silent in the churches.
သူတို့သည် ဟောပြောရသော အခွင့်မရှိကြ။	They have no permission to preach.	for it is not permitted unto them to speak;	They are not allowed to speak,
ပညတ်တရားစီရင်သည့်အတိုင်း သူတို့သည် ယောက်ျား၏ အုပ်စိုးခြင်းကို ဝန်ခံရကြမည်။	As the Law says, they should consent to man's ruling.	but they are *commanded* to be under obedience, as also saith the law.	but must be in submission, as the law says.
မိန်းမတို့သည် တစုံတခုကို သင်လိုလျှင်၊ အိမ်၌ မိမိခင်ပွန်းတို့ကို မေးမြန်းကြစေ။	If women want to learn something, let them ask their own husbands at home.	³⁵ And if they will learn anything, let them ask their husbands at home:	³⁵ If they want to inquire about something, they should ask their own husbands at home;
မိန်းမသည် အသင်းတော်၌ ဟောပြောလျှင် ရှက်ဘွယ်သော အကြောင်း ဖြစ်၏။	For a woman to preach in the church, it is a shameful thing.	for it is a shame for women to speak in the church.	for it is disgraceful for a woman to speak in the church.

6.3.4 Rethinking Hermeneutical Methods

Another challenge in reading a difficult passage like 1 Corinthians 14:34–35 is selecting a method of approach to the text. Quite apart from denominational teachings, the common practice of biblical studies in Myanmar is a traditional methodological approach handed down by the missionaries. This assumes objectivity and normativity and prevents interpreters from looking at the text from a different perspective. Although contextual factors impinging on the interpreter play an influential role in determining how one approaches and interprets Scripture, this role has been ignored in hermeneutical practices in Myanmar.

Many Myanmar Christians would agree generally with Ling's statement that "doing theology in Myanmar should be concerned with the need to study current issues in Myanmar. These issues include economic poverty, religious freedom, gender, women and children, health, development and environment."[54] However, the same Christians would be reluctant to accept the view that all interpreters approach the text with culturally or denominationally conditioned presuppositions. Texts concerning women and silence found in 1 Corinthians 14 and 1 Timothy 2 are examples of sources of tension for women doing theology in Myanmar. If they raise hermeneutical issues, they are immediately branded as feminist, Western, and anti-male. Typically, their views are ignored and their methodologies are deemed to be a case of "bias" rather than critical analysis.

This raises the crucial issue of how Myanmar Christians can explore and evaluate new hermeneutical approaches to contentious texts such as 1 Corinthians 14 and 1 Timothy 2. Some contemporary interpreters in Myanmar do approach biblical texts in a way similar to their counterparts in "Latin America, Africa and Asia, where people are reading and studying the Bible in direct relation to the often trying circumstances of their daily lives."[55] Due to the constant struggles and instability caused by longstanding political crises in Myanmar, the Bible is largely read and studied by these interpreters in direct relation to daily experiences of struggle, whether knowingly or unconsciously. This is different from hermeneutical methodologies in the West, where interpreters approach texts more abstractly.

The need for Myanmar interpreters to understand and respond to the Myanmar context when approaching biblical texts is echoed in the 1978 Lausanne Consultation on Gospel and Culture *Willowbank Report*, which states that biblical interpreters "cannot come to the text in a personal vacuum

---

54. Ling, "Challenges, Problems, and Prospects," 8.
55. Luz, *Bible in a World Context*, back cover.

and should not try to. Instead, they should come with an awareness of concerns stemming from their cultural background, personal situation, and responsibility to others."[56] This includes an awareness of the interpreter's role in the hermeneutical process, as well as considering the effects of contextually influenced interpretation on the lives of people. This also means that Myanmar interpreters should not try to ignore or suppress concerns and questions, but rather allow themselves to be challenged by the text and be willing to be corrected by the process of critical analysis. This approach gives interpreters freedom from fear of being labeled exemplars of "bias" and the liberty to raise all concerns arising from texts and contexts, while at the same time generating theological reflections that are relevant for Myanmar.

6.3.5 Rethinking Leadership

Another area in need of rethinking in the development of a critical contextual hermeneutics is the Myanmar understanding of leadership. The observations of Chin Do Kham, who conducted a study on Myanmar church leaders, clarify how leadership is viewed in Myanmar. He points out that "in churches today, including Myanmar, many seem to preach biblical leadership principles such as servanthood, yet their day to day actions reflect secular, dictatorial, authoritarian leadership styles."[57] He links this to traditional cultural understandings of leadership that are deeply rooted in the hierarchical system of Burmese Buddhism (with its longstanding influence on Myanmar monarchs throughout the centuries), British colonial values, and Western missionary values. In this light, he concludes that "servant leadership is seen as a weakness in the Burmese context."

Kham's study finds that the concept of leadership in Myanmar is based on a traditional understanding that a leader's legitimacy derives from his position, "which is a symbol of power, authority, superiority and control."[58] In this view, leaders "who can command others are seen as competent, influential, and effective." He also notes that since the dominant image of leadership in Myanmar is "performance oriented," autocratic leaders with many

---

56. Lausanne Committee for World Evangelization, *Willowbank Report*, 6.
57. Kham, "Historical Values and Modes," 92.
58. Kham, 157.

followers are seen as successful, and thus the character traits of leaders are deemed to be secondary.

Kham sees Jesus's teaching on servant leadership as in direct contrast to this dominant cultural view of leadership in Myanmar. This teaching of Jesus is found, for example, in Mark 10:35–45, where he taught that those who aspire to be in leadership must become servants among God's people; and in John 13:5, where Jesus demonstrated servant leadership by washing the feet of his disciples. Since the word "servant" is a negative term in the worldview of people in Myanmar, Kham acknowledges that "all Burmese Christian leaders are living with a strong tension between the culturally acceptable authoritarian leadership style and biblical servant leadership."[59] Therefore, although servant leadership is accepted conceptually in Myanmar, men cling to their positions of power, authority, superiority, and control in the hierarchy of the church.

Given this conceptual clash between the servant leadership demanded and exemplified by Jesus and the strong hierarchical understanding of leadership in Myanmar culture, it was inevitable that a literal interpretation of 1 Corinthians 14:34–35 that commands women to be silent always has not been questioned. It is also understandable that rereading this text with a critical eye will be met with great resistance. This illustrates the crucial impact of cultural understandings of concepts such as leadership on the interpretation of texts like 1 Corinthians 14:34–35, and thus the need for critical analysis of both the interpreter's context and the context of the text.

6.4 Obstacles to a Critical Contextual Myanmar Hermeneutic

This section focuses on ways to address the obstacles and challenges to developing a critical contextual Myanmar hermeneutic that have been identified in this chapter. This will require a willingness to review the Myanmar context and to learn from other approaches to interpretation. But such openness will only be possible through greater exposure to the world of scholarship. This will lead not only to a more honest appraisal of the Myanmar context,

---

59. Kham, 152.

but also to rethinking the translator's role, rereading the text considering its historical context, and embracing servant leadership.

6.4.1 Need for Increased Exposure to the World

A major issue we have identified in interpreting passages that concern women in the church is a literal reading of such texts. As demonstrated in previous sections, this approach can be linked to the cultures of respect and obedience, and it is problematic because it does not critically analyze the contextual influences on the translators' choices. This shows the need for greater willingness and ability to understand and analyze all contexts (biblical, translator, and interpreter) in Myanmar hermeneutics. Yet, this will only be possible through increased exposure to different approaches to interpretation around the world. While actual travel to other centers of biblical scholarship is unfeasible for most Myanmar interpreters, the explosion of respected online sources now makes this exposure more possible.

However, awareness of these reservoirs of knowledge has been very limited in Myanmar to date, for two reasons: lack of theological materials, especially developments in contextual theologies from around the world, and lack of access to the internet. The shortage of theological materials does not mean that theologians in Myanmar have not been writing about or raising contextual questions. Yet, as noted in chapter 2, a related challenge has been the lack of freedom of expression and ability to publish, as well as very strict government regulations that have prohibited the import of religious materials until recently. Since resources have only circulated within certain organizations, exposure to information, from both within and outside the country, has been limited. With the opening up of Myanmar society since the restoration of democracy, it is hoped that this exposure will increase.

6.4.1.1 Exposure through Online Resources

Many contextual theologians and biblical scholars around the world, including Asia, other parts of the non-Western world, and in the West, have written extensively on the importance of context in biblical interpretation. Many of these resources are now available online. Following Myanmar's years of self-imposed isolation from the rest of the world, which only ended in 2010, mobile SIM card prices began to drop from 20 lakhs (nearly 2000 USD) to

1500 kyats (1.50 USD) in 2014.⁶⁰ Although the internet was introduced in Myanmar in 1997, only 1 percent of the population had internet access in 2011.⁶¹ However, price drops have meant an increasing affordability of cellphones, and this has led in turn to increased use of internet services.

The legacy of isolation from the world explains the difficulties entailed in accessing theological materials online, something which theologians and biblical scholars from other countries have enjoyed for many years. Myanmar thus lags far behind in theology and biblical studies in comparison to the rest of the world. Although internet access is now more widely available for public use in Myanmar, the internet speed is widely referred to as "slower than a turtle." However, the hope for Myanmar is that as internet speed and access continue to improve, the exposure to different approaches to interpretation, especially those open to critical contextual analysis, will raise awareness among Myanmar interpreters of ways to overcome the obstacles to critical contextual hermeneutics. They will gain the ability and confidence to approach all contexts critically – biblical, translator, and interpreter.

6.4.1.2 *Exposure through External Publications*

Increased exposure to published resources, particularly online sources, will mean greater acquaintance with a variety of scholars writing on feminism, women in leadership, contextual theology, developments in hermeneutics, and other related fields. This will assist Myanmar interpreters in understanding that not all who advocate feminism in Christianity are women, and that not all Western feminists are antagonistic toward males. Many well-known Western male scholars, such as Ben Witherington, Gordon Fee, Craig Keener, and Stanley Grenz, are among a host of respected biblical scholars who hold a "biblical feminist" view.⁶² They differ from proponents of "Christian feminism" represented by scholars such as Elisabeth Schüssler Fiorenza, who advocate for "suspicion of biblical authority" and who seek to "denounce all texts and traditions that perpetuate and legitimate oppressive patriarchal structures in the 'Word of God' for contemporary communities and people."⁶³

---

60. Di Certo, "Building a Digital Future," 16.
61. Freedom House, "Burma," *Freedom on the Net 2011*, 77.
62. Mickelsen, ed., *Women, Authority and the Bible*. The authors were participants in a 1984 Evangelical Colloquium on Women and the Bible.
63. Schüssler Fiorenza, "Will to Choose or to Reject," 130.

Biblical interpreters in Myanmar will benefit from knowledge of both "biblical feminist" and "Christian feminism" approaches. "Biblical feminists" affirm the authority of the Bible and see the issue of oppression of women as one which can be addressed through careful interpretation. They argue that the Bible advocates for the mutuality of men and women in all spheres of life, including marriage and ministry in the church. Both views of feminism consider the role of the interpreter in the process of interpretation, but they differ in their views of the authority of the Bible, and this leads to differences in their approaches to biblical passages about women. These approaches can be instructive for biblical interpreters in Myanmar, as they evaluate these different views in dialogue with the contextual realities of Myanmar, to reread biblical texts about women with effective critical contextual hermeneutics.

6.4.1.3 Exposure through Myanmar Publications

There is also a critical need for growth in academic publications by biblical scholars from Myanmar, specifically on passages that concern women. This will not only help increase awareness of the role of our context in the process of interpretation but will also stimulate a more relevant theology that seeks to answer questions that arise from within our context. This is "contextualizing theology," to borrow from Kosuke Koyama,[64] rather than contextual theology. This contextualizing is a dynamic, ongoing process that will raise awareness of the complex nature of our social reality in Myanmar, where poverty, deeply held religious beliefs (both Christian and Buddhist), violence, communal conflict, authoritarianism, colonial history, entrenched patriarchy, and the reality of discrimination co-exist at all levels of society. Contextualizing theology raises consciousness of all the ways in which our theological reflection, praxis, and our reading of Scripture are deeply influenced by the interplay of political, cultural, and religious dynamics.

Within this enterprise of contextualizing theology, some biblical scholars have already begun grappling with questions that arise from the social realities of Myanmar. For example, Samuel Ngun Ling has raised the issue of the linkage between violence and poverty in Myanmar, where ethnic violence and conflicts are extensive, due to the long history of oppression. In this light, his comment on women and violence mentioned earlier sheds further light

---

64. Koyama, "New Heaven and New Earth."

on the need to engage in contextualizing theology and biblical study in Myanmar. He points out various forms of violence, including sexual violence, suffered by women in Myanmar, and links these harsh realities to the long history of the submissive role imposed on women by the patriarchal political, religious, and cultural worldview of Myanmar. He concludes that "physical violence against women has become an important gender-related dimension."[65] He therefore suggests that the issues of violence and poverty in Myanmar require a "radical change of human attitude and mentality, spirituality and lifestyle – the creation of a new praxis, from passive co-existence to active pro-existence according to the model and way of Christ." This orientation has profound implications for Myanmar interpreters' approach to biblical texts affecting women.

6.4.2 Rethinking Judson's Translation

The exploration of ways to overcome obstacles to a Myanmar hermeneutic that addresses biblical passages concerning women also suggests the need to rethink the translator's context in Myanmar. As discussed earlier, due to Myanmar's culture of respect that has led interpreters to revere the translator Adoniram Judson, his translation work has seldom been questioned. Yet, rethinking Judson is a necessity if we are to overcome obstacles to an adequate Myanmar hermeneutics. I argue that there are two issues which interpreters in Myanmar must address in the translation work of Judson: learning from his usage of Burmese terminologies in his translation (along with related mistakes in his approach to mission) and analyzing the influence of his own context on his translation. We must rethink Judson's translation from a critical point of view rather than from the perspective of incontestable respect.

6.4.2.1 Terminology and Translation

According to La Seng Dingrin, as cited earlier, the legacy of Judson must be understood in terms of two conflicting facts. First, Judson borrowed Burmese Buddhist terminologies for his translation, reappropriating them for Christian use. At the same time, he held a very negative view of Buddhism and attempted to replace Buddhist ideology with a Christian ideology. Dingrin believes that understanding both aspects of Judson is important for evaluating

---

65. Ling, "Violence, Poverty, Justice," 54.

his work. He argues that the first aspect – Judson's usage of Burmese Buddhist terminologies for Christian purposes – was largely a success, while his negative attitude toward Buddhism was a failure.[66] A contextually conscious hermeneutics in Myanmar must evaluate both to make an accurate assessment of his translation.

I argue that the fact that Judson borrowed Burmese Buddhist terms and turned them into Christian terms accentuates the need for Myanmar interpreters to undertake a serious analysis of Judson's translation choices. It also requires a dialectical study of Buddhism and Christianity. Judson sought to spread the gospel in the vernacular to convert the Burmese people, and an essential part of this mission was his production of a Bible translation and Bible tracts using the Burmese language.[67] He did this with the understanding that the "formation of Christian literature in Myanmar indicates the meeting of the Christian gospel with Theravada Buddhism."[68]

This is seen in his usage of the word *bhura* for God, a term borrowed from Burmese Buddhism.[69] Since *bhura* has a wide range of meanings, such as one who is "the highest and holiest of human beings" or the "noblest religious term" for the Buddha and monks, La Seng Dingrin argues that this concept is "not only very Theravada Buddhist but also contradictory to the Christian concepts of God, creation, and the atonement of Jesus Christ." He believes that it was for this reason that Judson added *thavara* (eternal) before *bhura*, meaning "eternal God," to better describe the Christian concept of God. He sees this choice, along with other Burmese Buddhist terminologies, as evidence that Judson was "perfectly acquainted with the terms he employs" in his translation, since this term looks "very Christian" and "at the same, truly Burmese Buddhist too, though it does not refer at all to the Buddha."[70] Looking at just this one example of Judson's borrowing and reframing of Burmese Buddhist concepts indicates that he was contextually aware to some extent in his thinking.

---

66. Dingrin, "Conflicting Legacy," 4.
67. Judson, *Life of Adoniram Judson*, 564.
68. Dingrin, "Adoniram Judson's Tracts," 53.
69. Dingrin, "Conflicting Legacy," 4.
70. Dingrin, 6.

Judson's contextual awareness is further seen in terminology that he avoided using. Nyunt notes that Judson was clearly aware that the Buddhist understanding of heaven is quite different from the Christian concept. Since the "ultimate need of Buddhists is enlightenment or obtaining *Nibbana* . . . [which is] not a perpetuation of reincarnation,"[71] Judson avoided using this term to describe the Christian concept for the result of one's faith, and he thus translated as "eternal life" or "heaven" the terms *htawara a-that or kaung kin bon*. He understood that the Christian concept of heaven or eternal life is quite different from the Buddhist concept that sees heaven as a continuation of a miserable state of suffering, although it is to some degree better than earthly existence. In this view, heaven is the biggest curse for Buddhists, since "it is understood in terms of a predestined process, a miserable cyclic rise and fall of one meaningless, aimless reincarnation after another."

In examining these and other examples from Judson's borrowed as well as avoided terminologies in his Bible translation, Myanmar interpreters need to have an in-depth knowledge of Burmese Buddhism in order to be able to evaluate Judson's usage of Buddhist terminology. In Nyunt's research among local missionaries, mainly from minority ethnic groups in Myanmar who are working among the Bamar Buddhists, he notes their lack of contextualization in communicating the gospel.

> Significantly, most respondents were still not ready to exchange traditional approaches with more culturally relevant and contextually appropriate approaches. In the area of language, all communicators strongly emphasized using Burmese language but still many of them were not yet familiar with Buddhist terms. In general, most churches were hesitant to make use of the Buddhist Scripture. This may be a sign of their negative attitudes towards the Buddhist religion and its scriptures.[72]

La Seng Dingrin links these negative attitudes toward the Buddhist religion and scriptures to Judson's negative view of Buddhism, which he refers to as a conflicting legacy. He gives several examples of Judson's view of Burmese Buddhism, which he referred to as "atheistic," "false," "fictitious,"

---

71. Davis, *Poles Apart*, viii.
72. Nyunt, "Toward a Paradigm," 162.

"idolatrous," and "offering no escape," and refers to Judson's prediction of "the fall of Buddhism and the worldwide victory of Christianity."[73]

Because of Judson's attitude, in Pe Maung Tin's view, "the missionaries evidently came neither to learn from nor to make Buddhists the object of their missionary love and concern. Rather, the Buddhists are seen only as the object of the missionaries' preaching."[74] Nyunt links Judson's negative perspectives on Burmese Buddhism to his failure in his mission work, where it took him around six years to win one convert.[75] The clash between what the Burmese think of themselves and what Westerners like Judson thought of them clarifies this dynamic. Nyunt describes this disjunction clearly in the following way:

> Leaving aside the history, the Bamar people assume themselves as the descendants of Buddha's clan and assume that they know more about life and religion than any other ethnic group in the world.[76] For this reason, when Western missionaries came and preached the gospel to them, they felt insulted instead of accepting it. They could not endure to hear any better knowledge than they had. It reflects their belief that they had arrived on this earth earlier than others. Consequently, they presumed that they knew more about life and religion than the Westerners who came to preach. This heritage produced a mentality of superiority in the Bamar people and has been a challenge to the missionary task of the Church.[77]

The above observations show that rethinking Judson must include a critical examination of his familiarity with Buddhist terms and his appropriation of them in his translation. Rethinking Judson also necessitates an evaluation of the mistakes of Judson the missionary, and learning from them as an important task for critical analysis. This is relevant today since Judson's negative attitudes toward Buddhism remain prevalent among the missionaries and clergy in Myanmar, as well as in theological education. Noting these

---

73. Dingrin, "Conflicting Legacy," 3.
74. Tin, "Presenting the Gospel," 28.
75. Nyunt, "Toward a Paradigm," 145.
76. Bischoff, *Buddhism in Myanmar*, 4.
77. Nyunt, "Toward a Paradigm," 109.

negative attitudes in the Myanmar church today, Nyunt points out that "the Christian missionaries in Myanmar did not seem to be so active in indigenizing the gospel and in adapting themselves to the Bamar situation;" for this reason, the "foreignness of Christianity as introduced and practiced in Myanmar constitutes a difficult barrier for the present-day missionary to overcome."[78] Ling observes these same negative attitudes toward Buddhism in theological education in Myanmar, where "less or even no attention [is paid] to questions posed by multi-faith traditions (Buddhist, Christian, and others), their spiritual experiences and moral values."[79]

This legacy of Judson points out the need for Myanmar interpreters to take into better account the cultures and languages within the Myanmar context. This process entails a thoroughgoing reconsideration of Judson's translation. In that context, a reexamination of texts that concern women, particularly texts on women and silence like 1 Corinthians 14:34–35, would mean engaging dialogically with both the translator's choices and the cultural context of contemporary interpreters and readers.

6.4.2.2 The Influence of the Translator's Context

Rethinking Judson also entails critically analyzing how his own context influenced his translation. Since translation is already the translator's interpretation, the influences of the translator's own cognitive environment are inevitable, and they are visible in the translator's choice of words. Paul Ellingworth's explanation of this dynamic is instructive. He claims that if the work of the translator is effective, "it will challenge its readers, potentially a whole language community, to undertake a reverse pilgrimage from B (*interpreter's own situation*) to A (*world of the Bible*); that is, in translational terms, to 'analyze' its own situation and presuppositions; to relate or 'transfer' them to the world of the Bible, and relate them by a process of 'restructuring' to the biblical message" (emphasis added).[80]

I would argue that when a translation has been accepted in the interpretive community as a good translation, interpreters often go directly from their context to the context of the Bible without considering the historical gap, the

---

78. Nyunt, 145.
79. Ling, "Challenges, Problems, and Prospects," 5.
80. Ellingworth, "Theory and Practice," 164.

language gap, and the time gap between the contexts. This explains an important aspect of the uncritical nature of most interpretation that relies on Judson's translation. Since the translation is well received in Myanmar, the interpreter often does not pause to consider that one's own context influenced the translator. It is important for Myanmar interpreters to understand that Judson's translation is itself interpretation, and that it thus needs to be subject to critical analysis like any other work. This entails understanding factors in Judson's own nineteenth-century Protestant American cultural and religious background that would have predisposed him to come to texts such as 1 Corinthians 14 with a view on the roles and status of women. As discussed in chapter 3, Judson's views on women preaching, and broader issues surrounding women's leadership in the church, are important factors in understanding the choices he made in translating such texts.

6.4.3 Rereading the Text in Light of the Historical Context

Given the Myanmar culture of obedience and respect, which leads to a literal reading of biblical texts, Myanmar interpreters tend to equate the present situation with the historical context described or implied in the text. These interpreters thus often appropriate the patriarchy they find in the Bible as normative for today and use it to reinforce the subservient role of women in family, church, and society, without considering the text within its own context. This form of spontaneous adoption through literal interpretation does not critically consider the gaps between the world of the Bible and the present context of the interpreter – the "historical gap," the "cultural gap," similarities or differences in worldviews (also called the "philosophical gap"), and the "linguistic gap."[81] The remedy is to explore the meaning of the text in light of its historical context, for "the meaning of a text cannot be interpreted with any degree of certainty without historical-cultural and contextual analysis."[82]

Regarding this investigation of the historical context of a biblical text, Osborne's suggestions are helpful for the Myanmar interpreter. He argues that understanding the historical context is the first stage in serious biblical study, for this process is a consideration of "the larger context within which

---

81. Virkler and Ayayo, *Hermeneutics: Principles and Processes*, 19.
82. Virkler and Ayayo, 81.

a passage is found."[83] Without this, "interpretation is doomed from the start," because "statements simply have no meaning apart from their context."[84] In addition, the interpreter must investigate issues of authorship, dating, the audience being addressed in the text, and, most importantly, the purpose and themes of the text in light of the larger context, because the interpreter "should not study any passage without a basic knowledge of the problems and situation addressed in the book and the themes with which the writer addressed those problems."[85] All of these concerns are important aspects of critical analysis of the historical context.

The purpose of this historical study is to discover what the text meant in its original setting, and how it relates to the rest of Scripture, to apply the originally intended meaning in a contextually relevant way today. With regard to this important role of historical context in forming theological meaning, the Myanmar scholar Khin Swe Oo argues that passages that concern women in ministry today must be "properly examined and interpreted in the light of the overall teachings of the Scripture, and the cultural environment of those days for which they were originally intended, as well as practical theological implications in our present context."[86] In that light, she notes that problematic passages such as 1 Corinthians 11, 14, and 1 Timothy 2 "were originally written to different audiences and places, regarding different specific situations, contexts, times and problems encountered." This knowledge of the historical context of the texts should condition our application of such texts for our own context today.

An understanding of the nature of contextual theology is also helpful in looking at the text in historical context. Contextual interpretation studies the original context and language, but also with an eye toward listening to God's word and heeding it. In other words, the interpreter appropriates the text in its historical context and, in that light, seeks to discern "what Scripture is affirming"[87] to apply it in culturally appropriate forms in the present. As mentioned earlier, in the discussion of selective literalism in Myanmar

---

83. Osborne, *Hermeneutical Spiral*, 36–37.
84. Osborne, 36–37.
85. Osborne, 38.
86. Oo, "Theological Understanding of Women," 5.
87. Lausanne Committee for World Evangelization, *Willowbank Report*, 4.

interpretation, the fact that women's head covering advised in 1 Corinthians 11 is rejected solely because head covering is not a Myanmar tradition, and that "Burmese Christians do not wear veils or avoid teaching,"[88] indicates the need to pay greater attention to the historical context of the text.

This example indicates the complexity of interpretation in Myanmar, where readers are more selective in their interpretational process than their claim for a literal approach would suggest, as well as less contextual than their claim for contextualization would suggest. This bolsters my call for greater availability in Myanmar of resources in biblical studies, specifically those on the historical background of texts, such as commentaries, dictionaries, and encyclopedias, and works on cultural customs in the biblical period. A tremendous effort is also needed to translate these into Burmese languages, so that theological students, pastors, and others can read biblical texts in the light of their historical context.

6.4.4 The Need to Embrace Servant Leadership

As discussed, the hierarchical system in Myanmar society is one of the obstacles to doing contextual hermeneutics, because this ideology understands leadership as "power-over" – exercising coercive authority over others and viewing the servant as the lowest form of human experience. This concept of hierarchical power clashes with the concept Jesus introduced in Mark 10:42–45, where he says to his disciples that the greatest person is the one who serves others. Myanmar interpreters know this precept, but although they have accepted it conceptually it has been difficult to apply it in the church, given the cultural embrace of "power-over" leadership. This once again calls for a reevaluation of our theology and practice as Myanmar Christians, so that we can embrace servant leadership more fully.

Aye Nwe suggests that embracing servant leadership in Myanmar necessitates a redefinition of power. She sees this as key to overcoming obstacles in the way of greater involvement of women in leadership in the Myanmar churches. She claims that the current practice of "power-over" leadership is destructive since this is the power of domination, which "creates dualism between the powerful and powerless, rich and poor, strong and weak, advantaged and disadvantaged, man and woman, perpetrator of violence and

---

88. Gay, "Authority and Submission," 300.

victim, oppressor and oppressed."[89] This occurs, she says, due to misinterpretations of the power that God has given to both male and female in creation. The power they have been given through God's gift of "dominion" is a gift of stewardship or care for creation, which is different from the "militaristic and patriarchal understanding of power as domination." Such domination serves the interests of the ruler rather than the well-being of the weak.

In contrast, Jesus's servant model of leadership is "the real imperative to the existing chaos. It is a calling to serve for the well-being of others rather than for self. It is different from hierarchical and patriarchal power. It is constructive power that recognizes 'the power in all.' In the servant model of power, or 'the power to serve,' it is essential for all, men and women, to be included."[90] Nwe concludes that God's originally intended ideal form of power is modeled by Jesus in Matthew 20:14–30, and that Jesus also admonishes his followers to serve others rather than self by his own example in Mark 10:42–45, where he says to his disciples, "but whoever would be great among you must be servant and whoever would be first among you must be slave of all."[91] This power that Jesus modeled and bequeathed to his followers is "the power which sets people free from bondage, oppression, exploitation, abuse, injustice, inhumanity and domination. It is the power that embraces all [so as] to have peace, restoration, order, self-esteem, and harmony with each other."[92]

Embracing the ideal of servant leadership by redefining the meaning of power is also a key to addressing hermeneutical obstacles in Myanmar, especially in relation to passages that concern women in the church. This suggests that when we interpret passages that relate to ministry and church life, we must look at these texts considering Jesus's pattern of servant leadership. This includes our approach to interpretations of passages about women such as 1 Corinthians 14 and 1 Timothy 12. If ministry is serving and a locus of servanthood, and if the church fully accepts ministry as serving the body of Christ in Myanmar, our understanding of these passages will be amended,

---

89. Nwe, "Empowerment as Constructive Power," 2.
90. Nwe, 3.
91. Nwe, 3.
92. Nwe, 3.

since no one will fight over being the waiter. Embracing servant leadership will mean that no one can "lord it over" anyone, including women.

6.5 Conclusion

Having examined the many obstacles and challenges Myanmar interpreters face in interpreting passages that concern women in the church such as 1 Corinthians 14, and having advocated ways to overcome these obstacles, I would like to point out that there are a variety of opinions on the issue of women's silence in the church, and I have only presented three hermeneutical approaches that deal specifically with 1 Corinthians 14:34–35. I find that understanding a variety of opinions on this passage and comparing them is not only helpful in gaining insight, but also more liberating than focusing only on one perspective. Due to the traditional practices of biblical study in Myanmar, interpreters often remain trapped in only one interpretation. However, for Myanmar biblical studies to be both critical and contextually relevant, interpreters need to become more aware of a variety of interpretations of passages. This indicates the need to introduce a range of hermeneutical approaches in our theological institutions. This does not mean that all interpretations are correct but considering them critically necessitates looking at them alongside one another to gain greater insight.

Opening ourselves to a range of hermeneutical approaches also brings challenges to the way we approach biblical texts in Myanmar. As mentioned elsewhere, due to Myanmar's missionary teachings from evangelical traditions, many Myanmar interpreters approach texts solely from the point of view of reverence for the authority of the Bible. Some contemporary interpreters who are more conscious of contextual theology tend to be critical of the missionaries and their approach to mission, and these interpreters are attempting to deal with contextual issues. However, Myanmar interpreters very rarely deal with the implications of the fact that our translation of the Bible came from a missionary. To create well-informed and contextually relevant hermeneutics in Myanmar, interpreters must reread biblical texts with fresh eyes, taking into account all the contexts that inform the texts.

CHAPTER 7

Revisiting the Text through Critical Contextual Hermeneutics

Drawing on the proposed principles and methodology of a critical contextual hermeneutic for Myanmar as outlined in chapter 6, this chapter revisits issues surrounding the interpretation of 1 Corinthians 14:34b-36. It reexamines the primary textual issues raised earlier, as well as contextual issues affecting translation and interpretation. The first section looks at the contextual issues arising from the text that concern women, particularly relating to the historical context. This section argues for an analysis of the historical context as an interpretive key in revisiting the text. The second section reconsiders the primary textual issues in considering the identified hermeneutical keys. This is done by means of a comparative analysis across the contemporary interpretations discussed earlier. These tasks contribute to an understanding of what the texts are likely to have meant to the original readers in their historical context and help identify criteria for a culturally appropriate application of the text in the contemporary context of Myanmar.

7.1 Interpretive Keys in Revisiting the Text

Despite the widespread use of *Lectio Divina* and other devotional practices that focus on the immediate sense of a reading of Scripture without reference to a background knowledge of the text, biblical interpreters generally agree that an understanding of the historical background of the text is critical for hermeneutics. Contextual critical hermeneutics understands the historical context of the biblical text as an important hermeneutical key in determining textual meaning. In this light, this section argues for two interpretive keys in any examination of Pauline passages that concern women in the church. The first key concerns the role of women in the historical context when the text was written, and the second key concerns the general attitude of Paul toward women.

In analyzing the 1 Corinthians 14:34b-36 passage regarding women and silence, then, the hermeneutical keys would include an analysis of the historical context as it related to the role of women in first-century Corinth, and an analysis of Paul's attitude toward women.

The first interpretive key, an analysis of the historical context of the 1 Corinthians 14:34b-36 text, highlights the sociopolitical setting of Corinth as well as the role of women in Corinthian society. The sociopolitical background is relevant because it reveals the attitudes toward women in first-century Greco-Roman society and the influences which shaped such attitudes.

The next part of this analysis examines the role of women in Corinth. Three analytical foci are relevant to the issue of women and silence in 1 Corinthians 14:34b-36: the general role of women in society, how silence was understood in Corinthian society, and the role of women in the religious setting. Addressing these issues can assist the interpreter in undertaking a contextual critical analysis of the text in question.

This analysis is undertaken to demonstrate how these hermeneutical keys can contribute to interpreting difficult texts in Pauline literature. The presupposition is that a critical form of analysis in contextual hermeneutics must seriously consider the historical context before revisiting the meaning and significance of the text. My claim is that the critical analysis of historical contexts is responsible hermeneutics, for it seeks both to be faithful to the historical context and to uncover relevant applications for contemporary settings today.

This critical analysis aspect of contextual hermeneutics recognizes that any interpretation must go through a process of historical reconstruction. Historical analysis requires that the interpreter draw informed conclusions about the circumstances surrounding the text. This means that interpreters need to reconstruct the context to explain the situation in the Corinthian church at the time of Paul's writing. In this process, contextual critical hermeneutics acknowledges the role of interpreter bias in historical analysis, because, like all interpreters of Paul, we are forced to concede a degree of speculation regarding the social circumstances in which his letters were written.

Interpretation of the available information is also likely to be influenced by "our own and other's predilections, preconceived ideas about Paul, views on men and women, limited knowledge of Greco-Roman culture, and a whole host of other subjective and elusive factors."[1] These factors are at work with respect to the three contemporary interpreters (Grudem, Schüssler Fiorenza, and Witherington) whose approaches were explicated in chapter 4. Each of these three scholars' interpretations construct the historical setting slightly different from the others, although all three view the broader context of 1 Corinthians 14 in relation to prophecy. The following section examines important features to consider in a historical reconstruction of the social setting of Corinth in Paul's time.

7.1.1 Women in Corinth

The first part of the analysis of the historical context of 1 Corinthians 14:34b-36 focuses on the social and cultural background during the time of Paul. As Fee notes, understanding "the various sociological, economic, and religious factors that made up the environment of the city of Corinth has a profound influence on one's understanding of Paul's letters to the church there."[2] From the perspective of critical contextual hermeneutics, this analysis is an important process given our concern for the role of women in the Myanmar church, since it helps to provide a critical awareness of the historical gap between the Corinthian context and the Myanmar context. Moreover, as Crocker points out, this makes "one aware of how time-bound some of the problems are that the Corinthians are dealing with and that Paul is discussing."[3]

The city of Corinth was situated about two miles from the Gulf of Corinth, at the southern gateway of the isthmus connecting mainland Greece with the Peloponnesian peninsula.[4] The city had been the largest and most prosperous

---

1. Peppiatt, *Women and Worship*, 9.
2. Fee, *First Epistle to the Corinthians*, 1.
3. Crocker, *Reading First Corinthians*, 25.
4. Fee, *First Epistle to the Corinthians*, 1; Murphy-O'Connor, *St. Paul's Corinth*, 6–10.

city in Greece before it was destroyed by Roman forces in 146 BC.[5] It was reestablished as a Roman colony by the order of Julius Caesar in 44 BC,[6] and repopulated mainly with Roman freedmen, army veterans, and urban tradespersons and laborers.

The city was ruled by Roman officials and even the architecture of the city took on the look of a Roman city.[7] Greeks who lived in and around Corinth, even in its ruins, became "resident aliens," since only Romans and their descendants were now considered citizens.[8] However, once it was rebuilt, many immigrants, including Jews, migrated into the city due to its economy.[9] The kinds of people living in the city mentioned in 1 Corinthians 12:13 and their social status, were described as being "Jew, Greek, slave, free."[10] Many scholars[11] agree with Thiselton that the culture of Corinth after the Roman takeover was "formed after a Roman model" and deemed to be "prosperous and self-sufficient" based on the inhabitants' success in trade and business.[12] Witherington notes that evidence from architecture, arts, and inscriptions depicts a city that was deeply rooted in Roman culture, beyond the official language being Latin[13] and governed according to Roman law. Therefore, he sees the term "Greco-Roman" as the most accurate way to describe Roman Corinth.[14]

Understanding the historical context of Corinth as Roman is important for interpreting passages in 1 Corinthians and helps shed light on the contextual realities which informed Paul's writings. Since "the church was in

---

5. Fee, 1; Murphy-O'Connor, 6–10, 51–54; Witherington, *Conflict and Community*, 4–5. Strabo, *Geography* 8.6.20, cited in Murphy-O'Connor, 51–54, writes: "Corinth is called 'wealthy' because of its commerce, since it is situated on the Isthmus and is master of two harbours, of which one leads straight to Asia, and the other to Italy; and it makes easy the exchange of merchandise from both countries."

6. Fee, 1; Murphy-O'Connor, 6–10, 51–54; Witherington, 4–5.

7. Thiselton, *First Epistle to the Corinthians*, 3; Witherington, 4–5.

8. Thiselton, 3; Witherington, 4–5.

9. Thiselton, 4–5.

10. Fee, *First Epistle to the Corinthians*, 1; Friesen, Schowalter, and Walters, eds., *Corinth in Context*.

11. Fee, 1; Murphy-O'Connor, *St. Paul's Corinth*, 6–10, 51–54; Witherington, *Conflict and Community*, 4.

12. Thiselton, *First Epistle to the Corinthians*, 4–5.

13. Friesen, Schowalter, and Walters, *Corinth in Context*, 23.

14. Witherington, *Conflict and Community*, 8.

many ways a mirror of the city,"[15] many of the practices within the Corinthian church derived from the influence of Roman culture. Thiselton highlights the "impact of the culture of Corinth upon the developing faith of newly converted believers."[16] For Paul, this cultural influence was problematic and so he called for new practices to infuse the life of the church. For example, 1 Corinthian speaks repeatedly of problems of boasting and false pride in the Corinthian church (e.g. 1 Cor 1:28–31; 5:1–2). These behaviors reflected the concept of honor and shame in Roman culture. Witherington points out that this culture of honor and shame was prominent in Corinth, such that public boasting and self-promotion were common practice, and indeed a highly-developed art form. The Corinthians had brought such attitudes into the church. It is in this light that Paul beseeched the Corinthians to allow these Roman cultural values to be transformed by the gospel.

Another aspect of Roman culture which Paul addresses is the custom of veiling for women in public. This is found in the head covering passage of 1 Corinthians 11:2–16. There has been great debate among scholars regarding what Paul meant by "head covering." For example, Payne,[17] Bloomberg,[18] and Murphy-O'Connor[19] see head covering as referring not to an actual head covering, but to appropriate hairstyles for both men and women in Roman culture. However, Fee,[20] Winter,[21] and Thiselton[22] conclude that the passage refers to an actual head covering, based on another aspect of Roman culture. All their arguments focus on what was deemed appropriate in Roman culture. This is captured by Thiselton's comment that "for a married woman in Roman society to appear in public without a hood sent out signals of sexual availability or at the very least a lack of concern for respectability."[23] Understanding

---

15. Fee, *First Epistle to the Corinthians*, 3.

16. Thiselton, *First Epistle to the Corinthians*, xviii.

17. Payne, "Wild Hair and Gender Equality," 9, differentiates between hairstyles for men and women, where long hair for men was associated with homosexuality and respectable women's hair had to be pinned up and not let loose.

18. Blomberg, *1 Corinthians*, 211, sees Paul as warning Corinthian Christian men to keep their hair short and Christian women to keep their hair tied up.

19. Murphy-O'Connor, *Keys to First Corinthians*, 132.

20. Fee, *First Epistle to the Corinthians*, 1; Winter, *Roman Wives, Roman Widows*.

21. Winter, 77.

22. Thiselton, *First Epistle to the Corinthians*, 5.

23. Thiselton, 5.

the dress codes for married women in Roman culture helps explain why wearing a head covering became such an issue. This also sheds light on the reason behind Paul's command for women to prophesy with their heads covered.

This leads to the second concern of the historical analysis, the role of women in Corinthian society. Since our focus is 1 Corinthians 14:34b-36, which speaks of women and silence in the religious setting, this setting becomes our specific concern regarding the role of women. The question is how Corinthian society understood women speaking in relation to the role of women in the religious setting. Focusing on this question is helpful in assisting interpreters not only to understand the issue of women and silence in the primary text, but also to bring critical judgment to bear on what Paul meant by prohibiting women from speaking.

Although he detects a new attitude developing among Roman women in Paul's time, Winter acknowledges that women in the Roman world lived in a deeply patriarchal and hierarchical society where "the power of husbands over their wives can be paralleled with that of the father over his children."[24] Crocker also points out that the Corinthian congregation existed in a hierarchical and patriarchal culture that envisioned an ideal family as one in which "men should be dominant over women."[25] In this culture, the man as the head or *pater familias* "cared for and was obeyed by his wife and children as well as all clients, servants, and slaves."[26] In this culture of paternal

---

24. Winter, *Roman Wives, Roman Widows*, 17. For Winter, Paul's prohibition has to do with the attitudes that women were bringing into the church that reflected those of the new women of Roman Corinth, which were in defiance of the imperial rule. The penetration of Roman culture meant that the transfer of the values relating to Roman women were both traditional and new. In the first century, "the Roman women, unlike their Greek sisters in Hellenistic times, appeared in the public domain," and "imperial wives appear to have set a precedent for wives of senatorial rank and others in the social hierarchy" (37). Material published by ancient historians supports the view that wives praying and prophesying with their heads uncovered were replicating the attitudes and actions of new wives which were contrary to both the traditional Roman and the Corinthian norms for wives engaging in religious activity (77). He sees the "angels" in 1 Cor 11:2–6 as messengers or spies whom the imperial court would have sent to investigate whether women were breaking the law (91). Therefore, he sees Paul as asking the wives to wear "marriage veils" while "praying and prophesying" so that their actions would not be "misunderstood" (93–94). He concludes that "the filtering down of the new roles for women enabled Christian women to contribute to a wider sphere of service" (204).

25. Crocker, *Reading First Corinthians*, 129.

26. Crocker, 129–130.

headship over the household, the father had the right to put his children to death and the husband could put his wife to death in the case of murder.[27] In both Greek and Roman culture, chastity was expected only from wives.[28]

Ciampa and Rosner argue that understanding this cultural background sheds light on the impact of mutuality in Paul's comment on the role of women. They conclude that Paul's comment in 1 Corinthians 7 on the husband and wife both being faithful in marriage, and the authority that both husband and wife had over each other's bodies, was "revolutionary in the ancient world where patriarchy was the norm."[29]

This leads to our primary question related to passages that concern women's silence in Paul's writing: whether cultural issues are behind his rebuke. Were women allowed to speak in Corinthian society? Were there different norms for different classes of citizens? These questions lead us to examine how women speaking was understood in this cultural setting.

In the Greco-Roman world, there was strong prejudice against women speaking in public. Generally, in a society with strictly defined gender and social roles, and a strong view of the rights of a husband over his wife, such behavior was viewed as inappropriate, and, in particular, a married woman carrying on a conversation with another woman's husband was considered shameful.[30] Cases are recorded where husbands divorced their wives for having even a private conversation in a public setting with a common freedwoman.[31] Plutarch wrote that a wife was "to do her talking either to her husband or through her husband," implying that a woman's personal speech was a way

---

27. Winter, *Roman Wives, Roman Widows*, 18.
28. Winter, 20.
29. Ciampa and Rosner, *First Letter to the Corinthians*, 280–281.
30. Ciampa and Rosner, 725.
31. "In his *Memorable Deeds and Sayings*, Valerius Maximus (from the early first century AD), speaking of the harsh treatment of some husbands toward their wives, mentions Quintus Antistius Vetus, who divorced his wife because he had seen her in public having a private conversation with a common freedwoman. For, moved not by an actual crime but, so to speak, by the birth and nourishment of one, he punished her before the crime could be committed, so that he might prevent the deed's being done at all, rather than punish it afterwards." According to this text, "a wife should not be having a private conversation (where was her attendant?) with a stranger, certainly not a 'common freedwoman' (and even more certainly not someone else's husband)." Ciampa and Rosner, 726.

of exposing herself.[32] Marcus Porcius Cato (195 BC) denounced women speaking to other women's husbands in public as immodest.[33]

Regarding women speaking in a legal setting, Roman law prohibited married women from arguing in court due to the cultural mores that considered women speaking in public immodest behavior. Winter notes that forbidding women to "intervene (intercede) in public settings" on behalf of their husbands was already an imperial ban in the time of Augustus.[34] In the time of Claudius, this prohibition – "the Velleian Decree of the Senate" – was legally validated to discourage women from speaking on behalf of others, especially on behalf of their husbands, in a legal setting.[35]

From all of this evidence, it is clear that married women in Greco-Roman culture were not allowed to speak to other women's husbands or to speak on behalf of their husbands in a public setting. This leads to the question of whether women could speak at all in public in Roman Corinth.

Although the notion of married women speaking in a public setting was considered shameful in the Greco-Roman world, women could speak in a religious setting. Witherington notes that this was the case in temple worship near Corinth,[36] where women could be priestesses and "young girls apparently served there as priestesses as in other Greek Demeter shrines and may have worn a distinctive ceremonial hat."[37] He connects this to the issues addressed

---

32. Ciampa and Rosner, 726.

33. The original quote states, "What kind of behaviour is this? Running around in public, blocking streets, and speaking to other women's husbands! Could you not have asked your own husbands the same thing at home?" Livy, *History of Rome*, 34.1, in Lefkowitz and Fant, eds., *Women's Life in Greece and Rome*, 143–144. Also Ciampa and Rosner, *First Letter to the Corinthians*, 726.

34. Winter cites *The Digest*, 16.1.2 (Ulpian). Winter, *Roman Wives, Roman Widows*, 178. See also Grubbs, *Women in the Law*, 55.

35. Although Winter quotes this, he notes that "it is not clear what incident occurred at that time or what follows from it." Valerius might be referring to his regrets over allowing women to engage in "speaking in *politeia*, i.e. the courts and, in one instance, the forum." Winter, 115. This is also suggested in relation to 1 Cor 11 in Winter, "Veiled Men and Wives," 178.

36. Witherington, *Conflict and Community*, 17, explains that the oracle was past its heyday in Paul's time, "but it was still functioning, and there was a close connection between Apollo and the oracle. There was a temple of Apollo in Corinth, and Delphi is only about 50 km from Corinth. Apollo was the god of prophecy, and . . . the Corinthians would have understood prophecy in the light of this part of their context."

37. Witherington's interpretation of the head covering in 1 Cor 11 is that it was like the distinctive ceremonial hat that the priestess wore as a sign of her authority to prophesy. He notes that "there is evidence that secret rites, perhaps initiatory rites, were carried out in a room directly behind a dining room in a building in the shrine precincts." Witherington, 17.

in 1 Corinthians 11–14 and argues that the issue there likely concerned a ceremonial headpiece rather than an actual head covering or hairstyle.[38] He points out that "it is very believable that these women assumed that Christian prophets or prophetesses functioned much like [those at] the oracle at Delphi, who only prophesied in response to questions, including questions about purely personal matters."[39]

Looking at this historical data on women speaking in the Greco-Roman setting of Corinth as a whole, a point of agreement among these interpreters is that the role of women in Corinth was situated in a strongly patriarchal setting. All of them see Christian behavior in Corinth influenced by the Greco-Roman culture of the time. However, what they make of this historical data appears to depend on their view of Paul: whether they are convinced he was committed to patriarchy, held views of patriarchy and egalitarianism in tension, or was committed to egalitarianism.

This dynamic is also evident in the interpretations of Grudem, Schüssler Fiorenza, and Witherington, where they refer to religious practices at Delphi. Although all of them situate women's silence within the context of prophecy, Grudem argues that their prophetic role should not be compared to that of prophetesses at Delphi, because the prophecy at Delphi consisted of "unintelligible utterances."[40] Schüssler Fiorenza contends that the practice of unbound hair and heads thrown back that was typical of prophetesses at Delphi was something the Corinthian Christian pneumatics copied.[41] Witherington also relates the Corinthian Christian context to the practice of prophetic utterances in the temple worship at Delphi.[42]

Regardless of one's view regarding women and silence in Paul's writing, understanding the historical background is significant. It provides an awareness that the historical context in Paul's Corinth was considerably different from that of contemporary interpreters. This also highlights the fact that Paul's writings were in response to contextual issues which arose for a specific historical audience, among people who were very much influenced by their

---

38. However, Payne, Bloomberg, and Murphy-O'Connor see the head covering as referring to hairstyles, and Fee, Winter, and Thiselton see it as an actual covering.
39. Witherington, *Conflict and Community*, 17.
40. Grudem, *Gift of Prophecy*, 224.
41. Fiorenza, *In Memory of Her*, 228.
42. Witherington, *Conflict and Community*, 17.

surrounding culture. This acknowledgment assists contemporary interpreters in being more appreciative of the influential role of culture in our own understanding of biblical texts.

This leads to the second interpretive key for our passage on women and silence: an analysis of Paul's overall view of women, particularly his attitude toward women in ministry. Our critical contextual hermeneutic argues from the perspective that Paul's attitude toward women in general and women in the church needs to be seriously considered when revisiting a difficult passage like 1 Corinthians 14:34b-36. It also argues that Paul's attitude toward women in ministry should be analyzed considering his overall view on ministry. Without such an analysis, the intended meaning of the author will likely be misinterpreted.

7.1.2 Paul's Attitude on Women in the Church

The questions surrounding Paul's views on women center on two seemingly contradictory statements. First, he acknowledges in 1 Corinthians 11 that women pray and prophesy, yet two chapters later he commands women to be silent in the church. How can women exercise their ministries of praying and prophesying if they are to be silent in the church? Some interpret these contradictory statements as evidence of Paul changing his attitude. Others argue that the prohibition against women speaking in church cannot be made by Paul and therefore conclude that 1 Corinthians 14:34b-36 must be an interpolation. A hermeneutical decision considering this conundrum depends on an interpreter's honest attempt to gain an understanding of Paul's overall view of women, whether they see him as a traditionalist or a feminist.

Paul's attitude toward women can be discerned from his treatment of women leaders in the church. Paul mentions several women in his writings as *co-workers* in the churches. Paul used the term συνεργός ("coworkers") most commonly to refer to those who helped him in ministry.[43] This term is used thirteen times in the New Testament, "all but one of which are in the

---

43. Witherington, *Women in the Earliest Churches*, 111, following Ellis, *Prophecy and Hermeneutic*, 3–22.

Pauline corpus" of writings.⁴⁴ Paul used this term and another similar term, κοπός, to refer to several women.⁴⁵

For example, in Philippians 4:2–3, Paul mentions Euodia and Syntyche as αἵτινες ἐν τῷ εὐαγγελίῳ συνήθλησάν μοι μετὰ καὶ Κλήμεντος καὶ τῶν λοιπῶν συνεργῶν μου,⁴⁶ that is, those who "struggled together with me in the gospel along with Clement also and the rest of my co-workers." In Romans 16:3 and 1 Corinthians 16:19, he mentions Priscilla, along with her husband Aquila, as συνεργούς, "coworkers" who "risked their necks" for Paul. They were both leaders in the church. Acts 18:26 mentions them as those who discipled Apollos in the faith. In Romans 16:6, Paul sends a greeting to Mary who "worked very hard" (NIV and NRSV), πολλὰ ἐκοπίασεν, which is related to κοπίαω. In Romans 16:7, Paul mentions Junia. Some commentators suggest that, since Junia's name is mentioned together with Andronicus, it is possible that they were another husband-and-wife team.⁴⁷ Other scholars argue that, although Junia is a female name, this must have been a male.⁴⁸ However, it is now clear that Junia was a woman.⁴⁹ Junia and Andronicus were both called ἐπίσημοι ἐν τοῖς ἀποστόλοις, "well known among the apostles."⁵⁰ Also in Romans 16:12, Paul mentions Tryphena and Tryphosa as τὰς κοπιώσας ἐν κυρίῳ, "workers in the Lord" (NRSV).

Paul also refers to Phoebe in Romans 16:1 as διάκονον τῆς ἐκκλησίας, meaning "deacon." Witherington notes that Romans 16:1 and 1 Timothy 3:11 are the "only two places where women are given the title διάκονον in the New Testament."⁵¹ Our question at this point is whether they spoke in public in the churches where they were considered as co-workers or deacons. Bassler is helpful in focusing attention on the role these women played in the church. She asks how these women could "function as co-workers in the churches if they cannot speak in those churches? How can Phoebe fulfill the role of

---

44. Witherington, 111. The other is in 3 John 8.
45. Witherington, 111, following Ellis, *Prophecy and Hermeneutic*, 7.
46. AN²⁸, 610.
47. Witherington, *Women in the Earliest Churches*, 115.
48. Epp, *Junia*; McKnight, *Junia Is Not Alone*.
49. Epp, *Junia*.
50. Witherington, *Women in the Earliest Churches*, 115.
51. Witherington, 113; Payne, *Man and Woman*, 61–63.

deacon (Rom 16:1–2) if she cannot speak out in the assembly? Something is seriously amiss here."[52]

Considering Paul's references to these women, all noteworthy enough to be singled out by name, it seems clear that Paul worked together with women in ministry. Grudem and Schüssler Fiorenza agree that Paul offered words of appreciation to these women. Nevertheless, as noted earlier, Grudem believes that the roles these women played in the early churches did not involve authoritative speaking and Schüssler Fiorenza sees Paul as recognizing the role of these women out of obligation. As I have argued, both views are problematic and misrepresent Paul. Grudem's view is problematic since the New Testament does not provide a clear reference as to what is an authoritative or a non-authoritative form of speech. Schüssler Fiorenza's view is problematic because it stereotypes Paul as being insincere. I find Witherington's view more persuasive. Witherington sees the roles these women played as necessarily involving a speaking role, and that Paul was recognizing the ministries of these women not out of a sense of obligation but in genuine appreciation.

Regardless of one's view on Paul's attitude toward women, no interpreter can fail to note that Paul allowed women to pray and prophesy in public in 1 Corinthians 11. In the church mentioned in Acts 21:9, Philip's four daughters were known as prophets. This fact and the role of other women as co-workers and deacons lead to the question of Paul's views on ministry. In 1 Corinthians 12:28, Paul describes the gift of prophecy as a gift from the Holy Spirit that edifies the whole church. He mentions the gift of prophecy before the gift of teaching. There is nothing in Scripture that alludes to the gift of prophecy being gender-specific.

Paul's theology of ministry is relevant in this regard. In 1 Corinthians alone, Paul portrays himself as God's servant together with Apollos in 3:5–9, and as a servant of Jesus Christ in 4:1. In Romans 1:1, he mentions that he is "Paul, a servant of Jesus Christ." Like Jesus, Paul sees a leader in the church as someone who serves. Given this theology of servant leadership, one could conclude that Paul recognized and accepted women as co-workers in the church. He expected them to serve in ministry. Considering the historical background of women's role in Roman Corinth highlighted earlier, and Paul's

---

52. Bassler, "1 Corinthians," 564.

attitude toward women in the church, the following section revisits the 1 Corinthians 14:34–35 passage to understand what Paul was saying when he admonished women to be silent in the church.

7.2 Revisiting 1 Corinthians 14:34–35

As noted previously, scholars have differed greatly on what they believe Paul meant in this passage and how it should be interpreted. In my research on three contemporary interpreters – Grudem, Schüssler Fiorenza, and Witherington – it became clear that there are five areas where Pauline interpreters are required to make decisions relating to the intended meaning of this particular passage: authorship, context, women, submission, and the law in historical context, in relation to the concept of silence.

A critical analysis of Adoniram Judson's translation of this text in the Myanmar context shows evidence of similar conscious or unconscious decision-making by him as a translator. In reaching my own exegetical conclusions, I follow the same pattern of analysis and also take the perspective that the problem presented by women and silence in Corinth is most helpfully seen as a specific situation which needs to take note of Paul's overall attitude toward women in the church and his theological perspective.

7.2.1 Pauline Authorship

The significance of the concept of silence in 1 Corinthians 14:34–36 is also influenced by the interpreter's understanding of authorship and decisions about textual variants. This is also raised by the apparent contradiction between 1 Corinthians 14:34–36 and 1 Corinthians 11:3–16, where Paul encourages all believers to participate in praying and prophesying, without specifying gender. Due to the difficulty of reconciling the apparent differences between these two texts, and the sense in which 1 Corinthians 14:34–36 sounds "un-Pauline," many egalitarian scholars such as Fee[53] and Payne[54] take 14:34–36 to be an interpolation. Some other egalitarian scholars see this text as Paul's

---

53. Fee, *First Epistle to the Corinthians*.
54. Payne, *Man and Woman*.

citation of others' views in order to refute them.[55] However, all three contemporary interpreters that I have presented in this thesis see Paul as the author of 1 Corinthians 14:34–36.[56] This would also have been the case with Judson. My proposed reading of 1 Corinthians 14:34–36 likewise takes Paul as the author. Nevertheless, the interpolation theory needs to be considered seriously.

As noted in chapter 5, there is a textual variant issue in 1 Corinthians 14:34–35, where in some manuscripts, verses 34–35 come after verse 40. This transposition of verses 34–35 is found in Western manuscripts such as uncials D (06),[57] F (010),[58] G (012),[59] a b[60] (old Latin witnesses of the fourth and fifth centuries), vg^{ms} (Vulgate manuscript),[61] and the fourth-century church father Ambrosiaster.[62] In addition to these manuscripts, UBS^4 also mentions codex 88 and Seduliu-Scottus.[63]

However, the very early papyri $\mathfrak{P}^{46}$ together with uncials ℵ (01), B (03), Ψ (044), and most $\mathfrak{M}$ manuscripts[64] read these verses in their traditionally accepted order. UBS^4 also identifies manuscripts that witness to this text. They include all that NA^{27} mentions plus four more uncials, A K L 0150 0243,[65] and 22 minuscules.[66] Although transpositions in copying are common, and it is therefore not surprising that such transpositions have occurred in different manuscripts, transposition alone does not provide sufficient reason for an interpolation theory. Fee attaches more weight to the usage of words, such as speaking, silence, submission, and the law, which he sees as contradicting Paul's linguistic usages in other accepted texts.

---

55. Flanagan and Snyder, "Did Paul Put Down Women," 10–12; Flanagan, "Let the Women Speak," 90–93; Allison, "Let Women Be Silent," 27–60; Peppiatt, *Women and Worship*.

56. Wire and Keener also consider Pauline authorship as authentic. Wire, *Corinthian Women Prophets*, 146–158; Keener, *Paul, Women and Wives*, 70–100.

57. Codex Claromontanus.

58. Codex Augiensis.

59. Codex Boernerianus.

60. Old Latin manuscripts entitled Armachanus and Veronensis.

61. Codex Fuldensis.

62. NA^{28}, 466.

63. UBS^4.

64. NA^{28}, 466.

65. UBS^4.

66. They are: 6 33 81 104 256 263 365 424 436 459 1175 1241 1319 1573 1739 1852 1881 1912 1962 2127 2200 2464. UBS^4.

Although I agree with Fee that Paul's linguistic usages here seem different from elsewhere, the fact that there is no manuscript that dismisses verses 34–35 entirely makes the authorship of Paul a stronger possibility than the interpolation theory. Then, the question becomes why such a textual variant occurred. Ebojo argues that the variant occurred because of various scribes' personal beliefs or their churches' views of what they thought Paul was saying.[67] In other words, the repositioning of verses 34–35 after verse 40 reflects the scribes' own interpretation of the text.[68]

7.2.2 Silence: The Context

It is vitally important for our interests to attempt to understand the context of 1 Corinthians 14:34–36. As mentioned above, some interpreters see this passage in the context of a rhetorical argument in which Paul is quoting the negative views of Corinthians themselves about women in the church in order to refute them.[69] Some interpreters also see this text as part of the larger debate about speaking in tongues in worship, which Paul has just been addressing.[70] Grudem, Schüssler Fiorenza, and Witherington all see these verses in the context of prophecy.[71] However, they disagree on who Paul is restricting within the context of prophecy. Grudem sees Paul as restricting all women, Schüssler Fiorenza sees the restrictions as applying only to Corinthian wives, and Witherington sees them as referring to Corinthian prophetesses.

Regardless of one's views on the overall context, or to whom the restrictions apply, there is still a question concerning whether verse 33b, ὡς ἐν πάσαις

---

67. Ebojo, "Should Women Be Silent?," 6; Thiselton, *First Epistle to the Corinthians*, 1149. See also Witherington, *Paul's Narrative Thought World*, 288; *Women in the Earliest Churches*, 90–92; Ebojo, "Sex, Scribes and Scriptures," 380–382.

68. Metzger and Ehrman, *Text of the New Testament*, 259, mentions several possible reasons for the repositioning of the text. Witherington, *Conflict and Community*, 288 (see also 91–92), also argues that "Displacement is no argument for interpolation. Probably these verses were displaced by scribes who assumed that they were about household order, not order in worship, scribes working at a time when there were church buildings separate from private homes." Comfort, "Scribes as Readers," 28–53, suggests reader-reception analysis, which sees textual variants as the process of scribal readings and interpretations.

69. As noted, although Thiselton believes this passage is authentic, he sees this view as "not farfetched, for Paul appears to do precisely this in 6:12; 7:1; 10:23; and perhaps elsewhere (e.g. in 8:1–6)." Thiselton, *First Epistle to the Corinthians*, 1150.

70. Kroeger, "Strange Tongues?" 10–13.

71. Other scholars also understand this passage in the context of prophecy. See Wire, *Corinthian Women Prophets*, and Thiselton, *First Epistle to the Corinthians*.

ταῖς ἐκκλησίαις τῶν ἁγίων, meaning "as in all the churches of the saints," is related primarily to verse 33a or to verse 34. If verse 33b is linked with 33a, the sentence will read, "For God is not [a God?] of confusion but of peace *as in all the churches of the saints*." If verse 33b is linked with verse 34, then it will read, "*As in all the churches of the saints*, women should be silent in the churches."[72] The crux of the debate rests on whether this command for silence is situation-specific or universal, to be applied to every church. The argument is that, if verse 33b goes with verse 34, the command becomes a universal requirement for women to be silent in the church.[73]

Although Grudem, Schüssler Fiorenza, and Witherington disagree on who they think Paul is prohibiting from speaking in this context, they all agree that verse 33b is linked logically with verse 34. Greek texts in NA[27] and UBS[4] also link verse 33b with 34.[74] It is true that several other scholars[75] and Bible translations link verse 33b with the preceding verse.[76] However, a number of other scholars[77] and Bible translations,[78] including the Judson Burmese translation, support the reading of verse 33b with 33a. The Judson Burmese translation reads, "God does not administer things that cause confusion. As it happens in all the churches of the saints, he administers harmonious peace." Grudem, in particular, finds this form of reading the text problematic.[79]

Nevertheless, Judson's view remains plausible. First, the link between verses 33b and 33a is less problematic than the link with verse 34, because linking verse 33b with verse 34 results in two occurrences of ταῖς ἐκκλησίαις in one sentence.[80] The challenge for scholars who link verse 33b with verse

---

72. NRSV.

73. Grudem, *Evangelical Feminism*, 234, maintains that Paul's instruction cannot be restricted to a specific church only but is a universal requirement for all the churches.

74. Ciampa and Rosner, *First Letter to the Corinthians*, 717, notes that "the point of v. 40 may be understood as the bridge between the two parts of this verse such that the thought is that God is not a God of disorder but of peace, [therefore everything should be done in a fitting and orderly way] as in all the congregations of the Lord's people."

75. Ebojo, "Should Women Be Silent?"

76. NRSV, REB, NIV, NJB, and GNB take 33b with 34.

77. Ellingworth and Hatton, *Handbook on Paul's First Letter*, 324; Ebojo, "Should Women Be Silent?," 21.

78. KJV, RV, NBV, LB, and *The Message* all see 33b attached to 33a.

79. Grudem, *Gift of Prophecy*.

80. (33b) Ὡς ἐν πάσαις ταῖς ἐκκλησίαις τῶν ἁγίων; (34) αἱ γυναῖκες ἐν ταῖς ἐκκλησίαις σιγάτωσαν.NA[27], 1 Cor 14:33b-34.

34 is reconciling these two appearances of ταῖς ἐκκλησίαις. Some explain the first usage of ταῖς ἐκκλησίαις as being a reference to universal believers and the latter ταῖς ἐκκλησίαις as referring only to the Corinthian believers.[81] I agree with Ebojo that taking these two occurrences as separate units is the "most natural reading"[82] and the most logical.

A rationale for this conclusion is that Paul used ταῖς ἐκκλησίαις in the conclusions of both 1 Corinthians 4:17 and 7:17. Further, the expression used in 33b is similar to the usage in 1 Corinthians 4:17 (ἐν πάσῃ ἐκκλησίᾳ, meaning "in every church") and in 1 Corinthians 7:17 (ἐν ταῖς ἐκκλησίαις πάσαις, meaning "in all the churches"). Both phrases occur at the end of a sentence. The use of this similar phrase indicates that verse 33b is likely to be a concluding statement to all that Paul has argued in the whole paragraph. Agreeing with this, Ellingworth explains that "verse 33b will form the conclusion, not only of verses 32–33a, but also of the whole paragraph,"[83] including verses 26–33.

Moreover, the transposition of verses 34–35 without verse 33b is another indicator that verse 33b goes with the previous verse rather than the following verse.[84] Ebojo sees this transposition as a clue that shows the scribal understanding of where this verse belongs and concludes that this clue indicates a "context-specific" instruction. He thus shares Ellingworth's view and points out that connecting verse 33b to 33a "localizes the validity of the prohibition and universalizes the call for an orderly exercise of the pneumatic experience." This way of understanding the verse appears to be the case for Judson as well.

After connecting verse 33b to the preceding verse, the question then becomes where verses 34–35 fit into the larger picture. Like the three contemporary interpreters, I see this text in the context of prophecy.[85] It is part of

---

81. Witherington, *Women in the Earliest Churches*, 96; Witherington, *Conflict and Community*, 287; Garland, "1 Corinthians," 670.

82. Ebojo, "Should Women Be Silent?," 20.

83. Ellingworth and Hatton, *Handbook on Paul's First Letter*, 324, notes that this should be translated as a separate sentence: "This is what happens in all the churches of God's people." Ebojo, 20.

84. Ebojo, 21.

85. Witherington, *Women in the Earliest Churches*, 102; Thiselton, *First Epistle to the Corinthians*, 1158, notes that "with Witherington, we believe that the speaking in question denotes the activity of sifting or weighing the words of prophets, especially by asking probing questions about the prophet's theology or even the prophet's lifestyle in public."

the instructions given by Paul for orderly worship in the churches.[86] Within the context of prophecy, I see Paul as admonishing Corinthian prophetesses[87] who were wives,[88] to be silent in the church. The following section explains further the reason behind this exegetical decision.

7.2.3 Silence: The Women

Scholars also differ regarding the question of who Paul is restricting in this passage. This is seen in the interpretations of Grudem, Schüssler Fiorenza, and Witherington. All their differences rest on whether αἱ γυναῖκες in 1 Corinthians 14:34 is referring to all women or just to wives. Grudem sees αἱ γυναῖκες as referring to all women, including unmarried women.[89] He argues from the culture of patriarchy in Corinth at the time of Paul's writing, where all women, married and unmarried alike, were under the authority of men. From that perspective, he sees Paul as restricting all women from speaking in the church.[90] Schüssler Fiorenza sees αἱ γυναῖκες as referring to wives.[91] She assumes that Paul is prohibiting only the wives, who had been praying in tongues and prophesying in the worship of the community. Witherington views αἱ γυναῖκες as referring to "married women" who are the Christian "prophets."[92] He sees Paul as restricting Christian women prophetesses from asking questions during the worship service.

A decision on who αἱ γυναῖκες is referring to hinges on two things: the interpreters' understanding of the textual variant issue on the omission of ὑμῶν in verse 34 following αἱ γυναῖκες, and the interpreters' understanding of τοὺς ἰδίους ἄνδρας in verse 35. For the textual variant issue of ὑμῶν in verse 34, the appearance of this word is supported by manuscripts such as D F G

---

86. Witherington sees the order in worship as the theme of 1 Cor 14. See *Conflict and Community*, 287; Thiselton, 1146–1149.

87. This is the view of Witherington, who also notes that these prophetesses are likely to be wives.

88. This is emphasized by Schüssler Fiorenza.

89. As noted in chapter 4 Ciampa and Rosner rebut this view, stating that "it is not at all clear that very young and immature girls would have been permitted to speak in the church at all." Ciampa and Rosner, *First Letter to the Corinthians*, 722.

90. Grudem, *Gift of Prophecy*, 248. Origen supported this view. Coyle, "Fathers on Women."

91. Fiorenza, *In Memory of Her*, 230–231.

92. Witherington, *Conflict and Community*, 287.

𝔐 (ar b) sy; Cyp (Ambst), but ℵ A B Ψ⁹³ 0243 33 81 104 365 1175 1241 1739 1881 2464 support the reading without ὑμῶν.⁹⁴ As noted, the manuscripts that support the insertion, such as D F G, are Western manuscripts, Greek-Latin bilingual texts that have a sixth and ninth century dating. The reading of just αἱ γυναῖκες without ὑμῶν is supported by the Alexandrian witnesses such as ℵ A B, which are fourth and fifth century documents. Judson follows the tradition of the Western manuscripts and translates this passage with ὑμῶν.

The preferred reading here is the reading of αἱ γυναῖκες without ὑμῶν due to the earlier dating of the supporting manuscripts.⁹⁵ The dating of the Alexandrian manuscripts is generally considered to be earlier than the Western manuscripts. The question once again is the reason for such a variation. Scholars like Metzger see this as "probably a scribal addition."⁹⁶ Other scholars such as Thiselton explain this addition as the scribes' attempt to "localize the rule" to Corinth.⁹⁷ Perhaps, this was also the view of Judson when he selected αἱ γυναῖκες with ὑμῶν and translated ἐν ταῖς ἐκκλησίαις, the plural "churches," into the singular "church." By translating the plural into the singular, the instruction becomes context-specific to the Corinthian church rather than to the "churches" as a whole. Although all of the above reasons for variation are plausible, the scribal interpretation of what Paul meant in this passage is more likely the reason behind such an addition.⁹⁸ As noted, this is the same reason for the textual variant issue, the transposition of verses 34–35 after verse 40. Although the reading without ὑμῶν after αἱ γυναῖκες is the preferred reading, as noted, αἱ γυναῖκες is more likely a reference to the "wives," for the following reasons.

The usage of τοὺς ἰδίους ἄνδρας in verse 35 points to the women in this context being "wives." As noted, the phrase τοὺς ἰδίους ἄνδρας can be translated as either "their own men"⁹⁹ or "their own husbands,"¹⁰⁰ depending on the

---

93. Codex Athous Lavrensis.
94. NA²⁷ 466.
95. Metzger and Ehrman, *Text of the New Testament*, 109.
96. Metzger and Ehrman, 500.
97. Thiselton, *First Epistle to the Corinthians*, 1150.
98. Ebojo, "Should Women Be Silent?," 23.
99. Grudem, *Gift of Prophecy*; Wire, *Corinthian Women Prophets*, 156.
100. "Their own husbands" in NIV, NRSV, REB, ASV, and NJB; "their husbands" in KJV and ESV.

interpreters' understanding of the text. Although "your own men" as inclusive of all men is possible considering the patriarchal cultural setting, Witherington argues that "husbands" is more likely what Paul had in mind in this context.[101] The reason is that Paul used the phrase τὸν ἴδιον ἄνδρα in 1 Corinthians 7:2[102] in the context of the husband-and-wife relationship. Paul also used the same phrase in Ephesians 5:22 and Titus 2:4[103] regarding the husband-and-wife relationship. This consistent usage indicates that τοὺς ἰδίους ἄνδρας is more likely "husbands," and that therefore the women in this context are "wives." Similarly, the paired usage of "ὁ ἀνήρ" with "ἡ γυνή" in verse 35 likely refers to wives and husbands. Scholars such as Garland,[104] Johnson,[105] and Ebojo[106] argue that this pair usage is a significant indicator that Paul is referring to wives and husbands. The same pair usage is found in other 1 Corinthians texts, particularly 1 Corinthians 7:3–4, 10–16, 34, and 39, where the reference is clearly to marital relationships.[107]

My analysis of the above findings leads to the conclusion that the women in this passage are the Corinthian Christian wives. The overall context of Paul's concern, orderly worship in the churches and orderly practice of prophecy, suggests that the wives in this context are prophetesses[108] or at least participating in prophecy. These conclusions lead to the next question, regarding what Paul meant by αἱ γυναῖκες ἐν ταῖς ἐκκλησίαις σιγάτωσαν[109] ("women should be silent in the church"), since he has already acknowledged that women pray and prophesy in worship in 1 Corinthians 11:5.

---

101. Witherington, *Conflict and Community*, 287; Garland, "1 Corinthians," 667.

102. NA[27], 450.

103. Paul's authorship of the pastoral epistles is disputed.

104. Garland, "1 Corinthians," 667. He points out similar usage in 1 Cor 7:25 and 11:3. Schüssler Fiorenza, *In Memory of Her*, 230–231.

105. Johnson, *1 Corinthians*, 275. As noted ιν chapter 4.2.3: whenever "ἡ γυνή" is used in the same context with "ὁ ἀνήρ," then 'wife' is the "correct translation (1 Cor 7:14; Eph 5:22; 1 Tim 3:2; 1 Pet 3:1)," but adds that "on the other hand, there are places such as in this context where 'woman' and 'man' may be more appropriate (Acts 5:14; 8:12; 22:4; 1 Cor 11:11–12)."

106. Ebojo, "Should Women Be Silent?," 18. Paul uses this pair 31 times, more or less with regard to the marital status of the woman in focus.

107. Other passages include Rom 7:2–3; Eph 5:22–25; Col 3:18–19; Titus 2:4–5. Ebojo, "Should Women Be Silent?," 18.

108. Witherington, *Conflict and Community*, 287.

109. NA[27] 465.

7.2.4 Silence: The Speaking

The next interpretive challenge is Paul's usage of the word σιγάω ("silence") in verse 34. As noted previously, Grudem, Schüssler Fiorenza, and Witherington all view this text in the context of prophecy. Grudem sees Paul as using σιγάω ("to be silent") to prohibit any woman from asking evaluative questions about a prophecy given by a man during a worship service.[110] He interprets λαλέω here as "judging or evaluating" in the sense of an authoritative form of speech that only the male leadership is permitted to use in the church. Schüssler Fiorenza concludes that Paul is using σιγάω to prohibit only the wives of men in the church from a general sense of λαλέω,[111] "speaking to and questioning" their husbands during the Christian worship assembly.[112] She argues that the reason for this injunction was so as not to give the wrong impression to unbelievers who, based on their cultural mores, would consider such questioning inappropriate.

Witherington also understands λαλέω in the general sense of asking questions, including questions about purely personal matters, and concludes that Paul was using σιγάω to silence wives from asking disruptive questions during the prophetic worship service itself.[113] These interpretations highlight two areas of concern in determining the meaning of σιγάω, which are the interpreters' understanding of Paul's usage of σιγάω in the particular context, and the usage of σιγάω in relation to λαλέω from verses 34 and 35.

Generally, interpretive differences regarding Paul's usage of σιγάω hinge on the interpreters' understanding of the context and how this affects decisions about whether this word is referring to a temporal or a permanent command, or to an absolute or specific form of silence. These differences among interpreters' understandings of Paul's usage of σιγάω are seen in Bible translations, where some simply use σιγάω to mean that women "should be

---

110. Grudem, *Gift of Prophecy*, 233; Hurley, *Man and Woman*, 185–194; Carson, "Silent in the Churches," 129. Agreeing with Grudem, Thiselton comments, "We believe that the speaking in question denotes the activity of sifting or weighing the words of prophets, especially by asking probing questions about the prophet's theology or even the prophet's lifestyle in public. This would become especially sensitive and problematic if wives were cross-examining their husbands about the speech and conduct which supported or undermined the authenticity of a claim to utter a prophetic message and would readily introduce Paul's allusion to reserving questions of a certain kind for home." Thiselton, *First Epistle to the Corinthians*, 1158.

111. Nida, *Greek-English Lexicon*, 363.

112. Schüssler Fiorenza, *In Memory of Her*, 228.

113. Witherington, *Women in the Earliest Churches*, 102.

silent,"[114] while others say that women "should keep silence"[115] or "should remain silent."[116] Unlike some interpreters who see Paul as relegating women to "absolute silence,"[117] the three interpreters that I have highlighted in this study (Grudem, Schüssler Fiorenza, and Witherington) see Paul as restricting women to a specific form of speech in the context of worship in the church.[118] They argue that Paul could not have meant absolute silence for women in 1 Corinthians 14:34 since the women were given permission to pray and prophesy in 1 Corinthians 11.[119]

The question is whether the present active imperative usage of σιγάω offers such a meaning. The word σιγάω appears in two other verses, in 1 Corinthians 14: 28 and 30. These two usages of σιγάω are in the present active imperative form in the singular, and verse 34 is in the present active imperative plural form. The nature of the imperative mood in the present tense does offer the meaning of "the action as an ongoing process."[120] Grudem and Witherington render the word as "keep" and Schüssler Fiorenza renders it as "remain." These words, "keep" or "remain," possibly indicate two things: They acknowledge that the role of silence for women was already a familiar practice for

---

114. NRSV

115. KJV, ESV, NASB.

116. *New Living Translation.*

117. Phillips, *Exploring 1 Corinthians*, 324, notes that Paul here is referring to three things. "First, there is *an absolute rule* (14:34). There is *a blunt prohibition*: 'Let your women keep silence in the churches (14:34a); there is *a biblical precept*: 'for it is not permitted unto them to speak; but they are commanded to be under obedience, as also saith the law' (14:34b). The word for *silence* here is a strong one. It is *sigao*. It means 'absolute silence.'" He contends that the command for women to keep silence as cultural and confined to Corinth is contrary to Paul's statement in 1 Cor 11. He argues that absolute silence here is supported by Paul's statement, "it is not permitted for them to speak" and "let them ask their husbands at home," in line with the usage of "shame" in 1 Cor 14:35. Mare, "1 Corinthians," 275–276, notes that "women were not to speak in public worship. . . . The command seems absolute: Women are not to do any public speaking in the church." Fee, *First Epistle to the Corinthians*, 706–707, also contends that "the plain sense of the sentence is an absolute prohibition of all speaking in the assembly" and thus argues for interpolation theory.

118. Schüssler Fiorenza includes "remain silent."

119. Interpreters like Barrett argue that Paul meant absolute silence and that 1 Cor 14 is about the public worship setting, whereas 1 Cor 11 is about the private worship setting (formal vs. informal settings). Barrett, *First Epistle to the Corinthians*, 332. Also Conzelmann, *1 Corinthians*, 246. The problem with this view is that there is no such indication in the text. Hurley notes that the flow of chapter 14 suggests that "the verses regulating women's speaking are to be understood as making it all the more unlikely that two radically different kinds of service are in view." Hurley, *Man and Woman*, 187.

120. Wallace, *Greek Grammar Beyond the Basics.*

Corinthian women in the church; or, conversely, this command for women to be silent has a timeless claim on women in the church. Our three interpreters conclude that it is the former to which σιγάω is referring in the text. They see the phrase in 1 Corinthians 14:33b, "as in all the churches of the saints," as a clue that this practice is already normative in Corinth, and, thus, they see Paul's command here as limited to a specific situation and not to an absolute command.[121]

Other interpreters see σιγάω as meaning "stop speaking"[122] or "refrain from speaking."[123] Ciampa and Rosner[124] maintain that Paul probably means "refrain from speaking," since he had already asked different participants in worship to do likewise, in the context of speaking in tongues in verse 28 as well as in the weighing of prophecy in verse 30. In his proposal to translate σιγάω as "should allow for silence," Thiselton maintains that the verb σιγάω could mean "to stop speaking" or "to hold one's tongue, or hold one's peace, or to refrain from using a particular kind of speech, or speech in a presupposed context," depending on the context.[125] He notes that the REB translates σιγάω as "stop speaking" in 1 Corinthians 14:30, although it translates it in verse 34 as "should keep silent."[126]

One could argue that the translation of σιγάω as "to stop speaking" is plausible in the context of 1 Corinthians 14, where the prohibition of Paul should relate to resolving problems related to pneumatic practices in the church. Two other occurrences of σιγάω, in 1 Corinthians 14:28 and 30, support the translation of "stop speaking" for 1 Corinthians 14:34 as well. The reason is that the first verse (1 Cor 14:28) admonishes a speaker who was

---

121. I have argued in this chapter that 1 Cor 14:33b is to be linked with 1 Cor 14:33a and not with 34.

122. Thiselton, *First Epistle to the Corinthians*, 1153.

123. Ciampa and Rosner, *First Letter to the Corinthians*, 720. Ellis, "Silenced Wives of Corinth," 213–220, argues that "the catch-word connection" between vv. 28, 30, 34 connotes "'to be silent,' 'to stop speaking,' 'to refrain from speaking.'" Although Witherington sees the word here as referring to "keep silence," he argues that it is in keeping with the catchwords in previous verses. Witherington, *Women in the Earliest Churches*, 9.

124. Ciampa and Rosner, *First Letter to the Corinthians*, 720; Ellis, "Silenced Wives of Corinth," 213–220.

125. Thiselton, *First Epistle to the Corinthians*, 1153.

126. Ellingworth and Hatton, *Handbook on Paul's First Letter*, 322, notes that "the situation is probably not exactly the same as that in verse 28. That is why the same verb is translated 'keep silence' in verse 28 and 'be silent' in verse 30. In the present verse, 'stop speaking' as in TEV is a better translation."

speaking in tongues to stop speaking[127] when no interpreter is available to provide an interpretation. The second verse (1 Cor 14:30) is an instruction to a prophet to stop speaking if someone else receives a revelation. In both cases, Thiselton notes that σιγάω could be referring to "stop speaking" or to "sifting prophetic speech."[128] The idea of "stop speaking" links well not only with the context where Paul's primary concern is correcting disorderliness and promoting decency in worship, but also with the usage of λαλέω in the following verses, 34 and 35.

As noted, many interpreters' understanding of σιγάω links to the usage of λαλέω, especially in terms of the kind of speech to which Paul refers in this context. The question focuses on whether Paul is referring to formal or informal forms of speech. Schüssler Fiorenza and Witherington see the usage of the word λαλέω in this context as conveying a general sense of speaking that includes questioning, while Grudem understands λαλέω as referring to a more inspired form of speaking, "judging or evaluation."[129] As noted, this is also likely the view of Judson, where he translated λαλέω as an authoritative form of speaking, particularly "preaching." This translation of the word λαλέω as "preaching" in all the twelve times it is used in the context of prophesying and speaking in tongues, rather than as "speaking," highlights a significant change of meaning in relation to the requirement that women should be silent.

The next question, then, is whether the text alludes to such a meaning. As noted in Grudem's interpretation, the usage of the same word λαλέω in 1

---

127. Ciampa and Rosner, *First Letter to the Corinthians*, 720. Interpreters differ widely on the meaning in all three verses. For example, Ciampa and Rosner see v. 28 as "remaining silent" and v. 30 as "stop speaking." They see the v. 34 usage as being the same as "remain silent" in v. 28. Ebojo sees vv. 28 and 30 as "let [a person] be silent" but v. 34 as absolute silence. Ebojo, "Should Women Be Silent?," 17.

128. Thiselton, *First Epistle to the Corinthians*, 1153.

129. Interpreters like Barrett understand λαλέω as referring to a form of inspired speech, "speaking in tongues." Barrett, *First Epistle to the Corinthians*, 332. Henry, *Commentary*, 2271, notes that women "are not permitted to speak (v. 34) in the church, neither in praying nor prophesying. The connection seems plainly to include the latter, in the limited sense in which it is taken in this chapter, namely, for preaching, or interpreting scripture by inspiration. And, indeed, for a woman to prophesy in this sense was to teach, which does not so well befit her state of teacher of others, [means that she] has in that respect a superiority over them, which is not allowed the woman over the man, nor must she therefore be allowed to teach in a congregation: I suffer them not to teach. But praying, and uttering hymns inspired, were not teaching."

Timothy 2:11–15, which prohibited women from teaching, is the link to this interpretation.[130] It is from this perspective that Grudem sees the word λαλέω in 1 Corinthians 14:34 as referring to women not participating in judging or evaluating their husband's prophecies,[131] which would mean that they could question their authoritative role which was reserved only for male leaders who were preachers and teachers. The problem with this view is that the word λαλέω is referring to the informal sense of "speak or talk," not to inspired forms of speech.[132] Moreover, the fact that the speech is described as "shameful" suggests that the form of speech to which the verse refers could not be an inspired form of speech. Paul also does not differentiate the judgment entailed in prophecy as higher than the general gift of prophecy or anything related to prophecy as a gender-specific gift.[133] Furthermore, in the context of the evaluation and judging of prophecy, Paul used the term διακρίνω for "judging" in verse 29, not λαλέω.[134]

The clearest contextual clue regarding what Paul meant by λαλέω is found in verse 35, where there is the conditional clause εἰ δέ τι μαθεῖν θέλουσιν ("but if they [women] want to learn").[135] The emphasis here is on μαθεῖν, which has the meaning of "to learn" or "a process of learning."[136] This implies that the reason behind women's speech is their desire to learn. Judson's translation

---

130. Ebojo contends that the dissimilarities between 1 Cor 14:34–35 and 1 Tim 2:11–12 are greater than the similarities. He also notes that the mandate to be silent in 1 Tim is a didactic problem in the Ephesian church, whereas 1 Cor 14 addresses the problem of pneumatic practices in relation to church order and decency. Ebojo, "Should Women Be Silent?," 16. Keener argues that "Paul here actually opposes something more basic than women teaching in public . . . he opposes them learning too loudly in public." Keener, *Paul, Women and Wives*, 80.

131. Thiselton, *First Epistle to the Corinthians*, 1158, notes that Witherington shares this view as well. However, Witherington points out that the problem was being "disrespectful or they may have been asked in a disrespectful manner." He sees Paul as telling the wives that "questions should not be asked in worship. The wives should ask their husbands at home. Worship was not to be turned into a question-and-answer session." Witherington, *Women in the Earliest Churches*, 102.

132. Louw and Nida, *Greek-English Lexicon*, 396. See also "λαλεῖν," in BDAG, 582.

133. As noted, a rebuttal of Grudem's view is found in Greenbury, "1 Corinthians 14:34–35," 721–731.

134. Greenbury, 721–731.

135. μαθεῖν, from μανθάνω. NRSV translates this as "If there is anything they desire to know," ESV as "if there is anything they desire to learn," NIV as "If they want to inquire about something," NASB as "If they desire to learn anything," NET as "to find out about," KJV as "if they will learn anything," and NLT as "if they have any questions." It is translated as "inquire about" in the *New English Translation*.

136. μανθάνω in Nida, *Greek-English Lexicon*, 381.

captures this in translating the phrase "If women want to learn something."[137] The emphasis is on the fact that whatever questions the women asked were considered acceptable at home, but unacceptable in the context of public worship. It is in this context that Paul says that the women should ask their own husbands at home. This fits with the Greco-Roman cultural worldview that considered it "scandalous for a married woman to carry on conversation with other women's husbands" even in private, but even more in a public setting.[138]

Considering all the above, I find that the usage of the word σιγάω in 1 Corinthians 14:34 makes sense given the overall context of Paul's concern in 1 Corinthians 14, which is, correcting disorderly behavior in the worship of the church. When it is translated as a command to married women to "stop speaking," this is not about inspired forms of speech such as prophecy or tongues, but a specific form of informal conversation such as questioning, and relates to being disruptive in worship. Given this understanding, the following section examines what Paul meant by using the word ὑποτάσσω in verse 35.

7.2.5 Silence: Submission

Another debated issue is the significance of ὑποτάσσω in 1 Corinthians 14:34–35, meaning "submission." Various translations say that women "should be subordinate,"[139] should "be under obedience,"[140] that "they must not be in charge,"[141] or that they "should keep their place as the law directs."[142] Differences center on the translators' understanding of whom the women should submit to and the context in which they are to submit.

The passage does not give a clear indication about whom it is the women are to submit to. Grudem argues that Paul's main concern was "the principle of submission," and that such submission is to "male leadership in the church." Schüssler Fiorenza sees it as referring to submission of wives to their

---

137. As cited in Chapter 3.2.2.5

138. Ciampa and Rosner, *First Letter to the Corinthians*, 725; Forbes, *Prophecy and Inspired Speech*, 724.

139. RSV, NRSV.

140. KJV.

141. TEV.

142. REB.

husbands.¹⁴³ Witherington understands it as referring to the submission of wives to the principle of order in the worship service.¹⁴⁴

To me, Witherington's understanding of ὑποτάσσω seems the most likely given the context. As noted, the scribe of codex A¹⁴⁵ added τοῖς ἀνδράσιν after ὑποτάσσω, which carries the sense that the submission here is the submission of the wives to their husbands. Although a preferred reading is ὑποτάσσω without τοῖς ἀνδράσιν (since the reading with τοῖς ἀνδράσιν appears in only one manuscript), it is likely that ὑποτάσσω is referring to submission of wives to husbands. The reason is found in the usage of ὑποτάσσω in relation to the words "ὁ ἀνήρ" and "ἡ γυνή." These words appear together in 1 Corinthians 14:34–35, Ephesians 5:21, and in Titus 2:4. In Ephesians 5:21 and Titus 2:4, Paul refers to the relationship between husband and wife.¹⁴⁶ This was probably the view of Judson as well, since he translated the text with the insertion of τοῖς ἀνδράσιν after ὑποτάσσω.

The question then is, what was the context in which Paul was asking the wives to submit?¹⁴⁷ The way Paul asked the wives to submit influences the context of ὑποτάσσω. The occurrence of ὑποτάσσω in verse 32 before verse 34 offers two possibilities. First, the middle voice usage of ὑποτάσσω in verse 32¹⁴⁸ gives the meaning of submission as denoting "self-control, or controlled speech."¹⁴⁹ Second, the usage in verse 32 suggests that the middle voice usage of ὑποτάσσω in verse 34 should be read in the same context.¹⁵⁰ Translators differ here on whether to take ὑποτάσσω as infinitive or imperative due to an

---

143. She reasons from the "Greco-Roman exhortations for the subordination of wives as part of the law." Schüssler Fiorenza, *In Memory of Her*, 231.

144. He notes the usage of ὑποτάσσω in terms of the relationship between husband and wife in Eph 5:22; Col 3:18; Titus 2:5; between child and parents in Luke 2:51; slaves and masters in Titus 2:9; 1 Pet 2:18; submission by all to secular authority in Rom 13:1; Titus 3:1; 1 Pet 2:13; Christians to church officials in 1 Pet 5:5; everyone in relation to God in Jas 4:7; 1 Pet 5:5; and believers in relation to Christ in Eph 5:22.

145. Codex Alexandrinus.

146. Ebojo, "Should Women Be Silent?," 22.

147. Witherington notes that the only time silence is associated with submission in the Old Testament is out of respect for God in Hab 2:20; Isa 46:1; Zech 2:13; Judg 3:19; Job 29:21; and Ps 37:17.

148. ὑποτάσσεται is in the present middle/passive indicative. "The spirits of prophets are *subject to* the prophets" (NRSV, ESV), "subject to the control of" (NIV), and "in control" (NLT).

149. Thiselton, *First Epistle to the Corinthians*, 1155.

150. ὑποτασσέσθωσαν, present middle/passive imperative. NA²⁷, 465.

apparent textual variant.¹⁵¹ A preferred reading is ὑποτασσέσθωσαν, supported by ℵ A B 33 81 104 365 (1175) 1241 2464.¹⁵² These manuscripts are dated earlier than the manuscripts with ὑποτασσέσθαι in the infinitive. The middle voice usage provides the nuance of submission as being voluntary. As noted, Judson's usage of *won khan* ("accept") instead of *nar khan* ("must obey") shows his view of submission in this text as self-voluntary action of wives to their husbands.

These reasons provide a framework for understanding what Paul is saying in the larger context of his concern for order. With Witherington, I find that the reference here is to order in the worship service, not in the family.¹⁵³ The usage of ὑποτάσσω in this text is often understood by scholars as subordination of wives to husbands based on Genesis 3:16.¹⁵⁴ However, Genesis 3:16 is about the stage after the fall. Thiselton points out that patterning the understanding of submission on the fall is in conflict with Paul's affirmation of a new model of relationality for Christian believers in Galatians 3:28, where there is no longer any division between male and female, slave or free, Jew or Greek (NRSV).¹⁵⁵ Given this understanding, he proposes that the most accurate meaning of ὑποτάσσω is "let them keep to their ordered place" in the context of Christian worship.¹⁵⁶

This explanation by Thiselton fits well within the overall context of 1 Corinthians, where Paul was correcting the abuses of Christian liberty in

---

151. "They are commanded to be under obedience" (KJV); "should be subordinate" (NRSV); "must be in submission" (NIV); "should be in submission" (ESV); "should be submissive" (NLT).

152. Variant reading from ὑποτασσέσθωσαν is ὑποτασσέσθαι, which is in present passive infinitive. This is supported by (D F G) Ψ 0243 𝔐 lat(t) sy.

153. Witherington, *Women in the Earliest Churches*, 102–103. Witherington argues that the submission "is not gender specific" since "Paul requires respect, submission, and silence of any listener when any prophet is speaking" (vv. 28–32), and that in admonishing some women who are asking questions (vv.34.) Paul is arguing from the same principle. Witherington, *Conflict and Community*, 276. Also see Thiselton, *First Epistle to the Corinthians*, 1155.

154. Grudem, *Gift of Prophecy*, 253. Grudem notes the problematic nature of Gen 3:16 and later changes this to pattern after the Gen 2 pre-fall created order. Scholars who see this text referring to Gen 3:16 include Barrett, *First Epistle to the Corinthians*, 330. See also Robertson and Plummer, *First Epistle of St. Paul*, 325.

155. Thiselton, *First Epistle to the Corinthians*, 1155. Wire, who sees Paul as an insecure authoritarian, states that the issue here is whether "order" still applies to a charismatic gospel community. *Corinthian Women Prophets*, 13–38.

156. Thiselton, *First Epistle to the Corinthians*, 1155. REB takes the same usage of ὑποτάσσω and translates it as women "should keep their place as the law directs."

worship. The "ordered place" then refers to order in worship, not order in the family relationship. This kind of submission in 1 Corinthians 14:28–32 is expected by Paul of any listener when any prophet is speaking. In that same context, Paul requires voluntary submission of wives, who were the violators in this context, to the principle of order in the worship service. Based on this understanding, the following section examines what Paul meant by saying ὑποτασσέσθωσαν, in relation to ὁ νόμος.

7.2.6 Silence: The Law

Interpreters also disagree extensively over what Paul means in his references to ὁ νόμος. Those who regard 1 Corinthians 14:34–45 as an interpolation see the usage of ὁ νόμος here as "the ultimate problem for Pauline authorship"[157] since the usage of ὁ νόμος in this context is different from Paul's usages elsewhere. This is the only place where Paul does not give a supporting text for his arguments, and the only usage of ὁ νόμος in relation to "Christian behaviour;" moreover, there is nothing in Old Testament law that talks about women or silence.[158] For those who accept Pauline authorship, the debate centers on whether ὁ νόμος is referring to the Mosaic law,[159] to Jewish custom as law,[160] to the rabbinic law,[161] the Old Testament Scriptures as law,[162] or to Roman

---

157. Fee, *First Epistle to the Corinthians*, 791.

158. Fee describes the problem: "when Paul elsewhere appeals to 'the Law,' he regularly cites the text (e.g. 9:8; 14:21), usually to support a point he himself is making. Nowhere else in the entire corpus does he appeal to the Law in this general, but absolute, way as binding on Christian behavior. More difficult yet is the fact that the Law does *not* say any such thing. An early passage in Genesis (3:16) is often appealed to, but that text does not say what is argued by this glossator."

159. Nash, *1 Corinthians*, 382, holds that the law of Moses did teach the subordination of wives to their husbands, and husbands' duty to teach the law to their wives.

160. Fitzmyer, *First Corinthians*, 533. From his view of this passage as the words of the Corinthian men, he sees "the law" here as referring to Jewish tradition.

161. Martin, *Spirit and the Congregation*, 87. Paul's own teaching under the rabbinic tradition. Mollenkott, *Women, Men and the Bible*, 96, and Fung, "Ministry in the New Testament," 192, see Paul as appealing to the oral tradition of his day and note that this term is used in this manner elsewhere, for example, in Acts 22:3; Rom 2:17–20; Eph 2:15; and Phil 3:5–6.

162. Interpreters differ as to what law Paul had in mind. Barrett, Robertson, and Plummer see this passage in relation to Gen 3:16, as the subordination of wives. Barrett, *First Epistle to the Corinthians*, 330; Robertson and Plummer, *First Epistle of St. Paul*, 325. Grudem sees it in relation to Gen 2. Grudem, *Gift of Prophecy*, 223. Witherington sees Job 29:21 as the law, in *Women in the Earliest Church*, 103. Grenz notes that "the ancient authors did enjoin submission and silence in certain contexts. This attitude reflects respect for God (Isa 41:1; Hab 2:20; Zech

law.¹⁶³ Bible translations reflect these disagreements among interpreters on Paul's usage of ὁ νόμος.¹⁶⁴

These different views on the usage of the word ὁ νόμος ("the law") in 1 Corinthians 14:34 are generally linked to the interpreter's understanding of σιγάω ("silence") and ὑποτάσσω ("subordination"). The fact that Paul does not specify the object of women's submission in the text generates debate on whether this law is referring to σιγάω or ὑποτάσσω. Assuming ὑποτάσσω as subordination of all women to male leadership, Grudem sees ὁ νόμος as referring to the Old Testament, particularly the creation order in Genesis 2.¹⁶⁵ Schüssler Fiorenza explains ὑποτάσσω as subordination of wives to husbands and assumes ὁ νόμος as the Greco-Roman law that prohibited wives from "speaking" in public.¹⁶⁶ Unlike Grudem and Schüssler Fiorenza, Witherington links this passage directly to silence. He takes ὁ νόμος as alluding to the Old Testament as the law, particularly noting Job 29:21, which mentions respectful silence when a word of counsel is spoken.¹⁶⁷

These interpreters also examine Paul's usage of ὁ νόμος elsewhere in their efforts to determine what he most likely meant in the context of 1 Corinthians 14:34. The term ὁ νόμος appears 123 times in Pauline writings, 9 times in

---

2:13), for those in authority (Judg 3:19) and for wise persons noted for their knowledge and counsel (Job 29:11). In addition, God himself imposes silence on someone who speaks insolently to a righteous person (Ps 31:17–18)." Grenz and Kjesbo, *Women in the Church*, 120. Thiselton sees the law here as the principle of order in the Old Testament, where God turns chaos into order. Ciampa and Rosner relate this passage to Num 12:1–15, where Miriam criticized Moses the prophet. Ciampa and Rosner, *First Letter to the Corinthians*, 2010.

163. Schüssler Fiorenza, *In Memory of Her*, 231; Wire, *Corinthian Women Prophets*, 135.

164. For example, "Law" (NIV, NBV), "Jewish Law" (GNB), "Law of Moses" (CEV), "Scriptures" (Living Bible).

165. As cited in chapter 4, at first he saw this passage as referring to Gen 3:16 but later changed his opinion to Gen 2. He argues that in 119 usages of ὁ νόμος, Paul never once uses it about rabbinic law or Roman law. Church fathers such as Clement of Alexandria assumed the subordination view, which believed that men are superior to women. This is discussed in Coyle, "Fathers on Women," 117–167.

166. As cited in chapter 4, she maintains that the "Jewish-Hellenistic missionary tradition" was derived from Greco-Roman law.

167. Witherington, *Women in the Earliest Church*, 103. Ciampa and Rosner see this passage as alluding to Num 12:1–1, in which Miriam criticized Moses. They see Miriam as violating her role of submission and silence. Ciampa and Rosner, *First Letter to the Corinthians*, 727. Thiselton sees the word ὁ νομος referring to the Pentateuch, which "declares the ordered character of creation and human life and the regulative character (especially Leviticus, Deuteronomy, Numbers) of boundaries or differentiations." Thiselton, *First Epistle to the Corinthians*, 1153.

1 Corinthians and none in 2 Corinthians.¹⁶⁸ The phrase ὁ νόμος λέγει ("the law says") appears only two times elsewhere, in Romans 3:19 and 1 Corinthians 9:8. Fee, who sees the 1 Corinthians 14:34–35 text as not authored by Paul, provides helpful explanations on Paul's usages of the term ὁ νόμος elsewhere. He points out that whenever Paul appeals to ὁ νόμος, a specific Old Testament text is cited, as in 1 Corinthians 9:8 and 14:21.¹⁶⁹ An issue for 1 Corinthians 14:34 is that Paul does not hint at or cite any specific text from the Old Testament. Paul elsewhere "does *not* say" the law is binding on "Christian behavior."¹⁷⁰ Furthermore, there is nothing in the entire Old Testament that discusses women speaking.¹⁷¹ Winter also notes that there is no specific command about women's vocal participation in the Mosaic law.¹⁷²

While acknowledging that there is no specific Old Testament command that can be directly linked to what Paul is saying about ὁ νόμος in this context, Grudem and Witherington nevertheless argue that the term alludes to some Old Testament passage. Other scholars argue that the meaning of the term must consider the perspective of Old Testament law, given Paul's Jewish background.¹⁷³ Some interpreters assume that ὁ νόμος is a reference to Genesis 3:16,¹⁷⁴ while others state that it refers to Genesis 2:21–24.¹⁷⁵ This was probably the view of Judson as well when he translated ὁ νόμος as *"pyit nyat tayar,"* meaning "the Law." His translation of ὑποτασσέσθωσαν ("women should accept men's ruling") alongside καθὼς καὶ ὁ νόμος λέγει ("as the Law commands") suggests that he sees the law here as referring to Genesis 3:16.

---

168. NA²⁷.
169. Fee, *First Epistle to the Corinthians*, 791.
170. Fee, 791.
171. Fee, 791.
172. Winter, *Roman Wives, Roman Widows*, 93.
173. Aland, Aland, and Bauer, *Griechisch-Deutsches Wörterbuch*, argue that νόμος in Rom 3:27; 4:15; and 5:13, refers to the law in general or the Roman law, that Rom 7:21–25 and 8:2 are referring to "rule," Rom 3:27, 8:2, and Gal 8:2 are referring to the new law, and all the other references in Pauline writings refer to the Jewish law, the law of Moses or the holy Scriptures. Garland, "1 Corinthians," 672; Hodge, *First Epistle to the Corinthians*, 1953.
174. Robertson and Plummer, *First Epistle of St. Paul*, 325; Barrett, *First Epistle to the Corinthians*, 330. Also, translations such as KJV, NIV, and NRSV see the law here as referring to Gen 3:16.
175. Bruce, *1 and 2 Corinthians*, 136 rejects the view that refers to Gen 3:16. This "is unlikely, since in MT and LXX Gen 3:16 speaks of a woman's instinctive inclination . . . towards her husband, of which he takes advantage so as to dominate her. The reference is more probably to the creation narratives."

I find that Schüssler Fiorenza's view of ὁ νόμος as referring to Greco-Roman law offers the more convincing argument. First, this view connects the usages of σιγάω ("silence") and ὑποτάσσω ("subordination") to ὁ νόμος. Although Paul's reference to ὁ νόμος links both submission and silence to women in the text of 1 Corinthians 14:34, interpreters often make only one such linkage. As mentioned in the usage of ὑποτάσσω, linking ὁ νόμος to Genesis 3:16 is problematic since this passage is talking about the relationship after the fall. Likewise, in linking ὁ νόμος to Genesis 2:20–24,[176] "the created order" is problematic since this interpretation of created order conflicts with Paul's concept of the new creation in Galatians 3:28.[177] Moreover, the Genesis 2 passage does not mention anything about speaking or asking questions.

Although Witherington's view is promising, the connection with Job 29:21 is unconvincing since that text is about respectful silence, not about women.[178] However, Schüssler Fiorenza convincingly connects the usages of σιγάω ("silence") and ὑποτάσσω ("subordination") to ὁ νόμος by explaining the law here as a reference to the Roman law, particularly the Velleian decree of the Roman Senate that banned wives from speaking and asking questions in public.[179] She sees Paul as prohibiting wives from speaking and questioning in the public worship assembly because such behavior was regarded as contradictory to the submissive and silent role of wives in Greco-Roman culture.[180]

Second, the usage of αἰσχρον ("shame") with γάρ ἐστιν γυναιξὶ λαλεῖν ("for a woman to speak") in 1 Corinthians 14:35 further supports Schüssler Fiorenza's argument for the Roman law being a fit with the Greco-Roman cultural background of Corinth.[181] Since there is no law in the Old Testament

---

176. Grudem, *Gift of Prophecy*, 239–255. See also Carson, "'Silent in the Churches,'" 152; Hurley, *Man and Woman*, 192.

177. Thiselton, *First Epistle to the Corinthians*, 1155. Wire contends that the issue here is whether "order" still applies to a charismatic gospel community. Wire, *Corinthian Women Prophets*, 13–38.

178. Thiselton, 1155.

179. As in chapter 4, this is also the view of Winter, *Roman Wives, Roman Widows*, 96. Kroeger and Kroeger, "Pandemonium and Silence," 51–52, understand the law here as the legal efforts of Greco-Roman society to control ecstatic female behavior and translate submission as "they must control themselves."

180. As noted, she argues that the "Jewish-Hellenistic missionary tradition" derived from Greco-Roman law.

181. She sees Paul prohibiting wives from speaking and questioning in the public worship assembly referring to the Velleian decree of the Roman Senate that banned women from speaking in public.

that specifically mentions women speaking, the silence of women, or the submission of women, it is possible that Paul is referring to a law that the Corinthians would naturally understand. Regardless of the interpreter's understanding of the nature of women or wives' participation in worship, the usage of the word αἰσχρόν ("shame") suggests that the command here refers to cultural mores regarding propriety, where certain actions of wives were considered shameful for themselves and their husbands.

The culture in the historical setting of Corinth was a mixture of Greek, Roman, and Jewish. Ciampa and Rosner argue that since this Greco-Roman culture was strongly patriarchal and hierarchical, in terms of the law, a woman's submission would normally be understood "to refer to her submission to the authority of her husband" regardless of the specific subcontext, whether Jewish, Greek, or Roman.[182] Therefore, the term ὁ νόμος ("the law") in this text may plausibly be understood as referring to the prevailing legal framework in the cultural construct of propriety in Greco-Roman Corinth.

The question here is whether Paul would use ὁ νόμος in reference to Roman law. As noted above, interpreters who focus on the influence of Paul's Jewish background argue that Paul never uses ὁ νόμος, "the law," to refer to Roman law.[183] However, at issue is also the fact that there is no specific reference that supports the prohibition of women speaking or submission in the Old Testament.[184] A similar argument can therefore be made here in support of the influence of the Greco-Roman cultural setting in Corinth.

This is highlighted by Hollander in his explanation of the double usage of ὁ νόμος in 1 Corinthians 9, where he sees the first ὁ νόμος as referring to "the law" in general and the latter to "the Law of Moses."[185] In Hollander's view, "all this makes it wholly understandable that Paul, as a Hellenistic Jew and Christian living in the Greco-Roman culture, could refer first to 'the law' in general, and next to 'the Law of Moses' as a specimen of a larger class of national laws, given by a God-inspired man, Moses, to the people of Israel (or the Jews)."[186] He therefore argues that it is very doubtful that the law in

---

182. Ciampa and Rosner, *First Letter to the Corinthians*, 722.
183. Fung, "Ministry in the New Testament," 192.
184. Fee, *First Epistle to the Corinthians*, 791.
185. Hollander, "Meaning of the Term 'Law,'" 119.
186. Hollander, 123.

1 Corinthians 14:34 is the Jewish law, since his "(Gentile) readers in Corinth would not have understood the Pauline phrase this way."[187] From this same perspective, it is possible that Paul could use ὁ νόμος to refer to the Roman law in this context. Winter notes that the concern for propriety, shame, and obligations in the Corinthian context provides "powerful arguments to invoke in Roman culture."[188] It is within this framework that Paul is anxious not to cause unnecessary social offence.

The next question, then, asks what lies behind Paul's reference to the Roman law. The sentence ἐν οἴκῳ τοὺς ἰδίους ἄνδρας ἐπερωτάτωσαν in verse 35, meaning "they should ask their own husbands at home," serves as a clue to the reasoning behind Paul's usage of the term law. The fact that these women were asking questions would be considered "inconsistent with this manner of respecting the husband" in Greco-Roman culture.[189] Winter links such behavior of the wives to "the new women" who were emerging in the Greco-Roman world at that time, and points out that such women "asking questions" may have been a reason for the imperial decree that banned wives from speaking on behalf of their husbands.[190]

Witherington also concludes that 1 Corinthians 11 and 14 "seem to be Paul's reaction to those whom he perceived to be overly liberated women."[191] Agreeing with this view, Ebojo notes that the presence of this new attitude among women at this time in "the church, as a public assembly, was not spared either."[192] Winter thus sees Paul as referencing the Roman law in this context, because "the wrong impression being given to the outsider is also central to the issue of order in the service, and particularly prophetic activity which is for the unbeliever (14:22–25) and in which women also engage (11:5)."[193]

However, when we evaluate these explanations, the sentence is not only about speaking or asking questions as a shameful act. The fact that Paul

---

187. Hollander, 123.
188. Winter, *Roman Wives, Roman Widows*, 93.
189. Ciampa and Rosner, *First Letter to the Corinthians*, 722.
190. Winter, *Roman Wives, Roman Widows*, 96.
191. Witherington, *Women in the Earliest Churches*, 126.
192. Ebojo, "Should Women Be Silent?," 25–29, mentions church leaders before the fourth century, such as Ambrosiaster, John Chrysostom, and Tertullian, making overtures against women's apparently disrupting presence.
193. Winter, *Roman Wives, Roman Widows*, 93.

commands the wives to ask these questions at home in verse 35, ἐν οἴκῳ τοὺς ἰδίους ἄνδρας ἐπερωτάτωσαν ("let them ask their husbands at home"), supports the view that Paul's concern is the *way* the wives ask, not just the fact of their asking.[194] If so, it is the disruptive manner of the wives' questioning that Paul considered shameful and which was of primary concern. This is the view of Witherington,[195] who points out that the purpose of Paul's command was "correcting an abuse of a privilege, not taking back a woman's right to speak in the assembly," which he had already acknowledged in 1 Corinthians 11.[196]

In light of the concern in these passages about maintaining order in worship and the immediate issue of prophesying in worship services, the wives are commanded to respect the good order of the service; in effect, they are to avoid being disorderly. The motive behind using the Roman law, then, could be as Schüssler Fiorenza sees it, that of not giving the wrong impression to unbelievers and protecting the Corinthian Christian community from being seen as an "orgiastic" cult.[197] Agreeing with this, Garland also concludes that "Paul's instructions are conditioned by the social realities of his age and a desire to prevent a serious breach in decorum."[198]

7.3 Contextual Application of the Text

Considering the translation work of Judson in Myanmar, contemporary interpretations, and the historical-cultural background, a possible reading of the interpretive problem concerning women's silence is that it is a situation-specific command for the context of Corinth in Paul's day. All of the above

---

194. Witherington, *Women in the Earliest Churches*, 102; Thiselton, *First Epistle to the Corinthians*, 1159; Wire, *Corinthian Women Prophets*, 152–158; Keener, *Paul, Women and Wives*, 70–100.

195. Witherington, *Women in the Earliest Churches*, 287, writes, "It is very believable that these women assumed that Christian prophets or prophetesses functioned much like the oracle at Delphi, who only prophesied in response to questions, including questions about purely personal matters. Paul argues that Christian prophecy is different: Prophets and prophetesses speak in response to the prompting of the Holy Spirit, without any human priming of the pump. Paul then limits such questions to another location, namely home. He may imply that the husband or man who was to be asked was either a prophet or at least able to answer such questions at a more appropriate time."

196. Witherington, *Women in the Earliest Churches*, 287.

197. Schüssler Fiorenza, *In Memory of Her*, 232; Winter, *Roman Wives, Roman Widows*, 93.

198. Garland, "1 Corinthians," 673.

findings show that the prohibition against women speaking in 1 Corinthians 14:34–35 is plausible when this text is seen in historical context as: (1) a problem of the church in the specific context of Corinth; (2) directed to a specific group, the wives in the Corinthian church; (3) intended to stop these women from a specific kind of speaking (asking questions during times of prophetic utterances in the church's worship services); (4) for a specific problem, namely, that their questions had disrupted the worship order of the church; and (5) making use of a specific social framework, the Roman law, as a reminder that such questioning by the wives would be considered inappropriate and shameful in their cultural setting. Paul mentioned the wives since they were the ones who were disrupting worship.[199] Paul asked them to stop what they were doing and to submit voluntarily to maintain the orderliness of the worship service. (6) He did not stop them from learning but directed their questions to another setting for a specific purpose, that of not giving the wrong impression to unbelievers about the Corinthian Christian community.

These findings fit well within the context of 1 Corinthians 14, where Paul talks about the proper use of spiritual gifts, tongues, and prophecy. This includes speaking in tongues and prophetic utterances during worship in 1 Corinthians 14:28–30. He urges the Corinthians to stop speaking in tongues without meaningful interpretation and to take turns to prophesy. In both cases, Paul's main concern is about order in the worship service. The above explanation of 1 Corinthians 14:34–35 also fits well with Paul's concluding statement in 1 Corinthians 14:39–40, where he urges both Corinthian men and women to "be eager to prophesy, and do not forbid speaking in tongues," and to minister in the gifts of the Spirit "decently and in order."[200] This suggests that Paul is here arguing that "disorder and division were created not by the gifts themselves, but by the way in which they were used."[201]

Further, our findings fit well within the overall context of 1 Corinthians, where Paul allowed women to prophesy in 1 Corinthians 11:5 with a head covering, and where he dealt with the proper conduct of believers during the Lord's Supper in 1 Corinthians 12, given the concern for propriety especially in relation to sensitivity to outsiders. Finally, our findings cohere with Paul's

---

199. Witherington, *Women in the Earliest Churches*, 276.
200. NRSV.
201. Witherington, *Women in the Earliest Churches*, 275.

concerns for the broader context, where he speaks of limiting one's freedom in Christ for the sake of others; he addresses this concern regarding lawsuits among believers (1 Cor 6), married life (1 Cor 7), food sacrificed to idols (1 Cor 8), Paul's use of his own freedom (1 Cor 9), and believers' freedom (1 Cor 10).

The next question, then, is whether the command for women's silence is still applicable in the church today, since all our findings suggest that Paul's command is situationally specific for the first-century Corinthian context. As we have seen, contemporary interpreters differ on whether the text is normative or a context-specific command. From Grudem's perspective that sees all teachings of the Bible as normative and applicable for Christians in all times and places, he views this text as normative for women in the church today. He reasons that if Paul does not want this rule to be applied in other churches, then he would not say that "women should remain silent *in the churches.*"[202] Witherington shares this view. However, they differ on what they see as normative. Grudem sees Paul as prohibiting women from speaking an authoritative form of speaking that includes judging and evaluating, which were reserved for male leadership only. Witherington sees Paul as prohibiting wives from asking disruptive questions to the prophets in the worship service.[203]

Critical contextual hermeneutics seeks not only to understand the text as it was received in its historical context, but also to identify an appropriate application of the text for the present context, from the perspective of faith and the authority of the Bible. My view is that the 1 Corinthians 14:34–35 text is situation-specific, and therefore normative only in similar situations. After examining the historical background and agreeing with Witherington's view of Paul's main concern in this passage, my conclusion is that the general principle for 1 Corinthians 14:34–35 is showing appropriate respect when another is speaking in a worship service. The principle is not about gender, even though it is relevant to understand the significance of gender issues in first-century Corinth. The text is not about stopping Christian women from speaking generally or restricting women from speaking authoritatively in the church.

---

202. Grudem, *Evangelical Feminism*, 245.
203. Witherington, *Conflict and Community*, 274.

This leads to the next question, concerning how this text is best applied in the church today in the Myanmar context when similar situations occur. This requires Myanmar interpreters' awareness, following Ciampa and Rosner, of the extent to which Paul was being sensitive to issues of cultural appropriateness in the places where the church found itself.[204] The challenge in applying such a text to the church in Myanmar is that the biblical interpreter must have a critical awareness of the social realities in the Myanmar cultural context. This means being able to understand and articulate what is considered an appropriate way of showing respect in Myanmar culture. As noted earlier, biblical interpreters in Myanmar often view social practices of Myanmar as like the social norms of Paul's day. From that perspective, interpreters in Myanmar have typically appropriated this text uncritically and have therefore accepted the silent role of women as normative for today in Myanmar.

The challenge for Myanmar interpreters is not only to understand that we bring our own questions and life situations to the text, but also allow the biblical texts to function as Scripture. This requires allowing "the texts to ask questions of us, to confront our cultural presuppositions, to challenge and reshape our default readings."[205] Therefore, the challenge for Myanmar interpreters is to understand that there are not only similarities but also differences between contemporary Myanmar culture and first-century Greco-Roman Corinth culture, and that these similarities and differences must be analyzed critically in their search for the meaning of biblical texts.

In general, the culture of Myanmar is a shame-based culture, as was Corinth in Paul's day. It is also a strongly patriarchal and hierarchical culture, as was Corinth. Women are less likely to ask questions than their husbands in Myanmar society. Although there is no overt restriction on women's participation in public settings, speaking with other women's husbands in public or in private would be considered shameful, as in Corinth. Additionally, for a woman to speak with a loud voice is considered too authoritative and therefore shameful in Myanmar culture.

Yet, exhibiting sensitivity to this cultural reality, as Paul urged the Corinthian Christians to do, is not a straightforward matter with respect to Myanmar Christians. The obvious reason is that there is no law in Myanmar

---

204. Ciampa and Rosner, *First Letter to the Corinthians*, 720.

205. Flemming, *Contextualization*, 171.

that prohibits women from speaking in public or representing their husbands in court, as there was in Corinth. Moreover, although women were less educated than men in the past in Myanmar, as in Corinth (which was a possible reason for Paul to ask women to ask their husbands questions at home if they wanted to learn),[206] this is no longer the case in Myanmar today, where education is open to females as well as males. These areas of possible convergence and divergence mean that biblical interpreters cannot apply this text to the Myanmar Christian context without a critical contextual hermeneutical approach.

One could argue that respectful silence is already a normative value in Myanmar culture. This culture of respectful silence is required for younger persons in relation to older persons, and for those who are lower in social rank in relation to someone who is higher in rank. This cultural value has been reinforced throughout the authoritarian and hierarchical history of Myanmar. In this culture, asking questions to anyone in an authoritative role, such as leaders, elders, parents, and teachers, is considered inappropriate and disrespectful, regardless of which gender is doing the asking. At the same time, it is also true that there may be a deeply engrained assumption that "the respect given by someone in a lower position to someone in a higher position" would include women as "lower than" men. But, this assumption would be contrary to Paul's theology of ministry without hierarchy and his theology of inclusivity and "oneness in Christ."

Paul's command in 1 Corinthians 14:34–35 to show respect when another is speaking in worship is best understood by considering Paul's purpose in giving such a command. Paul's intention was to protect the Corinthian Christian community from giving the wrong impression to unbelievers. Paul asks believers to limit their own freedom for the sake of others throughout 1 Corinthians. In this light, the contextually appropriate application of 1 Corinthians 14:34–35 for Myanmar is the challenge to limit our own freedom for the sake of others, in the contemporary Myanmar context, so that Myanmar Christians too can build up the body of Christ. It is for this reason, as Paul reminds the Corinthians in 1 Corinthians 14:40, that "all things should be done decently and in order."

---

206. Keener, *Paul, Women and Wives*, 81.

7.4 Conclusion

Drawing on the principles and methodology of a critical contextual hermeneutics for Myanmar, this chapter has examined the issues surrounding the interpretation of 1 Corinthians 14:34–35, keeping in mind the Myanmar context. In chapter 3, I identified the ways in which the translation work of Adoniram Judson was similar to or different from the Greek New Testament texts and how Judson's interpretations were like or different from contemporary interpreters such as Grudem, Schüssler Fiorenza, and Witherington. Considering all the evidence, I can only conclude that Judson's translation was itself an interpretation that was influenced by his presuppositions and cultural worldview. The challenge for Myanmar interpreters who read Judson's translation today is to recognize that "the gospel must challenge the presuppositions of the missionary's culture if it has any hope of speaking prophetically to the new culture in which it is being contextualized."[207]

My analysis of the interpretations of Grudem, Schüssler Fiorenza, and Witherington also highlighted the role of the interpreter's context.[208] Considering the information derived from Judson's Bible translation and these contemporary interpreters, the challenge for Myanmar interpreters is to recognize that our own presuppositions inevitably influence our interpretations of biblical meaning. This means that interpreters must allow the gospel to challenge those influences that shape our understanding of Scripture. This is what happened to Paul as well. Although Paul's interpretations of the meaning of the gospel for the emerging church were influenced by three cultures (Jewish, Greek, and Roman), he also challenged the worldviews, values, and practices of Greco-Roman society that were normative in Corinth. An example in 1 Corinthians is his challenge to "the culture of status, power and self-promotion" that characterized Roman Corinth in light of the cross, which makes 'the cross' and everything it stands for offensive in that culture (1 Cor 1:18).[209]

---

207. Flemming, *Contextualization*, 140.

208. Flemming sees context as "a variety of boundaries: regionality, nationality, culture, language, ethnicity, social and economic status, political structures, education, gender, age, religious or theological tradition, worldview or values (the 'life world' of the audience)." Flemming, 20.

209. Flemming, 171.

My analysis has highlighted the complexity and challenges that interpreters face in determining the meaning of 1 Corinthians 14:34–35, both in its historical context and in terms of its application for contemporary Christians, including Myanmar Christians. I argue that both translation decisions and views of the historical context of Corinth in Paul's day must be viewed as products of the interpreters' cultural worldviews. The hope is that this approach to hermeneutics will give hope to Myanmar interpreters who approach biblical texts from the perspective of faith to see the benefits of engaging in this kind of critical contextual analysis.

CHAPTER 8

Summary and Conclusion

In chapter 1, the introductory chapter, I introduced the problem of the interpretation of biblical texts concerning the role and status of women in the church in Myanmar. To address this challenge, Part One focused on the interpretation of 1 Corinthians 14:33b-36, and the influential translation by Adoniram Judson in his Burmese Bible, first published in 1840. Part Two evaluated representative contemporary interpreters in the search for hermeneutical tools that could aid those (particularly Myanmar biblical scholars) who wish to take both the authority of the Bible and the significance of biblical, historical, and cultural contexts seriously in addressing such texts and their application for the church in Myanmar today.

Considering these concerns, Part One focused on two problematic areas, culture and translation, surrounding interpretations of 1 Corinthians 14:33b-36 in Myanmar. Part Two highlighted the strengths and weaknesses of different hermeneutical schools of thought when applied to biblical interpretation in Myanmar, and then articulated a proposed critical contextual hermeneutic that takes the Myanmar context seriously. Below is a summary of these contributions to biblical interpretation in Myanmar.

8.1 Culture and Hermeneutics

In Part One, concerning problematic issues surrounding the interpretation of 1 Corinthians 14:33b-36 in Myanmar, I examined the contributions of translation and culture to Christian attitudes which have defined the role of women in the church. In chapter 2, I discussed how the concept of silence has been understood in Myanmar culture and how this understanding has contributed to Myanmar Christians' attitudes about the role of women in the church. I noted how the conceptual framework for understanding the word "silence" is deeply rooted in people's experiences of authoritarian rule throughout the imperial, colonial, and postcolonial periods of Myanmar history. The religious teachings of Buddhism, the major religion in Myanmar, also reinforced this concept of silence. The concept of silence as a sign of submission to authority became inseparable from Myanmar culture and was understood as submission not just to national authorities but also to anyone in a position of authority. This understanding strengthened the control of every perceived authority over people in all areas of life, including the political, societal, and religious spheres. It governed the relationship between rulers and ruled, men and women, and parents and children.

Generally, biblical interpreters' understanding and usage of words is intertwined with symbols from the past, their own experiences, and their own worldviews. This same dynamic would be expected to occur in Myanmar as well. This intertwined nature of the interpreter's understanding of words generates a situation where the translation communicates ideas and ideologies that go beyond the intent of the original author. For instance, Judson translated a generic term meaning "speaking" in the original New Testament Greek as "preaching" in 1 Corinthians 14:34b-36, which as a specific form of speaking has serious implications for the issue of women's silence in the Myanmar church. This translation choice by Judson helps explain how the word "silence" in this text has been construed by subsequent Myanmar interpreters in a way that goes beyond the meaning the original author intended, as far as this can be discerned. The evidence suggests that the cultural understanding of silence has influenced Myanmar interpreters in a way that has affected the received understanding of the meaning of 1 Corinthians 14:34b-36 and other texts, with those involved not being aware of the influential role of their cultural assumptions.

In short, Myanmar's contextual understanding of the concept of silence contributed to the ongoing uncritical acceptance of a translation that has reinforced the practice of silencing women in the church. Thus, one could conclude that Myanmar culture has contributed to negative attitudes toward women in the church in Myanmar today by reinforcing assumptions about what 1 Corinthians 14:34b-36 and other biblical texts mean. From the perspective of contextualization, denying cultural influences in one's hermeneutics or accepting everything in one's culture without reflecting on it in the light of the Scripture, is to fall into the trap of uncriticality. With this understanding of how our reading of Scripture is affected by our social and cultural location, we can only conclude that Christians in Myanmar need to have a basis for analyzing all cultures that impinge on biblical interpretation – that of the translator, contemporary interpreters, the Bible, as well as our own culture.

8.2 Hermeneutics and Translation

Chapter 2 further investigated how Bible translation in Myanmar supported an understanding of silence as a proper sign of submission. Bible translation contributed significantly to Myanmar Christian attitudes on the role of women in the church. The Burmese Bible translation work of the nineteenth-century missionary Adoniram Judson has been the most significant translation in this regard. This translation's influence was reinforced by the revered status of Judson as the pioneer Protestant missionary in the country and the popularity of his translation. To demonstrate this influence, I explained how 1 Corinthians 14:33b-36 was translated in Judson's Burmese Bible and the impact of that translation on Myanmar Christians' views of the role of women in the church.

Particularly, I noted in chapter 3 that Judson's Burmese translation of 1 Corinthians 14:34–35 interpreted silence to mean that women should not be "preaching." As noted in the previous section, this is an example of how translators' understanding of words are intertwined with their own worldviews. Due to his literal approach, as opposed to a critical approach, Judson's linguistic choice was taken literally without considering usages in the original first-century context (not to mention the Myanmar context). This approach greatly impacted views and practices surrounding the role of women in the Myanmar church. Considering all the issues surrounding the interpretation of 1 Corinthians 14:33b-36 in Myanmar, one could conclude that the translator's literal approach to interpretation, together with other influences, led to an uncritical acceptance of the silent role of women in church.

In other words, Adoniram Judson's understanding of the role of women in society contributed to his choice of words in his translation of 1 Corinthians 14:33b-36, and consequently to Myanmar Christian views about the role of women in the church. His understanding of the role of women in society was like that of the popular teachings of his day, rendering this text as an injunction that women should not preach in the church.

Judson most likely believed that he was being true to what the Bible is saying. And although his translation of 1 Corinthians 14:33b-36 contributed to present-day restrictions on the role of women in the church, it is important to note that he did support giving some freedom for women to be involved in the Myanmar church during his time. Missionary women in those days, including his wives, were actively involved in evangelism and teaching in the church, and were very occasionally involved in preaching. It was through their active involvement in ministry and their contributions to mission work that many more women in their home countries were encouraged to become missionaries and the women's missionary movement flourished.

An added dynamic in understanding Judson's views and how they affected his usage of words in texts is that he was not asking the questions that we are asking now. When he translated the Bible, his main interest was a missionary concern. From this missionary concern, he adopted many terms from Burmese culture, including religious terms, and adapted them to present the Christian message in a familiar linguistic and cultural framework. However, his translation shows that, while some local linguistic terms worked well, others suggested meanings different from what Judson or the original text may have intended, due to the complex nature of the language and associations and nuances in meaning of which he might not have been aware. The usage of the word "silence" in Judson's translation is one of those instances which resulted in more than what the translator might have intended. We as interpreters today are now looking back at Judson's translation and noting these dynamics in his translation work. As discussed in the previous section, this dynamic of translation offers a contribution to understanding our own cultural assumptions and their influential role in interpretation.

One can also conclude that Judson's association of "silence" with "not preaching" in 1 Corinthians 14:33b-36 supported a preexisting view of the role of women in Myanmar society. His translation helped enable the church in Myanmar to maintain this patriarchal authority structure. It reinforced a belief that women should be silent in the church as in other spheres in Myanmar society. For some, it restricted women from preaching in the presence of men. For others, it restricted women from preaching entirely.

To summarize, although in certain respects Judson's translation work and personal faith were liberating for women in Myanmar during that period, they have nevertheless contributed to the restricted role of women in preaching positions in the church in Myanmar today. Given the respect owed to Judson for what he accomplished, adopting a different view of women's roles is difficult for Myanmar Christians in the family, society, and the church today. Whether one attempts to deny the impact of the translator's role or accept everything in a translation without critical analysis – both amount to uncritical contextualization. With this understanding of how patriarchal culture influenced translation and how translation in turn reinforced cultural attitudes towards women in the church in Myanmar today, it is possible to critique the translation while still being respectful of the translator.

8.3 Schools of Interpretation

Chapter 4 analyzed the strengths and weaknesses of different hermeneutical schools of thought when applied to the abovementioned interpretive issues in Myanmar. They were examined to assess hermeneutical tools in resolving problems of interpretation in passages concerning women. This was done from the perspective of those who wish to take both the authority of the Bible and the significance of context seriously. To this end, I examined three different hermeneutical schools of thought in chapter 4 and identified the principles and presuppositions behind each hermeneutical school to learn how they contributed to their interpretations of 1 Corinthians 14:33b-36. This chapter then unpacked their detailed explanations of 1 Corinthians 14:33b-36. Drawing on the insights from this chapter, chapter 5 proposed a critical contextual hermeneutic for Myanmar, focusing on issues related to the role of women highlighted in the Corinthians text.

Leading up to this, I addressed the principles underlying the approaches of different hermeneutical schools from different contexts in interpreting 1 Corinthians 14:33b-36, by highlighting two approaches. First, in chapter 4, I explored how hermeneutical schools that prioritize either Scripture over culture, or the rights and interests of women over Scripture, have both contributed to contemporary interpretations, despite their differences in perspective. This exploration highlighted how all interpreters' presuppositions are linked to their sociological and cultural positioning and to their understanding of the nature and authority of the Bible. It also highlighted how these presuppositions undergird the theoretical frameworks that influence their hermeneutical approaches to biblical passages affecting women. This in turn accentuates the important function of the interpreter in the interpretive process, which includes determining the starting point for interpretation and establishing the meanings of texts.

However, although both the hermeneutical schools that prioritize Scripture over culture and those prioritizing the rights and interests of women over Scripture have contributed to our understanding, neither adequately addresses the perspective of interpreters who wish to hold together a serious concern for the status of women, the authority of the Bible, and the significance of context for interpretation and translation. Hermeneutical schools that prioritize Scripture over culture tend to see biblical interpretation as a culturally straightforward process without realizing how their own cultural worldviews and corresponding values have influenced their interpretations.

I have therefore advocated for a critical contextual hermeneutic, a different form of interpretation that deals adequately with both Christian tradition and biblical authority, on the one hand, and relevant cultural concerns in the Myanmar context on the other hand. This need for critical hermeneutics which takes seriously the Christian and cultural traditions in Myanmar was elaborated further in chapter 6, where I demonstrated the problematic nature of Myanmar hermeneutics given the fact that it has not adequately considered the influence of our cultural presuppositions in biblical interpretation.

Incorporating all of the issues raised and addressed in chapters 3 and 4, I then articulated a critical contextual hermeneutic for Myanmar in chapter 5. Drawing on aspects of the abovementioned schools of interpretation, together with a theology of critical contextualization, this hermeneutic provides a way to analyze certain perspectives of Christian tradition in Myanmar, particularly related to the status and roles of women. This approach seriously considers the significance of context in interpretation and translation. It provides a framework which makes it possible to contest traditional interpretations that have restricted the roles and status of women in Myanmar, while retaining a high view of the authority of Scripture and its role in the Christian church.

8.4 Critical Tools for a Contextual Hermeneutic

In light of the hermeneutical problems surrounding the interpretation of 1 Corinthians 14:33b-36 in Myanmar, I have presented a critical hermeneutic grounded in three contexts: the Myanmar context, the Bible translator's context, and the biblical context in its historical setting. Within this contextual framework, this book has examined the impact of Myanmar culture and religious teachings to identify Myanmar Christians' view on the role of women in the church and the attitudes behind their interpretations of biblical texts. We have also revisited the impact of Adoniram Judson's Bible translation on Myanmar Christians' view of the role of women in the church. All of this was done to identify problems in interpreting biblical texts concerning women's role in the church that the thesis intended to address.

Then, from a perspective which takes the authority of the Bible and the significance of context seriously, I revisited 1 Corinthians 14:33b-36 in chapter 7, considering all the principles proposed in my critical contextual hermeneutics. This focused on the biblical context of Corinth to better understand what the text meant to the original readers of that historical time. This was done to show the importance of understanding the hermeneutical distance between historical context and contemporary context. To accept all Scripture as literal and normative for all times, without critical analysis, is uncritical contextualization. With this understanding of how the context influenced the meanings of biblical texts, and how these historical contextual meanings, through critical analysis, can help create culturally appropriate applications for the church in Myanmar today, it is possible to critique traditional interpretations of 1 Corinthians 14:33b-36 based on the Judson Burmese Bible translation, in terms of how they have influenced the role and status of women in the Myanmar church.

Through analyzing all of the influences of translation in determining our understanding of the meaning of silence in the Myanmar church, I concluded that Judson's translation of 1 Corinthians 14:33b-36, and his own personal positioning, led to two oppositional effects: one that supported a degree of freedom for the women of his day to be involved in ministry, in that his translation of λαλέω as "preaching" meant women in Myanmar were not expected to be totally silent in church. At the same time, however, Judson appears to have reinforced the preexisting concept of the silent role of women in society whereby women could not preach and could not lead. Thus, critical questions about the exact situation Paul was addressing were not asked. However, I have also noted that Judson's concern was not the same as that of interpreters today. We are now looking back at Judson's translation and observing retrospectively all the influences on his translation and have concluded that his views were shaped by a culture of patriarchy which, in turn, reinforced the silent role of women in the church of Myanmar. In the same way, we are also now looking back at what happened in Corinth from the perspective of Myanmar today and noticing all the influences of patriarchy in that culture.

At the same time, when we analyze what happened in Corinth and its implication for Myanmar today, elements of Paul's teaching about Jesus also challenged the prevailing views of patriarchy in the ancient world (e.g. Gal 3:28). In the case of 1 Corinthians 14:33b-36, Paul appears to have gone along with patriarchal conventions in a specific situation. It can also be argued that Paul was restricting what women were actually saying, rather than restricting them solely because of their gender. So, while at times Paul appears to have gone along with patriarchal views in dealing with a specific situation, his overall teaching, when it is in line with the teaching of Jesus, reflects a more inclusive view of women. Therefore, one could conclude that the situation addressed in 1 Corinthians 14:33b-36 was normative only in that specific situation. With this understanding of how Scripture is interpreted and how our reading of Scripture is affected by people's social setting, both in the time and context of Scripture and throughout history, it is possible to have a clearer understanding of how attitudes toward the role and status of women in the church in Myanmar today should be constructed.

8.5 The Example of Katharine Bushnell

The role of women in the church has become an issue of serious concern in Myanmar today. Women leaders in and out of the church have raised this concern, especially since the recent opening of society, accelerated by changing events in the political situation as well as the impacts of globalization. The question that this thesis has raised is what should be done with this concern. Often, when women raise questions like this, they are labelled as not taking the Bible seriously. However, it is important to know that there are other ways of interpreting biblical texts from the perspective of faith. This faith perspective views the Bible as an authoritative text, not one approached solely from the hermeneutics of suspicion.

A prime example of such reading, which shares the conviction that the Bible is a book of freedom and empowerment for women that I propose, was undertaken by Katharine Bushnell, who questioned traditional biblical interpretations affecting women in the nineteenth century.

Katharine Bushnell (1856–1946)[1] was an American medical missionary of the Women's Christian Temperance Union (WCTU), the influential nineteenth-century women's movement.[2] When she went to China as a missionary, she discovered that the Chinese Bible was mistranslated in a way that supported cultural prejudices against women preaching, leading her to conclude that the struggles surrounding the social and spiritual suppression of women in the Chinese church in her day could be directly linked to such "mistranslations" of the Bible. Consequently, she began to compare her English translation to the original Greek language of the New Testament and found mistranslations there. She attributed these mistranslations to male translators who allowed their cultural bias against the equality of women to influence their translations.[3]

Bushnell argued from the perspective of one who took both the authority of the Bible and the experiences of women seriously, and thus advocated that seemingly contradictory statements in the Bible should not be rejected out of hand or embraced uncritically but studied with careful analysis. In certain Pauline passages in the Bible, she believed that the "ego-centric" view of patriarchal male interpreters distorted the original meaning of Paul.[4] She therefore insisted that the problem of women's suppression would be resolved when sufficient woman-power was invested in "translations, research, and hermeneutical endeavors."[5]

From this perspective and her conviction of the Bible's message of liberation for women, Bushnell composed one hundred biblical studies on passages

---

1. Bushnell, *God's Word to Women*. Bushnell's book was originally published in 1921 when she was 65 years old. Kroeger, "Legacy of Katharine Bushnell"; Du Mez, *New Gospel for Women*; Hoppin, "Legacy of Katharine Bushnell"; Bushnell, *Dr. Katharine C. Bushnell*.
2. Bushnell, *God's Word to Women*, 2
3. Kroeger, "Legacy of Katharine Bushnell," 2.
4. Bushnell, *God's Word to Women*, 218.
5. Kroeger, "Legacy of Katharine Bushnell," 2.

concerning women in the Bible, and compiled them in her book, *God's Word to Women*, in 1921.[6] For this achievement, Bushnell has been called the forerunner of the feminist movement and the most prominent egalitarian voice of her day in declaring the Bible to be a source of liberation for women.

I am seeking to raise, for today's Myanmar context, the kinds of questions on the role of women in the church that Bushnell raised in the nineteenth century in the Chinese context. The risk of asking these questions in Myanmar is like that in Bushnell's day, namely, that some will hold on to the domesticating model of patriarchy and try to force the church and Scripture into this mold, or else move away from Christianity altogether.

When Bushnell advocated that the Bible, rightly interpreted, supported women's liberation, the women's movement of her day quickly faded and women became less active. As the movement became further liberalized, many traditional Christians did not want to deal with this issue any more, since they associated any questions on the role of women in the church with rejecting the authority of the Bible. They also felt that challenges to specific passages by women were not necessary since Paul advocated that women be treated with respect by admonishing men to love their wives as they would love themselves.[7] These Christians felt that the Bible was sufficient and they were no longer interested in dealing with the questions that women like Bushnell had raised.

Despite these challenges from all sides, which persist in Myanmar today, this book has presented a critical contextual evangelical feminist reading within the Myanmar context. It critically evaluates our own past customs in the light of a careful consideration of recent biblical understanding. This includes careful detailed analysis of a difficult text in Pauline literature, considering Paul's overall view of women in the church, as well as his view of ministry. From this understanding, one can conclude that Paul's comment on women's silence in 1 Corinthians 14:34–36 is situationally specific and thus only normative for the specific situation in Corinth at that time.

Due to the strong patriarchal cultural background in Myanmar, this way of approaching interpretation is likely to face resistance. At the same time, the far-reaching implications of Paul's teaching on slavery give us hope

---

6. See also, *Dr. Katharine C. Bushnell*.
7. Eph 5:22.

regarding the possibility of attitudes changing on the issue of women in the church in Myanmar. Although Paul did not specifically condemn slavery in Philemon, his exhortation to accept one other as brothers and sisters in Christ centuries later helped change people's attitudes toward slavery in North America. Perhaps this is the nature of the gospel – that the gospel continually challenges us to form new attitudes toward others, in every time and place. From this understanding of how Scripture is interpreted and how our reading of Scripture is affected by our social situation, all contextual questions require critical dialogue with the gospel. Through such critical dialogue, there is hope that the always unfolding teaching of the gospel will form new attitudes toward women in the church in Myanmar today, and in the years to come.

Bibliography

Bible Versions and Translations

Aland, Barbara, Kurt Aland, J. Karavidopoulos, C. M. Martini, and B. M. Metzger, eds. *The UBS 4 Greek New Testament: A Reader's Edition*. Stuttgart: German Bible Society, 2007.

Aland, Barbara, Kurt Aland, and E. Nestle. *Greek-English New Testament*. 27th ed. Stuttgart: Deutsche Bibelgesellschaft, 1993. (NA[27])

Aland, K., and B. Aland. *Der Text des Neuen Testaments*. Grand Rapids MI: Eerdmans, 1995.

Easy-to-Read Burmese Bible. World Bible Translation Center, 2006.

The English Standard Version of the Bible. Crossway Bibles, 2008.

Good News Bible: With Deuterocanonical Books/Apocrypha: Today's English Version. United Bible Societies, 1979.

Griesbach, Johann Jakob. *Novum Testamentum Graece*. Vol 2. London: Impensis J. Mackinlay, et Cuthell et Martin, 1809.

The Holy Bible in Myanmar Common Language (Burmese). Yangon, Myanmar: The Bible Society of Myanmar, 2005.

Judson, Adoniram. *The Holy Bible: Containing the Old and New Testaments*. Maulmain, Burma: American Baptist Mission Press for the American and Foreign Bible Society and the American Baptist Board of Foreign Missions, 1840.

———. *The Holy Bible: Containing the Old and New Testaments*. United Bible Societies, 2007. (JB)

———. *The New Testament in Burmese*. Maulmein, Burma, 1832.

———. *The New Testament of Our Lord and Saviour Jesus Christ*. Maulmein: American Baptist Mission Press, 1837.

———. *The New Testament of Our Lord and Saviour Jesus Christ*. Rangoon, Burma: American Baptist Mission Press, 1866.

———. *The New Testament of Our Lord and Saviour Jesus Christ*. Rangoon, Burma: American Baptist Missionary Union, 1885.

Knapp, Georg Christian. *Hē Kainē Diathēkē – Novum Testamentum Graece*. Novum Testamentum Graece. Halae: Orphanotrophei, 1813.

———. *The Holy Bible Containing the Old Testament: Translated Out of the Original Hebrew, and with the Former Translations Diligently Compared and Revised: And the Greek New Testament; Printed from the Text and with the Various Readings of Knapp: Together with the Commonly Received English Translation. Designed for the Use of Students*. New York: Charles Starr, 1835.

———. *Novum Testamentum Graece: Recognovit Atque Insignioris Lectionum Varietatis Et Argumentorum Notationes*. Halae: e libraria Orphanotrophei, 1797.

Kyaw, Fr. John Aye, and Catholic Bible Translation Committe. *The New Testament, Psalms and Proverbs*. Myanmar: Catholic Bishops' Conference of Myanmar, 2005.

Nestle, Eberhard, and Erwin Nestle. *Novum Testamentum Graece*. 28th ed. Stuttgart, Germany: Deutsche Bibelgesellschaft, 2012. (NA[28])

New American Standard Bible. LaHabra, CA: Lockman Foundation, 1995.

New English Translation. Biblical Studies Press, 2005.

New International Version. Grand Rapids, MI: Zondervan, 2011.

New King James Version. Nashville, TN: Thomas Nelson, 1982.

New Living Translation. Carol Stream, IL: Tyndale House Publishers, 2013.

New Revised Standard Version. Nashville, TN: Thomas Nelson Publishers, 1989.

Revised English Bible (with Apocrypha). Oxford: Oxford University Press, 1990.

Robinson, Maurice A. *Elzevir Textus Receptus (1624): With Morphology*. Bellingham, WA: Logos Bible Software, 2002.

———. *Stephen's 1550 Textus Receptus: With Morphology*. Bellingham, WA: Logos Research Systems, 2002.

The German Bible Society. *The Greek New Testament, Fifth Revised Edition*. Stuttgart: Deutsche Bibelgesellschaft, 2014. (UBS[5])

References Cited

Aland, B., K. Aland, J. Karavidopoulos, C. M. Martini, and B. Metzger, eds. *The Greek New Testament: Apparatus. Fifth Revised Edition*. Stuttgart: Deutsche Bibelgesellschaft; American Bible Society; United Bible Societies, 2014.

Aland, Kurt, Barbara Aland, and Walter Bauer. *Griechisch-deutsches Wörterbuch zu den Schriften des Neuen Testaments und der frühchristlichen Literatur*. Berlin: De Gruyter, 2012.

Allison, Robert W. "Let Women Be Silent in the Churches (1 Cor 14:33b–36): What Did Paul Really Say, and What Did It Mean?" *Journal for the Study of the New Testament* 32 (Fall 1988): 27–60.

Anderson, Courtney. *To the Golden Shore: The Life of Adoniram Judson*. Valley Forge, PA: Judson Press, 1987.

Anderson, Justice C. "Review of *Translation as Mission: Bible Translation in the Modern Missionary Movement, The Modern Mission Era, 1972–1992: An Appraisal* by William A. Smalley (Macon, GA: Mercer University Press, 1991)." *Church History* 64, no. 1 (1995): 149–150.

Anonymous, *Golden Balance 21*. Yangon, Myanmar: n.p; n.d., 2.

Asbury Theological Seminary. "Dr. Ben Witherington III." http://asburyseminary.edu/person/dr-ben-witherington-iii/.

Baird, William. *History of New Testament Research*. Vol. 1. Minneapolis, MN: Augsburg Fortress, 1992.

Baker, Joyce B. "An Analysis of the Leadership Challenges Facing the Dallas Theological Seminary Women Alumnae." DMin thesis, Dallas Theological Seminary, 2005.

Balz, Horst, and G. M. Schneider. *Exegetical Dictionary of the New Testament*. Grand Rapids, MI: Eerdmans, 2004.

Barr, James. *The Semantics of Biblical Language*. London: SCM, 1983.

Barrett, C. K. *A Commentary on the First Epistle to the Corinthians*. London: A&C Black, 1971.

———. *The First Epistle to the Corinthians*. London: A&C Black, 1968.

Bassler, J. M. "1 Corinthians." In *Women's Bible Commentary*, edited by C. A. Newsom, J. E. Lapsley, and S. H. Ringe, 411–419. Louisville, KY: Westminster John Knox Press, 2012.

Bauer, Walter. *A Greek-English Lexicon of the New Testament and Other Early Christian Literature*. 3rd ed. (BDAG). Chicago, IL: University of Chicago Press, 2000.

Beaver, R. Pierce. *All Loves Excelling: American Protestant Women in World Mission*. Grand Rapids, MI: Eerdmans, 1968.

Beduhn, Jason David. *Truth in Translation: Accuracy and Bias in English Translations of the New Testament*. New York: University Press of America, 2003.

Bevans, Stephen B. "Models of Contextual Theology." *Missiology* 13, no. 2 (1985): 185–202.

———. *Models of Contextual Theology*. Maryknoll, NY: Orbis Books, 1992.

Bilezikian, Gilbert. *Beyond Sex Roles: What the Bible Says about a Woman's Place in Church and Family*. Grand Rapids, MI: Baker Academic, 2006.

Bischoff, Roger. *Buddhism in Myanmar: A Short History*. Kandy: Buddhist Publication Society, 1995.

Blevins, Carolyn D. "Diverse Baptist Attitudes toward Women in Ministry." *Baptist History and Heritage* 37, no. 3 (2002): 71–76.

Blomberg, Craig L. *1 Corinthians.* The NIV Application Commentary. Grand Rapids, MI: Zondervan, 1994.

Bratcher, Robert G. "The Nature and Purpose of the New Testament in Today's English Version." *The Bible Translator* 22, no. 3 (July 1971): 97–107.

Brekus, Catherine A. *Female Preaching in Early Nineteenth-Century America.* Waco, TX: The Center for Christian Ethics, Baylor University, 2009. . *Strangers and Pilgrims: Female Preaching in America 1740-1845.* Chapel Hill, NC: University of North Carolina, 1998.

Bruce, F. F. *1 and 2 Corinthians.* The New Century Bible Commentary. Grand Rapids, MI: Eerdmans, 1971.

Brumberg, J. J. *Mission for Life: The Story of the Family of Adoniram Judson, the Dramatic Events of the First American Foreign Mission, and the Course of Evangelical Religion in the Nineteenth Century.* Florence, MA: Free Press, 1980.

Burns, Evan Daniel. *"A Supreme Desire to Please Him": The Spirituality of Adoniram Judson.* Eugene, OR: Pickwick, 2015.

Bushnell, Katharine. *God's Word to Women.* Minneapolis, MN: Christians for Biblical Equality, 2003.

———. *Dr. Katharine C. Bushnell: A Brief Sketch of Her Life and Work.* Hertford: Rose and Sons, 1932.

Cairns, Alan. *Dictionary of Theological Terms.* Greenville, SC: Ambassador Emerald International, 2002.

Caldwell, Larry W. "How Asian Is Asian Theological Education?." In *Tending the Seedbeds: Educational Perspectives on Theological Education in Asia,* edited by Allan Burke David Harkness, 23–46. Quezon City, Philippines: Asia Theological Association, 2010.

———. "Interpreting the Bible with the Poor." In *The Church and Poverty in Asia,* edited by Lee Wanak, 171–180. Manila, Philillipines: OMF Literature, 2008.

———. "Scripture in Context Part 1: Reconsidering Our Biblical Roots: Bible Interpretation, the Apostle Paul and Mission Today." *International Bulletin of Missionary Research* 29, no. 2 (Summer 2012): 91–100.

———. "Scripture in Context Part 2: Reconsidering Our Biblical Roots: Bible Interpretation, the Apostle Paul and Mission Today." *International Journal of Frontier Missiology* 29, no. 3 (Fall 2012): 113–121.

———. "Towards the New Discipline of Ethnohermeneutics: Questioning the Relevancy of Western Hermeneutical Methods in the Asian Context." *Journal of Asian Mission* 1, no. 1 (1999): 223–232.

Carson, D. A. "'Silent in the Churches': On the Role of Women in 1 Corinthians 14:33b-36." In Piper and Grudem, *Recovering Biblical Manhood and Womanhood,* 120–153.

Chain, Anna May. "Wives, Warriors and Leaders: Burmese Christian Women's Cultural Reception of the Bible." Society of Biblical Literature, SBL Forum Archive, Oct 2005. https://www.sbl-site.org/publications/article.aspx?ArticleId=455.

Chin Human Rights Organization. *Threats to Our Existence: Persecution of Ethnic Chin Christians in Burma*. Bangkok: Wanida Press, 2012.

Christie, Vance. *Adoniram Judson: Devoted for Life*. Tain, UK: Christian Focus Publications, 2013.

Ciampa, Roy E., and Brian S. Rosner. *The First Letter to the Corinthians*. The Pillar New Testament Commentary. Grand Rapids, MI: Eerdmans, 2010.

Cing, Cin Lian. "Women Roles, Rights and Pastoral Leadership in the 21st Century: Inter-Denominational and Inter-Ethnic Cultural Perspective (Evangelical Perspective)." In *Engagement: Judson Research Center Bulletin*. Yangon, Myanmar: Myanmar Institute of Theology Judson Research Center, 2008.

Clark, Catherine, and Richard Kroeger. "Strange Tongues or Plain Talk?" *Daughters of Sarah* 12, no. 4 (1986): 10–13.

Clarke, Adam. *The New Testament, "Romans-Revelation."* Vol. 6. Reprint, New York: Abingdon-Cokesbury, 1851.

Clement, J. *Adoniram Judson: Being a Sketch of His Life and Missionary Labors*. Auburn, AL: Derby and Miller, 1852.

Comfort, Philip Wesley. "Scribes as Readers: Looking at New Testament Textual Variants according to Reader Reception Analysis." *Neotestamentica* 38, no. 1 (2004): 28–53.

Convention on the Elimination of All Forms of Discrimination against Women. "Concluding Observations of the Committee on the Elimination of Discrimination against Women: Myanmar." United Nations CEDAW/C/MMR/CO/3, November 7, 2008. https://undocs.org/CEDAW/C/MMR/CO/3.

Constitution of the Republic of the Union of Myanmar (2008). Rangoon: Printing & Publishing Enterprise, Ministry of Information, 2008.

Conzelmann, H. *1 Corinthians*. Hermeneia: a Critical and Historical Commentary on the Bible. Philadelphia: Fortress, 1975.

Couch, M. *Dictionary of Premillennial Theology*. Grand Rapids, MI: Kregel Publications, 1996.

Coyle, J. Kevin. "The Fathers on Women and Women's Ordination." In *Studies in Early Christianity: A Collection of Scholarly Essays*, edited by David M. Scholer, Everett Ferguson, and Paul Corby Finney. New York: Garland, 1993. [Originally published in *Église et Théologie* 9 (1978): 51–101.]

Crocker, Cornelia Cyss. *Reading First Corinthians in the Twenty-First Century*. New York: T&T Clark International, 2004.

Cross, F. L., and Livingstone, E. A., eds. *The Oxford Dictionary of the Christian Church*. 3rd ed. Oxford: Oxford University Press, 2005.

Davis, John R. *Poles Apart: Contextualizing the Gospel in Asia*. Bangalore, India: Theological Book Trust, 1993.

De Jong, John. "A Nineteenth-Century New England Exegete Abroad: Adoniram Judson and the Burmese Bible." *Harvard Theological Review* 112, no. 3 (2019): 319–339.

———. "A 'Sin Offering' Crouching at the Door? Translation Lessons from an Exegetical Fossil in the Judson Bible." *The Bible Translator* 61, no. 2 (1 April 2010): 89–92.

de Mesa, José M., and Lode L. Wostyn. *Doing Theology: Basic Realities and Processes*. Manila: Wellspring Books, 1982.

Delap, Lucy. "Uneven Orientalisms: Burmese Women and the Feminist Imagination (Report)." *Gender & History* 24, no. 2 (August 2012): 389–410.

Di Certo, Bridget. "Building a Digital Future in Myanmar." *Reach* (March 2014): 16–21.

Dietrich, Walter, and Ulrich Luz, eds. *The Bible in a World Context: An Experiment in Contextual Hermeneutics*. Grand Rapids, MI: Eerdmans, 2001.

Din, Aung. "Wanted, Christian Daughter-in-Law," *Myanmataman* (December 1967): 1–15.

Din, Tha. *Comparative Study of Buddhist and Christian Scriptures*. Rangoon, Burma: CLS, 1963.

Dingrin, La Seng. "The Conflicting Legacy of Adoniram Judson: Appropriating and Polemicizing against Burmese Buddhism." *Missiology* 37, no. 4 (2009): 485–497.

———. "A Literary Study of Adoniram Judson's Tracts with Respect to the Mutual Relationship between Christian and Buddhist Terminology." In *Our Theological Journey: Writings in Honor of Dr. Anna May Say Pa*, edited by Festschrift Committee. Yangon: Myanmar Institute of Theology, 2006.

Du Mez, Kristin Kobes. *A New Gospel for Women: Katharine Bushnell and the Challenge of Christian Feminism*. New York: Oxford University Press, 2015.

Duesing, Jason G. *Adoniram Judson: A Bicentennial Appreciation of the Pioneer American Missionary*. Nashville, TN: B&H Publishing Group, 2012.

Dunn, James D. G. *Jesus and the Spirit*. Philadelphia, PA: Westminster Press, 1975.

Ebojo, Edgar. "Sex, Scribes, and Scriptures: Engendering the Texts of the New Testament." *Journal of Biblical and Theological Research* 39 (2016): 367–394.

———. "Should Women Be Silent in the Churches? Women's Audible Voices in the Textual Variants of 1 Corinthians 14:34–35." *Trinity Theological Journal* 14 (2006): 1–33.

"The Editor: Translations—1970, a Review of the Year." *The Bible Translator* 22, no. 2 (April 1971): 61–67.

Ellingworth, Paul, and Howard Hatton. *A Handbook on Paul's First Letter to the Corinthians*. New York: United Bible Societies, 1994 [1985].

Ellingworth, Paul. "Theory and Practice in Bible Translation." *The Evangelical Quarterly* 55, no. 3 (July–September 1983): 159–168.

Ellis, E. Earle. *Prophecy and Hermeneutic in Early Christianity*. Grand Rapids, MI: Eerdmans, 1978.

———. "The Silenced Wives of Corinth (1 Cor 14:34–35)." In *NT Textual Criticism and Its Significance for Exegesis: In Honour of Bruce Metzger*, edited by Eldon J. Epp and Gordon D. Fee, 213–220. Oxford: Clarendon, 1981.

Elwell, Walter A. *Evangelical Dictionary of Theology*. Grand Rapids, MI: Baker Academic, 2001.

En, Simon Pau Khan. *Called to Be a Community: Myanmar's [sic.] in Search of New Pedagogies of Encounter*. Yangon, Myanmar: Association of Theological Education in Myanmar, 2002.

———. "Engagement, Women Roles, Rights and Pastoral Leadership in the 21st Century: Inter-Denominational and Inter-Ethnic Cultural Perspective (Denominational Perspectives)." In *Engagement: Judson Research Center Bulletin*. Yangon, Myanmar: Myanmar Institute of Theology Judson Research Center, 2008.

———. "*Nat* Worship: A Paradigm for Doing Contextual Theology for Myanmar." PhD, University of Birmingham, 1995.

England, John C., Jose Kuttianimattathil, and John M. Prior, eds. *Asian Christian Theologies: A Research Guide to Authors, Movements, Sources*. Vol. 2. Southeast Asia. Maryknoll, NY: Orbis, 2003.

Epp, Eldon J. *Junia: The First Woman Apostle*. Minneapolis, MN: Fortress Press, 2005.

Fee, Gordon D. *The First Epistle to the Corinthians*. Rev. ed. The New International Commentary on the New Testament. Grand Rapids, MI: Eerdmans, 2014.

———. "Hermeneutics and the Gender Debate." In *Discovering Biblical Equality: Complementarity without Hierarchy*, edited by R. W. Pierce and R. M. Groothuis, 364–381. Downers Grove, IL: InterVarsity Press, 2005.

Fielding-Hall, H. *The Soul of a People*. London: Macmillan, 1898.

Fink, Christina. *Living Silence: Burma under Military Rule*. New York: Zed Books, 2001.

Fitzmyer, Joseph A. *First Corinthians: A New Translation with Introduction and Commentary*. New Haven, CT: Yale University Press, 2008.

Flanagan, N. M., and E. H. Snyder. "Did Paul Put Down Women in 1 Cor 14:34–36?" *Biblical Theology Bulletin* 11 (1981): 10–12.

———. "Let the Women Speak in Church: An Egalitarian Interpretation of 1 Cor 14:34b–36." *Biblical Theology Bulletin* 13 (1983): 90–93.

Flemming, Dean. *Contextualization in the New Testament: Patterns for Theology and Mission*. Downers Grove, IL: InterVarsity Press, 2005.

Forbes, Christopher. *Prophecy and Inspired Speech in Early Christianity and Its Hellenistic Environment*. Tübingen: Mohr Siebeck, 1995.

Freedom House. "Burma." *Freedom on the Net 2011*, 77. https://freedomhouse.org/sites/default/files/inline_images/Burma_FOTN2011.pdf.

Friesen, Steven J., Daniel N. Schowalter, and James C. Walters, eds. *Corinth in Context: Comparative Studies on Religion and Society*. Leiden: Brill, 2010.

Fung, Donald Y. K. "Ministry in the New Testament." In *The Church in the Bible and the World*, edited by D. A. Carson, 154–212. Grand Rapids, MI: Baker, 1987.

Garland, David E. *1 Corinthians*. Baker Exegetical Commentary on the New Testament. Grand Rapids, MI: Baker Academic, 2003.

Gay, Naw Eh Tar. "Authority and Submission in Some New Testament Letters: Postcolonial Feminist Reading from Myanmar." PhD Thesis, University of Birmingham, 2011.

———. "Exegesis on 1 Timothy 2:11–15: Debate on Women Leadership." *RAYS: MIT Journal of Theology* 4 (2003): 41–50.

Gender Equality Network. "Myanmar Laws and CEDAW: The Case for Anti-Violence against Women Laws." January 2013. https://www.burmalibrary.org/docs20/Myanmar_Law+CEDAW-en-red.pdf.

Grant, Robert, and David Tracy. *A Short History of the Interpretation of the Bible*. Philadelphia, PA: Fortress Press, 1984.

Greenbury, James. "1 Corinthians 14:34–35: Evaluation of Prophecy Revisited." *Journal of the Evangelical Theological Society* 51, no. 4 (December 2008): 721–731.

Grenz, Stanley J., and Daniel M. Kjesbo. *Women in the Church: A Biblical Theology of Women in Ministry*. Downers Grove, IL: InterVarsity Press, 2010.

Groothuis, Rebecca Merrill. *Good News for Women: A Biblical Picture of Gender Equality*. Grand Rapids, MI: Baker, 1997.

Grubbs, Judith E. *Women in the Law in the Roman Empire: A Sourcebook on Marriage, Divorce and Widowhood*. London: Routledge Press, 2002.

Grudem, Wayne A. "1 Corinthians 14:20–25: Prophecy and Tongues as Signs of God's Attitude." *Westminster Theological Journal* 41, no. 2 (1979): 381–396.

———. "Are Only Some Words of Scripture Breathed Out by God?." In *Translating Truth: The Case for Essential Literal Bible Translation*, edited by Wayne Grudem, Leland Ryken, C. John Collins, Vern S. Polythress, and Bruce Winter, 1–21. Wheaton, IL: Crossway Books, 2005.

———. *Bible Doctrine: Essential Teachings of the Christian Faith*. Edited by Jeff Purswell. Grand Rapids, MI: Zondervan, 1999.

———, ed. *Biblical Foundations for Manhood and Womanhood*. Wheaton, IL: Crossway Books, 2002.

———. *Business for the Glory of God: The Bible's Teaching on the Moral Goodness of Business*. Wheaton, IL: Crossway Books, 2003.

———. *Christian Beliefs: Twenty Basics Every Christian Should Know*. Grand Rapids, MI: Zondervan, 2005.

———. *Countering the Claims of Evangelical Feminism: Biblical Responses to the Key Questions*. Sisters, OR: Multnomah, 2006.

———. *Evangelical Feminism: A New Path to Liberalism?*. Wheaton, IL: Crossway Books, 2006.

———. *Evangelical Feminism and Biblical Truth: An Analysis of More Than One Hundred Disputed Questions*. New York, NY: Doubleday, 2009.

———. *The First Epistle of Peter: An Introduction and Commentary*. Tyndale New Testament Commentaries. Grand Rapids, MI: Eerdmans, 1988.

———. *The Gift of Prophecy in the New Testament and Today*. Wheaton, IL: Crossway Books, 1988.

———. "The Meaning of Kephalē ('Head'): A Response to Recent Studies." *Trinity Journal* 11, no. 1 (1990): 3–72.

———. "The Perspicuity of Scripture." *Themelios* 34, no. 3 (2009): 288–308.

———. *Politics According to the Bible: A Comprehensive Resource for Understanding Modern Political Issues in Light of Scripture*. Grand Rapids, MI: Zondervan, 2010.

———. "Prophecy – Yes, but Teaching – No: Paul's Consistent Advocacy of Women's Participation without Governing Authority." *Journal of the Evangelical Theological Society* 30, no. 1 (1987): 11–23.

———. *Systematic Theology*. Grand Rapids, MI: Zondervan, 1995.

———. "Why Christians Can Still Prophesy." *Christianity Today*, 16 September 1988, 29–35.

Gunanto, M. Emmanuel. "Biblical Apostolate in Southeast Asia in the Light of Dei Verbum." *East Asian Pastoral Review* 47, no. 2 (2010): 190–200.

Guo, Luo, ed. *Understanding Burma (Myanmar): History, Geography, Economy*. Beijing, China: Intercultural Press, 2013.

Hall, D. G. E. *A History of South-East Asia*. London: Macmillan, 1964.

Hall, Douglas John. *Professing the Faith: Christian Theology in a North American Context*. Minneapolis, MN: Fortress Press, 1993.

Hambrick-Stowe, C. E. *Charles G. Finney and the Spirit of American Evangelicalism*. Grand Rapids, MI: Eerdmans, 1996.

Harriden, Jessica. *The Authority of Influence: Women and Power in Burmese History*. Copenhagen: Nordic Institute of Asian Studies, 2012.

Hassey, Janette. *No Time for Silence: Evangelical Women in Public Ministry around the Turn of the Century*. Grand Rapids, MI: Baker Academic Books, 2008.

Henry, Matthew. *An Exposition of All the Books of the Old and New Testament: Practical Remarks and Observations*. Edited by W. Baynes. Vol. 5. London: W. Lochhead, 1806.

———. *Matthew Henry's Commentary on the Whole Bible: Complete and Unabridged in One Volume*. Peabody: Hendrickson, 1994.

Hiebert, Paul G. *Anthropological Reflections on Missiological Issues*. Grand Rapids, MI: Baker, 1994.

———. "Critical Contextualization." *International Bulletin of Missionary Research* 11, no. 3 (July 1987): 104–111.

———. *The Gospel in Human Contexts: Anthropological Explorations for Contemporary Missions*. Grand Rapids, MI: Baker, 2009.

———. *Transforming Worldviews: An Anthropological Understanding of How People Change*. Grand Rapids, MI: Baker, 2008.

Higgins, Kevin. "Biblical Interpretation Diverse Voices: Hearing Scripture Speak in a Multicultural Movement." *International Journal of Frontier Missiology* 27, no. 4 (Winter 2010): 189–196.

Hiu, Elim. *Regulations Concerning Tongues and Prophecy in 1 Corinthians 14:26–40*. New York: T&T Clark, 2010.

Hluan, Anna Sui. "Analysis on the Leadership Challenges Facing the Women Alumnae among the Evangelical Seminaries of Yangon." DMin, Asia Graduate School of Theology-Philippines (Myanmar Extension), 2007.

Hodge, Charles. *First Epistle to the Corinthians*. Grand Rapids, MI: Eerdmans, 1953.

Hollander, Harm W. "The Meaning of the Term 'law' (Νόμος) in 1 Corinthians." *Novum Testamentum* 40, Fasc. 2 (April 1998): 117–135.

Hoppin, Ruth. "The Legacy of Katharine Bushnell." *Priscilla Papers* 9, no. 1 (Winter 1995): 8–10.

Horsey, Richard. "New Religious Legislation in Myanmar." *SSRC Conflict Prevention and Peace Forum*, 13 February 2015.

Horsley, H., and S. Horsley. *The Book of Psalms*. Translated with Notes, by S. Horsley. Edited by H. Horsley. 1815. Neuilly sur Seine, FR: Ulan Press, 2012.

Houtman, Gustaaf. *Mental Culture in Burmese Crisis Politics: Aung San Suu Kyi and the National League for Democracy*. Tokyo: Tokyo University of Foreign Studies Institute for the Study of Languages and Cultures of Asia and Africa, 1999.

Hulse, Erroll. *Adoniram Judson and the Missionary Call*. Florida: Chapel Library, 2007.

Hunt, Robert. "Bible Translation." In *The Encyclopedia of Protestantism*, edited by Hans J. Hillerbrand, 246–250. New York: Routledge, 2004.

Hunt, Rosalie Hall. *Bless God and Take Courage: The Judson History and Legacy*. Valley Forge, PA: Judson Press, 2005.

Hup, Cung Lian. "A Brief Survey of Mission in Myanmar from a Missiological Perspective." In *Our Theological Journey: Writings in Honor of Dr. Anna May Say Pa*, edited by Festschrift Committee, 78–92. Yangon: Myanmar Institute of Theology, 2006.

Hurley, James B. *Man and Woman in Biblical Perspective*. Eugene, OR: Wipf and Stock, 2002.

Ikeya, Chie. "Gender, History and Modernity: Representing Women in Twentieth Century Colonial Burma." PhD, Cornell University, 2006.

———. "The 'Traditional' High Status of Women in Burma: A Historical Reconsideration." *Journal of Burma Studies* 10, no. 1 (2005): 51–81.

James, Sharon. "The Life and Significance of Ann Hasseltine Judson (1789–1826)." *Southern Baptist Journal of Mission* 1, no. 2 (Fall 2012): 22–33.

———. *My Heart in His Hands: Ann Judson of Burma*. Darlington, England: Evangelical Press, 1998.

Jewett, P. K. *Man as Male and Female*. Grand Rapids, MI: Eerdmans, 1975.

Johnson, Alan F. *1 Corinthians. IVP New Testament Commentary Series*. Illinois: InterVarsity Press, 2004.

Judson, Adoniram. *A Dictionary of the Burman Language*. Calcutta, India: Baptist Mission, 1823.

———. *A Dictionary, Burmese and English*. 2nd ed. Edited by Edward Abiel Stevens. Maulmain, Burma: American Baptist Mission Press, 1852.

———. *A Dictionary, English and Burmese*. Maulmain, Burma: American Baptist Mission Press, 1849.

———. *A Digest of Scripture, Consisting of Extracts from the Old and New Testaments: On the Plan of "Brown's Selection of Scripture Passages."* Maulmain, Burma: American Baptist Mission Press, 1838.

———. *Grammar of the Burmese Language*. Edited by E. O. Stevens. Rangoon, Burma: American Baptist Mission Press, 1883.

———. *The Septenary, or Seven Manuals*. 3rd ed. Maulmain, Burma: American Baptist Mission Press, 1860.

———. *The Threefold Cord: Eccles. IV. 12*. Philadelphia, PA: Baptist General Tract Society, 1829.

———. *A View of the Christian Religion in Three Parts, Historic, Didactic and Preceptive*. Maulmain, Burma: American Baptist Mission Press, 1860.

Judson, Ann Hasseltine. *An Account of the American Baptist Mission to the Burman Empire: Letters*. London: Joseph Butterworth and Son, 1827.

Judson, Edward. *The Life of Adoniram Judson*. New York: Anson D. F. Randolph, 1883.

Keener, Craig S. *Paul, Women and Wives: Marriage and Women in the Letters of Paul*. Peabody, PA: Hendrickson, 1992.

Keller, Rosemary Skinner, Rosemary Radford Ruether, Marie Cantlon, and Edith Waldvogel Blumhofer. *The Encyclopedia of Women and Religion in North America*. Vol. 1. Bloomington IN: Indiana University Press, 2006.

Khai, Chin Khua. *Cross amidst Pagodas: A History of the Assemblies of God in Myanmar*. Baguio, Philippines: APTS Press, 1995.

Khaing, Mi Mi. *The World of Burmese Women*. London: Zed Books, 1984.

Kham, Chin Do. "Historical Values and Modes of Leadership in Myanmar: Assessment of Roots of Values among Christian Leaders in Yangon." PhD, Trinity International University, 1988.

Khawsiama, Khin Maung Yee. *Towards a Ludu Theology : A Critical Evaluation of Minjung Theology and Its Implication for a Theological Response to the Dukkha (Suffering) of People in Myanmar (Burma)*. Bern: Peter Lang, 2013.

Kim, Eunjoo Mary. *Women Preaching: Theology and Practice through the Ages*. Cleveland, OH: Pilgrim Press, 2004.

Kittel, Gerhard, Gerhard Friedrich, and G. W. Bromiley, eds. *Theological Dictionary of the New Testament*. Abridged in One Volume. Grand Rapids, MI: Eerdmans, 1985.

Knapp, Georg Christian. *Lectures on Christian Theology*. Translated by Leonard Woods. New York: G&C&H. Carvill, 1831.

Knowles, James D. *Life of Mrs. Ann H. Judson: Late Missionary to Burmah, with an Account of the American Baptist Mission to that Empire*. Philadelphia, PA: American Sunday School Union, 1830.

———. *Memoir of Ann H. Judson, Late Missionary to Burmah; Including a History of the American Baptist Mission in the Burman Empire*. Boston: Gould, Kendall, and Lincoln, 1844.

Koyama, Kosuke. "New Heaven and New Earth: Theological Education for the New Millennium." Keynote address given at the General Assembly at ATESEA, Hong Kong, 1997.

Kroeger, Catherine Clark. "The Legacy of Katharine Bushnell: A Hermeneutic for Women of Faith." *Priscilla Papers* 9, no. 4 (Fall 1995): 1–5.

Kroeger, Catherine Clark, and Richard C. Kroeger. "Strange Tongues or Plain Talk?." *Daughters of Sarah* 12, no. 4 (1986): 10–13.

Kroeger, Catherine Clark, and Richard Clark Kroeger. "Pandemonium and Silence at Corinth." *Reformed Journal* 28, no. 6 (1978): 6–7.

Kyi, Aung San Suu. *Freedom from Fear: And Other Writings*. Edited by Michael Aris and Vaclav Havel. London, England: Penguin Books, 2010.

———. *The Voice of Hope*. London: Rider Books, 2008.

Lausanne Committee for World Evangelization. *The Willowbank Report: Consultation on Gospel and Culture*. Lausanne Occasional Paper 2. Lausanne Committee for World Evangelization, 1978. https://www.lausanne.org/content/lop/lop-2.

"Law on the Practice of Polygamy." Burma Library. https://www.burmalibrary.org/sites/burmalibrary.org/files/obl/docs21/2015-08-31-Law_on_the_Practice_of_Monogamy-54-bu.pdf.

Lee, Archie C. C. "Cross-Textual Hermeneutics on Gospel and Culture." *Asia Journal of Theology* 10, no. 1 (1996): 179–204.

Lee, Sidney, ed. *Dictionary of National Biography*. Vol. 27. London: Macmillan, 1891.

Lefkowit, Mary R., and Maureen B. Fant, eds. *Women's Life in Greece and Rome: A Source Book in Translation*. Baltimore, MD: John Hopkins University Press, 1992.

Lewis, Jonathan, M. Crossman, and S. Hoke, eds. *World Mission: An Analysis of the World Christian Movement*. Pasadena, CA: William Carey Library, 1994.

Lieberman, Victor B. *Burmese Administrative Cycles: Anarchy and Conquest, c. 1580–1760*. Princeton, NJ: Princeton University Press, 2014.

Ling, Samuel Ngun. "A Burmese Christian's Responses to Social Values of Work, Consumption, and Economic Options in Myanmar." In Samuel Ngun Ling, ed. *Theological Themes for Our Times: Reflections on Selected Themes of the Myanmar Institute of Theology*. Yangon, Myanmar: Judson Research Center of Myanmar Institute of Theology, 2007.

———. "Challenges, Problems, and Prospects of Theological Education in Myanmar." *CTC Bulletin* 12, no. 1 (April 2006). Christian Conference of Asia. https://www.cca.org.hk/ctc/ctc06-01/ctc06-01e.htm .

———. *Christianity through Our Neighbors' Eyes: Rethinking the 200 Years Old American Baptist Missions in Myanmar*. Yangon, Myanmar: Judson Research Center of Myanmar Institute of Theology, 2014.

———. *Communicating Christ in Myanmar: Issues, Interactions and Perspectives*. Yangon: Association for Theological Education in Myanmar, 2006.

———. "Doing Theology under the Bo Tree: Communicating the Christian Gospel in the Bama Buddhist Context." *RAYS: MIT Journal of Theology* 2 (January 2001): 73–84.

———. "The Encounter of Missionary Christianity with Resurgent Buddhism in Post-Colonial Myanmar" International Conference on Religion and Globalization. Thailand: Payap University, 2003.

———. *Theological Themes for Our Times: Reflections on Selected Themes of the Myanmar Institute of Theology*. Yangon, Myanmar: Judson Research Center of Myanmar Institute of Theology, 2007.

———. "Violence, Poverty, Justice and Peacemaking: A Burmese Christian Response." *Ministerial Formation* 104 (January 2005): 45–54.

Luther, Calista V. *The Vintons and the Karens: Memorials of Rev. Justus H. Vinton and Calista H. Vinton*. Boston: W. G. Corthell, 1880.

Lwin, Tint. "Contextualization of the Gospel: An Effective Strategy for the Evangelization of the Theravada Buddhists in Myanmar." PhD, Southern Baptist Theological Seminary, 1997.

Lynn, Soe Than. "NLD Can Spur Judicial Reform: Hluttow Reps." *The Myanmar Times*, April 9, 2012.

Ma, Agatha, and Kyoko Kusakabe. "Gender Analysis of Fear and Mobility in the Context of Ethnic Conflict in Kayah State, Myanmar." *Singapore Journal of Tropical Geography* 36, no. 3 (2015): 342–356.

MacHaffie, Babara J. *Her Story: Women in Christian Tradition*. Minneapolis, MN: Fortress, 2006.

Mananzan, Mary John. "Woman and Christianity." *Praxis* 1, no. 2 (May–August 2005): 16–22.

Mang, Aung. "Training to Effectively Communicate the Gospel in a Multi-Cultural Society." In *Educating for Tomorrow: Theological Leadership for the Asian Context*, edited by Manfred Waldemar Kohl and A. N. Lal Senanayake, 89–104. Bangalore: SAIACS Press, 2007.

Mare, W. Harold. "1 Corinthians." In *The Expositor's Bible Commentary: Romans through Galatians*, edited by Frank E. Gaebelein, 275–277. Grand Rapids, MI: Zondervan, 1976.

Marshall, I. Howard, ed. *Moulton and Geden Concordance to the Greek New Testament*. London: Bloomsbury Publishing, 2014.

Martin, Ralph. *The Spirit and the Congregation: Studies in 1 Corinthians 12–15*. Grand Rapids, MI: Eerdmans, 1984.

Martin, Robert P. *Accuracy of Translation*. Carlisle, PA: Banner of Truth, 1989.

Matthews, Shelly, Cynthia B. Kittredge, and Melanie Johnson-Debaufre. *Walk in the Ways of Wisdom: Essays in Honor of Elisabeth Schüssler Fiorenza*. London: Trinity Press, 2003.

McKim, Donald K. "Griesbach, Johann Jakob." In *Historical Handbook of Major Biblical Interpreters*. Downers Gove, IL: InterVarsity Press, 1998.

McKnight, Scot. *Junia Is Not Alone*. Denver, CO: Patheos Press, 2011.

McLeish, Alexander. *Christian Progress in Burma*. London: World Dominion Press, 1929.

McQuilkin, J. Robertson. "Problems of Normativeness in Scripture: Cultural Versus Permanent." In *Hermeneutics, Inerrancy and the Bible*, edited by Earl D. Radmacher and Robert D. Preus, 219–282. Grand Rapids, MI: Zondervan, 1984.

Melanchthon, Monica Jyotsna. "Graduate Biblical Studies in India." In *Transforming Graduate Biblical Education Ethos and Discipline*, edited by Elisabeth Schüssler Fiorenza and Harold Richards Kent, 119–146. Atlanta, GA: Society of Biblical Literature, 2010.

Melton, J. Gordon. *Encyclopedia of Protestantism*. New York: Infobase Publishers, 2005.

Metzger, Bruce M. *The Bible in Translation: Ancient and English Versions*. Grand Rapids, MI: Baker Academic, 2001.

———. *A Textual Commentary on the Greek New Testament*. London and New York: United Bible Societies, 1971, 1994.

Metzger, Bruce M., and Bart D. Ehrman. *The Text of the New Testament: Its Transmission, Corruption, and Restoration*. New York: Oxford University Press, 2005.

Mickelsen, Alvera, ed. *Women, Authority and the Bible*. Downers Grove, IL: InterVarsity Press, 1986.

Middleditch, R. T. *Records of the Life, Character, and Achievements of Adoniram Judson: Burmah's Great Missionary*. New York: E. H. Fletcher, 1854.

Midgley, Clare. "Can Women Be Missionaries? Envisioning Female Agency in the Early Nineteenth-Century British Empire." *Journal of British Studies* 45, no. 2 (2006): 335–358.

Milhaven, Annie Lally. *The Inside Stories: Thirteen Valiant Women Challenging the Church*. Mystic, CN: Twenty-Third Publishers, 1987.

Moffett, Samuel Hugh. *A History of Christianity in Asia*. Vol. 2: 1500–1900. New York: Orbis Books, 2005.

Mollenkott, Virginia. *Women, Men and the Bible*. Nashville, TN: Abingdon, 1977.

Mon, Nang Thuzar. "Victimization of Women in Kenlung Area." BTh Thesis, Myanmar Institute of Theology, 1994.

Moore, Elizabeth H. *Early Landscapes of Myanmar*. Thailand: River Books, 2007.

Moulton, H. K. *The Analytical Greek Lexicon Revised*. Grand Rapids, MI: Zondervan, 1978.

———. *The Challenge of the Concordance: Some New Testament Words Studied in Depth*. London: S. Bagster, 1977.

Mundhenk, Norman A. "Punctuation." *The Bible Translator* 32, no. 2 (1 April 1981): 227–234.

Munro, Winsome. *Authority in Paul and Peter. The Identification of a Pastoral Stratum in the Pauline Corpus and 1 Peter*. Cambridge: Cambridge University Press, 1983.

Murphy-O'Connor, Jerome. *Keys to First Corinthians: Revisiting the Major Issues*. Oxford: Oxford University Press, 2009.

———. *St. Paul's Corinth: Text and Archaeology*. Collegeville, MN: Liturgical Press, 2002.

Myanmar Language Commission. *Myanmar-English Dictionary*. Kensington, MD: Dunwoody Press, 1996.

Myint, Khin Maung. *Christian Marriage: Compilation of Articles and Sermons*. Yangon, Myanmar: n.p., 1999.

———. *How to Choose Your Mate according to the Will of God, before You Marry*. Yangon, Myanmar: n.p., 1999.

Nan, M. Seng Tsin. "Submission to the Government (Rom 13:1–7): Biblical Perspective with Christian Ethical Reflection for Present Day Myanmar." ThM thesis, MF Norwegian School of Theology, 2011.

Nash, Robert S. *1 Corinthians*. Macon, GA: Smyth & Helwys, 2009.

Nawl, Cung. *Why Myanmar Church Fails in Evangelizing the Buddhist Bamar People*. Yangon: n.p., 2004.

Ng, Esther Yue L. *Reconstructing Christian Origins? The Feminist Theology of Elisabeth Schussler Fiorenza: An Evaluation*. Cumbria, UK: Paternoster Press, 2002.

Nida, J. P., and E. A. Louw. *Greek-English Lexicon of the New Testament Based on Semantic Domains*. Vol. 1. New York: United Bible Societies, 1996.

Nikaya, Anguttara. *The Book of the Gradual Sayings (Anguttara Nikaya). The Book of the Fives*. Translated by F. L. Woodward. Pali Text Society Translation Series. Vol. 3. Oxford: The Pali Text Society, 2001.

Noll, Mark A. *A History of Christianity in the United States and Canada*. London: SPCK, 1992.

Nunn, H. P. V. *The Elements of New Testament Greek*. Cambridge: Cambridge University Press, 1923.

Nwe, Aye. "Empowerment as Constructive Power for Gender." *CTC Bulletin* 20, no. 3 (December 2004). https://www.cca.org.hk/ctc/ctc04-12/ctc04-12m.htm.

———. "Gender Hierarchy in Myanmar." *RAYS: MIT Journal of Theology* 10 (January 2009): 131–139.

———. "Women's Roles, Rights and Pastoral Leadership in the 21st Century: Inter-Denominational and Inter-Ethnic Cultural Perspective (Baptist Perspective)." *RAYS: MIT Journal of Theology* 9 (January 2007): 32–39.

Nyunt, Khin Tida. "Myanmar Women in Church and Society." *In God's Image* 23, no. 3 (June 2004): 19–20.

Nyunt, Peter Thein. *Missions amidst Pagodas: Contextual Communication of the Gospel in Burmese Buddhist Context*. Carlisle, Cumbria: Langham, 2014.

———. "Toward a Paradigm of Christian Communication for the Bamar Buddhists in Yangon City." PhD Thesis, South Asia Institute of Advanced Christian Studies, 2010.

Odell-Scott, David W. "Let the Women Speak in Church, an Egalitarian Interpretation of 1 Cor 13:33b-36." *Biblical Theology Bulletin* 13, no. 3 (1983): 90–93.

Økland, Jorunn. *Women in Their Place: Paul and the Corinthian Discourse of Gender and Sanctuary Space*. New York: T&T Clark, 2004.

Omanson, Roger L. "Robert Galveston Bratcher (1920–2010)." *The Bible Translator* 61, no. 4 (17 August 2016): 169–175.

Oo, Khin Swe. "Theological Understanding of Women in Ordained Ministry." In *Women in Ministry and Theological Education: A Chance and Challenge for the Churches in the Mekong Region*, edited by Christa von Zychlin, 17–30. Hong Kong: Mekong Mission Forum, 2013.

Ortlund, Raymond C. "Male-Female Equality and Male Headship: Genesis 1–3." In Piper and Grudem, *Recovering Biblical Manhood and Womanhood*, 86–104.

Osborne, G. R. *The Hermeneutical Spiral: A Comprehensive Introduction to Biblical Interpretation*. Downers Grove, IL: InterVarsity Press, 1991, 2006.

Pa, Anna May Say. "Because of Eve: Reading Genesis 2 and 3 from Feminist Perspectives." *Engagement* 5 (December 2005): 31–36.

———. "Birthing an Asian Feminist Theology in the Face of the Dragon: A Burmese Perspective." *RAYS: MIT Journal of Theology* 3 (February 2002): 21–28.

———. "Boundary Crossers and Risk Takers: Ruth and Justa in the Struggle for Life." *CTC Bulletin* 26, no. 1 (June 2010): 83–89.

———."A Place at the Round Table Equipping Burmese Women for Leadership." *RAYS: MIT Journal of Theology* 5, no. 1 (January 2004).

Partners Relief and Development. *Crimes in Northern Burma: Results from a Fact-Finding Mission to Kachin State* (November 2011). https://www.burmacampaign.org.uk/images/uploads/Crimes_in_Northern_Burma.pdf.

Payne, Philip Barton. "Is 1 Corinthians 14:34–35 a Marginal Comment or a Quotation? A Response to Kirk MacGregor." *Priscilla Papers* 33, no. 2 (Spring 2019): 24–30.

———. *Man and Woman, One in Christ: An Exegetical and Theological Study of Paul's Letters*. Grand Rapids, MI: Zondervan, 2009.

———. "Vaticanus Distigme-obelos Symbols Marking Added Text, Including 1 Corinthians 14:34–5." *New Testament Studies* 63 (2017): 604–625.

———. "Wild Hair and Gender Equality in 1 Cor 11:2–16." *Priscilla Papers* 20 number 3 (July 2006): 9–15.

Pears, Angie. *Doing Contextual Theology*. Hoboken, NJ: Taylor and Francis, 2009.

Peppiatt, Lucy. *Women and Worship at Corinth: Paul's Rhetorical Arguments in 1 Corinthians*. Eugene, OR: Cascade Books, 2015.

Philip Schaff, Samuel M. Jackson, and D. S. Schaff. *A Religious Encyclopaedia or Dictionary of Biblical, Historical, Doctrinal, and Practical Theology*. New York: Funk & Wagnalls, 1882–1883.

Phillips, John. *Exploring 1 Corinthians*. John Phillips Commentary Series. Grand Rapids, MI: Kregel Publications, 2005.

Piper, John, and Wayne A. Grudem. "An Overview of Central Concerns: Questions and Answers." In Piper and Grudem, *Recovering Biblical Manhood and Womanhood*, 60–94.

———, eds. *Recovering Biblical Manhood and Womanhood: A Response to Evangelical Feminism*. Wheaton, IL: Crossway Books, 1991.

Pleasants, Phyllis Rodgerson. "Beyond Translation: The Work of the Judsons in Burma." *Baptist History and Heritage* 42, no. 2 (2007): 19–35.

Pope-Levison, Priscilla, and John R. Levison. *Return to Babel: Global Perspectives on the Bible*. Westminster John Knox Press, 1999.

Porter, Stanley E., and Craig A. Evans. *New Testament Interpretation and Methods*. Sheffield: Sheffield Academic Press, 1997.

Porter, Stanley, and Mark J. Boda. *Translating the New Testament: Text, Translation, Theology*. Grand Rapids, MI: Eerdmans, 2009.

Pwint, Zon Pann. "Ceremony Celebrates Revised Bible Translation." *Myanmar Times* (Yangon, Myanmar), 3 December 2012.

Rack, Henry D. *Reasonable Enthusiast. John Wesley and the Rise of Methodism*. 2nd ed. Nashville, TN: Abingdon Press, 1992.

The Republic of the Union of Myanmar. *The 2014 Myanmar Population and Housing Census. The Union Report*. Nay Pyi Taw, Myanmar: Department of Population, Ministry of Immigration and Population, 2015.

The Republic of the Union of Myanmar. *The 2014 Myanmar Population and Housing Census. The Union Report: Religion, Census Report Volume 2-C*. Nay Pyi Taw, Myanmar: Department of Population, Ministry of Labour, Immigration and Population, 2016.

Reuther, Rosemary Radford. *Sexism and God-Talk: Toward a Feminist Theology*. Boston: Beacon Press, 1993.

Reventlow, Henning Graf. *History of Biblical Interpretation, Volume 4: From the Englightenment to the Twentieth Century*. Atlanta, GA: Society of Biblical Literature, 2010.

Ricoeur, Paul. *The Conflict of Interpretations: Essays in Hermeneutics*. Edited by Don Ihde. Evanston, IL: Northwestern University Press, 1974.

———. "The Critique of Religion." In *The Philosophy of Paul Ricoeur: An Anthology of His Work*, edited by Charles E. Reagan and David Stewart, 213–222. Boston, MA: Beacon Press, 1978.

Robert, Dana Lee. *American Women in Mission: A Social History of Their Thought and Practice*. Macon, GA: Mercer University Press, 1997.

———. "Judson, Ann ('Nancy') (Hasseltine)." In *Biographical Dictionary of Christian Missions*. Edited by Gerald H. Anderson. New York: Macmillan, 1998.

Robertson, Archibald, and Alfred Plummer. *A Critical and Exegetical Commentary on the First Epistle of St. Paul to the Corinthians*. Edinburgh: T& T Clark, 1914, 1986.

Robinson, J. M. "Die Hodajot-Formel in Gebet und Hymnus des Fruhchristentums." In *Apophoreta: Festschrift Für Ernst Haenchen*. Berlin: A. Töpelmann, 1964.

Rogers, Benedict. *Than Shwe: Unmasking Burma's Tyrant*. Chiang Mai, Thailand: Silkworm Books, 2010.

Rowe, Henry K. *History of Andover Theological Seminary*. Newton, MA: 1933.

Russell, Letty M. *Human Liberation in a Feminist Perspective*. Philadelphia, PA: Westminster Press, 1974.

Sangermano, Vincentius. *A Description of the Burmese Empire*. London: Susil Gupta, 1833.

Scanzoni, Letha, and Nancy Hardesty. *All We're Meant to Be*. Waco, TX: Word Books, 1974.

Scholer, David M. "Contours of an Evangelical Feminist Hermeneutics." *Catalyst* 15, no. 4 (April 1989): 3–15.

———. "Feminist Hermeneutics and Evangelical Biblical Interpretation." *Journal of the Evangelical Theological Society* 30, no. 4 (1987): 407–420.

Scholer, David M., Everett Ferguson, and Paul Corby Finney, eds. *Studies in Early Christianity: A Collection of Scholarly Essays*, New York: Garland, 1993.

Schreiner, Thomas R. "An Interpretation of 1 Timothy 2:9–15: A Dialogue with Scholarship." In *Women in the Church: An Analysis and Application of 1 Timothy 2:9–15*, edited by Andreas J. Kostenberger and Thomas R. Schreiner, 85–120. Grand Rapids, MI: Baker, 2005.

Schreiter, Robert J. *Constructing Local Theologies*. Maryknoll, NY: Orbis Books, 1985.

Schüssler Fiorenza, Elisabeth. "Biblical Interpretation and Critical Commitment." *Studia Theologica – Nordic Journal of Theology* 43, no. 1 (1989): 5–18.

———. *Bread Not Stone: The Challenge of Feminist Biblical Interpretation*. Boston, MA: Beacon Press, 1995.

———. *But She Said: Feminist Practices of Biblical Interpretation*. Boston, MA: Beacon, 1992.

———. "Changing the Paradigms." *The Christian Century*, 5–12 September 1990, 796–800.

———. *Discipleship of Equals: A Critical Feminist Ekklesia-logy of Liberation*. New York: Crossroad, 1993.

———. "The Ethics of Biblical Interpretation: Decentering Biblical Scholarship." *Journal of Biblical Literature* 107, no. 1 (1988): 3–17.

———. "Feminist Theology and New Testament Interpretation." *Journal for the Study of the New Testament* 22 (1982): 32–46.

———. "Feminist Theology as a Critical Theology of Liberation." *Theological Studies* 36, no. 4 (1975): 605–626.

———. *In Memory of Her: A Feminist Theological Reconstruction of Christian Origins.* New York: SCM, 1983.

———. *Jesus: Miriam's Child, Sophia's Prophet.* London: SCM, 1995.

———, ed. *The Power of Naming: A "Concilium" Reader in Feminist Liberation Theology.* Maryknoll, NY: Orbis Books, 1996.

———. "The Power of the Word: Charting Critical Global Feminist Biblical Studies." In *Feminist New Testament Studies: Global and Future Perspectives,* edited by Althea Spencer Miller Kathleen O'Brien Wicker, and Musa W. Dube, 43–62. New York: Palgrave Macmillan, 2005.

———. *The Power of the Word: Scripture and the Rhetoric of Empire.* Minneapolis, MN: Fortress, 2007.

———. *Rhetoric and Ethics: The Politics of Biblical Studies.* Minneapolis, MN: Fortress, 1999.

———. "Rhetorical Situation and Historical Reconstruction in 1 Corinthians." *New Testament Studies* 33, no. 3 (1987): 386–403.

———. "The Will to Choose or to Reject: Continuing Our Critical Work." In *Feminist Interpretation of the Bible,* edited by Letty M. Russell, 125–136. Philadelphia, PA: Westminster Press, 1985.

———. *Wisdom Ways: Introducing Feminist Biblical Interpretation.* Maryknoll, NY: Orbis Books, 2001.

Seekins, Donald M. *Historical Dictionary of Burma (Myanmar).* Lanham, Maryland: Scarecrow Press, 2006.

Sein, Ma Sein. "The Position of Women in Hinayana Buddhist Countries." MA thesis, University of London, 1958.

Shepherd, Loraine MacKenzie. *Feminist Theologies for a Postmodern Church: Diversity, Community, and Scripture.* New York: Peter Lang, 2002.

Skidmore, Monique, and Trevor Wilson. *Dictatorship, Disorder and Decline in Myanmar.* Canberra: ANU Press, 2008.

Smalley, William A. "Language and Culture in the Development of Bible Society Translation Theory and Practice." *International Bulletin of Missionary Research* 19, no. 2 (1995): 61–71.

———. *Translation as Mission: Bible Translation in the Modern Missionary Movement.* Marcon GA: Mercer University Press, 1991.

Society of Biblical Literature. "Robert Galveston Bratcher 1920–2010." SBL Forum Archive, https://www.sbl-site.org/publications/article.aspx?ArticleId=863.

Spoorenberg, Thomas. "Myanmar's First Census in More Than 30 Years: A Radical Revision of the Official Population Count." *Population & Societies (INED)* 527, November 2015, 1–4.

Stanton, Elizabeth Cady. *The Woman's Bible.* Monroe, WA: Pacific Publishing Studio, 1990.

Steinberg, David I. *Burma: the State of Myanmar*. Washington DC: Georgetown University Press, 2001.

Stendahl, Krister. *The Bible and the Role of Women*. Philadelphia, PA: Fortress Press, 1966.

Stine, P. C. "Eugene A. Nida: Theoretician of Translation." *International Bulletin of Missionary Research* 36, no. 1 (2012): 38–39.

———. *Let the Words Be Written: The Lasting Influence of Eugene A. Nida*. Leiden: Brill, 2004.

Strack, Hermann Leberecht, and Paul Billerbeck. *Kommentar Zum Neuen Testament Aus Talmud Und Midrasch*. Edited by Paul Billerbeck. Whitefish, MT: Kessinger Publishing, 2010 [1922].

Stringer, Phil. "The Word of God for All Nations: Myanmar." http://textus-receptus.com/wiki/Article:_The_Word_of_God_for_All_Nations_by_Phil_Stringer#Mymanmar.

Stuart, Arabella W. (Arabella M. Willson). *Lives of the Three Mrs. Judsons: Mrs. Ann H. Judson, Mrs. Sarah B. Judson, Mrs. Emily C. Judson, Missionaries to Burmah*. Boston, MA: Lee and Shepard, 1855.

Sugirtharajah, R. S. "Introduction, and Some Thoughts on Asian Biblical Hermeneutics." *Biblical Interpretation* 2, no. 3 (1994): 251–268.

Sunquist, Scott W., ed., *A Dictionary of Asian Christianity*. Grand Rapids, MI: Eerdmans, 2001.

Thang, Khoi Lam. " 'Baptism' in Myanmar Bible." The Second Workshop on Bible and Bible Translation. Yangon, Myanmar: Association for Theological Education in Myanmar and the Bible Society of Myanmar, 25–27 October 2017.

Thang, Khoi Lam. "Eagle in the Myanmar Bible." *The Bible Translator* 60, no. 4 (2009): 195–200.

Thiselton, Anthony C. *The First Epistle to the Corinthians: A Commentary on the Greek Text*. Grand Rapids, MI: Eerdmans, 2000.

———. *The Two Horizons: New Testament Hermeneutics and Philosophical Description with Special Reference to Heidegger, Bultmann, Gadamer, and Wittgenstein*. Grand Rapids, MI: Eerdmans, 1980.

Thoung, Samo. "Being a Man." *Myanmartaman*, January 1995, 11–12.

Thwin, Thanlwin Pe. *Myanmataman*, May 1972, 1–15.

Tin, Pe Maung. "Presenting the Gospel of Christ within the Given Culture and Its Context." *Southeast Asia Journal of Theology* 3, no. 2 (October 1961): 28–36.

———. "Women in the Inscriptions of Pagan." *Journal of Burma Studies* 25, no. 3 (1935): 149–159.

———. *Women in the Inscriptions of Pagan*. Fiftieth Anniversary Publications, no. 2. Rangoon: Burma Research Society, 1960.

Topich, William J., and Keith A. Leitich. *The History of Myanmar*. Santa Barbara, CA: Greenwood, 2013.

Toungoo Baptist Mission. *Minutes of a Council Held at Toungoo 8 October 1863*. Rangoon: Baptist Mission Press, 1863.

Trager, Helen G. *Burma through Alien Eyes: Missionary Views of the Burmese in the Nineteenth Century*. Bombay: Asia Publishing House, 1966.

Tucker, Ruth A. *Women in the Maze: Questions and Answers on Biblical Equality*. Downers Grove, IL: InterVarsity Press, 1992.

Tucker, Ruth A., and Walter L. Liefeld. *Daughters of the Church: Women and Ministry from New Testament Times to the Present*. Grand Rapids, Michigan: Academie Books, 1987.

U, Alan Saw. "Professor U Pe Maung Tin: A Gentle Genius, a Meek Master." *Journal of Burma Studies* 9, no. 36 (2004): 35–41.

Vanhoozer, Kevin J., Craig G. Bartholomew, Daniel J. Treier, and N. T. Wright, eds. *Dictionary for Theological Interpretation of the Bible*. Grand Rapids, MI: Baker Academic, 2005.

Vincent, S. V. "The Use of Honorifics in Burmese." *The Bible Translator* 14, no. 2 (October 1963): 196–197.

Virkler, H. A., and K. Ayayo. *Hermeneutics: Principles and Processes of Biblical Interpretation*. Grand Rapids, MI: Baker, 2007.

Vuta, Kawl Thang. "A Brief History of the Planting and Growth of the Church in Burma." DMiss, Fuller Theological Seminary, 1983.

Wa, Maung Shwe, G. Sowards, and E. Sowards. *Burma Baptist Chronicle*. Rangoon: Board of Publications, Burma Baptist Convention, 1963.

Wah, Eh Eh. "The Outstanding Baptist Women Leaders in Myanmar." BD Thesis, Myanmar Institute of Theology, 1991.

Wallace, D. B. *Greek Grammar Beyond the Basics: An Exegetical Syntax of the New Testament*. Grand Rapids, MI: Zondervan, 1996.

Walsh, W. Pakenham. "Adoniram Judson." In *Modern Heroes of the Mission Field*. New York: Fleming H. Revell, 1915.

Warburton, Stacy R. *Eastward! The Story of Adoniram Judson*. New York: Round Table Press, 1937.

Wayland, F. *A Memoir of the Life and Labors of the Rev. Adoniram Judson*. Vols. 1 and 2. Boston: Phillips Sampson, 1853.

Weiss, A. *Women at Prayer: A Halakhic Analysis of Women's Prayer Groups*. Jersey City, NJ: KTAV Publishing House, 2001.

Willans, H. C. "Translators' Conference in Burma." *The Bible Translator* 4, no. 1 (1 January 1953): 21–25.

Williams, J. B. *Memoirs of the Life, Character, and Writings of the Rev. Matthew Henry*. London: J. O. Robinson, 1829.

Wilson, H. B. *The History of Merchant-Taylors School, from Its Foundation to the Present Time: In Two Parts. I. Of Its Founders, Patrons, Benefactors, and Masters. II. Of Its Principal Scholars.* London: Marchant and Galabin, 1814.

Win, Aye Aye. "Women in Creation and Today." BTh Thesis, Myanmar Institute of Theology, 1998.

Winter, Bruce. *Roman Wives, Roman Widows: The Appearance of New Women and the Pauline Communities.* Grand Rapids MI: Eerdmans, 2003.

———. "Veiled Men and Wives and Christian Contentiousness: 1 Corinthians 11:2–16." In *After Paul Left Corinth: The Influence of Secular Ethics and Social Change*, 121–141. Grand Rapids, MI: Eerdmans, 2001.

Wire, Antoinette Clark. *The Corinthian Women Prophets: A Reconstruction through Paul's Rhetoric.* Minneapolis: Fortress, 1990.

Witherington III, Ben. *The Acts of the Apostles: A Socio-Rhetorical Commentary.* Grand Rapids, MI: Eerdmans, 1998.

———. *The Christology of Jesus.* Minneapolis, MN: Augsburg Fortress, 1990.

———. *Conflict and Community in Corinth: A Socio-Rhetorical Commentary on 1 and 2 Corinthians.* Grand Rapids, MI: Eerdmans, 1995.

———. "The Eternal Subordination of Christ and of Women." *Ben Witherington*, 22 March 2006. http://benwitherington.blogspot.com/2006/03/eternal-subordination-of-christ-and-of.html.

———. *The Gospel Code: Novel Claims About Jesus, Mary Magdalene and Davinci.* Downers Grove, IL: InterVarsity Press, 2004.

———. *Grace in Galatia: A Commentary on St. Paul's Letter to the Galatians.* Grand Rapids, MI: Eerdmans, 1998.

———. "Hermeneutics: A Guide for Perplexed Bible Readers." 21 August 2007, http://benwitherington.blogspot.com/2007/08/hermeneutics-guide-for-perplexed-bible.html

———. *The Indelible Image: The Theological and Ethical Thought World of the New Testament.* Vol. 2. Downers Grove, IL: InterVarsity Press, 2010.

———. *The Jesus Quest: The Third Search for the Jew of Nazareth.* Grand Rapids, MI: Inter-Varsity Press, 1995.

———. *Jesus the Sage: The Pilgrimage of Wisdom.* Edinburgh: T&T Clark, 1994.

———. *John's Wisdom, a Commentary on the Fourth Gospel.* Louisville, KY: Westminster John Knox Press, 1995.

———. *Letters and Homilies for Hellenized Christians.* Downers Grove, IL: InterVarsity Press Academic, 2006.

———. *The Living Word of God: Rethinking the Theology of the Bible.* Waco, TX: Baylor University Press, 2009.

———. *The Many Faces of the Christ, the Christologies of the New Testament and Beyond.* New York: Crossroad Publishing, 1998.

———. *The Paul Quest: The Renewed Search for the Jew of Tarsus.* Downers Grove, IL: Inter-Varsity Press, 2001.

———. *Paul's Letter to the Romans: A Socio-Rhetorical Commentary.* Edited by Darlene Hyatt. Grand Rapids, MI: Eerdmans, 2004.

———. *Paul's Narrative Thought World: The Tapestry of Tragedy and Triumph.* Louisville, KY: Westminster John Knox Press, 1994.

———. "Rite and Rights for Women – Galatians 3.28." *New Testament Studies* 27, no. 5 (1981): 593–604.

———. *What's in the Word: Rethinking the Socio-Rhetorical Character of the New Testament.* Waco, TX: Baylor University Press, 2009.

———. "Why Arguments against Women in Ministry Aren't Biblical." 2009, http://www.beliefnet.com/columnists/bibleandculture/2009/10/why-arguments-against-women-in-ministry-arent-biblical.html#ixzz35mTqZbIh.

———. *Women and the Genesis of Christianity.* Cambridge: Cambridge University Press, 1990.

———. "Women and Their Roles in the Gospels and Acts." PhD Thesis, University of Durham, 1981.

———. "Women in Ministry." *Asbury Herald* 108, no. 1 (Winter 1997): n.p.

———. *Women in the Earliest Churches.* Cambridge: Cambridge University Press, 1988.

———. *Women in the Ministry of Jesus: A Study of Jesus' Attitudes to Women and Their Roles as Reflected in His Earthly Life.* Cambridge: Cambridge University Press, 1984.

Womack, William. "Contesting Indigenous and Female Authority in the Burma Baptist Mission: The Case of Ellen Mason." *Women's History Review* 17, no. 4 (2008): 543–559.

Women's League of Burma. *Breaking the Silence.* Paper submitted to the Forty-Sixth Session of the Commission on the Status of Women. Thailand, March 2002.

Wyeth, Walter Newton. *Ann H. Judson: A Memorial.* Cincinnati, OH: The author, 1891.

———. *The Wades: Jonathan Wade, Deborah B. L. Wade; A Memorial.* Philadelphia, PA: The author, 1891.

Yarchin, William, ed. *History of Biblical Interpretation: A Reader.* Peabody, MA: Hendrickson, 2004.

Langham Literature, with its publishing work, is a ministry of Langham Partnership.

Langham Partnership is a global fellowship working in pursuit of the vision God entrusted to its founder John Stott –

> *to facilitate the growth of the church in maturity and Christ-likeness through raising the standards of biblical preaching and teaching.*

Our vision is to see churches in the Majority World equipped for mission and growing to maturity in Christ through the ministry of pastors and leaders who believe, teach and live by the word of God.

Our mission is to strengthen the ministry of the word of God through:
- nurturing national movements for biblical preaching
- fostering the creation and distribution of evangelical literature
- enhancing evangelical theological education

especially in countries where churches are under-resourced.

Our ministry

Langham Preaching partners with national leaders to nurture indigenous biblical preaching movements for pastors and lay preachers all around the world. With the support of a team of trainers from many countries, a multi-level programme of seminars provides practical training, and is followed by a programme for training local facilitators. Local preachers' groups and national and regional networks ensure continuity and ongoing development, seeking to build vigorous movements committed to Bible exposition.

Langham Literature provides Majority World preachers, scholars and seminary libraries with evangelical books and electronic resources through publishing and distribution, grants and discounts. The programme also fosters the creation of indigenous evangelical books in many languages, through writer's grants, strengthening local evangelical publishing houses, and investment in major regional literature projects, such as one volume Bible commentaries like the *Africa Bible Commentary* and the *South Asia Bible Commentary*.

Langham Scholars provides financial support for evangelical doctoral students from the Majority World so that, when they return home, they may train pastors and other Christian leaders with sound, biblical and theological teaching. This programme equips those who equip others. Langham Scholars also works in partnership with Majority World seminaries in strengthening evangelical theological education. A growing number of Langham Scholars study in high quality doctoral programmes in the Majority World itself. As well as teaching the next generation of pastors, graduated Langham Scholars exercise significant influence through their writing and leadership.

To learn more about Langham Partnership and the work we do visit **langham.org**

www.ingramcontent.com/pod-product-compliance
Lightning Source LLC
Chambersburg PA
CBHW061704300426
44115CB00014B/2563